# FREEDOM TO WIN

A Cold War Story of the Courageous
Hockey Team That Fought the Soviets for
the Soul of Its People—and Olympic Gold

ETHAN SCHEINER

PEGASUS BOOKS
NEW YORK LONDON

FREEDOM TO WIN

Pegasus Books, Ltd.
148 West 37th Street, 13th Floor
New York, NY 10018

First Pegasus Books cloth edition July 2023

Map on page iv. Copyright © Shutterstock/Peteri

Map on page v. Created by Emily Torres.

Interior design by Maria Fernandez

Library of Congress Cataloging-in-Publication Data is available.

ISBN: 978-1-63936-351-3

10 9 8 7 6 5 4 3 2

Printed in the United States of America
Distributed by Simon & Schuster
www.pegasusbooks.com

*To Melanie, Casey, & Serena*

*and*

*To the people of Czechoslovakia, the Czech Republic (Czechia), and Slovakia.*

*This is your story.*

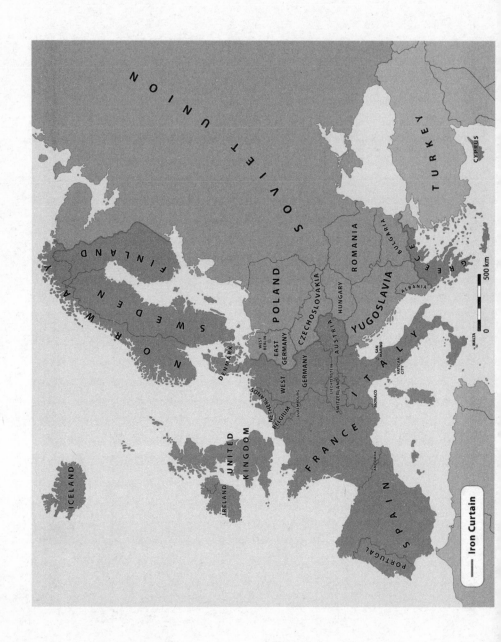

Iron Curtain

# Cold War Czechoslovakia
## Cities and Towns Featured in *Freedom to Win*

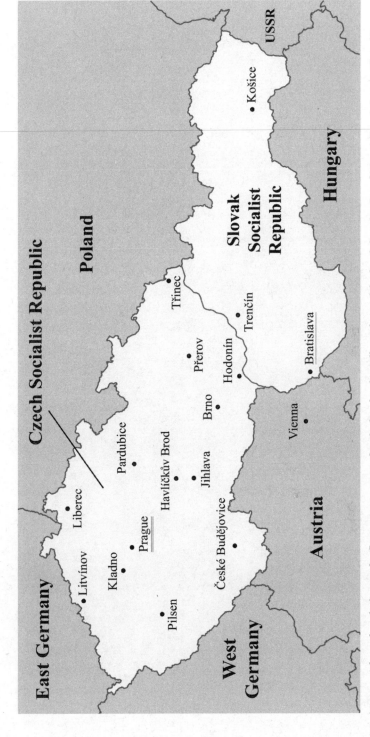

*Cities/towns not located perfectly to scale. Beginning in 1969: Czechoslovakia formally made up of the Czech Socialist Republic and Slovak Socialist Republic.*

# Contents

# Replay of a Lost War

M arch 21, 1969. Three small-town men and their hockey teammates from the little country of Czechoslovakia found themselves in the midst of a scene unlike any they had ever encountered. When Jaroslav Holík, his younger brother Jiří, and their friend since childhood Jan Suchý took to the ice in Johanneshov Stadium in Stockholm, Sweden, a crowd of thousands engulfed them, shaking the arena with a mad roar for Czechoslovakia's hockey squad. In the stands, people chanted, *Revenge for August '68!* As the players looked around, they saw fans holding banners supporting their team. One in particular stood out: "You Send Tanks, We Bring Goals."

This was no normal sporting event.

Just months earlier, the Soviet Union—"the Russians"—had invaded their country. Jaroslav, Jiří, Jan, and all of Czechoslovakia watched as, each day, piece by piece, their freedoms disappeared. In desperation, Czechs and Slovaks searched for a sign that the Soviets had not stolen everything from them. Powerless against thousands of tanks and half a million troops, they knew they could never take down the soldiers in a military battle. But what if they defeated the Soviets in a different kind of fight? What if they could show that even though Moscow held them physically captive, there were freedoms that it could never take from them?

They turned to their country's heroes, the representatives of Czechoslovakia's national hockey team. The task for these men? Nothing less than bringing defeat to the greatest hockey squad on the planet. The Soviet Union had won the previous six world titles, including the last two Olympic Games. Nevertheless, everywhere the Czechoslovak players went, people told them, "We don't care what else you do. Just beat the Russians!" For the people of Czechoslovakia, the March 1969 World Ice Hockey Championships in Stockholm turned into a battlefield.

On March 21, seven months to the day since Soviet tanks first appeared on their streets, Czechs and Slovaks—through Jaroslav, Jiří, Jan, and their teammates—could finally fight back. By the end of the evening, the Czechoslovakia-Soviet rivalry would be all anyone at the tournament talked about. The front-page headlines in the Western press described it aptly: *Hate Match*. Alexander Dubček, Czechoslovakia's leader, would describe it as much more: "It was a replay of a lost war."

For years to come, people would speak of that week in Stockholm when Czechoslovakia's hockey players spit on the Communist coat of arms that adorned their jerseys, took out their anger on the ice in ways that no one had ever seen in a sporting event, and inspired the people of their demoralized country.

The inspiration would shape the lives of a new generation. Hockey players twenty-nine years later and thousands of miles from home would kiss a new coat of arms and try to achieve the one thing that eluded the heroes of 1969.

Through it all, the ice warriors fought for far more than just hockey victories. They battled to show that the people of their long-overlooked country had the *freedom* to win.

# PART I

# FROM WINTER TO SPRING

*Lenka interrupts. "In the West no one knows anything about Prague. They try to forget Prague after they betrayed us in 1938. Do you know about 1938?"*

*"The Munich accord?"*

*"Accord? Does accord mean agreement? But we did not agree to anything.* Mnichovská zrada, *that is what we call it. The Munich betrayal. And because of this betrayal we are forgotten, our country is forgotten, Prague is forgotten, and who cares that it is most beautiful city in Europe? So we need people like you to help the world rediscover our city and our country. And to protect it against the Russians."*

—Simon Mawer, *Prague Spring*[1]

CHAPTER 1

# The Butcher Shop on Thin Ice

I n 1942, in a little town in what was once known as Czechoslovakia, a twenty-year-old man named Jaroslav Holík ["ya-RO-slav ho-LEEK"] opened a butcher shop. In the years to come, he and his family put their hearts and souls into the shop. It would become the center of their world.

The young man could hardly have chosen a more difficult place and time to open a new business than the town of Brod in 1942. Just a few months earlier, in late September 1941, Reinhard Heydrich, a high-ranking German official, had arrived in the Czech capital of Prague seemingly straight out of central casting. Six feet, three inches tall, with neatly slicked blond hair and pale blue eyes, Heydrich personified the ideal Aryan. Adorned with nicknames such as the Blond Beast, the Hangman, Himmler's Evil Genius, and the Young Evil God of Death, Heydrich had helped organize the Kristallnacht reign of terror on German and Austrian Jews and served as the official planner of "The Final Solution," the Nazi plan for the genocide of the Jewish people. Heydrich instantly lived up to all of his nicknames, executing more than 140 people within five days of his arrival in the Czech lands.

To many, Heydrich's landing in Prague felt sudden, but really it had been centuries in the making. Today Brod sits in the very center of the Czech Republic, almost exactly equidistant between the country's two biggest cities, about seventy miles from the capital, Prague, to the northwest and Brno to the southeast. But once upon a time the area was all forest-covered frontier. Settlement began in the mid-1200s with the discovery of silver ore deposits. Soon German settlers made up the majority of the population, leading the town to name itself Německý Brod (German Ford) in 1308. Over the years the town was visited by numerous calamities, from plagues to fires to floods, but the greatest threat arose because of its location in the middle of the continent. One after another, the powers of Europe sought to hold sway over the region, and by the late 19th century it had become part of the Austro-Hungarian Empire.

After intense lobbying by Czech and Slovak nationalists and the collapse of the Austro-Hungarian Empire at the end of the first World War, in 1918 the Allies supported the creation of a new country, Czechoslovakia, out of a small part of the lands that had been under the Empire's control. Czechoslovakia was immediately among the world's most industrialized countries, and established a parliamentary democracy. In Brod, jubilant citizens marched through the streets to celebrate the establishment of the free Czechoslovak state. As they did, they tore down all Austrian signs, pictures of the Austrian emperor, and any other symbols of the imperial state, which they burned in a huge bonfire in the main square. [1]

But Czechoslovakia faced a major problem. The western corner of the country jutted nearly 150 miles into Germany, with German lands to the north and the south, and ethnic Germans made up nearly a quarter of Czechoslovakia's population. As a result, Czechoslovakia included numerous German-speaking enclaves, especially in the area surrounding Brod.

Over time, German nationalists in Czechoslovakia increasingly demanded that their border regions be made part of the "homeland," and once Hitler rose to power in the 1930s, Germany threatened to use force to accommodate them. Desperate to prevent war across Europe, in 1938 Britain and France signed the Munich Agreement with Germany, thus giving Hitler effective control over large swaths of Czechoslovakia. As he prepared to give Germany much of what it wanted, British prime minister Neville Chamberlain explained the decision to his people over the radio: "How horrible, fantastic, incredible it is that we should be digging trenches and trying on gas masks here because of a quarrel in a far-away country between people of whom we know nothing." Czechoslovakia was not even invited to the negotiations over its lands and felt betrayed by the western powers, all the more so because it had a military alliance with France. This would not be the last time that the world abandoned Czechoslovakia.

On March 15, 1939, German military forces entered the Czech lands. News of the invasion arrived in Brod first thing that morning, and heavily armed German soldiers entered the town at 1 P.M. In Jihlava, a town with a large German population sixteen miles to the south, the residents celebrated the new arrivals. But in Brod—where the Hussite Wars had driven out much of the German population in the 15th century—the mood was largely one of indifference, and only a few representatives of the city came to greet the invaders. [2] In the following weeks, that mood changed. Posters started to appear all over town, in German and broken Czech, listing new ordinances for the residents, most notably a nightly curfew. [3] Brod was permitted to maintain its own mayor, but Germans controlled the rest of the administration and opened an office for the Gestapo, the Nazi secret police. [4] Over time, the Germans sent hundreds of thousands of Czechs to concentration camps, but at the beginning the Nazis showed greater restraint than they demonstrated elsewhere in Europe because of their desire to mobilize the Czech population for the German war effort. Eventually, though, Hitler grew impatient with what he saw as overly lenient treatment of the Czechs by his deputies. In September 1941 he sent in Heydrich, one of his favorite lieutenants, to whip the country into submission.

Appropriately fearing for its country's fate under the rule of the Nazi that Adolf Hitler affectionately called "the man with the iron heart," in the late spring of 1942 the Czechoslovak resistance assassinated Heydrich. Hitler immediately ordered devastating reprisals. German forces killed more than 1,300 Czechs, and in June entirely eliminated two helpless villages.

It was at this very time, as the threat of violence from German forces swirled around him, that young Jaroslav Holík decided to carve out a new life for himself. Earlier in the year he had convinced the beautiful Věra Kašparová to marry him. On August 3, 1942, as Nazi terror rained down upon the country, Jaroslav and Věra's first child was born. They named him Jaroslav, just like his father. Given the utter madness that surrounded his birth, perhaps the Holíks should have anticipated that the child would grow up to be wild.

As if marriage, a new child, and the Nazi occupation weren't enough, in 1942 Jaroslav Sr. also decided to open a butcher shop. The decision had actually been made by his father, who said to his son, "Look! There is an open butcher shop. Rent it, and show me what you can do." [5] Meat was the family business. Jaroslav's father was a butcher. So was his brother. And even though little more than 10,000 people lived in Brod during the war, the town had enough demand to accommodate multiple butchers. [6]

Jaroslav and Věra's shop sat in a nearly perfect location on Horní Street, a three-block-long, narrow gray-brick lane lined with local businesses. Horní Street led diagonally into the beautiful town square, which was surrounded on four sides by distinctive two-story Renaissance and Baroque houses with decorated gables. In the square's northeast corner, a centuries-old church tower allowed visitors to view the quiet town and the vast countryside beyond.

By the time Jaroslav and Věra wed in 1942, the German occupation had hit Věra's family hard. Věra had been born in 1922 to a woman who worked on a nearby farm and died after childbirth. A kind Brod couple, Robert and Marie Horák, adopted the little girl and brought her to live with them. Robert had long been deeply concerned about the plight of the poor and the grave inequality he saw around him. He became a devoted member of the Communist Party and even served under the Party banner as Brod's deputy mayor. In 1941, the Germans carried out a series of arrests of Communists in the town. The occupiers executed the editor of the Communist newspaper for his "resistance activities" and shipped Horák off to Buchenwald concentration camp. Věra spent the next four years caring for her ill mother and waiting for news of her father.[7]

The period following Jaroslav and Věra's wedding, the opening of the butcher shop, and the birth of little Jaroslav proved no less terrifying. In 1943, the Germans took complete control of Brod's administration and established German as the town's official language. Former officers in the Czechoslovak army organized resistance groups, which the Gestapo quickly crushed, putting to death two of their members and sending others off to concentration camps, some never to return. The Holíks' worries only grew after their second son, Jiří ["YI-rzhee"], was born on July 9, 1944. Allied air raids focused on a local airfield and dropped bombs on the town, which damaged buildings and killed four schoolchildren.[8]

Life in the butcher shop didn't feel much safer. For the rest of his life, Jaroslav Jr. would vividly remember German soldiers confiscating smoked meats. Věra hid the boy under a table, holding his head down so he couldn't see, but he never forgot the pounding of the soldiers' heavy boots as they shouted in German at his father.[9] The Holíks had to confront a series of difficult questions in their shop: "Will we have enough?" "Will we have the products that the Germans want?" "*Should* we sell to them?" "Will we have enough for our regular customers?" "Will the Gestapo come take our store?" Then, toward the end of the war, when local partisans came to buy products, the question became, "If we sell to them, will someone rat us out?" One day, a Czech partisan bought sausages and salami. Several hours later, Věra saw German soldiers carrying the man away . . . dead.[10]

Nevertheless, needing to make a living, Jaroslav Sr. and Věra threw themselves into the shop. Jaroslav Sr. lacked both a formal education and the glad-handing panache of a typical salesman, but he had good sense and simply outworked everyone else. A disciple of Dale Carnegie and his book *How to Win Friends and Influence People*, the young man became a skilled negotiator, able to get products and rent services and space at good prices.[11] Věra, who had previously worked in a hairdressing salon in Prague, handled sales.[12] The Holík butcher shop not only survived, but even became popular.[13]

With the tide turning against the Germans in early 1945, a civilian resistance group in Brod formed to fight back. In early May, as Czechs in Prague spontaneously rose up to fight their occupiers, civilians in Brod revolted as well. In response, German forces carried out brutal countermeasures, including executing Brod locals. The repression continued until May 8, when the Germans fled, fearing the approaching Soviet Red Army. On May 9, Soviet forces liberated the town. Only then did the people of Brod learn just how cruel the occupiers had truly been, as they uncovered mass graves of tortured patriots.[14]

In the weeks after the liberation, the Holíks received a welcome shock: Věra's father, Robert, abruptly appeared on the doorstep of the butcher shop, thin as a pole and weighing less than ninety pounds.[15] Many Germans had lived in the area around Brod prior to the war, and Grandpa Horák had learned quite a bit of the language. His knowledge of German had helped him survive in Buchenwald.[16] A die-hard Communist, Horák was grateful to the Soviets for their part in freeing him and his country from Germany's clutches.

In truth, US army forces had entered Czechoslovakia by early May 1945, prepared to support the effort to defeat the Germans. However, American president Harry Truman and General Dwight Eisenhower wanted to avoid a showdown with Soviet leader Joseph Stalin, who saw Eastern Europe as his payment for the millions of Soviet soldiers who had died fighting the Nazis. The American leadership ordered its forces to stay back, thus giving the Soviets time to carry out the liberation. It was a decision that many leaders on the US side came to regret and that millions in Eastern Europe, including the Holíks, came to despise. Once again, Czechoslovakia's geography—this time, its shared eastern border with the USSR—proved to be a curse.

But in the immediate aftermath of the war, the people of Brod thought little about that; instead they focused on rebuilding. Wanting no more to do with its long-gone German heritage, the town changed its name to Havlíčkův Brod ["hav-LEECH-koov brodt"] (Havlíček's Ford), honoring local nineteenth-century writer Karel Havlíček Borovský. Residents volunteered nearly 100,000 hours to remove damaged buildings and vehicles, repair and repave roads and squares, and restart city gas distribution. One year after liberation, visitors were hard pressed to find any clear evidence of war damage in the town.[17]

The town's population was growing, which was great news for the young entrepreneurial family. Jaroslav Sr. and Věra worked from dawn to dusk in the shop, and the boys helped whenever they were needed. Yet money was hardly plentiful for the young couple, both just twenty-four years old, with two small children. They lived in a small town, with a population now close to 12,000, in a small country of just twelve million that was struggling in the postwar world. The kids had little beyond the bare necessities: each had two pairs of shorts, one pair of cloth pants, and a "disgusting" pair of sweatpants.[18] Jaroslav Sr. and Věra poured their earnings back into the business, purchasing machinery and devices to expand into a large meat cannery, the first of its kind in Brod.

Even still, they didn't put *every* crown (Czechoslovakia's currency) into the shop. For Christmas in 1946 they gave four-year-old Jaroslav Jr. a gift that would shape the rest of his life: his first ice skates, a detachable pair that affixed to the bottoms of his boots.

The gift was a rare luxury for the Holík family. When it came time to exchange presents that year, Jaroslav's father handed his wife a hat. It was the very hat he'd given her the year before, which he rewrapped so she would have something to open. It was the same hat that he would give her the next year as well.[19]

When the Holíks awoke on Christmas morning, the scene was bleak. On the first floor, their one-room kitchen, living, and dining space was also used by the butcher shop, so the wooden floor was usually covered in meat mess and grease. Věra got up at 3 A.M. three times a week to scrub it, with only a wood-stove to warm her. Upstairs they had just a single bedroom in which they all slept. During the winter they used a single heating drum to warm the apartment and to heat water for bathing. It had no separate bathroom. Instead, a single toilet sat in the hallway. The toilet space was so poorly lit that Jiří avoided relieving himself in the house because of his fear of the dark. [20]

Little Jaroslav's Christmas gift was part of the effort Jaroslav Sr. and Věra made to create a joyful childhood for their boys. Despite the poverty of the time, life for the Holík kids looked a lot like that for children elsewhere. With their parents working all day, they were able to mostly just run free when not at school. Somehow, even in small-town Czechoslovakia, kids got their hands on magazines from the West filled with stories of exotic lands like "Texas." At night they hid under the covers, reading these magazines by flashlight. In the summer they created elaborate maps of the town wherein the local creek became "The Amazon." So it was for the young Holík boys. Brod covered only a total of twenty-five square miles, markedly smaller than American towns such as Middlebury, Vermont, and Bend, Oregon, and even a shade smaller than tiny Oshkosh, Wisconsin. The Holík boys, with their closely shorn towheads, could be seen running all around town throughout the year. Although Jaroslav towered over his just two-years-younger brother, there was little doubt that they were siblings. As little boys, both were so skinny that their ribs stuck out when they frolicked in their swimsuits at the lake. [21]

The kids in Brod especially loved winter games. On cold winter evenings, they poured water onto the streets so they could get up early the next day and slide around town on makeshift sleds. [22] But the older Holík brother yearned to do something else on the ice.

When he opened his new skates on Christmas Day, Jaroslav Jr. could not contain his excitement. Brod contained numerous ponds of varying sizes, some just tiny patches of water. Jaroslav Sr. took his older boy out to one such patch behind a nearby park and taught him how to skate. From that day on, whenever young Jaroslav had a free moment in the winter, he went from pond to pond, skating to his heart's content. [23] Two years later, when Jiří was four, Věra started making Jaroslav bring his little brother with him. Until the boys were old enough for school, on winter mornings the parents headed off early to work, then around lunchtime took the boys to the pond.

Most often, Jaroslav Jr. and Jiří went to Cihlář (Brickworker) Pond, so-called because it sat by the brickwork factory. The pond sat nestled near Vršovice, just outside of Brod, where Věra's parents lived. In the winter the pond typically froze over by the end of November and remained frozen through the end of February. But the first signs of ice were hardly reliable. The neighborhood children were largely unsupervised, and as the surface began to solidify, they all went out to test it. From time to time, one of the kids took a step too many, the thin surface collapsed, and the child fell into the icy water. No one ever drowned, but many had to run home to change clothes. As the temperature turned colder, the kids watched with fascination as ice makers cut big chunks from the frozen pond for the local brewery. Once the adults left, the Holík boys would jump onto floating ice sheets, pretending that they were Inuits.[24] With all the kids skating around, the ice became chipped and uneven, so the Holík boys turned their grandparents' old metal tub into a Zamboni. They filled the tub with water, dragged it down to the pond, and poured it onto the ice to smooth out the surface.

Jaroslav Jr. loved his time at the pond, but complained about having to bring his brother: "Why do I have to tie his shoelaces and watch over him?!" Jiří followed his brother around on the ice until around 6 P.M. when their parents came to get them. As she picked up the boys, Věra always girded herself, ready to hear the latest from other parents about her older son's poor behavior.

From the earliest age, Jaroslav Jr. drove his parents to distraction. Much like the neighborhood crusty elderly man who knew better than everybody else, he never hesitated to let anyone within earshot know his opinion. The other kids nicknamed him "Old Timer" (*Starej*). People with big mouths often find themselves in conflict with others, and the Holíks saw their firstborn starting fights at a young age, even with children older and bigger than he was. Jaroslav Sr. was beside himself. "You jackass, why do you have to fight with everyone? Just look at your brother, he smiles and everything is good."[25]

When he started attending school, Jaroslav Jr. made life miserable for his teachers, whom he talked back to on a regular basis. He was a natural leader in the classroom and directed his followers to join him in causing a general ruckus. They hid under their desks to play blackjack and invented new games, such as seeing who could spit through the classroom window and come closest to nailing the horse that carried the town's mail.

Corporal punishment was the norm in Brod schools at the time, so Jaroslav found himself getting smacked repeatedly by his teachers, but it was his mother's lectures that he most feared. In the house, Věra handled academics and had to suffer through reports at parent-teacher conferences that not only was Jaroslav performing poorly on his schoolwork, he also was constantly in trouble. Jaroslav usually argued with her, but once she started haranguing him, his eyes glazed over and he felt his mind melting. He decided to take steps to reduce the torture. Each student had a special notebook in which teachers recorded students' grades and noted disciplinary issues. As Jaroslav racked up the punishments, he got himself a second notebook, where many of his worst citations would get listed. When his parents asked to see the notebook, he only showed them the first book, so they never learned of half his shenanigans.[26]

Jaroslav developed such a reputation that when Jiří entered the school that his older brother attended, one teacher recoiled. "You are Holík's brother? Jesus Christ, what an ordeal this is going to be!"[27] But, in reality, Jiří couldn't have been less like his brother. Jaroslav Jr. had inherited his father's fiery temper, but everyone described Jiří as more like the sweet-tempered Věra. Whereas Jaroslav ran from one place to the next, Jiří strolled. At times Jaroslav wished he could borrow the peace that seemed part of his younger brother's inner nature, but he quickly became infuriated at the thought of staying so still. The younger boy followed instructions and did well in school. Whenever she looked at her sweet little boy, Věra's heart melted. She told Jiří that all it took was a smile and everyone fell in love with him.[28]

So it was that when Věra came to pick her boys up from the pond, she could always expect to hear complaints about Jaroslav. But when both boys had been skating together for about a year, she began to hear something else as well. People of all ages were awestruck by her son. *Not* Jaroslav—it was Jiří that everyone gawked at. At no more than five years old, Věra's baby glided around the ice with extraordinary grace and speed. No one had ever seen anything quite like it, and it made an impression on an important person in the town.[29]

Brod had a rich tradition of hockey, going back well before World War II.[30] In the early years after the war, kids played pickup hockey on any pond that would freeze. In 1949, when Jaroslav and Jiří were seven and five years old, the Holík boys began to notice a gray-haired man in his fifties watching them play. The man was Jaroslav "Dad" Tománek, who worked in the local revenue service office but was also the area's godfather of youth hockey, serving as team organizer, manager, treasurer, and occasional coach. In the years that followed, none of the kids could think of a time that he was missing from Brod's Kotlina rink, even if it was freezing or snowing. He never played hockey, and had never been seen on skates. But he loved children and knew what sports meant to them. Tománek didn't know the first thing about coaching, but he focused on one core principle: He forced the boys to skate while looking at him. He held up various numbers of fingers and instructed the skaters to tell him how many he was holding up. If they looked down, he gave them a quick smack with a stick. Because of this one drill, the boys learned to see everything around them on the ice while also controlling the puck.[31]

Kotlina was an open-air, natural-ice rink surrounded by wooden boards. As was common throughout the country, the base of the skating surface was concrete, which was sprayed down with hose water that turned to ice when the temperature dropped low enough. When resurfacing was required, volunteers dragged barrels of hot water all over the ice. There was a small bleacher stand next to the rink, but many fans stood on snowbanks to watch. An old house abutted the rink and provided miserable, cramped changing rooms floored with wooden planks. Upon entering, players needed to immediately start a fire in the heater or they would freeze while changing.[32]

At seven years old, Jaroslav Jr. caught Tománek's eye, and with the prodding of Jaroslav Sr., decided to join the organized hockey team. The boy had to look after his brother while his parents worked, so the Holíks insisted that Jiří also join the squad as one of its youngest members.[33] From the beginning, they were joined by one other boy Jiří's age.

Jan Suchý ["Yaan SU-khee"] was born in Brod on October 10, 1944, three months after Jiří. When Jan was born, both his parents worked at the local hospital. His twenty-year-old mother, Jarmila, was a cook, and his twenty-eight-year-old father, František, drove the ambulance. František rarely talked about his work and, in fact, was rarely home at all. Every day after work, he returned to the apartment, changed out of his work clothes, and headed to one of his two favorite pubs, where he hung out and played cards with a group of friends. The routine there was always the same: a pack of cigarettes, three beers, and four rums.

The Suchýs lived near the hospital, about half a mile due east of the Holíks, in an apartment building nicknamed "The Pigsty" (*Prasečák*) because it used to house pigs. Their apartment had a kitchen and a single bedroom in which they all slept. Cash was extremely tight, and they had to scrimp to be able to afford anything beyond the necessities. Despite the lack of money and the close quarters, František and Jarmila got along well, and Jan never once heard his parents fight.

Each morning during the winter, Jarmila dropped little Jan off with a lunch at a local frozen pond, and he spent the day there playing on the ice with other boys from the neighborhood. When the boys got hungry, they built a fire out of twigs to heat their food and then continued playing. When Jan was just four years old the bigger kids taught him how to skate. He didn't have his own skates, but he begged the other kids to let him play hockey with them. The big kids set him up as the goalie, having him stand in the scoring area in his regular walking shoes. They shot hard but somehow the little boy didn't flinch. The kids didn't have much beyond their clothes to cover themselves, but they did make protective hockey gear out of whatever they could find. They stole any materials that might be turned into equipment and brought them to Jan's mother, who sewed everything together. Thanks to František's work at the hospital, Jan had ready access to a huge store of cotton balls, which he stuffed into his father's big winter gloves to catch pucks in the goal. After begging his father throughout the start of the winter season, little Jan got his first skates for Christmas in 1948, the same detachable kind Jiří also received that year. To the little Suchý boy, there was no greater feeling than flying around the ice.

In general, František Suchý gave his son little attention, until one day when he went to pick the boy up from the pond. František had been a soccer player for Brod and appreciated real athleticism. As he arrived to bring five-year-old Jan home, he couldn't believe what he saw. His son raced around the ice as fast as any of the older boys and played hockey with them as an equal. In a town as small as Brod, František knew Dad Tománek, and he signed his boy up to play with the group at Kotlina. Jan leaped at the chance to play more seriously. When the kids learned that practices ran early in the morning, six-year-old Suchý was the only one from his class to sign up. [34]

Jiří and Jan were the same age, but they could not have been more different. Little Jan's thick dark brown locks stood in sharp contrast to Jiří's blond hair. Whereas Jiří's constantly smiling boyish face gave him a cherubic image, Suchý's more angular features made him appear older than he actually was, and his smirk left those around him wondering what hijinks he had up his sleeve. Jan was tall and skinny, while Jiří was just small all over, leading Suchý to refer to him as "Runt" (*Mrňous*). Jiří quickly got to work figuring out a nickname that he could throw back. He finally came up with *Souška*, a play on Suchý's last name that translates to "dry tree," a reference to how skinny and weak Jan appeared. The younger Holík boy later grew to be a stocky five feet, eleven inches tall, but Suchý never stretched above five-nine, and even though he grew stronger and more muscled, everyone called him Souška for the rest of his life. [35]

The behavior of the two boys contrasted even more than their physical appearances. Everyone knew Jiří for his happy-go-lucky disposition, his excellent behavior, and the fact that he did as he was told by his teachers and coaches. Suchý, meanwhile, was a completely different story. Souška didn't mind mixing it up with other kids and simply refused to follow the rules. When the circus came to town, a young Jan skipped school to shovel sawdust in exchange for free tickets. He developed a reputation for his mischief, such as well-planned heists of local farmers' strawberries, apples, and watermelons or sneakily filching fish from a breeding pond. [36] And though Suchý *loved* hockey and played to win at all costs, he refused to follow his coach's instructions.

Despite all these differences, Runt and Souška quickly bonded as the youngsters of the team. Jiří was the only person Jan had ever met who could outskate him, while Jiří quickly realized that Suchý was by far the most naturally talented of all the young hockey players he had seen. Each morning in the winter, long before the sun rose, the two met in front of the local painter's cottage and set out together for the arena. Already in their gear, they would immediately clean the ice and get to work. [37]

Training was difficult. As soon as nightly temperatures hit freezing, Jaroslav Sr. yanked his groggy boys out of bed long before the sun could rise and possibly thaw the ice. As he shouted at them, Jaroslav Jr. and Jiří begged to stay in bed, but their father had plans for them. A 5 A.M. wake-up, a quick breakfast, and then the boys took off for the half-mile walk to Kotlina for 6 A.M. practice. Ordinarily, the walk might have been quick, but since the youth teams weren't permitted in the locker rooms, they had to carry all their very heavy gear—skates, pads, sticks—to and from the rink. After practice, the boys stopped at the butchery, where Jaroslav Sr. gave them each a piece of salami or sausage. [38]

It was hard to get quality hockey equipment in 1950s Czechoslovakia, espe-cially out in the boonies of Brod. In particular, little was available in young kids' sizes, so everyone had to get creative. One of the regulars at the Holík butcher shop was a carpenter and cabinetmaker named Mareš. When Jiří was just five years old, the little boy carefully hid away one of the sharp butcher knives, cut off a few slices of dry salami, and made a secret visit to see the man: "Mr. Mareš, here is some salami. Please make me a hockey stick." Before you knew it, the little boy had himself several sticks! For protective gear, Jaroslav Sr. comman-deered sheet metal from local factories, which he used to construct pads. Věra handcrafted protection from random pieces of plywood and stitched together padded pants. Still, even with the makeshift protection, it was incredibly painful when the boys got hit by the puck, and their elbows were constantly swollen. [39]

None of the boys' families was rolling in money, but life was good. The boys had their hockey. The Holíks had their butcher shop.

And then the Communists stepped in . . .

In March 1946, early in the year that Jaroslav Jr. received his first skates, British statesman Winston Churchill traveled to the United States to talk about the part of the world where the Holíks lived. After the war, the Soviet Union and its clients in the region employed a range of tactics—from rigging elections and threatening force to outright violence—to ensure the rise of Communist regimes throughout much of Central and Eastern Europe. On March 5, at Westminster College in Fulton, Missouri, Churchill, who had led Britain throughout the war, spoke passionately about the threat:

> An iron curtain has descended across the Continent. Behind that line lie all the capitals of the ancient states of Central and Eastern Europe. Warsaw, Berlin, Prague, Vienna, Budapest, Belgrade, Bucharest and Sofia, all these famous cities and the populations around them lie in what I must call the Soviet sphere, and all are subject in one form or another, not only to Soviet influence but to a very high and, in some cases, increasing measure of control from Moscow. . . . The Communist parties, which were very small in all these Eastern States of Europe, have been raised to pre-eminence and power far beyond their numbers and are seeking everywhere to obtain totalitarian control.

Jaroslav Jr. knew nothing about the speech and had only heard the name "Churchill" in passing, but the former prime minister was very familiar with the Holíks' little country. The most positive words in the address came when he noted that Czechoslovakia remained the one true democracy in the region. Prior to the war, Czechoslovakia had been the most democratic country in Eastern Europe. On May 26, 1946, nearly three months after Churchill's speech, the country held free and fair parliamentary elections. Czechoslovakia's Communists were the big winners, taking 38 percent of the vote, by far the most for any party.

It was no surprise that the Communists performed so well. In 1946 life was still difficult in Czechoslovakia, which was struggling to rise from the ashes of the war. People faced a deteriorating economy, severe shortages of all goods, and high unemployment. They remembered that historically the country's Communists had tried to work within the democratic system, that capitalist countries had abandoned Czechoslovakia before the war, and that Czechoslovak Communists had fought hard against the Germans. It also didn't hurt that it had ultimately been the Communist-led USSR that liberated the country. Following the election, the Communist Party formed a coalition government that sought to address the country's economic crisis.

It was not immediately clear how much things would change with the Communist Party in power, but there were ominous signs. The Communists now controlled the country's police, military, agriculture, and propaganda. In addition, the government took steps to control large-scale businesses, which instantly affected people across the country. The Holíks saw the results immediately as the government took over the Veselý Textile Company in Brod, which employed 900 people.[40] On the whole, though, the new policies didn't appear too radical, and the government seemed open to working with the capitalist West. When the US began preliminary discussions on the Marshall Plan, which would offer massive economic aid to help European countries rebuild after the war, Czechoslovakia's government announced in July 1947 that it would participate.

But the Soviets grew worried about Czechoslovakia drawing too close to the West. Stalin immediately summoned Klement Gottwald, Czechoslovakia's prime minister and Communist Party chairman, who rushed to Moscow. Stalin berated Gottwald for betraying the Communist partnership. Czechoslovakia's leader quickly volunteered to pull out of the Marshall Plan deliberations. When he returned home, Czechoslovakia's government withdrew its stated intention to discuss economic aid with the West.

Meanwhile, Czechoslovakia's economic problems continued to mount. In turn, increasingly Czechoslovak citizens and politicians lost confidence in the Communists. It became clear that the Party would not do very well in the planned 1948 election.

Stalin and Czechoslovakia's Communists saw the writing on the wall and decided to act. In February 1948, Stalin sent to Prague one of his top diplomats, Valerian Zorin, whose mere presence offered a reminder that Czechoslovakia's Communists had the backing of the Soviet Red Army. To bang home the point, Gottwald requested that Soviet forces set up along Czechoslovakia's border. Stalin also sent "consultants" to Prague. Following the consultants' blueprint, Czechoslovakia's Communists purged critics from the national police force and mobilized militias of supporters, who took to the streets. [41] Czechoslovakia's non-Communist leaders saw no good options. They could risk civil war and possibly a Soviet invasion by pushing back against the Communists, or they could give in.

People like the Holíks knew little about these behind-the-scenes machinations. But they did know that over the course of February 1948, police and armed militia groups took over Prague and began a purge of all non-Communists in the government and the bureaucracy. And they knew that, on February 25, 1948, Czechoslovakia's non-Communist parties and leaders stepped down, permitting the Communists to take full control of the country. In the weeks that followed, the Holíks watched with horror as their new government banned all opposition to the regime and imprisoned non-Communist politicians who continued to resist. [42] The one remaining member of the cabinet not sympathetic to the Communists was found dead, having "jumped" out of a third-story window.

Within less than three years, Czechoslovakia had traded a German occupation for a homegrown—but Soviet-supported—authoritarian regime of its own. Initially, following the coup, the police arrested relatively small numbers of potential dissenters from the military, police, and non-Communist political parties, and many of them were soon released. However, in the fall of 1948, the government passed the Law for the Defense of the Republic, which made it a crime to speak ill of Czechoslovakia or its leaders, or even to criticize the Soviet Union. In the coming years, tens of thousands of Czechs and Slovaks would be sentenced to prison for these crimes.[43] The StB (*Státní bezpečnost*), the secret police, detained and then released tens and possibly hundreds of thousands more.[44] The secret police also swept thousands of potential opponents out of Czechoslovakia's cities—opposition party leaders, business owners, lawyers, pensioners. Large numbers were sent to labor camps and uranium mines while their homes were turned over to Communist Party notables. Travel beyond the country's borders without permission became prohibited.

The government followed Stalin's cue in calling dissenters the "enemies of the people" and "enemies of the republic." It carried out a purge of teachers who might not be sympathetic to the Communist cause. In school, children learned Russian—and about both the virtues of communism and the failings of capitalism. Instead of a free press, the media delivered whatever "news" was useful to the regime. The Ministry of Information and Culture took over and "purified" the country's libraries and bookstores. More than fourteen million books were removed from private collections.[45]

The Holíks felt the pressure. On a daily basis, Czechs and Slovaks had every reason to fear the secret police, whose network of informants allowed the government's reach to be everywhere. Throughout the country, coworkers, neighbors, friends and, at times, even family members now reported each other's actions and words to the government. The Holíks' good friend Dr. Horníček often came to the house to talk politics and listen to Radio Free Europe with Jaroslav Sr. so they could learn about the news from abroad. When Věra got angry and closed the windows to make sure no one could hear them, the men turned the volume way down and leaned in close to the receiver. Dr. Horníček insisted, "Look, I'm telling you within a year it's going to blow up and the Communists will be out of power!" One day he said those same words in a local café, and then found himself imprisoned for a year.[46]

At home, Jaroslav Sr. and Věra constantly cursed the regime, but the moment they stepped outside they zipped their mouths shut. The problem they faced, though, was that Jaroslav Jr. had no filter. No matter how much they pleaded, and no matter where he was or whom he was with, the younger Jaroslav never shied away from expressing his views on the Communists.[47] Fortunately, his tirades never came back to haunt the family. Perhaps his years of antics had most of the town already turning a blind eye—and deaf ear.

Following the 1948 coup, Czechoslovakia's Communist leaders feared that the USSR might remove them from power and possibly even send in troops if they didn't demonstrate complete loyalty. The government went to great lengths to demonstrate its allegiance to Moscow. "Friendship with the Soviet Union" became a national slogan, and now-President Gottwald became the object—although only as a junior partner to Stalin—of a cult of personality pushed across Czechoslovakia. Czechoslovak officials placed portraits of Stalin and Gottwald everywhere, always careful to describe Gottwald as "Stalin's best disciple."[48] Work began in Prague on an enormous granite statue of Stalin—some fifty feet high, seventy feet long, and weighing seventeen thousand tons—the largest depiction of the Soviet leader in the world.[49]

In the years 1949–52, Stalin sent Soviet advisors to help the Czechoslovak government "prove" that it was under threat and rally support around the country for the regime. A series of show trials played out, relying on fabricated charges and evidence, including torture-induced confessions. The torture included direct physical pain, as well as sleep deprivation to muddle the defendants' thinking, and threats of devastating consequences for wives and children. The trials were broadcast live over the radio and included an audience that the government bused in to watch. Everyone followed a script that all the participants, including the charged, were forced to memorize and rehearse. The outcome, always pre-established, included lengthy prison terms and even the death penalty.[50] In the end, some two hundred people were executed.

Beginning in 1949, the government went after the Catholic Church, which stood as a competitor for the hearts and minds of the working class. The regime seized monasteries. It also imprisoned hundreds, if not thousands, of Catholic priests, monks, and nuns, subjected many to torture and abuse, and in some cases put them to death.[51]

Perhaps the most distressing of the show trials focused on Milada Horáková. Horáková had worked tirelessly as a social justice and women's rights activist. When she campaigned in favor of democracy and in opposition to the Communists after the 1948 coup, the government arrested her as the "criminal mastermind of a terrorist conspiracy." In late spring 1950, Horáková's trial was broadcast not just on the radio but also through public address systems in workplaces and in the streets. Even after brutal torture by the secret police, the forty-eight-year-old Horáková refused to follow the script and calmly disputed the charges. But the court found her guilty and sentenced her to death. On June 27, 1950, the government hanged her.[52]

Still, many in the country believed in the communist system; to them, it was kinder than capitalism, which left those at the bottom defenseless. Supporters rejoiced in May 1948 when a new constitution declared that the economy would be founded on nationalized industry and the government began to take over privately owned businesses. Věra's father, Robert Horák, was one of those people who believed deeply in the idea of communism. He loved the idea of a society and government that would take care of everyone. Grandpa Horák volunteered as the head of the local homeless shelter. He got up at 4 A.M. every day to walk three miles to the train station to pick up a large stack of *Rudé právo*, the Communist Party's newspaper, which he then distributed around town. Even at a very young age, Jaroslav Jr. recognized the extraordinary kindness of his grandfather and decided that if he ever had a son, he would name him "Robert."[53]

When it came to communism, Grandpa Horák and Jaroslav Sr. totally disagreed. The Communists' actions directly threatened the Holíks' lives. Jaroslav Sr. and Věra spent 1949 moving from a state of disbelief to growing unease to downright fear and misery as the government gradually took control of Havlíčkův Brod's establishments.[54] In 1948–49 the regime nationalized all of Brod's large textile factories and seized local Brod farms, which it transferred to state farm collectives. At first, the government assured the people of Czechoslovakia that it would only take over businesses with at least fifty employees, but over time it extended its reach to smaller and smaller ones as well. The Holíks feared for their cannery but felt safe in their butcher shop, which employed only a few workers. Then they watched in horror as the government moved in on the shops of small craftsmen and even took over the one-man barbershop in town. One night in 1950, the Holíks' smokehouse burned down when an employee fell asleep on the job. The government used the fire as an excuse, blaming the Holíks for "sabotaging the national economy and harming a workplace of the people." It gave Jaroslav Sr. two options: He could accept a tiny sum of cash in exchange for the entire business, or the government could simply take the business from the Holíks and send Jaroslav Sr. to jail.

Jaroslav Sr. agreed to the "sale," but he remained optimistic. Surely the Communist government would soon fall and he would get his business back. But his hopes never materialized. Every day offered a painful reminder to the Holíks of how their world had been turned upside down. They continued to live at the butchery, only the shop wasn't theirs anymore. They had lost—or rather, the Communists had taken—everything.

To make ends meet, Jaroslav Sr. faced the possibility of working in the mines until some friends helped him get a job at the brickwork factory. As he took up the new position, life for the Holíks took an even worse turn when Věra fell severely ill with tuberculosis. The family lived in constant fear as she spent the next two years in and out of the hospital. To compensate, Jaroslav Sr. picked up a side job of sifting sand.[55] Gradually Věra recovered, and after a few years she and her husband took over the management of a fast-food establishment. They made the business a success, but their shifts were twelve hours a day, and one of them had to be there most days.[56] Still, their situation was tolerable compared to what some people were facing.

Throughout his life, Jaroslav Jr. would vividly remember the most startling show trial, one making it crystal clear that *no one* was safe in Czechoslovakia. In 1951, following instructions from the highest levels in Moscow, the Soviet advisors insisted that Czechoslovakia investigate and put on trial leading members of the country's Communist Party. The authorities arrested as many as 25,000 members of the Party, government, military and security forces, and employees in nearly every sector of the economy.[57] At first the investigators arrested only minor figures, but increasingly over time they fabricated evidence against far bigger fish. On December 6, 1951, President Gottwald announced that they had found "proof" that his top deputy and the second most powerful figure in the country, General Secretary Rudolf Slánský—the man who had helped kickstart Czechoslovakia's show trials—was leading a conspiracy against the Party and the state.[58]

Nearly one year later, on November 27, 1952, Slánský's trial produced fourteen guilty verdicts. Eleven of the men, including Slánský, were Jewish, hardly surprising given the heavy antisemitism that was part of the 1950s purges. Slánský was publicly hanged on December 3.[59]

Jaroslav Sr. invited friends who shared his hatred of the Communists to come sit around his giant dining room table and listen to the radio broadcast of the Slánský trial. Following a behind-the-scenes barrage of mental and physical torture, Slánský confessed to the totally fabricated crimes and willingly followed the government's script. The men around the table exclaimed, "How could anyone confess to so many things? The people are being swindled!"

Jaroslav Jr. sat with them and listened to every word. As he did, the ten-year-old boy thought to himself, *This country is sick . . .* [60]

# CHAPTER 2

# Enormous Fish on a Tiny Pond

When his kids were little, Jaroslav Sr. decided to make them into ski jumpers. He drove them some twenty-five miles to Harus Hill, where they marched to the top of a one-hundred-foot ramp. From there, he could see the path to stardom. Then he looked at the boys. Terrified, little Jiří sobbed, begging not to have to jump. It probably wasn't going to work with that one. Jaroslav Sr. turned toward his firstborn and told him to begin. Jaroslav Jr. was iron-willed, never willing to admit fear, but his stomach now churned unpleasantly. He tried not to look at the ground far below, and he pushed off. He instantly felt his body sucked downward at an unimaginable speed before dropping off the bottom lip of the ramp . . . and immediately crashed onto his face. Down on the ground he lay in a crumpled heap. "Again!" Jaroslav Sr. barked at the boy. Jaroslav Jr. made his way back up the ramp and initiated his second descent. Same result. "Again!" Before long, the futility of these efforts dawned on the man. His sons were not going to become ski jumpers. Plus, it was just too much work to reach the mountains. [1]

Jaroslav Sr. relished the fact that his boys lived a life similar to kids in free countries all around the world. But he also believed that their freedom and joy would be fleeting. Before long, Jaroslav Jr. and Jiří would be grown, and life for the average citizen in Czechoslovakia was difficult. The government had taken away his business. Basic products like fruit, vegetables, meat, and appliances were in short supply. People had to wait in lines for everything and often couldn't get what they wanted. In a communist society, very few forms of upward mobility existed. The most straightforward path to a better life was to join the Communist Party and work one's way up within its ranks. Yet the notion of joining the group that had taken away his butcher shop made the Holík *pater familias* sick to his core. But there was one other way to succeed in a communist society: sports. It was a long shot, but he became convinced that between him and his boys, they could make it happen.

During the Cold War, Eastern Bloc governments placed a big emphasis on sports. They regularly highlighted their own athletes and teams, whose success created a distraction from the difficulties of daily life, inspired in their people a sense of pride in the country, and—when victorious—showed the world the "superiority" of the communist system. For these reasons, communist regimes gave their athletes favored status, allowing them benefits that few others in the country received. They got better pay, greater access to food and luxury items (like cars), and first crack at services such as good schooling and housing. And they were among the very few to be able to travel to lands outside the communist world. Athletes in Czechoslovakia were no exception.

At the very moment that Jaroslav Sr. looked to begin training his boys, he could see all this in the life of Emil Zátopek. In the 1940s and 50s, Zátopek was the finest long-distance runner in the world at a time in which track and field stood out as one of the most popular sports on the globe. Combined with his naturally ebullient and warm personality, Zátopek's success made him the most popular athlete in Czechoslovakia.

Born in 1922 in Czechoslovakia, Zátopek was a true believer in communism. He embraced the equality that communism purported to create and openly supported Czechoslovakia's government. In the 1950s, he would cooperate with the military counterintelligence branch of the secret police. In 1950, his signature even appeared on a letter that endorsed the execution of Milada Horáková—although there is debate over whether he had actually agreed to attach his name. [2]

The Communist regime took full advantage of Zátopek's athletic achievements in its propaganda efforts. As Zátopek set one world record after another, the government-sponsored newspaper placed his accomplishments on the front page, citing it as proof of the greatness of the country's administration of sports. [3] In the 1948 summer Olympics, Zátopek won a gold and a silver medal. Upon his return after the games, the government organized victory parades for the hero and sent him around the country to give morale-boosting speeches to workers' groups.

Because Zátopek brought glory to the country, he also had unique latitude to push back against the regime. While at the 1948 Olympics, Zátopek met a

Czechoslovak javelin thrower named Dana Ingrová, and the two fell in love. As a member of the military, Zátopek had to seek permission from the army to get married, but his request was quickly rejected because Dana's godfather had been associated with the country's pre-1948 democratic regime. When Zátopek announced that he would therefore quit the military, the army did an about-face and consented to the marriage.[4]

In 1952, Zátopek's friend Stanislav Jungwirth won Czechoslovakia's 1,500-meter track championship, thus qualifying to run the event in the Olympics in Helsinki, Finland. But Jungwirth's father was in prison, jailed for political dissidence, so Czechoslovakia's authorities informed their 1,500 meter champion that he would not be permitted to travel to Finland. Furious at the poor treatment of his fellow athlete, Zátopek refused to get on the airplane that was to carry the team, informing officials that he would only go if Jungwirth did as well. Czechoslovakia's officials blinked and agreed to send both men.

Zátopek knew the potential trouble he was in. Even under normal circumstances, he told friends that he feared imprisonment if he failed in athletic competitions. Now that he had directly taken on the regime, many assumed that anything less than a celebrated performance would lead Zátopek to a sentence of hard labor in the uranium mines. Indeed, a document proposing "the exemplary punishment of Staff Captain Emil Zátopek" was delivered to the defense minister's inbox.

Ordinarily, Zátopek ran only the 5,000 and 10,000 meter races at the Olympics. Now, though, to give himself a greater chance of winning gold, he added an event that he had never run before—the marathon. Over the course of eight days, Zátopek won gold in all three events, each in Olympic record time. The Defense Ministry tore up the document that had proposed his punishment.[5]

Back in Havlíčkův Brod, Jaroslav Holík Sr. was unaware of how Zátopek had asserted his independence, but he knew that he wanted his children to have the same opportunities Emil had.

Jaroslav Sr. had always been deeply involved in sports. His great love had been skiing, especially ski jumping, and he had trained with one of the country's legendary jumpers. As an adult with a wife and family, though, he had thrown himself into his butcher shop and insisted that his boys help the business succeed. But when the government took the shop, there wasn't any point to having the kids come to work with him anymore. Instead, they would become athletic stars! He told them time and again, "If you want to get anywhere in life, you have to play a sport. It won't happen any other way."[6] It became his obsession.

In the town of Havlíčkův Brod in the country of Czechoslovakia, the obvious sport was hockey.

By the early 1950s, Czechoslovakia already had a rich but sometimes troubling history with hockey.

Organized hockey in its current form, with a flat, circular puck, was codified and became popular in Canada in the last decades of the 19th century. Meanwhile, Europe focused on its own version of the sport, "bandy," in which players made big golf swings at a round ball.[7] Bandy soon attracted a healthy following in Prague, in what was then called Bohemia (Czech lands within the Austro-Hungarian Empire).[8] In the early 1900s, though, the popularity of the Canadian style of the game grew rapidly in Europe, and in 1908 a group of European countries founded what was to become the International Ice Hockey Federation (IIHF). Bohemia was among the early members.

In 1909, Bohemia sent a Canadian-style hockey team to its first-ever international tournament in Chamonix, France. Just a few weeks before the tournament, the team's goalie, a gynecologist by profession, sat down to translate the rules of the game from French into Czech, but an issue remained: the players from Bohemia had never actually played the game. On the train ride to France, a Belgian passenger showed them a puck, the first one they had ever seen. They were surprised by the shape, having thought until then that hockey pucks were square. When they arrived in France, they had to buy Canadian-style hockey sticks suitable for playing with a puck, because such sticks didn't exist in Bohemia. Not surprisingly, Bohemia lost every game it played.

Despite the losses, the men returned home excited about the game and eager to compete more, but they faced a new problem: ice, or more accurately, the lack thereof. In most years, Prague sees little snow and infrequent freezing temperatures. With no ice in Prague in 1910, the team found itself unable to practice, so it didn't attend the inaugural European hockey championships in Switzerland. In 1911, the climate proved more helpful . . . until three weeks before the tournament, when the Prague ice melted. Unwilling to miss out again, the men created a makeshift rink, where they laid down pieces of waxed wood boards on which they practiced shooting goals. Improbably, the approach worked. The team traveled to Berlin, where it won the European championships. [9]

With the victory, Bohemians went wild over the sport. By 1913 Bohemia had the most hockey clubs in Europe and became a European hockey powerhouse until World War I halted international play. [10] Once the games returned in the 1920s, the team from the newly minted Czechoslovakia remained one of the best in Europe (although it didn't hold a candle to squads from Canada).

During World War II, hockey served a surprising role in the Czech lands: helping maintain the spirit of the people in the face of an otherwise all-powerful foe. In 1940, Germany organized a pair of matches between its own players and those of the occupied Czech region. The plan was to highlight Aryan superiority in sports for propaganda purposes, and accordingly the games were broadcast live over the radio to tens of thousands of civilians from a Prague stadium, where most of the spectators were German soldiers. But things didn't go as planned for the Germans. The Czechs won 5–1 and 3–0. [11]

After the war ended, the sport became a joyful outlet for the people of Czechoslovakia. The national hockey team was aided by the fact that its players had been forced to stay in the country, where they had plenty of opportunity to play. Indeed, during the war, the leading teams played games as often as five times a week in exchange for food, one of the most sought-after commodities in occupied Europe.

The first ice hockey World Championships after the war were held in 1947 in Prague as the country tried to rebuild. In those days children went to school six days a week, and because the tournament began on a Saturday, ordinarily they would have been unable to attend. But a coal shortage made it impossible to heat the local schools an extra day, leaving hundreds of children free to watch the opening matches. When Sweden defeated Czechoslovakia 2–1 near the end of the round-robin tournament, it was assumed that all was lost for the home country team. The following day Sweden was matched up against Austria, and a victory by the Swedes would clinch the title. With defeat assuredly at hand, hundreds of Czechoslovakia fans chose to ignore the game and instead attended an afternoon production of *The Barber of Seville*. To their surprise, in the opera's final act, a well-informed but still in-character performer sang, "Say to the master that Austria is beating Sweden," inspiring mad cheering among the audience. Austria held on to defeat Sweden, which meant that Czechoslovakia had won its first ice hockey world championship. Given that ice only really stayed on the ground for around four months per year, Czechoslovakia didn't have the climate to favor winter sports. But the 1947 world title cemented the country's love of the game played on frozen water with sticks and a flat puck. [12]

However, the championship had a large asterisk attached to it, because Canada, winner of eleven of the thirteen prewar World Championships, had chosen not to attend in 1947. Returning to world action in 1948, it made its presence known in the Winter Olympics in St. Moritz, Switzerland. In their one game against each other, Canada and Czechoslovakia tied. The two countries finished the Olympics with identical 7–0–1 (seven wins, zero losses, and one tie) records, but Canada was awarded the gold medal because of its greater goal differential, the margin by which it had outscored its opponents.

Two weeks after Czechoslovakia's ice hockey team returned from the 1948 games, the Communists carried out their coup. Rather than live under a Communist regime, thousands of Czechs and Slovaks fled the country. In turn, the government imposed strict limits on travel. But the Communists recognized that allowing some movement out of the country could be beneficial. Czechoslovak athletes who performed well in international competition would promote national pride at home and demonstrate the superiority of the country's sports program. As such, it was important to permit athletes to compete abroad. But the regime also grew worried over what they might do once they left the country's borders.

In November 1948, Czechoslovakia's national hockey squad was slated to play a series of exhibition matches in England. The Czechoslovak players split up into two different airplanes—the first group left the continent a day early and then waited for their remaining teammates, who were supposed to come to London the next day. Game time arrived, but the rest of the team didn't. Later that night, those in London received the news: The air taxi carrying the remaining players had disappeared from radar over the English Channel. The men aboard had almost certainly perished.

The plane crash crushed morale, but hockey had become so popular in 1940s Czechoslovakia that the country retained a large pool of players. Just three months later, a reconstituted Czechoslovak squad traveled to Stockholm,

Sweden, to participate in the 1949 World Ice Hockey Championships. Opening the final round of play, the team defeated Canada to take the gold medal, inspiring wild celebrations back in Czechoslovakia.

By now, though, Czechoslovakia's Communist regime had grown paranoid about its athletes. After Zátopek, Czechoslovakia's greatest athlete at the time was Jaroslav Drobný. Drobný had been a star on Czechoslovakia's national hockey team. He was also ranked among the top tennis players in the world and in 1949 quit hockey to focus on tennis. Grateful for the prestige he brought the country, Czechoslovak officials prepared to bestow upon him the title "Master of Sport," which carried with it a lifetime pension. Ironically, as they finalized the honor, Drobný defected from Czechoslovakia, terrified of how easily the government could take everything away from him. [13] The regime temporarily imprisoned innocent friends of Drobný's as punishment for his departure and prohibited other tennis players from leaving Czechoslovakia at all for the next five years.

An easy-to-miss plaque on a city wall in Prague makes clear just how far the government was willing to go to prevent further escapes by its athletes. The bronze plaque bears the image of a hockey player and an inscription noting that the three-story building there was once a tavern, the spot where tragedy befell players from Czechoslovakia's beloved team.

In March 1950, the national hockey team arrived at Prague's airport, where it was to board a flight to London, this time to defend its world title, but abruptly the authorities announced that the trip was delayed and the team should go home to await further instructions. Perhaps the players should have been suspicious. Just days before, Alena Vrzáňová, Czechoslovakia's top figure skater, had decided not to return to Czechoslovakia after winning her second consecutive world ladies' singles title in London, and the regime was obviously concerned that more athletes might defect as well. On March 13, Czechoslovak officials informed the players that the trip to London was canceled because, they said, the British had not provided visas for Czechoslovakia's radio reporters. The entire story sounded fishy. Devastated, a number of the players headed to the U Herclíků tavern in Prague to drown their sorrows. As they drank, they grew boisterous, ranting against the Communist Party. Soon a fight broke out between the players and some other men . . . who turned out to be members of the secret police, who arrested them all.

The players assumed that the jailing was simply because of the bar fight and that everything would soon return to normal. But events took a very different turn. Before long, the police arrested other members of the team who had not been at the pub, including goalie Bohumil Modrý. The authorities announced that the players were "state traitors" who had planned to defect from Czechoslovakia and that Modrý was the ringleader of the planned escape.[14]

Since the Communists had taken power in 1948, the punishment for those considering defection had been meted out to thousands of people in the country. First, torture. Police commonly bound, blindfolded, and stripped the accused naked. The inquisitors then beat those they had captured and even sicced attack dogs on them. They routinely burned their captives and stuck needles under their fingernails. The accused typically confessed and then were sent to prison, often for many years, often in the country's uranium mines, where they worked with little protective gear, choked on radioactive dust, and used radioactive water for tea.[15]

As the police explained the case before them, the hockey players were flabbergasted. They had pondered defecting in 1948, but ultimately had chosen not to do so. As the players awaited trial, the jailers tortured them. One well-known official, Captain Pergl, used whips and batons and even an apparatus that he attached to the accused's temples and then tightened.[16]

The outcome of the trial was preordained: twelve players in all were found guilty, with sentences ranging from eight months to fifteen years. Modrý received the harshest sentence—fifteen years' hard labor in the Jáchymov mines. There prisoners dug up and carried uranium barehanded, which was then sent to the Soviet Union for the country's nuclear program. After five years, Modrý was released, but the time working with radiation took its toll, and he died at age forty-six.

To this day, no one knows for certain what the regime hoped to achieve by imprisoning the players. The most convincing explanation is that the authorities arrested the men simply for their behavior at the pub, but once they were in custody, the secret police realized that the event could be used to their advantage. Concerned about a wave of defections, they decided to send a message to the people—*no one* was beyond the reach of the government, not even star athletes, and even *considering* defection would be punished.[17]

-:::-

Despite the imprisonment of the national team, Czechoslovakia remained obsessed with the sport of hockey, nowhere more so than in Havlíčkův Brod. In part, the townspeople loved the sport because there was little else to do. Only a few families in Brod had a telephone. The only television in town was at the hospital—and even that was really more of a radio with a tiny screen. The Holíks owned a radio and a gramophone, and Jaroslav Sr. had a few vinyl records that he liked to play. For teenagers, there was no place to go dancing or listen to music—just "tea times," essentially a café or restaurant where teen boys could drink tea and glance awkwardly at girls. Adults didn't have many options outside the house either. They could go to one of the pubs or an occasional movie, but that was it. [18]

Brod's greatest living legend was a hockey player named Václav Chytráček, who was the only player in town good enough to make a full-time living off the sport. When Chytráček skated, he looked like he was floating and appeared to be able to do anything imaginable with a hockey stick. He often grabbed a puck behind his own goal, skated up the ice, and scored—all on his own. The people of Brod loved him when he was briefly appointed to play for the national B-squad, essentially the backup national team. They worshipped him when he declined offers to join top league teams because of his desire to stay in his hometown. And his legend only grew after he took a stick to the face, leaving him blind in one eye, but still continued to play and run every aspect of the Brod men's team. [19]

With the town's love of hockey and seeing Chytráček as inspiration, Jaroslav Sr. made his decision: his boys would become hockey stars. After he lost his business and thought about how he would stay afloat financially, Jaroslav Sr. told those around him his plan: "I have two small boys, and I want them to be athletes. I won't go work in the mines, but I will work in the brickworks so I can keep an eye on my kids."

Despite the enthusiasm for hockey in Brod, the youth hockey team was basically a ragtag group of a dozen kids with makeshift equipment and mismatched jerseys who were willing to get up at unspeakable hours to play. They didn't exactly attend rigorous practices. Occasionally, Chytráček came to coach. On those days, the boys learned a bit about hockey tactics and training. But most days the boys' "practices" at Kotlina looked a lot like their unstructured play on the pond. They skated for a while, and when they felt ready, they played practice games. With only about a dozen kids there, everyone played, giving them all a chance to hone their skills.[20]

In addition to Dad Tománek, one other adult was willing to coach: Jaroslav Sr. Like Tománek, Holík rarely set foot on the ice and didn't even have a pair of skates. Mostly he just told the boys how long to skate and then threw them some pucks. Despite knowing relatively little about the sport, he constantly criticized their play, and his highest praise was "That was weak, but passable." He focused on keeping his players disciplined. He took greater charge at games, where he roared before every match, "Score five goals in the first five minutes and you're good to go!" Then, if the boys went more than a few minutes without a goal, he berated them: "You jack-asses, how come you didn't score again?" When the boys were victorious, Jaroslav Sr. insisted they could do even better, informing them that they had only won "by a little."

It became clear that his boys and Suchý were a cut above the rest, and once Jan's father agreed to it, Jaroslav Sr. was tough on all three. If Jaroslav Sr. was unhappy with any of his three young stars . . . SMACK! Jaroslav Jr. of course argued ferociously with everyone everywhere. At home, Jaroslav Sr. didn't use corporal punishment to deal with his elder son's impertinence. But he never hesitated to strike him at the rink, especially when the boy talked back to him. During one match, Jaroslav Jr. tore into Jiří, telling the younger boy that he was causing them to lose the game. Their father grew so incensed that he chased young Jaroslav around the ice and only stopped when the referee came to the rescue. Yet, no matter how he acted with them on the ice, the former butcher felt incredible pride in his children's hockey prowess. After games, when he knew the boys couldn't hear him, he exulted to his wife: "Věruška, our boys crushed it on ice today!"[21]

Coming from a small town without public transportation, the greatest adventure for the boys was getting to travel to other towns to play. Dad Tománek was a skilled organizer and set up matches all around the region. Even just traveling twenty-five miles out of town felt like a huge trip. And going to the big city of Prague? It was like visiting a strange new land. The boys usually went by train, but the most exciting trips were taken in the backs of flatbed trucks. For the whole wintery drive, they lay down on a bed of fur underneath a tarp. Victory always made the freezing cold worth it. Whenever the boys won, Tománek bought them all hot dogs. In their memories, they were the most delicious that they would ever taste.[22]

Jaroslav Jr. instantly became the team's undisputed leader, a position he partly maintained by beating up any teammate who didn't follow his instructions.[23] As Old Timer and the boss on the ice, Jaroslav was a natural center forward, the player in the middle of all the action. But even though Jaroslav was better than most kids at most aspects of hockey, he was not an especially good skater or shooter.

It was other, less tangible features of Jaroslav's game that made him special. He was an indefatigably hard worker, with total control of the stick, a creative mind, and an ability to see possible moves no one else could. Even as a youngster he came up with unexpected and productive passes to his teammates. He never stopped fighting for the puck, no matter what the score or the time remaining in the game.[24] In any match he played, he waged a constant stream of battles with his opponents and the referees. He even drove his own teammates crazy with his constant criticism. He especially fought with Jiří and Suchý when he thought they had made poor passes.[25]

Jiří had a completely different style. With his exceptional natural skating ability, he could elegantly do anything he liked on the ice, even when moving at top speed. And with his great instincts, he always seemed to end up in the right spot to make a play work. He was also so fast that few opponents could keep up with him, making him a constant threat on offense. With that speed, he was one of those rare offensive players who could rush back on defense when needed. As soon as he did, he grabbed the puck and started a new offensive set, which usually began with a pass to his brother.[26]

The two Holík boys scarcely interacted off the ice, not even saying "goodnight" as they turned off the light in their shared room. During the freezing winter months, though, the boys spent hours every day together at the rink and usually played side-by-side on the offensive line. They balanced each other, in part because of their different but complementary skills. They fought constantly, but their years of focusing on trying to win—rather than on their own individual glory—allowed each to know instinctively what the other would do and made it possible to play completely in sync.

The boys' personalities played well off each other, too. Born into a family where his older brother and father sucked all the oxygen out of the room, Jiří never tried to be a leader. His cheerful presence acted as a counterweight to his over-the-top brother. Surprisingly, despite his upbeat personality, Jiří quickly became dejected when his team started to lose. If the team fell behind by even just one goal early in the game, Jiří glowered: "This is going to suck!" Jaroslav fumed at what he saw as his brother quitting, but usually the older boy's intensity fired Jiří back up. [27]

Even though Jaroslav Jr. drove his parents crazy, his father seemed to favor him over his younger brother. Jaroslav Sr. valued hard work above all else, and no one worked harder than his elder son. As a result, he was more likely to talk about the accomplishments of Jaroslav Jr., no matter how well Jiří did. [28] Nevertheless, Jaroslav Sr. always sought to keep both boys' egos in check. When Jaroslav Jr. was eleven, a sports magazine published a beautiful picture of him scoring a backhand goal after faking out the goalie in a big tournament in Prague. Věra could hardly contain her pride, but Jaroslav Sr. told his son, "Only when you win a World Championship can you say that you know how to play hockey." [29]

Unlike the Holíks on the offensive forward line, Jan Suchý positioned himself as a defenseman, even as a six-year-old. He had an extremely physical style, bodychecking offensive players who came into his zone and throwing himself into would-be shots by his opponents. However, whenever he got the puck near his own goal, he totally disregarded the coaches' instructions to stay back on defense and instead charged up the ice trying to score. When he joined the forwards in their attack, Jiří and Jaroslav yelled at him, "Why the hell are you up here?!" Unlike most who played his position, Suchý had amazing control over the puck. He didn't shoot with much power, but once he got near the goal, he could aim with stunning precision. He scored *a lot*, unusual for a defensive player. Coaches couldn't control Jan's decision to go on the offensive, and once they saw how well it worked, they gave up trying to stop him. [30]

By the time the boys were teenagers, hockey took up many hours a day, to the point that it created conflicts with school. It didn't help that Jaroslav and Suchý scarcely put any effort into their schoolwork. Most of the teachers were unimpressed with the boys' hockey prowess and weren't happy with their academic performance and frequent tardiness after getting back late from games. [31]

As the older one, the issue with school reared its head first for Jaroslav. Around the age of fourteen, students in Czechoslovakia who did well in the classroom could continue on to *gymnázium*, the standard academically oriented schools. Students who did poorly would have to briefly attend a vocational school and then get a full-time job. In Jaroslav's cohort, only ninety students would get to continue on the academic school path, and Jaroslav and two of his buddies ranked 91st, 92nd, and 93rd. Jaroslav Sr. grew deeply worried. He knew firsthand how hard life was for the average working person in Czechoslovakia and what a full-time job would mean: "You must go to school, because only then will you have time for hockey." In the end, though, Jaroslav Jr. lucked out. At the last moment, a few of the top ninety students chose to forgo the local academic school path, creating space for the troublesome Holík boy. [32]

Though academic doors were rapidly closing, it became increasingly clear that the boys of Brod could play hockey at a very, very high level. The town had a population at the time of only around 15,000 people, in contrast to the roughly one million who lived in Prague. The size of the hockey teams reflected this disparity. Brod's team had two goalies and around ten skaters, about half what the various city teams put forward. As they lined up to face each other prior to games, the other teams' roster stretched the width of the ice, while the Holíks, Suchý, and company barely filled up the middle. In addition, when the Brod boys showed up for games, the opposing team's supporters laughed at them. Kids from Prague hit the ice in beautiful new, ironed uniforms. The Brod boys often came wearing whatever they could find and have their mothers mend for them. It was a treat when Jiří and Suchý were in eighth grade and the Brod organizers got the boys matching green-and-white Brod jerseys, but the crowd still mocked them for their mismatched pants.

Despite—or perhaps because of—its disadvantages, the team bonded. The boys instinctively learned to play in constant motion, always aware of where their teammates were on the ice, but leaving opponents uncertain how to cover them. Hockey teams typically send out to the ice one goalie, three forwards, and two defensemen. Because hockey is so exhausting, most teams frequently cycle in new lines of skaters so players can get regular breaks. But with only ten or so on the Brod team, the Holíks and Suchý rarely rested at all during games.

It was remarkable that Suchý could handle it. When he was eleven years old, he had decided that he wanted to start smoking, but couldn't afford the cigarettes. A buddy of his, the son of a shopowner, suggested a way: they would take empty bottles out of the shop and then bring them back to the store, saying they had collected them around town, in exchange for money to buy cigarettes. By thirteen, Suchý was smoking regularly and drinking beer whenever he could sneak it.

Somehow, though, when he was on the ice the boy never seemed to need a break. When Suchý was forced to sit, he quickly grew bored and begged to be allowed back into the game. When he and the Holíks really got tired, the Brod team pretended that the goalie needed to retie his leg guards, which bought a bit of time to rest. The boys played until their muscles burned, and after games Suchý was so tired that he didn't have the energy to eat. But still, the country bumpkins from Brod played such outstanding hockey that they usually crushed the big-city teams. [33]

Much of the hockey team's success was clearly due to Jaroslav Jr., who grew into a man in his early teens. Very blond as a little boy, his hair turned somewhat darker as he got older. He was handsome, but not in a classical fashion. With his full lips and strong nose, he looked like an Eastern European version of present-day movie star Liam Neeson, albeit with lighter hair. As a fourteen-year-old, his size and strength foreshadowed the six feet in height and 180 pounds of solid muscle that he would one day carry. His tight, athletic build, neatly coiffed hair, and piercing sharp dark eyes gave the impression that he was a light heavyweight boxer or tough gang enforcer. Despite speaking with the scratchy, high-pitched voice that defined him for the rest of his life, he was clearly not someone to trifle with. It was no surprise, therefore, when he began to hang out with grown men in the town.

At fifteen years old, he became obsessed with gambling. Whenever he had time off from hockey or school, Jaroslav Jr. strolled over to the Brod Café to play cards with a group of local men. None of the group seemed to care that Jaroslav was much younger. In fact they got a kick out of having the teenage hockey prodigy in their group. Somehow, Jaroslav never lost too much money, probably because he didn't drink (he found both alcohol and tobacco repellent), giving him a significant advantage over those he played with. [34]

Even as a young teenager, Jaroslav was always on the move. He traveled constantly—by train, bus, even bicycle—to towns as far as 150 miles away to watch minor league hockey or soccer. He took up jobs that lasted throughout the summer. He delivered milk. He made a pretty sum of money pounding out bricks in the factory that employed his father, where workers were paid by the number of bricks they produced. Between his gambling and summer jobs, the boy was even able to buy his mother new rugs for the entire house. [35]

When he was seventeen, Jaroslav moved to the Brod adult team, leaving the focus of the youth team on Jiří and Suchý. Both boys had grown considerably, and their athletic bodies were filling out. They spoke with deep voices that belied their youth. Despite never quite reaching the height of his brother, Jiří became much stockier. His hair had darkened to a light shade of brown, and he was more conventionally handsome than his brother. With his easygoing expression, he could have passed for a young skier from Colorado. Suchý's appearance offered a contrast to Jiří's in every way. He had lost his skinny Souška frame, but his body never bulked up substantially. And his features—his slightly turned-up nose, thin upper lip, dark brown hair, and thick, dark eyebrows—made him look tougher than his friend.

Jan's and Jiří's lives often followed very different paths. Both boys were accepted into the same school, but in tenth grade Suchý failed math. František Suchý grew so angry that he marched into the school and bellowed at the teacher, "My boy will be a sports star and has no time for math!" and took his son away. [36] Jan went to work at the town's knitting factory, a cushy job provided by a company that was a major sponsor of the hockey team. Then, as he turned sixteen, Suchý made another major change in his life. Walking by a restaurant in town, he noticed a teenage girl inside eating gingerbread cookies. He watched her through the window, making faces until she invited him to join her. Before long, they were dating seriously and would do so for years. [37]

Still, Jiří and Suchý remained extremely close, both on and off the ice. Jan did his best to add more fun to Jiří's life. He tried setting his friend up with a girl he knew, but Jiří didn't take to her, complaining that her skirts were too short. [38] The two teenagers went on long bicycle rides to help with their training. Souška insisted that they take "rest stops" at pubs, where he smoked and ordered a beer while Jiří quietly sipped lemonade. [39] Unlike Suchý, Jiří made it all the way through school, graduating with a diploma. [40]

In the 1960–61 season, when Jiří and Jan were sixteen, Brod's youth team was invited to play in the prestigious national tournament for kids under the age of eighteen. Coming from such a small town, the boys entertained no serious fantasies of winning the title. They were thrilled just to make the final four against three far bigger cities. And yet, led by their two superstars, the Brod bumpkins triumphed over the big city kids. Throughout the rest of their lives, Jiří and Suchý would recall it as perhaps their proudest moment.[41]

For his part, Jaroslav Jr. was enjoying his own independence, especially as part of the adult Brod hockey team.[42] Everything about the Brod men's team entertained Jaroslav. As a young gun, he faced hazing when, for example, the newbies were required to carry the team's gear to the train, unaware that the older players had weighted the bags with bricks. The players' debauchery after out-of-town games became legendary in Brod. Because he didn't drink, Jaroslav was able to fully appreciate and even remember everything. The players especially loved playing in Prague—and visiting their favorite watering hole on historic Celetna Street. After games, the men spent the entire night drinking at the pub, where Jaroslav made them a "rainbow." When fans bought shots for the Brod players, Jaroslav placed the alcohol in his empty lemonade bottle. Once it was filled with a variety of alcohol types, the players declared the contents a rainbow, which they consumed on the ride home the next morning.

Hijinks aside, when Jaroslav played, the Brod team started to win more than in the past. Deciding that the team could afford to lose a few extra games, a couple of older players began to produce specific outcomes for a fee. Once when Brod took an early 1–0 lead in a game, one of the ringleaders pointed to a wad of cash in his glove and screamed at the young players: "Bloody hell, rookies, if you score even one more goal, I'm going to kill you all. I've got money here!" In other cases, the team's goalie let in extra scores to ensure a loss.[43]

Jaroslav enjoyed the fun, but the simple fact was that he wanted to make a career in hockey. As a fan, he worshipped icon Vladimír Zábrodský, the star of the 1940s world champion Czechoslovakia team, and had an autographed photo of the man with the inscription, "If you want to know more, you need to practice as if you know nothing." Those words would become Jaroslav's mantra for decades to come as he strove to be great.[44] In part, it was simply that Jaroslav was in love with hockey. In part, it was that he had a fire burning inside that drove him to fight to win in any competition he faced. But there was something else. He had seen what the Communists did to his father: they had deemed the butcher replaceable and treated him accordingly. Jaroslav Jr. refused to allow such a thing to happen to himself. He would make himself *indispensable*. He would make himself too good to be denied.[45]

The seventeen-year-old Jaroslav knew that he was good, and indeed made an instant contribution to the adult team. Chytráček brought the teenaged prodigy onto the forward first line with him. Despite being paired with men ten to fifteen years his senior, Jaroslav refused to alter his aggressive style, even when much of the team reprimanded him. Only one big critique stuck with him. It came from Chytráček, the team's star, who made clear how Jaroslav was to pass to him: "Bloody hell, kid, you have to pay attention to which one of my eyes works!"[46]

With Jaroslav and Chytráček leading the way in 1960–61, Brod had its greatest season. The best teams in Czechoslovakia, especially those in the big cities of Prague and Brno, played in the "first division" of the country's hockey league. Teams from smaller towns typically played in lower divisions. With a victory in its final game, though, Brod would be able to move into the top division, an extraordinary accomplishment for a town of its size. Kotlina stadium only held seating for 3,000–4,000 people, but more than 5,000 braved rainy weather to squeeze their way into the open-air arena. In anticipation of victory, fans played music and even brought makeshift coffins as a symbol of their plan to bury their spot in the lower division. The crowd alternately roared and prayed as the match remained close throughout. When it reached the final seconds of play, the Brod team needed one more goal to secure a place in the top league. The crowd bellowed its support. Jaroslav took the puck with a chance to score . . . and lost control of it, dashing the hopes of the team and the town it represented. The crowd went silent, as if someone had died.[47]

The lost puck turned out to be the best thing to happen to Jaroslav. Had the team moved up to the top division, he probably would have stayed in Brod for the rest of his life. Instead, a new opportunity appeared.

# CHAPTER 3

# The Boys from Brod in Army Town

F ollowing the disappointing end to Brod's season in 1961, Jaroslav Sr. began working out the next steps in his boys' hockey careers. He determined that Jaroslav Jr. would join the Dukla Jihlava ["YI-hla-va"] squad, which was the best team in the region and competed in the top hockey league in the country. Still, Dukla Jihlava was a relatively new team, with little track record to speak of, and the Holíks intended for Jaroslav's stay there to be brief. The plan was that Jiří would soon join the famed Sparta Prague club, and eventually Jaroslav would as well. However, it wouldn't be long before the Holíks learned that, just as in the rest of life, things in the hockey world don't always go as planned.

By the early 1960s, crazed hockey fandom was the norm across the country.

Following the arrival of hockey in the early 1900s, teams and competitions sprouted all over the lands that would become Czechoslovakia. In 1936, the Czechoslovakia First Ice Hockey League was founded. After the war, the league blossomed.

As the Communists consolidated their power in Czechoslovakia in the early 1950s, they followed the Soviet playbook of promoting sports, most notably in the leading hockey league. Just as the USSR had done, Czechoslovakia's government created sports teams to represent important parts of the security apparatus. In 1953, the Interior Ministry, led by Rudolf Barák, one of the most powerful men in the country, created its own hockey team in the city of Brno. With a nod to the symbol of communism, the Interior Ministry named its team "Red Star" (*Rudá hvezda*). At first, Communist leaders hoped Red Star players would come from the worker families of the proletariat, but before long all that mattered was if the kids could play. [1]

Red Star instantly dominated the hockey league. With its rapid rise, the team became known as Kometa ("The Comets") Brno. Kometa had a number of advantages. All Czechoslovak men were required at age nineteen to serve two years in the military. But talented young hockey players could serve instead as "border guards" and play for Kometa, even though the nearest border (with Austria) was thirty miles from Brno. Kometa was also able to steal strong players from other squads, in part thanks to pressure from Interior Minister Barák. [2] Brno became the best team in Czechoslovakia for more than a decade.

Because Kometa players could be paid as border guards, they didn't have to get "proper" jobs. In the 1950s players on other teams, in effect, worked two jobs—as employees of the company that owned their team *and* as hockey players. Because working at the company was their day job, they often had to hold practices in the evenings. Over time, however, teams canceled the company obligations, letting their members become full-time hockey players with brief appearances at their official jobs on pay days. Because they were officially employed in non-sports positions, they retained amateur hockey status and were therefore eligible to play in international competitions such as the World Championships and Olympics. In reality, though, they received salaries to play hockey and earned bonuses for games that their teams won.

In the mid-1950s, Czechoslovakia's military made a decision that would permanently shape the country's hockey program. In 1955, it dissolved the army hockey teams. But soon afterward, the country's military leaders went to the USSR for a series of meetings, where Soviet leaders informed the Czechoslovak visitors that an army sports program was essential to the prestige and success of a Communist regime. Accordingly, in 1956 Czechoslovakia's government reorganized its military sports program and gave all army sports teams the name "Dukla" in honor of those killed in a famous 1944 World War II battle at Dukla Pass. The government also announced the creation of a new hockey team, but faced the problem of where to put the squad. Cities like Prague and Brno were already spoken for. At last, the army found the spot it was looking for sixteen miles due south from Havlíčkův Brod, in the city of Jihlava. The authorities had practical reasons for choosing the town, but more than anything, the location was ideal because the people of Jihlava needed something to cheer about.

Similar to nearby Havlíčkův Brod, beginning with the discovery of silver in the 13th century, Jihlava had been a mining town. It became a powerful city in the region, enclosing itself within huge walls. As textiles replaced mining as the principal industry, Jihlava built an attractive mix of Gothic, Renaissance, and Baroque public buildings and private homes along quaint cobblestone streets. The centerpiece of the town was a nine-acre main square, one of the largest in Europe.[3]

From the beginning, Germans made up the largest group of town residents, but unlike in Brod, they remained in Jihlava even into the 20th century. By 1918, when independent Czechoslovakia was founded, Germans comprised roughly 60 percent of the town's population, and as Hitler set his sights on the Czech lands, Jihlava was one of the country's largest German-speaking enclaves. During World War II, the Nazi Gestapo set up a powerful presence in the town, where it executed hundreds who supported the resistance.

By the end of the war, some three million Germans still lived in Czechoslovakia and faced retribution. Beginning in 1945, Czechoslovakia's leaders confiscated the property of most Germans on Czechoslovak soil, created internment campus to hold them, and expelled them from the country. Between horrible conditions, abuse, and outright murder by Czechoslovak soldiers and police, thousands of Germans died in the process.

The expulsions sharply altered Jihlava. In 1937, the city held roughly 30,000 people. Following the evictions of the German population that began in May 1945, there were only around 17,000. Jihlava found itself with huge numbers of unoccupied homes.

The years that followed the Communist coup were trying for Jihlavans. Prior to the war, the Communists had not been popular in the town, and on the whole residents resented the new government's policies following the 1948 coup. Agriculture had been a major part of life around Jihlava, creating strong social bonds in the community, and many in the town pushed back against the new government's efforts to take their family-owned farms. The Communists responded over 1949–52 by punishing many hundreds of farmers in the Jihlava region who resisted, even imprisoning the most recalcitrant. The Communists also cracked down on the Catholic Church, which had a long, rich history in the region. To make an example of both farmers and the church, the government held show trials in Jihlava, ultimately executing a number of opponents of the Communists' farming reforms and two Catholic priests.

The Communist regime also decided to transform cities like Jihlava. Partly in an effort to engineer economic equality, the government moved thousands of poor citizens from other parts of the country into the often upper-middle-class homes now left empty in Jihlava. By 1953, the population of the city had jumped to more than 33,000. Because of the opportunities the government gave them to climb out of poverty, the new arrivals were strong supporters of the Communist Party, unlike the core of the preexisting population of the town. The awkward mix of longtime residents and newcomers, combined with the tragic history of displacement, meant the city now lacked a sense of community.

A hockey team would help unite them.

Even discounting the catastrophic events that had occurred after the end of World War II, daily life in Jihlava felt dreary. Residents tended to be fairly poor, and government restrictions limited what even those with more resources could do. By 1954, the Communists had banned clubs that were not affiliated with the Party.[4]

But on September 5, 1954, even before they knew they would have a team, the people of Jihlava broke ground on the construction of a hockey arena on the grounds of a former cemetery. The city had little that it could spend on the project, so Jihlava citizens used their own money to purchase and donate many key items, like the coolant tubes that were needed to freeze the ice.[5] By the time the Dukla squad arrived in 1957 and showed what it could do in the beautiful new outdoor hockey arena, the team had already qualified for the country's top hockey league. In an instant, Jihlavans found something to bring them together. Many locals didn't really understand the rules of hockey and were befuddled by the various lines and circles painted on the ice, but even they turned into rabid Dukla Jihlava fans.[6]

Much of the town's love of the team came to focus on Coach Jaroslav Pitner. Born in 1926, Pitner had briefly played goalie for the air force hockey team in the early 1950s. Although he was merely an adequate player, Pitner proved himself to be a natural leader with a sharp hockey mind. Seeing his great promise, the military sent Pitner to a special school designed to train coaches.

In 1958, following his training, the military instructed Pitner to move to Jihlava to take over the unified armed forces Dukla hockey team. Pitner was devastated. He had created a home for himself in the town of Olomouc, a hundred miles from Jihlava, and he wanted to stay where he was. Nearly as bad, the Dukla team was notorious for poor discipline and led the league in penalties. Pitner felt exhausted at the mere thought of taking over such a group. He repeatedly declined the offer until the Ministry of Defense made its position clear: "We sponsored your coaching training and a soldier never debates his orders." Pitner packed his bags for Jihlava.

Pitner did impressive work with the wild Dukla bunch during his initial years in Jihlava, winning about as many games as he lost. But he knew that he could create a much better team. He told his superiors that Dukla Jihlava needed to develop a stable core of young players, rather than spinning on a carousel of established ones who were merely there for two years while they completed their compulsory military service. Pitner realized that few young players were interested in playing for a middling team in a sleepy, poor town, so he turned his attention to more unheralded players on second-tier teams—players who would not choose to return to their former team when they completed their military service. Fortunately, thanks to his role as coach of the junior national squad, Pitner was familiar with many of the country's best young players, and he had contacts in numerous small towns who kept him informed about up-and-coming stars.[7]

One such town was Havlíčkův Brod. In 1961 Jaroslav Holík, still just a teenager, toiled in relative obscurity as the superstar forward on the minor Brod hockey team. But in the young player's all-consuming fighting spirit, brilliant passing skills, and leadership, Pitner saw exactly the foundational player he needed. The Dukla coach came to Brod to convince the young man to come to Jihlava.

Jaroslav of course knew who Pitner was, especially with the older man's distinctive piercing gray-blue eyes and dark brown hair combed back to highlight a sharp widow's peak. In talking to the Jihlava coach, Jaroslav quickly gleaned a funny habit the older man had. Whenever Pitner was intrigued or irritated by something, he would give a quick sniff of his nose. He also had a natural, easy way with people. Even before the meeting, Jaroslav absolutely wanted to join

Dukla. It was where he needed to go to take the next step as a player. After Pitner met with Jaroslav Sr., it was agreed. That April, eighteen-year-old Jaroslav joined Dukla Jihlava, and in the summer he began his mandatory military service.

Veterans on the team hazed all rookies, but they took special glee in trying to torment the young man from Brod with the big mouth and even bigger attitude. A group of four team "leaders" found it hilarious to hold him and the other rookies down so they could paint their derrieres with black shoe polish. They then forced the young men to stand, completely naked, atop the metal roof of the barracks until the polish hardened. The veterans also tried to teach Jaroslav a lesson on the ice, but that backfired. Assuming they could break him down with tough play, they hit Holík hard in practice. The problem was that he went back at them harder, willing to use his fists, hockey stick, and anything else available. [8]

Jaroslav became the center forward, leading the team's starting line. The veterans didn't like it, but there was no denying the results. Dukla Jihlava went from winning roughly half its games to winning two-thirds during Jaroslav's first season with the team in 1961–62. For the first time ever, it sat among the top teams in the league. Perhaps Jaroslav had flown under the radar before he joined Dukla Jihlava, but in his first year in army town he proved himself to be a star.

Meanwhile, back in Brod, Jiří and Suchý joined the top adult team as seventeen-year-olds. When they got paid for their first victory with the team, the two teens headed to the nearest café, where they spent their earnings on all the whipped cream and chocolate they could buy. Between their success on the Brod adult team and their reputation as the two stars of the country's top junior squad, they, too, were making a name for themselves.

In 1962, officials from the historic Sparta Prague team came to Havlíčkův Brod and worked out an agreement with Jaroslav Sr. Jiří was studying at a university in Prague and already training with Sparta. That summer, he would officially move to the Prague club. In 1963, Jaroslav Jr. would be done with his military service and join Sparta as well.

However, the Holíks soon had to worry about issues far more serious than where the boys would play hockey. In September 1962, the start of Jaroslav's second season in Jihlava, Dukla headed to Moscow for a series of friendly matches. Jaroslav and his teammates were taking a walk around the city when suddenly he felt a stabbing pain in his leg. He spat through gritted teeth, "I'm not feeling so well . . ." and began to collapse. The men rushed him in a taxi back to the hotel, where things got worse. He had a temperature of 104 degrees, but no one could figure out what to do. The team flew him back to Czechoslovakia, where he showed no signs of improvement. It appeared that he might be dying, and no one knew why. Finally, one of the top doctors in Jihlava determined that the bone marrow within Jaroslav's right leg had become infected. They would operate immediately, and if the infection had spread, they might need to remove his leg. When Jaroslav awoke from the surgery, his leg was still intact. The infection had not spread, and the doctor had successfully removed the tainted portions of the bone.

The question now was whether Jaroslav could ever play again. He went stir-crazy having to remain in a cast throughout the fall, but by December, felt better. Hyperconfident in his ability to power through anything, he decided to remove the cast and return to the ice. He started practicing, played a handful of league games, and then insisted on traveling with Dukla to Sweden for a post-Christmas tournament. As Dukla took on the Swedish team, one of the opposing players accidentally smacked Jaroslav's leg with his stick, breaking the bone precisely where the doctor had operated. To see how bad it was, the Dukla doctor told Holík to put his weight on the injured leg. As Jaroslav stepped down, the pain reached a crescendo. He screamed, cursed at the team doctor, and lost control of his bladder. When the doctors examined the leg further, it became clear that real damage had been done and that Jaroslav's career was in jeopardy.

Jaroslav Sr. sent Jiří to Jihlava to live with his brother and help him recover. The deal with Sparta Prague was off for both boys, who now committed to stay in Jihlava. As a small-town kid, Jiří had found living in Prague thrilling, but refusing his father was simply not an option. Jaroslav would be in a cast for months, making Jiří's help essential.

All the while, Jaroslav never took seriously the notion that he might not be able to return to hockey. This time, he didn't remove the cast until the doctors permitted it. But by then his leg had been in a cast for so long that he faced muscle atrophy. He needed to learn how to walk again. Unsurprising to anyone who knew him, Jaroslav used his newfound weakness as motivation and got himself ready by the start of Dukla Jihlava's fall 1963 season.[9]

As Jaroslav recuperated, two familiar faces joined him on Dukla. Pitner had taken the opportunity to recruit not just Jiří, but Jan Suchý as well. Suchý had become one of the best athletes in all of Czechoslovakia and even made the junior national soccer team. At nineteen years old, he had to decide whether he was going to play for the Dukla Prague soccer team or the Dukla Jihlava hockey squad. In the end, he preferred the greater speed of hockey and thought he had a better chance of becoming a star on the ice. Plus, he could remain with his buddy Jiří. Suchý's father tried to persuade him to choose soccer. When Jan told him of his decision, František Suchý exclaimed, "Don't run home complaining that you chose wrong. I'll just punch you in the mouth."

It didn't take long for Jiří and Suchý to figure out that playing for Dukla Jihlava meant more than just hockey—they were in the army! When they first arrived, they had to walk around in military uniforms and obey orders. Worse yet, most of the officers didn't like hockey players, who had a reputation for flouting the rules. On their very first day of military training, Jiří and Suchý picked up their gray uniforms but neglected to put them on correctly. As they set foot out of the supply warehouse, an officer nabbed them and sent them to military jail for being improperly dressed. It wasn't the last time the pair found themselves locked up. Their most common offense was going home to Havlíčkův Brod without permission. One time they tried hitchhiking to Brod and hopped into a fancy car going their way. Five seconds into the ride, the driver asked innocently if they had difficulty getting permission to go home. "Oh, we just snuck out." The driver responded with a grin. "Is that right? Well, just so you know, I am General Veselý, the commander-in-chief of the Havlíčkův Brod division." And off they went to jail. When incidents like this occurred, the boys were required to call their commander, Coach Pitner, who usually told them, "You were dumb. You let yourselves get caught, so you stay there overnight." So Jiří and Suchý would spend the night locked up. The next morning at 8 a.m., Pitner would come get them out.

Even hockey players had to go through real military training when they first arrived in Jihlava. They lived in old barracks, where they made their own mattresses from hay and collected coal and wood for heating, even having to go outside to grab more during the night to avoid freezing. Officially, the Dukla men were listed as "tank operators." Jaroslav feared guns, which he somehow managed to avoid using during his training. And, fortunately, he only had to enter a tank once. With the horrible noise and claustrophobia-inducing cramped space, he hated the experience, but didn't have to do it again.

But most of all, Jaroslav, Jiří, and Suchý were hockey players, and they quickly made their presence in the league known. Anyone reading the sports news in Czechoslovakia couldn't miss the fact that the young men were becoming stars. But articles about Jaroslav's performance couldn't properly capture his effect on the game. His impact went way beyond statistics and his ability to skate, pass, or shoot.

On March 15, 1964, a young sports reporter named Miloslav Jenšík went to cover the final match of that year's World Handball Championships, held in Prague. Not yet thirty, Jenšík had already lived a long lifetime's worth of sporting experiences. Born in 1936 in Prague to a sports-mad father, Jenšík had attended nearly every match of the 1947 Ice Hockey World Championships in Czechoslovakia, and from there his passion for the game only grew. Soon after he graduated from college, the weekly magazine *Svět v obrazech* (*World in Pictures*) hired him to write about sports.

On the whole, the handball match that Jenšík watched in 1964 didn't make much impression on the sportswriter, but at one point one of the handball players launched a primitive, earsplitting, animal-like scream as he released his shot. Without missing a beat, a high-pitched scratchy voice behind Jenšík belted out, "Holy crap! What the hell does that idiot eat?!" The entire section of the stands burst into laughter. When Jenšík turned around to find out who had entertained the crowd, he saw a well-groomed light-haired young man surrounded by a group of hockey players. The sportswriter quickly figured it out. "Ah, so *that* is Jaroslav Holík!"

Everyone who followed Czechoslovak hockey knew of the young man's horrible injury, the dreadful possibility that he would lose his leg, and the extraordinary effort he had made to get himself back to the ice for the 1963–64 season. Serious followers of the sport like Jenšík knew that Jaroslav now dominated by doing anything and everything he could think of to win. No one wanted to play against Holík. He put himself into the middle of every play, battling at all times to control the puck. He also worked tirelessly to set his teammates up for scores. When Dukla was on offense, Jaroslav stationed himself directly in front of the goalie and sneakily pounded the netminder over and over with his stick. He constantly got into fights, but his favorite move was slightly more restrained. If he saw the puck in the crease in front of the opposing goal, he took advantage of the opportunity to steamroll through the other team's goalie.

However, what Jenšík hadn't known until watching him up close was that twenty-one-year-old Jaroslav Holík had a *way* about him. He had no hesitation about blurting to anyone and everyone whatever popped into his head, and even off the ice, his magnetic personality made people take notice. Charisma. That was the word for it. When you met Jaroslav Holík, you didn't forget it.[10]

Incredibly, Jaroslav wasn't the most talented player on Dukla Jihlava. In fact, he might not even have been the best hockey player in his family.

Jaroslav's triumphant return to Dukla Jihlava for the 1963–64 season coincided with a truly exceptional year for his nineteen-year-old younger brother. Locked behind the Iron Curtain, people in Czechoslovakia rarely saw anything of the rest of the world. But when Dukla's Coach Pitner developed an interest in Jiří and Suchý in 1963, he brought the young men to a preseason junior national team tournament in Essen, West Germany. Having grown up on a steady diet of propaganda about the evils of the West, the boys worried something terrible might happen to them. Instead, they had the time of their lives. It was thrilling to see a world bathed in light at all hours. The neon signs were especially eye-popping. Confronted with limitless goods available for purchase that simply didn't exist back home, the boys went wild looking for things that they could bring back to their families. Suchý used his pocket money to buy his mother a shirt that he then carried around like a trophy. But that trip turned out to be small potatoes.

As Jiří prepared to make his place on the Dukla Jihlava team in 1963, he got word that he had been selected for Czechoslovakia's national hockey team that would play in the 1964 Olympics! With his brilliant skating, unselfish play, and high-quality all-around game, Jiří was a deserving choice. But in his usual unassuming, modest fashion, Jiří chalked up the selection at least as much to his likeability as to his skill. And indeed, across the country, people in the sport asked, "Jiří *who*?!"

National team training began and, still just a teen, Jiří felt terrified as he entered the Olympic squad locker room for the first time. But that was nothing compared to the fear he confronted when the team took its first major trip, to America for a pre-Olympic tournament. As the small-town kid boarded the Soviet-made airplane to start the trip, Jiří began shaking, certain the flimsy machine couldn't possibly stay airborne. It was all he could do to hold it together as the flight continued across the Atlantic. He would later learn to take sleeping pills when he got on planes to manage the anxiety. When he arrived in New York City, he briefly forgot the terror of the ride: on Broadway, the boy from Havlíčkův Brod stood dumbstruck, staring at the lights, the shops, and the people.

By comparison, the Olympics in Innsbruck, Austria, were a disappointment. The Czechoslovak team didn't perform especially well but still managed to take the bronze medal. Czechoslovakia's Communist officials restricted the hockey players' movements and didn't allow them to view a number of the competitions. In addition, Jiří was unprepared for what he saw when a pair of team veterans took him out of the Olympic Village. "Hey, rookie! Come with us to experience what life is about." As the men showed Jiří the windows where they might "select" any one of a group of pretty women, Jiří turned beet red and decided it was time to return to his room and then back to Czechoslovakia as soon as he could. [11]

When he wasn't training with the national team, Jiří was becoming part of an exciting new hockey lineup in Jihlava. Despite still quarreling, the Holík boys continued to play beautifully with each other. Jiří didn't have Jaroslav's imposing physical presence, but with his spectacular speed and all-around skill, he shaped play all over the ice. Seeing how well they gelled, Pitner kept them together on the offensive line, with Jiří on the left and Jaroslav in the center. Eventually, Pitner placed on the right side of the line the sharpshooting Jan Klapáč. Klapáč had joined Dukla the year before Jaroslav and shown such shooting skill that he had been named to the 1964 Olympic team with Jiří. When Jihlava controlled the puck, the three complemented each other: Jiří set up the offensive play and got the puck to his brother, who brought it into the offensive zone, where he found an open Klapáč, who smacked it into the net. Klapáč was among the league leaders in goals nearly every year, and the Holík-Holík-Klapáč line set records for scoring. [12]

At first, the transition to the higher league was a bit more difficult for Jan Suchý. The players were much faster and smarter than what he had been used to. More than once, he tried his patented trick of jumping in front of an opponent's shot, only to find that the best players simply faked, leaving him splayed out on the ice while they skated in for an easy score.

As he got used to the higher quality of play, though, Suchý excelled, and actually changed the way defensemen played in Europe. Suchý was only about five feet, nine inches tall and 170 pounds, but he used his body to the fullest, literally throwing it into the path of pucks shot anywhere near him. It was all instinct. He couldn't imagine *not* jumping in front of opposing shots. As a result, Suchý suffered numerous broken bones, including his ribs, and when he changed out of his hockey uniform after games his body was covered with bright purple bruises. Pitner grew frustrated with Suchý's regular trips to the offensive end, as it left the defense vulnerable. Yet Suchý was such a brilliant skater and prolific goal scorer that Pitner finally had to accept it.

It wasn't just in his play that Suchý did things his own way. He loved practical jokes. One of his favorites was to put tape on the bottoms of his teammates' skates, causing them to fall the moment they took to the ice. He poured water down a referee's pants when the man had his back turned. And knowing that both Holíks were terrified of flying, once during a flight to a tournament Suchý worked out an arrangement with the pilot to plunge the plane suddenly into a steep descent. As the rest of the men screamed, Suchý cackled with delight.

But it was for his drinking, smoking, and gambling that he was most famous. Somehow he could spend the entire night carousing and then, without having slept a wink, arrive for a match as strong as ever. Following games, Suchý had little interest in food or water. Instead he pounded down a tankard of beer and some plain bread while smoking a pack of cigarettes behind the team bus, where Pitner wouldn't see him. During their early years together, when Pitner caught Suchý drinking too much or smoking, the coach was quick to dock the defenseman's wages.[13]

In general, though, Pitner spoke a language that soothed even the wildest hockey beast, and his players talked of how he had been born to coach. He used hockey tactics to great effect, consistently chose the right players for his teams, and employed a training style that brought out the best in his players. Usually, Pitner simply responded to poor behavior with harder practices and fines until the players performed well, in which case all was forgiven. The long-time military man was a natural psychologist, able to understand instinctively which players required coddling and which thrived when he screamed at them. Even still, he rarely needed to raise his voice because of the respect he generated.

Jaroslav Holík typically ignored coaches' orders, but he listened to Pitner, who was one of the few people willing to stand up to him. [14]

Getting quality young players like the Holíks and Suchý was only one piece of Pitner's plan to develop Dukla Jihlava. Even in his early years with the team, Pitner was a strong believer in the importance of conditioning and ahead of his time in building endurance through non-ice training. Pitner's favorite summer workouts involved taking the team to the middle of the wilderness, where they spent days on end running on trails, climbing rugged, steep hills, and rowing crew. During summers, he also introduced what the players called the "Tour de Dukla," bicycle riding for hundreds of miles that included overnight stays in inns far from home. Jaroslav seemed to crave the bicycle battles, pushing himself to the extreme, and won most "tour" legs. Somehow, Suchý was also among the best riders in the group, even though he insisted on carrying beer rather than water, saying, "The rides get better once you have a beer or two."

In 1964–65, his second season in Jihlava, Suchý began to hit his stride on the ice and in his personal life. Souška regularly went to Havlíčkův Brod to visit his girlfriend, Marie, the gingerbread-eating girl he had made faces at through a restaurant window a few years earlier. Many a morning he silently jumped out of her window so her parents wouldn't catch them. In the fall of 1964, when Suchý was twenty years old, Marie informed him that she was pregnant.

Their wedding, held in February 1965, turned into precisely the sort of event one would expect from Jan Suchý. The ceremony was a simple town hall affair, with Jiří as the best man. Then the party got started in Marie's parents' four-room house in Havlíčkův Brod, where they put everything that wasn't bolted down into one room and crammed the hundred-plus guests into the rest of the house. The groom and his best friends had to leave for a few hours to play the Brno team over in Jihlava, but they managed to return to the party by 10 P.M. As the drinking got serious and the accordion music kicked into high gear, new Jihlava player Stanislav Neveselý chucked cake around the room and nailed Jaroslav. Soon the assembled all started throwing cake and even fruit at one another, and within minutes it seemed that every inch of exposed space was covered with splattered pastry. Jaroslav rarely drank, but when he did tended to get passed-out drunk. Late in the evening, some of the guests looked outside, where they saw a totally inebriated Jaroslav sitting atop a huge pile of soot, yelling "Bring me coffee! Bring me coffee!" The group did his bidding. Jaroslav

proceeded, then, to toss the empty cups around the garden, where they disappeared into the snow. The guests who remained conscious kept going until 6:30
the following morning. When people finally came to, they couldn't believe the
extent of the wreckage. Cigarette holes in the furniture. Cake and fruit everywhere. A broken chandelier. Marie, Suchý's bride, was less than thrilled, and
forced her husband to repaint the entire interior of the house.

The following month Suchý and Jaroslav played in their first World Championship tournament along with Jiří, who had cemented his position on the
national team the previous year. Still just twenty years old, Suchý worked closely
with František Tikal, the squad's captain and fellow defenseman. Heading into
the second-to-last game of the tournament, Czechoslovakia had the opportunity
to take the title if it could just beat the Soviet Union. Prior to the match, Tikal
handed the younger man a small pink pill. "This will give you a bit of edge here.
It won't hurt you at all. Take it, so you perform at your best." Suchý did as he
was told, watching as Tikal dropped three of the pills down his own gullet.
Suchý never learned just what they had taken, but he felt unstoppable on the ice.
Partway through the game, an injury knocked him out of play, but Tikal scored
Czechoslovakia's only goal and went on to be named best defenseman in the
tournament. Still, the Soviets won 3–1, taking home the 1965 team trophy. All
that mattered little to Suchý when he got to his hotel room that night. He was
unable to eat or sleep and his head pounded. Jiří, his roommate, kept begging
him to lie down, but Suchý couldn't sit still and walked the halls all night. He
would never take anything like that little pink pill again. [15]

Meanwhile, 1965 proved to be *the* pivotal year for Dukla Jihlava. In the
spring, as they neared the end of their compulsory military service, Jiří and
Suchý accepted an invitation to extend their contracts with the team and the
army. Previously, Jaroslav had extended his contract as well. All three were
promoted to officer, which led to much better pay than regular servicemen
received. Then, with each major hockey victory—including winning medals in
international competition—Dukla players found themselves promoted to higher
officer ranks, which in turn produced even better pay. [16]

Dukla had a group of committed, experienced, and talented players, and the
team ramped up its conditioning even more under the leadership of assistant
coach Stanislav Neveselý, who joined the team as a player, but had trained in
physical education at a university in Prague. Neveselý tried out a new series

of exercises with the men, including many of the harsher training practices introduced in the Soviet Union. Pitner sniffed excitedly with each new exercise. Neveselý favored aerobic training over everything else and had the players do three and a half months of conditioning work throughout the off-season. Some of his practices were unconventional. He introduced the first massage therapist into the league and even experimented with having the players hop on one leg for twenty minutes without a break. Before long, other Czechoslovak teams began to adopt his methods.

Jaroslav Holík knew that he couldn't skate as well as others, so he had to rely upon his physical strength and conditioning. Desperate to recover fully from his leg injury, he threw himself into Pitner and Neveselý's plans, dragging the rest of the team with him. Thanks to heavy weightlifting, Jaroslav grew stronger than any of his teammates. He became convinced that, through sheer willpower, he could achieve anything. On a bet, one year Jaroslav decided to run a marathon, which his teammates set up just for him. The course was lined with onlookers, who cheered him on for the first thirteen miles, which were a breeze for the exquisitely well-conditioned hockey player. Then things fell apart. Jaroslav completed the twenty-six miles, hallucinating for much of the final leg of the course, and then had to be carried to the car that was to take him home.[17]

Jaroslav and his mates became a massive draw in Jihlava. As the team got better, residents began to see themselves as *Jihlavans*, represented by the Dukla hockey team.[18] Tickets to matches became a red-hot commodity and even Jihlavan currency, which could be exchanged for services like car repairs.

The team performed especially well in front of its supportive home crowd. The terrific turnout for matches in Jihlava was all the more impressive given that until the 1967–68 season the games were played in one of the last open-air stadiums in the country. Sometimes when there was rain or snow, matches had to be temporarily suspended. When play resumed, the puck might ricochet oddly off a hole in the ice or a small mound of snow.

With things coming together for Dukla in 1965, the time finally seemed right to put the screws to the league's dominant team, Kometa Brno, which had won the league title every single year save one since 1955. In Jaroslav's first four seasons in Jihlava, Dukla never finished the regular season in better than third place, while Brno won the title year after year.

But over time, Dukla Jihlava saw an opening. Kometa lost its privileged government position when Minister of Interior Barák, caught on the wrong side of a political power struggle, was forced out of his position in 1962 and imprisoned. Brno no longer had a pool of young soldiers to choose from, and the government no longer went out of its way to help the team gain star players. Meanwhile, Pitner was able to nab, for a year or two, any young player who had not yet completed his military service. Just as important, Pitner and Neveselý's conditioning drills and tactical moves were bearing fruit, and Pitner was able to convince an extraordinary group of players, led by Jaroslav, Jiří, Suchý, Klapáč, Jan Hrbatý, and Ladislav Šmíd, to stay with the team permanently. In 1965, Josef Augusta, another terrific young forward from Havlíčkův Brod, added to the team's strong foundation.

That year, Pitner set a goal for the team to win the title within three years, which the men from Jihlava tried to achieve right away. Klapáč was a scoring machine and would lead the league with forty-one goals in thirty-six games. Jaroslav would have his breakout season. On top of his usual physically com-bative style of play, he would lead the league, by far, in points (goals plus assists). This included forty-two assists (passes to a teammate, who in turn scored), eighteen more than anyone else in the league. Behind such brilliant play, Dukla didn't lose a single one of its first eight games.

As Dukla grew stronger, the crowds at its away games became increasingly belligerent. Most of all, the Dukla players hated playing in Košice, in southeast Slovakia, near the borders of both Hungary and the USSR. In the dark, old Košice stadium, opposing players had to walk more than fifty yards along a narrow path between the locker room and the ice, at times with police protection when the fans got especially unruly. The Czech players spent half the journey wiping the Košice fans' spit from their eyes or shaking out the beer that had been poured down their jerseys.

The Dukla men's most terrifying experience on the ice occurred, in the 1964–65 season, against the great Slovan Bratislava team. As play turned rough during the game, someone in the crowd suddenly threw a knife in the direction of the Dukla Jihlava goalie. Pitner pulled his players off the ice. As the Dukla men changed in the locker room, the crowd outside started throwing rocks at the windows. The players refused to leave the changing room until police provided an escort for the Dukla bus to get out of town. [19]

While not as intense, Jihlava fans at home came out in full force for their team as well. As the Dukla hockey team caught fire, demand for tickets far exceeded what the arena could handle. On December 2, 1965, Slovan Bratislava came to town for a highly anticipated showdown, and overzealous organizers sold 3,000 more tickets than the stadium could safely hold. Thirty minutes before the puck was to drop, the people outside decided that they wanted in, and they began to push, some violently. In the crush, some in the crowd were trampled. Others were asphyxiated. The Dukla players went out to see what was going on. They saw where people had fallen over the protective railings that had bent from the pressure. The only way to get some of the injured to safety was to bring them to the center ice. Bloodied fans with torn clothes filled portions of the rink. Fourteen people were badly hurt. Seven were severely injured. Two were dead. [20] But not even such a disaster could quell the locals' obsession with their hockey team and the season continued on.

As Dukla became a real challenge to Brno during the 1965–66 season, Jihlava's matches in Brno produced an atmosphere of palpable electricity. The games usually began around 6 P.M. But even though the stadium was unheated, when the Dukla team arrived around 4 o'clock, it would already be packed with more than six thousand fans in the standing section waiting to unleash their hatred upon the visitors. There was no separation between the stands and the players' bench, leaving the Dukla men exposed as the crowd threw cups of beer at them. Naturally, it was Jaroslav Holík who attracted the largest share of the Brno crowd's ire.

Jaroslav had already become famous for his intensity, which he aimed at anyone in his orbit, even his teammates. Whether on the ice, in the changing room, or outside of the arena altogether, Jaroslav constantly told the men on Dukla what to do, screaming at them when they made mistakes or if he didn't think they were working hard enough. The positive side was a team that was dedicated to working hard in its practices, something that was far from universal across the league.

Jaroslav saved his greatest wildness for his opponents at his matches, where he pounded and fought with men from other squads. When it came to Jaroslav and violence, it didn't need to be during the game. In one game against Kometa, an opposing player jabbed the Dukla goalie with his hockey stick. As the teams lined up to shake hands following the match, Holík punched the man in the face. Jaroslav didn't even restrict his fisticuffs to players. In a match against the Košice army team, the opposing team manager, a lieutenant colonel, taunted Holík, so Jaroslav punched him as well. Somehow, after a detailed explanation of his actions, Jaroslav managed to avoid serious punishment.

When Dukla Jihlava came to play in Brno, the Kometa fans went ballistic the moment they saw Jaroslav, launching every expletive they could think of at him. "Holík, you motherfucker!" Jaroslav *loved* it, always feeling that he played his best when he was overwhelmed with emotion. As the fans screamed bloody murder, Jaroslav played to the crowd, raising his hands, laughing, encouraging them to scream louder. During warmups, he would put up an ungloved hand, showing the crowd all five fingers, as if to say, "We're going to score five goals against you!" The gesture raised their ire all the more. Then, as he began to leave the ice for the final pregame meeting in the locker room, he abruptly returned to the ice to show the crowd *ten* fingers. The Brno fans went insane. It wasn't just that the opposing fans hated him. It was more that they *loved* hating him. During intermissions, the Brno faithful openly admitted to one another, "When Old Timer Holík quits, it won't be so much fun to come watch anymore."

Despite Dukla's hot start to open the 1965–66 season, Dukla just missed snatching the title from the defending champions—but the Jihlava team came back even more determined the following season. Jiří now joined Jaroslav and Klapáč among the league's top goal producers, and the team performed exceptionally well. The Jihlava fans constructed a cardboard coffin that represented the death of the Brno squad. In the season's penultimate match, Dukla Jihlava clinched the league championship. As the horn sounded to end the game, Pitner tried to sneak away from the ice, but Jiří quickly nabbed him. The Holík brothers lifted their coach onto their shoulders and paraded him around the arena. In the aftermath of the victory, hundreds of Jihlavans did the same with the team's players, carrying the town's heroes aloft as they chanted "Long live Dukla," and began a wild celebration that lasted till morning. [21]

The Jihlava players had become their town's favorite sons, but despite their celebrity and privileged positions, most still felt a need to ingratiate themselves with the people running the country. Army officers made clear to Dukla's players who remained on the army team after their two-year mandatory service that they were expected to become members of the Communist Party. Indeed, nearly everyone on the team joined the Party, in part because they feared punishment if they didn't.

But Jiří wanted no part of it. He had grown up in a family that hated the Communists. Plus, he was apolitical and wanted to stay out of such things. Jiří lived his life as a rule follower, which had bought him years of peace and quiet. Now, though, he wasn't going along with what the Dukla political leaders wanted and, although no one threatened him, members of the Party wouldn't stop pestering him. Just wanting to be left alone, Jiří finally agreed. "Ok, I'll join, but only under the condition that I won't have to attend any Party meetings."[22]

Among the permanent members of the Dukla Jihlava hockey team, Jaroslav and Suchý were the only ones to refuse. Others on the team argued that they should join for the sake of their kids. Jaroslav just laughed at them. "If you play hockey well enough, you have nothing to worry about." Suchý told anyone challenging him on the issue that they could throw him off the team if they didn't like his choice.[23]

As the Dukla men became stars, there didn't seem to be much risk to staying out of the Party. Czechoslovakia's top hockey players received privileges available to few people outside of the highest Communist Party circles. When the police stopped a Jihlava player for driving under the influence of alcohol, a simple autograph got him out of the infraction and back on the road within minutes. Regular Jihlavans had to wait in line for hours or even days to buy basic goods. Dukla players were usually given priority and sometimes could even have things specially ordered. Often, when a player went to a pub or a restaurant, he didn't even have to cover his own tab. Big stars were able to benefit the most. When Jaroslav needed to find a new apartment or a car, leading Communist officials went out of their way to ensure that he got the very best there was to offer.[24]

The Holíks had become a huge deal. Local girls fawned over the more classically handsome younger brother with the sunny disposition. But one young woman saw something more appealing in Jaroslav. Born in late 1945, Marie Prchalová grew up in Jihlava, where her father served as an office clerk and her mother worked in an electronics company. Marie was talkative and charming, and her pale blue eyes provided a dramatic contrast to her light olive skin and dark brown hair. She had graduated from the local business high school in 1964, and the following spring she and her school friends held a reunion at a nearby café. Unlike the other eleven girls in her group—who all swooned when they heard the name "Jiří Holík"—Marie had always been drawn to the *older* Holík boy's charismatic personality. As she sat in the café with her friends, she looked across the room. There was Jaroslav playing cards with a group of his friends. At midnight, he walked up to Marie and asked her to dance. After a night of dancing at the café, Jaroslav asked if he could walk her back to her hotel. "Sure," she replied. "But you'll be walking all twelve of us." When Jaroslav had gotten the young women safely back to their hotel, he asked Marie out for the following day. Hockey players—particularly those from Dukla—were noted for wanting little more from women than a one-night stand, so Marie thought, "Oh please, with a Dukla player? He probably won't even remember me tomorrow." She never showed up for the date. She assumed she would never see him again and moved on happily with her life.

A year later, in late March 1966, Marie went to watch the national basketball championships hosted in Jihlava. As she waited in line to buy a hot dog, she felt a tap on her shoulder. It was Jaroslav. The two sat together throughout the game. By September, Jaroslav was already asking her to marry him, but Marie was only twenty and in no hurry to get hitched . . . yet. In June 1967, just months after Dukla's first title, they stood in the Jihlava town hall, exchanging their vows. Jaroslav's teammates made a path and gate for the couple with their hockey sticks.

As she left the hall after the ceremony, Marie gasped. A sea of humanity stood between the newlyweds and the photographer's office, where they had planned to go next. She and Jaroslav had invited only fifty people, and they hadn't even announced the event publicly. But the nine-acre Jihlava town square was filled with people, *thousands of them!* Jaroslav had become such a big figure in Czechoslovak hockey—especially in Jihlava—that the entire town wanted to attend. The Jihlava authorities even canceled school to make it possible for everyone to celebrate the wedding of their great hockey star. [25]

# CHAPTER 4

# Poking the Bear

By 1967, Jaroslav, Jiří, and Suchý had entered the prime of their careers, making Dukla Jihlava the best team in Czechoslovakia's top hockey league. However, for Czechs and Slovaks, hockey involved much more than just competition between towns and cities. Each year, the country held its breath as the national team sought to bring home glory in the World Championships or the Olympics. The imprisonment of the national squad in 1950 had set back the country's national hockey program for a decade, but in the 1960s Czechoslovakia moved closer to its former stature. In the summer of 1966, after the squad had taken the silver medal in consecutive World Championships, Jaroslav Pitner took over as head coach of the national team. Pitner knew that he would need to make significant changes and pull something extraordinary out of the squad if it were to have any chance of ever winning the gold. [1]

In the 1960s, a seismic shift had altered the international hockey landscape, so that by 1967 one profoundly dominant team routinely crushed every other national squad, including Czechoslovakia's. Amazingly, this leviathan had begun to play hockey in international competition only thirteen years earlier.

The seed for Soviet dominance in hockey was planted in 1917 when the Vladimir Lenin–led Bolsheviks kickstarted the Russian Revolution. By late 1922, following a lengthy civil war, Lenin's Bolshevik group, now known also as the Communist Party, controlled most of the former Russian Empire. It proclaimed the formation of what was in effect a new country, the Union of Soviet Socialist

Republics (USSR). The Communists eliminated private property—giving control of property to the state—and centralized all economic planning in the hands of the country's leaders.

Following Lenin's death in 1924, Joseph Stalin seized power and radically transformed the country. Stalin forced peasants to become part of collective farms and killed at least a million wealthier farmers who resisted. The collectives were required to turn over so much of their yield that famine ensued in 1932–33. At least three million people (and likely many more) starved to death, the majority in Ukraine's *Holodomor* famine. In the 1930s, Stalin drummed up paranoia across the country, which he used as a pretense for what became known as the Great Purge. On his orders, the authorities engaged in widespread surveillance and rounded up perceived "enemies of the state" in the military, the Communist Party, and all other walks of life, who were then executed or sent to the Gulags in Siberia. The result was at least another one million dead in 1937–38.

From the beginning, the world's democratic powers, especially the US, Britain, and France, had been suspicious of the Soviet Union, which remained relatively isolated. But in the late 1930s they became more concerned about the rise of Nazi Germany. In 1939, the Soviets and Germany signed a non-aggression pact, which Germany broke in 1941 by invading the USSR. Fighting on the World War II Eastern Front continued for four years, until at last the Soviets pushed the German forces back.

By 1945, the Soviet Union had become a world power, and Stalin met with Allied leaders to determine how to administer the end of the war and the new order to follow. The USSR had been essential to the Allied victory in World War II and had suffered an unimaginable loss of nearly thirty million people. Little wonder then that the West agreed to concessions sought by Stalin. As part of the agreement, the US halted its own advances into German-controlled territory, allowing the Soviets to liberate key parts of Central and Eastern Europe and then gain control over much of the region. In the initial years that followed, Communist parties took over in a number of the countries there, including eastern Germany, Hungary, Poland, and Czechoslovakia. In reality, Moscow called the shots in all of them.

With the birth of the totalitarian regimes that the USSR forced on countries in its sphere, sharp tensions emerged between the democratic, capitalist West and the authoritarian, communist East. Each side posed collective military and economic organizations against the other, seeking to show its superiority. Sports played a major role in this effort.

After the 1917 Revolution, the Soviets had largely avoided interaction with the West, including in sports. The Communists emphasized physical fitness for their citizens. But the USSR shunned international competitions, describing events like the Olympics as elitist "bourgeois" activities designed to get workers to ignore their own plight and prepare them for "imperialist wars."[2]

World War II changed everything. The Soviet Union had shown itself to be strong and essential to defeating Fascism. Stalin now sought propaganda victories that would drum up patriotism at home and show the world the excellence of the communist system. Soviet leaders pushed to build the world's largest steel plant and the world's biggest airplane. They challenged the United States in the space race and worked to show the world that the Soviet people were faster and stronger than those in the West. As the Cold War with the West got underway, sports became a way of defeating the enemy without having to fight a bloody war.[3]

The Soviets faced two potential impediments to achieving their international sporting aims. First, international competitions required participants to be amateurs, something the Soviet athletes most definitely were not. Soviet Communists opposed professional sports, which they considered to be a distraction for the masses and grotesquely commercial. But they had been unable to halt the professionalization of USSR sports in the 1920s and 1930s, when rival soccer teams competed with one another to hire the top players.[4] Moreover, the Soviet government paid bonuses to athletes who performed at particularly high levels. And many athletes competed as members of the military or security forces. The government paid them as members of the military, even though these competitors were in reality professional athletes, soldiers in name only. At that time, participation in the Olympics was officially restricted to amateur athletes. But because the International Olympic Committee (IOC) desperately wanted to globalize the games, it accepted the claim that Soviet athletes were not professionals and allowed them to compete.

The Soviets' second potential impediment was the fact that sports would be useful propaganda only if their athletes succeeded against the capitalist countries. Stalin threw the resources of the state into the country's athletic program and refused international competition unless the USSR team was likely to win. In the late 1940s and early 1950s, Soviet leaders exacted promises of victory before they would allow athletes to participate in international events. They also fired sports bureaucrats whose promises of sporting success did not bear out.

As its leaders grew more optimistic, the USSR agreed to send competitors to the 1952 Summer Olympics in Helsinki. The Soviet Union performed extremely well, winning the second largest number of medals, but Soviet officials were displeased. The United States had won more. Most upsetting, the Soviets had lost in soccer to Yugoslavia, a communist country, but one that had broken away from Soviet influence in 1948. The Soviet government immediately disbanded the Central Army Club, which trained the soccer players. Whatever the case, the Soviet approach soon bore fruit: after 1952, the Soviet Union consistently dominated the Olympic medal count.[5]

As the Soviet Union considered entry into the world of international sports, bureaucrats in the country's Sports Committee faced a major decision. Canadian-style ice hockey was the principal team sport contested in the Winter Olympics, but in the USSR people primarily played the bandy version. From an ideological perspective, the Sports Committee was reluctant to introduce a "bourgeois" form of the sport. But, to succeed on the world stage, the Soviet Union had to compete in the forms of play used there. Beginning in September 1945, a small group of Soviet men began to train in the Canadian version. In February 1946, the group offered public demonstrations. And in October 1946, the sports authorities announced to the country's bandy players that they were to begin league play of *Canadian-style* hockey in December.[6]

Deciding that its athletes needed coaching in the sport that it was imposing on them, the Soviet leadership forced Prague LTC, Europe's best hockey club, to come to the USSR in March 1948, just as the coup in Czechoslovakia was unfolding. The LTC squad was delivered to a stadium to play a series of matches against Soviet players. When the LTC men saw the home team players, they openly laughed at their poor equipment—soccer uniforms, leather bicycle helmets, short bandy sticks.

After two private matches that USSR authorities insisted upon calling "joint training sessions" (just in case the visitors totally destroyed the Soviet side), the players moved on to games in front of spectators. Soviet authorities instructed 10,000 factory workers to attend, but never having seen the game before, the crowd didn't know when to cheer. The Soviet players and even officials appeared nearly as clueless. Two referees officiated the game, one from Czechoslovakia, who understood the game thoroughly, and one Soviet, who didn't. At one point, the Czechoslovak referee called a penalty on a Soviet player, whom he ordered to the penalty box. The player smiled and shook the referee's hand, but didn't leave the ice. To avoid inflaming the situation, the Czechoslovak official decided not to push it. The Soviet referee inferred that this was the way one handled penalties and so, whenever he whistled someone from Czechoslovakia for a penalty, the official skated over to shake the player's hand.

However, on the whole, the Czechoslovak men came away impressed. It was obvious that the Soviets had little experience with a puck and Canadian-style hockey sticks, but they skated extremely well, with lightning-fast speed and seemingly without need to rest. The hosts knew nothing about proper hockey gear, so they sent officials to measure the LTC players' apparel. When the two squads met up again two days later, the Soviet players came out perfectly attired. In three matches, each country won one and they tied the third. Czechoslovakia's team captain Vladimír Zábrodský predicted that it would not be long before the Soviets made their way to the top of international hockey.[7]

From these humble beginnings, the Soviet Union rose quickly among the world's elite hockey programs, and one man, Anatoly Tarasov, would be the person most associated with that rise.

Tarasov was born in Moscow in late 1918. As a child, he was an unusually hard worker, with seemingly boundless energy and an active mind. He became obsessed with soccer and bandy at an early age, and as a teen performed at a high level in both sports. At nineteen, he entered the Coaching School of the Central Physical Culture Institute, and in 1939 started making a living as a professional soccer player. When winter arrived, he took up professional bandy as well.

During World War II, the Soviet military had promoted Stalin's twenty-four-year-old son Vasily to the rank of major-general, and following the war, Vasily turned his attention to creating a strong sports program in the air force. Tarasov coached the air force soccer and hockey teams but, not for the last time, the coach's abrasive personality and insistence on doing things his own way got him into trouble. The two men clashed and in 1947 Vasily sacked Tarasov, who then became player-coach of the army's new Canadian-style hockey team.[8] In future years, Tarasov would ingratiate himself with powerful figures in the government who, in turn, helped him to stack the army team with many of the best players in the country.

As they did in all areas of life, the Soviets treated sport as a science, searching for new formulas for excellence. In the view of Soviet coaches like Tarasov, there was little difference in natural ability across advanced players, so top-notch conditioning and tactics became the secret to success.[9] Indeed, Tarasov's greatest contribution to Soviet hockey was the training program he initiated. The USSR had little money to spend on equipment and facilities and would not have its first artificial rink until 1956. To compensate, in 1950, decades before the practice became common in the West, Soviet coaches introduced new and spectacularly intense approaches to dry-land conditioning.[10] One exercise had players lift rocks from shallow waters in the Black Sea, carry them to dry land, turn around to throw the rocks back in, and then repeat the action for hours.

On the ice, attendees at Tarasov's practices might see players riding on each other's shoulders, juggling heavy weights, or performing somersaults and other acrobatics while the coach wildly cheered them on.[11] Tarasov seemed like a mad Dr. Frankenstein, his mind whirling, frenetically searching for hockey's secret formula. But unlike the mad scientist who wanted to be left alone with his lab, Tarasov preferred being constantly on stage, performing for the world. Fiery and stubborn, Tarasov roared at his players, desperate for them to play out his visions.[12]

Ever the good socialist, Tarasov insisted that players subsume themselves to the collective and prioritize the proper implementation of *his* system. He didn't permit freelancing and lashed out at any player who worked on his own behalf rather than the team's. Tarasov demanded that his players execute their moves with precision and, most of all, that they remain disciplined at all times. Even in the rough sport of hockey, the Soviet men rarely lost their cool and lashed out at the opposition. To do otherwise would be selfish and cost the team. Tarasov proclaimed that his entire approach flowed directly from Soviet culture and values.[13]

Tarasov and other Soviet coaches of the time changed the game. In Canada, hockey was played vertically; players drove the puck directly toward the opposing goal. In the Soviet Union, the initial top performers on the ice were soccer players, who came into the winter sport with a (non-American) football mentality. Accordingly, in hockey the Soviets emphasized constant crisscrossing and circular weaving, combined with controlling the puck using short passes that built upon one another until a player found himself receiving the disk in the perfect spot to score.[14]

In reality, other coaches played a bigger part in the early development of Canadian-style hockey in the USSR, but Tarasov was a terrifically successful self-promoter. Because of his larger-than-life personality and the fact that he published prolifically on the sport, Tarasov's name and ideas permeated the country and eventually the international hockey world. For these reasons, it was Tarasov who would become known as the "father of Soviet hockey."[15]

The first ice hockey World Championships had been held as part of the 1920 *summer* Olympics (although the hockey matches were held fifteen weeks prior to the rest of the games), but they moved to the colder season when the Winter Olympics debuted in 1924. Beginning in 1930, the World Championships became an annual event. In leap years, the Olympic ice hockey competition simply counted as the World Championships. As was the case in all other sports, professional hockey players were not officially permitted in either the World Championships or the Olympics, but authorities were willing to look the other way for non-amateurs who did not also play in the openly professional North American National Hockey League (NHL).

When it came time to choose a coach for the USSR's first entry in the World Championships, the Soviet leadership tapped not Tarasov but his rival, Arkady Chernyshev, the well-respected coach of Moscow Dynamo. Chernyshev was born in March 1914, nearly five years before Tarasov. Like Tarasov, Chernyshev had shown skill as a youth in both soccer and bandy. As a young man in 1936, Chernyshev was drafted into the Ministry of Internal Affairs, through which he joined the Dynamo soccer and bandy squads.

Two people could hardly have been less alike than Tarasov and Chernyshev. Even in his thirties, Tarasov had a prominent round nose and emerging jowls, which made him appear likely to become overweight as he aged. As he got older and did in fact put on considerable weight, his nose grew disproportionately, making him look like someone who had been punched in the face. His eyebrows became bushy, giving him a slightly disheveled appearance. In contrast, Chernyshev was more slender and distinguished-looking, with dark eyebrows and piercing eyes.

Their temperaments also contrasted sharply. In joining Dynamo, Chernyshev had also become part of the NKVD, a predecessor to the KGB, the USSR's intelligence and secret police agency. Befitting this position, he typically appeared reserved. He wrote little and hardly spoke to the media, remaining careful and diplomatic when he did, unlike Tarasov. The two coaches' behavior during matches showcased their differences most starkly. In contrast to the theatrically boisterous Tarasov, Chernyshev was always composed on the bench, rarely raising his voice.[16]

In 1954, for the first time ever, the Soviets entered the World (Canadian-style) Ice Hockey Championships in Stockholm, Sweden, with Chernyshev at the helm. As usual, Canada came in as the favorite, despite not sending a true "national" team. Every year, Canada sent to the World Championships a middling-quality local squad, but they were usually so much better than the Europeans that they typically won. Sure enough, going into the final match of the 1954 tournament, Canada was undefeated in six games. The Soviets had surprised everyone by easily winning their first five matches and then tying the strong Swedish team. The final game, which matched up the USSR against Canada, shocked the hockey universe. The Soviets played unlike anyone else in the world, moving the puck at warp speed and repeatedly finding an open man for a score. They obliterated the Canadians 7–2. Word spread that the Soviet players were "machines" or futuristic hockey "robots."

Back in Canada, fans were dismayed that their country had sent such a weak squad, so the following year the Canadians selected a much stronger group for the World Championships. The new Canadian squad shellacked the robots 5–0. But in 1956, in the first Winter Olympics the Soviets ever entered (in any sport), the USSR won the hockey gold medal, beating Canada 2–0.

After that victory, the USSR found international hockey much more difficult.[17] In recognition of the USSR hockey team's rise, Moscow was invited to host the 1957 World Championships, but the Soviets' desire to maintain control over one of their satellite states interfered with the games. In late October 1956, the people of Soviet-controlled Hungary attempted to end the USSR's domination of their country. Stalin had died three years earlier, and many thought, optimistically, that Moscow might now permit greater freedom in Hungary. But in early November the Soviets arrived with tanks and tens of thousands of troops to snuff out the uprising and ultimately helped execute the leaders of the nascent multiparty government. The West denounced the invasion and the US, Canada, Norway, West Germany, Italy, and Switzerland all announced that, in protest of the Soviet action in Hungary, they would not attend the World Championships in Moscow. Without Canada, the Soviets became the heavy favorite to win the tournament, but they lost the final match—and the gold medal—to Sweden.[18]

Tarasov was now installed as the new head coach, but it didn't do any good. Canada bested the Soviets in 1958 and 1959. The Soviets then finished behind both Canada and the gold-medal-winning US team in the 1960 Olympics. The Soviet leadership removed Tarasov as head coach and returned control of the team to Chernyshev, who did no better: in the 1961 World Championships, the Soviet Union lost not only to Canada, but also to Czechoslovakia, leaving the USSR with a "disgraceful" bronze medal.[19]

The late 1950s and early 1960s were an era of mounting distrust between the West and the USSR, and that distrust would even affect the hockey world. In May 1960, the USSR shot down an American U-2 spy plane over Soviet air space. Relations grew even more fraught following the failed US-backed Bay of Pigs invasion, which sought to overthrow the Communist government in Cuba, in April 1961. In August of that year, Cold War antagonisms reached new heights as East Germany abruptly erected the Berlin Wall. The 1962 ice hockey World Championships had been set for Colorado Springs in the US, but in retaliation for the Communists' construction of the wall, the West refused to issue the visa documents needed by the East German team to attend the tournament. In protest, the Soviet Union and Czechoslovakia boycotted the games.[20]

Following the 1962 World Championships, the Soviet Sports Committee came up with an unusual plan. Chernyshev would be the senior coach, but Tarasov would now also join on as the second coach. They were to share duties as a team of rivals.[21]

The coaches set to work and first unveiled their new monster in the 1963 World Championships. After a poor opening game against Sweden, the USSR took to dominating its opponents. Coming into the final match, the Soviets needed to defeat Canada by a margin of at least two goals to win the gold medal. And they did, winning 4–2 for the world title. The new coaching duo had pulled it off.

From there, the Soviets reached a new level of hockey mastery. Canada realized that the local teams it had sent in the past were no match for the new European squads. In 1964, for the first time, it sent an actual national team, a collection of the best amateur players from across the country. But it didn't matter. The Soviet Union went undefeated in the 1964 Olympic Games. The Soviets proved even more dominant in the 1965 World Championships, winning every match by at least two goals. In 1966, aside from a shocking tie against the ever-resourceful Sweden, the Soviets won every match again, on their way to their fourth consecutive world title.

The coaching combination of Tarasov and Chernyshev had turned out to be wildly successful. Tarasov's overbearing nature often turned off his team, but now the players also had the diplomatic Chernyshev available to help soothe them in the aftermath. Tarasov continued to introduce his brilliant new tactics and introduced approaches to conditioning and practicing that kept the players engaged. At the same time, the more conservative Chernyshev kept Tarasov from pushing tactics so far as to be counterproductive. The result was a new, completely dominant form of the game.[22] The Soviets preferred to play in red jerseys and, with their brilliant skating and overwhelming play, appeared to blanket the ice like a red wave.

It wasn't just the creation of a two-headed coaching monster that produced the Soviets' new success. The raw materials had been developing since the 1950s, when the sports leadership mandated increased attention to elite sports throughout the country. The Soviet authorities demanded the creation of hundreds of new hockey clubs and opened hundreds of sports schools, where young athletes learned from a standard school curriculum but received hours of sports training during the day as well. By the time the young athletes of the 1950s became eligible for the national team in the 1960s, they already knew the Soviet style of movement and precision passing.[23]

The 1960s saw the birth of a new era of Soviet super players. By 1965, half the players named to the World Championship all-star team were from the USSR.[24] Teams preparing to play the Soviet Union scrambled to figure out what they were to do against a wide array of offensive stars like Veniamin Alexandrov, Alexander Almetov, Konstantin Loktev, and Vyacheslav Starshinov.

Nearly everyone on the Soviet team was a threat to score, but perhaps the most iconic of the players was a hulking defenseman who showed less interest in the puck and more in stopping the opposition. Born in 1941 in Moscow, Alexander Ragulin stood six feet, two inches tall and at least 220 pounds when barefoot and clad in nothing but his underwear. Standing on his skates and covered in pads, he looked like a giant. Ragulin joined the national team in 1961 and became a mainstay on the World Championship all-star team in the years that followed. Opposing players actually found him to be among the most approachable and affable players off the ice. If plied with enough vodka, Ragulin loved to entertain a room by playing the accordion and singing. But on the ice he threw his full weight into flattening opposing players. One Swedish player, who bred horses as his day job, named one of his steeds "Ragulin" after it kicked him in the face. [25]

In short, by 1967, the Soviet hockey team had it all, and no other national team in the ice hockey world could hold a candle to the Soviet Union's Red Machine. It was at this remarkable Soviet team that Pitner and Czechoslovakia's national hockey squad took aim.

Despite the fact that Czechoslovakia served as a loyal satellite of the USSR, the two countries' hockey teams had formed a bit of a rivalry. Following the imprisonment of its national team, Czechoslovakia didn't send teams to the World Championships in 1950 and 1951. Once the Soviets began to compete at a high level in the years to come, many Czechs and Slovaks—including some of the players who had been sent to prison—suspected Moscow had actually ordered the imprisonment of the team to get Europe's greatest hockey threat out of the way. [26] Czechoslovakia could only manage a fourth-place finish in the 1952 Olympics and had to fight to even medal in international competition in the 1950s. When the two countries' hockey teams faced off in the 1956 Olympics, the Soviet team accused Czechoslovakia's skaters of playing unnecessarily roughly and injuring several USSR players. Even worse, the Soviets claimed that two days later Czechoslovakia went easy in its match with the US, apparently to try to harm the USSR's medal chances. [27]

Four years later, the Olympics were held in high-altitude Squaw Valley, California, where the USSR and Czechoslovakia battled for the bronze medal. On the final day, Czechoslovakia could clinch third place if it won in its match with the US, and after two periods led 4–3. High-level hockey matches are divided into three twenty-minute periods. During the break prior to the third and final period, the Soviet team captain burst into the American team's locker room and pantomimed wearing an oxygen mask. Taking the hint, a few

American players used oxygen during the game's final frame, and the US went on to score six unanswered goals, giving the gold to the Americans and the bronze to the Soviets over fourth-place Czechoslovakia.[28] Angered by the move, the men from Czechoslovakia got revenge the following year as they defeated the Soviets in the 1961 World Championships and took the silver ahead of the USSR.

However, after the 1962 boycott of the World Championships in Colorado Springs, everything changed in 1963 with the arrival of the now-dominant Red Machine. Czechoslovakia found itself in a frustrating position. It consistently won medals and most other matches at the World Championships and Olympics, but always lost to the Soviets.

The games against the USSR also had a strongly political element. In the initial years after the Soviets had helped liberate the country from the Nazis, many in Czechoslovakia had been strongly "pro-Russian." But following the 1948 Communist coup, the Czechoslovak government put forward a steady stream of servile USSR adoration. There was a running joke in Czechoslovakia: "Before, you could be good, better, or best. But now, you can be good, better, best, or Soviet!" Even before the USSR won its first hockey World Championship, Czechoslovak journalists, who were tightly controlled by their own Communist government, extolled the brilliance of the Soviets in the sport: "The Russians have no equal and the Czechoslovak team can do nothing but learn from them!" By the 1960s, the propaganda proved counterproductive. Regular Czech and Slovak citizens had grown contemptuous of such sycophancy and came to see each hockey match against the Soviets as the most important of the year. Yet, in major tournament play, only once—in 1961—did Czechoslovakia manage to win one of those games. As they lost match after match to the USSR and Czechoslovakia's leadership continued to suck up to the Soviets, Czechs and Slovaks couldn't help but wonder if their boys were being forced to lose on purpose.[29]

As he took over the Czechoslovakia national team, Jaroslav Pitner saw a far more difficult problem. He knew that his players had not been instructed to lose to the Soviets and that they would have spat at anyone who told them to do so. The real problem was that the Red Machine was simply great. The USSR had fantastic individual players, partly because it had a huge pool of millions of prospective players to draw from and partly because players received outstanding training from an early age. Pitner could do nothing about that advantage held by the Soviet Union.

So, as he prepared to take on the role of national team coach in the summer of 1966, Pitner focused on addressing something within his control. For years, the Red Machine's greatest advantage had been its vastly superior conditioning. When he took over in 1966, Pitner set up a summer training camp in the city of Pardubice to try to get his players into better shape and begin preparations for the 1967 World Championships.

Pitner had years of experience with players who sought to escape conditioning, but still he was surprised when many from Czechoslovakia's national team begged off, claiming injury. Undaunted, Pitner sent telegrams, informing them camp was mandatory and that the national team doctor could evaluate them there. Despite his ultimatum, two players still refused to attend. Pitner counted himself lucky that it was just two, but felt deflated by the fact that it was two of the best: Jaroslav Jiřík and Jozef Golonka.

A fierce competitor on the ice, Jaroslav Jiřík of Kometa was one of the top offensive players in Europe. He was one of Czechoslovakia's top scorers and a member of the national team since 1958. Since it was Jiřík's first transgression, Pitner suspended him but only for a few months.

The bigger problem was Jozef Golonka, one of the great stars of European hockey in the 1960s. Born in Slovakia in 1938, Golonka entered Czechoslovakia's professional league with his hometown Slovan Bratislava team when he was seventeen years old. A natural showman on the ice, Golonka talked constantly to his teammates, the opponents, and especially the referees, whom he frequently and dramatically corrected on their officiating. One of the biggest characters in Czechoslovak hockey, he had a puckish sense of humor and a quick laugh. When he found something funny, which was often, his eyes bulged out of his face, his teeth became visible and squeezed together, and he laughed with an almost asthmatic wheeze.

He took every opportunity to ham it up in front of television cameras. In one tournament, as he was pushed up against the boards, he shoved his face toward one of the cameras, rolled his eyes around in their sockets, and collapsed to the ice as if he had been stabbed. [30] When he or his teammates scored important goals, Golonka was apt to roll around on the ice in celebration. Many opposing players found him annoying, with an unprofessional and tiresome act. Even a number of his teammates felt he was too much of an actor, whose whining about calls and getting hit went overboard.

However, Golonka was also a *great* hockey player, a brilliant shooter, among the top offensive players in the country's history, and a hockey hero whose antics energized Czechoslovak fans. He was one of the most inspirational players on the team and worked hard to fire up his teammates.[31]

Nevertheless, Pitner felt that his hands were tied. Golonka had a history of missing hockey events without permission, so Pitner suspended him from the squad until just before the March 1967 World Championships.[32] The resulting backlash highlighted a fissure within the national team and within Czechoslovak society more generally.

In general, Czechoslovakia's national hockey team had good chemistry. Even players like Jaroslav Holík, who constantly cursed out and fought all opponents within Czechoslovak league competition, instantly became friendly with the other players during their time together on the national team. With relatively little annual turnover in personnel, the national team players got to know each other well, and their bonds grew tighter over time.

The principal exception to this comradery was the relationship between Czechs and Slovaks. In the 1966–67 season, out of the ten teams in Czechoslovakia's top league, only two played in Slovakia, and the fans of those teams prioritized defeating squads from the Czech lands. A leading Slovak coach declared that, even more than Czechoslovakia wanted to defeat the Soviets for the world title, Slovaks craved victory over a Czech team for Czechoslovakia's championship.[33]

The roots of this tension dated back to the negotiations that had led to the creation of Czechoslovakia. The Central European territories associated with the Czechs and the Slovaks sit immediately adjacent to each other, with Czech lands in the northwest and Slovak lands in the southeast, and the people of both places speak similar languages. However, Czech and Slovak lands have had markedly different histories and fairly different cultures. Among other things, Slovakia was more Catholic and more rural than the Czech lands. But by the late 19th century, they had something important in common: the Austro-Hungarian Empire controlled them and they both wanted out. In an effort to create their own independent space, in the 1890s Czech and Slovak leaders began negotiations with each other.

When independent Czechoslovakia was founded in 1918, Czech leaders agreed that the Slovak territory would be given substantial autonomy in the unified country. These promises went unfulfilled, but before long a more dramatic problem arose. In 1939, German forces not only occupied the Czech lands, but also forced Slovakia to split off to form an "independent" state dedicated to supporting Germany. Once Czechoslovakia reunified after the war, leading Party members from Slovakia pushed for more independence for their part of the country. In response, following the 1948 coup, Czechoslovakia's authorities charged several Slovak leaders with the crime of "bourgeois nationalism" and punished them severely. From there, the Czechoslovak Communist Party worked to continue to centralize power and used a new constitution to eliminate the final pieces of independence of the Slovak regional parliament.[34]

In general, the relationship between the Czech and Slovak parts of the country held stable, but underlying discomfort always existed. Many Slovaks felt Czechs looked down on them as less educated younger siblings and second-class citizens. Moreover, it seemed to many that the government prioritized the Czechs. The capital sat in Prague, the heart of the Czech lands. Slovaks also complained that, despite making up roughly a third of the total population, they received a substantially smaller proportion of government posts.

There was even a fear among some Slovaks that Czech leaders hoped to assimilate all citizens of the country, which might then eliminate unique Slovak traditions and culture. When they first negotiated over the creation of the new country, many Slovaks pushed for a name that would be spelled to highlight the separate regions—"Czecho-Slovakia"—and worried the name "Czechoslovakia" would turn their region into an afterthought. Over the years, many bristled at the use of "Czechs" to describe people from Czechoslovakia, because the shortened name seemingly eliminated the very existence of the Slovak people.

For their part, many Czechs felt Slovaks were too sensitive. They suggested that many people from Slovakia were too quick to raise the banner of Slovak nationalism and ignore their part in a larger Czechoslovakia. Some Czechs felt Slovaks based their demands too much on proportionality and not enough on performance and talent.

This dynamic played out in the national hockey team. In 1967, out of eighteen players on the roster, only two were Slovaks. When people pointed out the disparity, many Czech players grew irritated as they thought that the quality of

Slovak players didn't merit proportionality. Even when there were more Slovaks on the national team, they and the Czech players generally got along, but usually didn't socialize much with one another.[35] Within this dynamic, Golonka provided an interesting mix. He was a staunch Slovak partisan, and many of his teammates felt that he resented them for being Czech.[36] But he was also a die-hard Czechoslovak patriot and fought with his soul for the national team.[37]

He was also one of Slovakia's greatest heroes, and the backlash to his suspension was severe. Pitner received numerous letters deriding his decision. One, in particular, stood out: "You seriously think that there should be no Slovaks on the national team? . . . Do you even realize what kind of a persona Golonka is to all the Slovaks? And then you—a Czech ass—leave him out of the national team? . . . All of us Slovaks cordially wish for your death."[38]

Even while Jiřík and Golonka were out temporarily, serving their suspensions, Czechoslovakia's roster was very strong, filled with a new generation of young players.[39] Jiří was now on his fourth national team, and Jaroslav and Suchý were both on their third. Players from countries around the world admired the way all three of the boys from Havlíčkův Brod conducted themselves in international competition, taking care of business in a professional manner. Moreover, seemingly from the moment he had joined the national squad for the 1965 World Championships, Jaroslav Holík had become one of the team leaders.

Probably the country's most skilled offensive player was sharpshooter Václav ["VAA-tslav"] Nedomanský, who, at twenty-three years old, would also be playing on his third national squad. Six feet, two inches in height and 210 pounds, "Big Ned," as he became known, was blessed with a physically intimidating presence and could seemingly hit the puck harder than any other player in Czechoslovakia.[40] Jan Havel and Josef Černý also stood out as strong scorers. Along with Suchý, František Tikal, Oldřich Machač, and František Pospíšil served as the backbone of the defense.

In March of 1967, a wave of optimism flowed across Czechoslovakia as Pitner prepared for his World Championship coaching debut. Jiřík and Golonka were back from their suspensions. Over the previous few months, the national team had twice beaten the USSR in more minor tournaments.[41] During the final two weeks of March, the World Championships would be played just across the border from Czechoslovakia in Vienna, thus making it feel like home ice.[42]

But the tournament went poorly for Team Czechoslovakia. After winning its first three matches, Czechoslovakia lost to a weak Finland team and tied in matches against both Canada and Sweden.

Meanwhile, the USSR exhibited its usual inspired hockey. On top of all its preexisting greatness, one of the Soviet players, Anatoly Firsov, had become the preeminent hockey forward in the world. Firsov had made his first national team in 1964, but in 1967 he took his play to an entirely different level in the World Championships, leading all players with eleven goals and eleven assists in a mere seven matches. An exceptionally fast skater, Firsov handled the puck, passed, and shot with unusual creativity—all while smiling constantly. He would one day be viewed by many as the greatest Soviet hockey player in history.[43]

Behind its usual stellar play and now the stardom of Firsov, the USSR had gone undefeated in its first six matches in Vienna, clinching the gold medal even before it took on Czechoslovakia in the final match of the tournament. Awestruck by the incredible Soviet team, an Austrian newspaper wrote, "The skills of the world champions are almost beyond possible."[44]

Despite having no chance to win gold, Team Czechoslovakia came into the final match deeply motivated. The players desperately wanted to show that they could beat the Soviets in a meaningful game, and a victory might also get Czechoslovakia the silver medal. Then there was the crowd that was to attend the match: As the 1960s progressed, Czechoslovakia's government had somewhat loosened its grip on its citizens and now permitted them more international travel. With the presence of thousands of fans from Czechoslovakia, the players felt as if they were playing in front of a home crowd. As a result, tension hung over the team in a way that a non-gold medal game usually didn't.

That tension mounted as the two squads matched up closely from the start. From the moment play commenced, Czechoslovakia's supporters in the crowd kept up a steady chant in Czech—*Do toho!* ("Let's go!").[45] Unlike North American sports fans, who boo to express their unhappiness, Europeans whistle. Periodically, Soviet partisans tried to cheer on their own team and immediately found themselves jeered and whistled down by those supporting Czechoslovakia. The two teams hadn't felt great animosity toward one another before, but something gradually shifted early in the match.

For the first time in his career, Jaroslav Holík had a strong World Championship tournament. Still just twenty-four years old, he had scored two goals and led the team with seven assists in just six games. But what most people would remember about Jaroslav in Vienna in 1967 was his meeting with Alexander Ragulin, which turned the two into archrivals. Off the ice, Ragulin was a gentle Russian bear—quiet, calm, and somewhat shy. [46] On the ice, though, everyone on Team Czechoslovakia feared the mammoth defenseman. Everyone, that is, except Jaroslav, who refused to give due consideration to the fact that Ragulin had two inches and *at least* forty pounds on him. [47]

As usual, from the opening moments of play Jaroslav clashed with nearly everyone on the USSR side. Although his hatred of the Soviets dated back to his childhood, the loathing had grown in the years that followed. Even though he had come of age in communist Czechoslovakia, when he visited Moscow as a member of the junior national team, the level of repression there startled him. He developed what he called a "Russia allergy." He felt sympathy for the plight of the people, but looked to get under the skin of the country's players. Prior to games against them, Communist "advisors" swarmed around Team Czechoslovakia to explain the appropriate modes of behavior in dealing with the men from the USSR. Jaroslav went out of his way to do the exact opposite, taking pleasure from provoking members of the Red Machine. [48] Throughout the match in Vienna, he poked, prodded, and slammed into Soviet players, including goalie Viktor Konovalenko. He even cursed out the USSR bench.

Midway through the first period, a Golonka goal gave Czechoslovakia a 1–0 lead, but within a minute the Soviets evened the score. Almost immediately after play resumed, Jaroslav slashed the USSR goalie with his stick, prompting the Soviet players as a group to converge on Holík, while the Czechoslovak players pushed forward to protect their teammate. The crowd whistled and the two sides looked like they might fight until the officials separated them.

Play continued. Ragulin, clearly tired of Holík's act, decided to give Jaroslav extra attention. With roughly six minutes left in the first period, he held Jaroslav near the boards surrounding the ice as USSR wing Vladimir Vikulov flew in at top speed, crushing Holík as if he were in the middle of a red Soviet trash compactor. Wild jeering and whistling rained down from the crowd. The officials sent two Soviet players to the penalty box. As the game continued, Jaroslav made sure to ram into Ragulin with full force whenever the defenseman got the puck. Finally, the giant Soviet man couldn't stand it anymore. He grabbed Holík with two hands and smashed him to the ice.

The first period ended with the two squads tied—and near their emotional breaking points. The game had been exceptionally rough for international hockey. Coaches in both locker rooms spent intermission trying to calm their players.

The Soviets scored once in the second period, leaving Czechoslovakia one goal back with twenty minutes left to play. Little more than a minute into the final period, Jaroslav grabbed the puck and drove toward a possible score, but Ragulin cut him off and pushed him into the boards behind the goal. As the whistle blew and Jaroslav tried to head back out to open space, Ragulin refused to let him go, even as a referee tried to separate the two men. Only after a second referee arrived and the two zebra-striped officials physically pushed him away did Ragulin finally give up his grasp of Holík. But meanwhile the big Soviet man had snatched Jaroslav's stick so Holík now had to slide back toward the Soviet defenseman to regain it. Chanting in Czech, the crowd boomed over and over, *Ragulin, fuj!* ("Ragulin, ew!").

Mere moments later, Jaroslav Jiřík got the puck behind the net, slid forward just in front of the goal, and snuck in a score to tie things up. Jiřík hugged Golonka, who pulled them both down onto the ice. The rest of the Czechoslovak players dogpiled the two men as the crowd went mad! As play continued, people in the stands cheered wildly for the men from Czechoslovakia, except when play stopped and they took the opportunity to return to the *Ragulin, fuj!* chant.

But then everything collapsed. Just minutes after Jiřík's goal, Firsov scored for the USSR to go back on top. Little more than sixty seconds later, the Soviets scored again, taking a commanding 4–2 lead. The arena grew sharply quieter. More than thirteen minutes remained in the match, but as time ticked away and the end of the game approached, the Soviets maintained their two-goal lead.

Despite the large deficit, and with a bit under five minutes remaining, Czechoslovakia continued to push to get back into the game, and things got wild. Czechoslovakia's Stanislav Prýl made a beautiful pass to Jaroslav, who had flown past the USSR defense with only the goalie to beat, but Holík found himself pulled down roughly from behind by a Soviet defenseman. When play resumed, the Czechoslovak men went on the offensive, urgently pushing to score. After getting stopped and temporarily losing control, Czechoslovakia snatched the puck on the Soviet end of the ice and drove to set up on offense. As Czechoslovakia's Prýl sprinted with the puck at center ice, a Soviet player slammed him down. Jaroslav collected the puck, drove forward, and returned the disk to Prýl, who had hustled to get back into the play and now smashed a shot at the Soviet goalie, Konovalenko. But no goal. As the puck bounced away from the net, a group of players, including Konovalenko and Jan Suchý, literally fell over one another in a mad scrum in front of the goal.

Until that point, play had merely been rough, but now, as the puck bounced into the right corner, a switch flipped. Soviet Viktor Polupanov skated to collect the puck. When Jaroslav flew in, knocked the Russian player away, and grabbed the disk, something appeared to snap in Polupanov. Swinging his stick wildly, Polupanov threw his arms down onto the back of Jaroslav's head and back, as though he were trying to pick up the Czechoslovak center from behind. Feeling himself pushed down, Jaroslav managed to pass the puck farther into the corner. Polupanov threw Jaroslav to the ice, and the crowd began to whistle loudly.

Then something surprising happened. Given the circumstances, it wasn't so much *what* happened that was unexpected as it was *who* did it.

Throughout *Jiří* Holík's life, people had frequently misread him. Because he tended to follow rules, spoke with a cheerful, gentle voice, and, especially, smiled a lot, most people expected Jiří to always be laidback and carefree. But Jiří was a Holík. He came from the same genes as his brother. And he had spent his youth fighting back when Jaroslav attacked him. Jiří Holík had a fiery side that came out when you least expected it.

After Polupanov tossed Jaroslav to the ice, Soviet player Valeri Nikitin nabbed the puck in the corner. Prýl tried to blanket the Russian, who skated skillfully around him. Suddenly, seemingly out of nowhere, Jiří flew in, leading high with his right elbow into the face of Nikitin, snapping back the Soviet's head.

Full-blown fighting rarely occurs in international hockey matches, but Jiří's act kickstarted an all-out melee, with players on both teams attacking one another on live television. Like a bull, Ragulin charged at Prýl, throwing punches to the Czechoslovak player's face and head as whistling from the crowd drowned out all other sounds. Defenseman Ladislav Šmíd, one of the toughest men on Team Czechoslovakia, appeared unhinged as he attacked any Soviet player he could reach. Simultaneously, multiple Soviet players shoved Prýl repeatedly. As Prýl tried to push back, they slammed him to the ice. Meanwhile, Jaroslav stepped in front of Ragulin to stop the massive defenseman from going back into the scrum of players. The big defenseman pushed forward as if he might kill the older Holík brother, his progress only halted when a referee jumped in between them. As Ragulin tried to get around the ref, Jaroslav tried to slash the lower legs of the other Soviet players in the pile. Ragulin pulled Jaroslav out and kept him from doing more damage until a referee came over to calm them both.

Nothing like this had ever happened before in a hockey match between Czechoslovakia and the USSR.

After they finally got the players under control, the referees sent five players, including Jaroslav and Ragulin, to the penalty box. The ever-innocent Jiří somehow managed to avoid punishment, despite throwing the elbow that started the brawl. The remainder of the game was played with only three skaters on the ice for each squad instead of the usual five. Just seconds after returning to play, the Soviets jabbed Golonka hard in the stomach, leading to a fourth Soviet in the penalty box. [49] Furious about the attack on his teammate, Czechoslovakia's Jan Havel began screaming at the Soviet players, one of whom immediately jerked his stick up as if he was about to smash it into Havel. Only at the last second did the Soviet player restrain himself. When the final horn blew to end the game, Czechoslovak players slammed their sticks down in fury as the crowd launched a tsunami of whistles and obscenities toward the Soviet men. [50]

Protocol dictates that following the end of World Championship hockey matches, the entire roster from each of the two squads stands at attention on the ice as the winning team's national anthem plays and the flag representing the country of the winner is raised. Then, following the anthem, the members of the two teams shake hands with one another. On this March 29, 1967, according to custom, the Czechoslovak and Soviet players stood on the ice for the USSR anthem. But the wild, fury-infused whistling from the Czechoslovak partisans in the crowd made it almost impossible to hear the music. When the anthem came to a close, photographers crowded around the USSR players, who awaited the presentation of their championship trophy. Looking visibly annoyed at the group crushing in on them, the Soviet men forcefully shoved back cameramen who got too close. Bunny Ahearne, vice president of the International Ice Hockey Federation, presented the trophy to Team USSR, announcing, "We have just seen a most fitting and perhaps a most fighting end to our 1967 championships." But many couldn't hear him because of the ear-piercing whistles from the crowd.

Amid the wild end, the trophy presentation, and shrill sounds raging from the crowd, few spectators noticed that the Czechoslovak players refused to carry out the required end-of-game handshake.[51] For them, the battle was only just starting.

# CHAPTER 5

# The Prague Spring

I n Czechoslovakia, people were furious about the events in Vienna. They had seen the tournament gold medal as ripe for the picking, and the fourth-place finish was beyond the pale. They sent the players telegrams: "Return home via the sewers, you cowards." When the team bus crossed back into Czechoslovakia, fans surrounded the bus and cursed out the players. [1]

There was a group in Moscow even more concerned about what had happened in Austria. The final match between Czechoslovakia and the USSR unleashed something that traveled beyond Vienna, and even beyond the borders of hockey fandom. The two hockey teams had a bumpy history, but they had not fought with this kind of intensity before, especially on a grand stage where the whole world could see it. The Czechoslovak fans' hostile reaction to the Soviets at the World Championships reinforced that image. It was as if someone had pulled back a curtain to show the true feelings of many Czechs and Slovaks toward the Soviet Union. The open fury that rained down onto the Vienna ice during the Soviet anthem made clear that the relationship between the USSR and Czechoslovakia was not exactly the friendly one the two countries' leaders claimed.

Beginning in the hours following the match, the Soviet Embassy in Prague received crude phone messages and letters from Czechoslovak citizens venting their disgust at the Soviet hockey players. During a lunch hosted by Iraq's ambassador for diplomats in Prague in the first days after the match, Czechoslovak guests congratulated USSR ambassador Stepan Chervonenko for the victory, but then suggested the Soviets had helped cause the brawl. One Czechoslovak foreign ministry official even brazenly told Chervonenko the Soviets were totally responsible for the fight. What is more, the official warned, nearly everyone in Czechoslovakia had watched the match on television, and the fight had sparked a wave of anti-Soviet feelings. Deeply worried, three days after the March 29 match Ambassador Chervonenko sent Moscow a cable describing how the "political character" of the game had harmed USSR-Czechoslovakia relations. Chervonenko suggested halting contact sports between the two countries on Czechoslovak soil for the time being.[2]

With Moscow becoming increasingly agitated, Czechoslovakia's Communist Party grew apprehensive. The leadership sent a memo to Party members that "the scandalous end of the match between the two best friends . . . [allowed members of the public] to voice their anti-Soviet attitudes and to ridicule and deride our friendship." As a result of the game, the memo noted, even school-children in Czechoslovakia had begun to speak "insultingly" about the Soviets.[3]

Czechoslovakia's authorities brought in the hockey players and ripped them for their actions in Vienna. Articles in the government-controlled newspapers blamed Jaroslav most of all for starting the fight . . . as well as for cursing out the Soviet bench and repeatedly stabbing at the Russian goalie with his stick. Jaroslav found himself pulled into one disciplinary hearing after another. One with the hockey federation. Another with the military. Another with the police. And still another with the Communist Party. Jaroslav didn't really see the problem. His behavior in Vienna looked precisely the same as it did in countless other games he had played. "So, what happened out there with Ragulin, Comrade Holík?" Jaroslav explained. "Well, he's an ass." Confused as to how to proceed, the commission continued, "Oh, but you are an officer in Czechoslovakia's army, he's an officer in the Soviet army, and we are together in this union. You should be comrades! Why did you get into a fight?" Holík's answer left the officials even more dumbfounded: "He called me a fascist. And I called him a Bolshevik."[4]

Jaroslav soon found that undercutting relations with the Soviets had consequences. He had been deeply disappointed to miss out on the 1964 Olympic team when he hurt his leg, and he could hardly wait for an opportunity to play in the 1968 games in Grenoble, France. However, following the investigation of the events in Vienna, Pitner called Jaroslav in to explain that the star Dukla center would not be on the Olympic roster. In public, Pitner announced that there had been fierce competition for the center forward position and he could easily have chosen any of a number of players for that spot. Pitner explained that Jaroslav was not playing at his best and, moreover, spent too much time in the penalty box.[5]

Jaroslav couldn't believe it. He was the emotional heart of the team. He was among the very top center forwards in the country, and at twenty-five he was in his physical prime. In the previous season, he had finished just behind Nedomanský for most points in Czechoslovakia's top hockey league and had by far the most assists. In 1968, he would again be among the league leaders. He also led all non-Soviets in assists at the 1967 World Championships. It seemed obvious to Jaroslav that Pitner, who did not get final say over team personnel, had been ordered by the authorities to demote him because of his actions in Vienna.[6]

Czechoslovakia's leadership had put its foot down: actions that created problems with the USSR would not be tolerated.

Yet in the months following the 1967 World Ice Hockey Championships, it gradually became clear that big changes were afoot in Czechoslovakia—changes that would alter the country's relationship with the superpower to the east. And these changes coincided with the rise to prominence of a quiet man who appeared to be nothing like the other Communists who had led Czechoslovakia since 1948.

Despite being very tall, Alexander Dubček ["DUP-check"] did not cast a big presence. He had a kind-looking face, with soft lips, gentle eyes, and a slightly pointy nose. He was neither heavy nor skinny. But because of his height—he was six feet, four inches tall—and the way he held his neck, he had more than a passing resemblance to a giraffe. With his dull speaking style, he hardly inspired or evoked images of the great revolutionaries in world history. However, Alexander Dubček would ultimately be at the center of dramatic changes in Czechoslovakia.

Dubček's parents had both been born in Slovakia, but they met as young adult émigrés in Chicago in the late 1910s. The couple became devout communists and were thrilled about the Russian Revolution, especially the creation of the Soviet Union. Disenchanted with America, in 1921 they moved back to Slovakia just before the birth of their second child, Alexander. Devoted to the ideals of the Soviet Union, in 1925 the Dubčeks moved to the USSR, where they lived until 1938, when they returned to Slovakia. When Slovakia split off from Czechoslovakia to become a Nazi ally in 1939, eighteen-year-old Alexander joined a group of guerrilla fighters who eventually helped drive out the Germans.

World War II strengthened what Dubček called "the socialist convictions of freedom and social justice" that his parents instilled in him, and in 1949 he became a full-time paid staff member in Slovakia's Communist Party.[7] Truly committed to socialism, he quickly began moving his way up within the Party's hierarchy. The Party recognized his commitment and in 1955 sent him to Moscow for three years' study of party ideology.

In Moscow, Dubček noticed some important nuances in communist thought that would shape his own views. Reading Karl Marx convinced him that communism was inherently democratic, since it was based on the majority rule of workers. This view ran completely against the practice in the Soviet Union and its satellites, where the population had no say in government. Dubček's reading of Lenin, the central thinker behind the creation of the USSR, led him to an even more surprising conclusion. In Dubček's view, Lenin believed that if an advanced country (like Czechoslovakia!) carried out a successful socialist revolution, that country could take the lead in shaping socialism around the world, persuading more economically backward countries (like the Soviet Union) to follow it.[8] Knowing that his superiors, especially among the Soviets, would not respond positively, Dubček kept these interpretations to himself, but he also tucked them away in the back of his mind.

Dubček was even more blown away by the new era of communism that he saw in the Soviet Union during the mid to late 1950s. Joseph Stalin died in 1953 after years of dominating nearly every aspect of Soviet life. Few expected the Soviet Union to look inward to criticize its own past, but in 1956, nearly three years after Stalin's death, Soviet leader Nikita Krushchev delivered a "secret" speech to the Party lambasting the horrors of Stalin's rule. The sentiment of the speech trickled downward, so eventually Soviet Party members felt comfortable enough to tell Dubček bluntly that Stalin had been a cruel, repressive dictator and a murderer. In the months that followed, the Soviets freed tens of thousands of political prisoners. The revelations of Stalin's evil deeds devastated Dubček, who had been raised with the view that the USSR had been virtuous, but he became energized as he watched the Soviet Communists' willingness to confront their country's ills.

At the same time, his excitement turned to trepidation as he looked to return home to Czechoslovakia in 1958. [9]

Czechoslovakia had been led since 1953 by Antonín Novotný, a dull, arrogant man known for his frozen, impassive face, who hewed as closely to the Stalinist hard-line as any major figure in the Eastern Bloc. Despite Krushchev's efforts at "de-Stalinization," Novotný quashed Czechoslovak efforts to carry out reforms or even acknowledge Czechoslovakia's most grotesque abuses. And with good reason. Novotný had entered the upper circle of power in Czechoslovakia in large part through his success in fabricating evidence during the reign of terror of the early 1950s, including in the infamous Slánský trial that had shocked the Holíks in 1952. In the years that followed, people who challenged Novotný's authority found themselves imprisoned. [10]

As the years passed following Dubček's return from Moscow, the Communist Party repeatedly promoted him, making him one of the highest-ranking Communists from Slovakia and giving him a front-row seat to Novotný's ignorance, incompetence, and corruption. Dubček stewed as Novotný's policies kept Slovakia economically underdeveloped and politically powerless. He became even more frustrated as Novotný spoke contemptuously of the region. And Dubček grew infuriated as he watched Novotný force economic sacrifice on the population of the entire country while building a luxurious recreational compound where Party officials could spend their weekends. [11]

Over time, though, Novotný began to feel pressure from abroad and at home to change. After a forceful nudge from the Soviets and his patron Krushchev, he agreed in 1962 to create a commission to investigate Czechoslovakia's purges and political trials of the 1950s. Novotný clearly expected the commission to whitewash these events. Instead, it reported in detail that the government had subjected the defendants to physical and psychological torture. Worse still, the commission made clear that the prosecutors had used fabricated evidence to convict—and even execute—numerous innocent people, including many loyal Communists. Dubček served as ranking member on the commission. What he learned about the Party that he loved left him sick to his stomach, and he steeled himself to push for real reform. [12]

Novotný's limited understanding of complex policy making showed in Czechoslovakia's economy. Prior to the 1948 Communist coup, the Czech lands had a well-developed industrial sector, but years of mismanagement by the Communists had produced serious economic decline. As a result, there were shortages of food and other basic consumer goods that even led the government, in 1963, to declare that restaurants and factory cafeterias should observe a policy of "meatless Thursdays."[13]

As public anger over the poor economy grew during the 1960s, Novotný tried to appease his critics by easing up on some of his regime's more draconian policies, especially reducing censorship and even permitting some travel to the West. It was thanks to this relaxation of travel restrictions that Czechs and Slovaks were able to attend the 1967 Hockey Championships in Vienna.[14] Despite these efforts, public criticism of the government increased and came to a head in 1967. In June, the Czechoslovak Writers Union, a group whose members had mostly supported the Party, openly attacked the leadership's hardline policies and pushed for changes in a more democratic direction. Novotný pushed back. Announcing that "democracy and freedom have their limits," he cracked down on dissent, demoting and even expelling a number of the Party members who had criticized him.

But Novotný's problems were not over. Earlier in the year, he had created unnecessary tension with a number of prominent Slovak Communists when he had made a series of insensitive statements regarding Slovak cultural traditions. The relationship between Novotný and the top-ranking Slovak Communists continued to worsen and, at a major Party meeting on the final two days of October, reached a breaking point. At the meeting, Dubček charged Novotný with "behaving like a dictator" and damaging Slovakia's economy with his interference and incompetence. Irate, Novotný denounced Dubček and his Slovak followers. Incredibly, rather than stand by Novotný, a group of Czech leaders and other Party members expressed support for the Slovak side and even pushed for Novotný's resignation.[15]

On the second night of the Party meetings, events elsewhere in Prague left even more egg on the face of the Novotný regime. Students from Prague's technical college lived under horrible conditions in the school's dormitories. Due to power failures, the students regularly lacked heat and electricity. When the power went out again the night of October 31, the students had had enough. A group of 1,500 students marched with candles through the streets chanting "We want light! We want to study!" Eventually, police intervened and ultimately turned violent, using batons and tear gas, even kicking and beating students who lay on the ground. Outraged, students and professors conducted sit-ins in November to press the authorities to address the police brutality. In an extraordinary response, in early December the government made an official statement that the police actions had, indeed, been over the line. The statement was a sign that the regime could no longer simply do as it pleased and, by extension, undermined Novotný's position of power. [16]

In December, Soviet leader Leonid Brezhnev came to Czechoslovakia, at Novotný's request, to attempt to quell the dissent. Although he was critical of Novotný, Brezhnev pushed Czechoslovakia's top Communists to cease their open quarreling. But the Soviet leader's nudge did not have its intended effect. Calls for the Czechoslovak leader's ouster grew louder and more numerous. Novotný was forced to resign from his position atop Czechoslovakia's Communist Party. In January 1968, he was replaced by the forty-six-year-old Dubček. [17]

Almost immediately, censorship in Czechoslovakia declined. Communist Party leaders pushed for more complete reporting, without a propagandistic spin, of government deliberations and actions. The leadership started to meet with the public and spoke openly with citizens on live television. And the government gave writers greater freedom to say and publish what they liked. [18]

A new mood and sense of hope started to bubble up, affecting even the way that people viewed their beloved national hockey team. Czechs and Slovaks were well aware that the USSR had held sway over them for two decades. This domination extended even to hockey, where the fall of Czechoslovakia's national team in the early 1950s coincided with the rise of the Soviet team. But what if the changes that were beginning to occur in Czechoslovakia under Dubček were real? What if the Soviet Union could no longer tell Czechoslovakia what to do? If so, people thought, *perhaps we can finally beat the Soviets on the ice . . .*

By 1968, Czechoslovakia's hockey team had indeed become more likely to defeat the Soviets, but not because of any changes in the country's politics. Rather, thanks to changes in training and strategy implemented under Jaroslav Pitner, Czechoslovakia's national hockey team was ready to jump up a level.

Among the most important changes: Pitner had found someone who was, in fact, a professor of hockey to join him in training the squad. Born in 1922, three and a half years before Pitner, Vladimír Kostka had been an unremarkable player but was obsessed with the way hockey was played. A deeply committed communist, Kostka hewed closely to Marxist principles about the importance of using theory to inform practice and believed scientific and theoretical thinking about hockey would lead to major improvements in the sport. In the 1950s, Kostka joined the Faculty of Physical Education and Sport at Charles University in Prague, a program dedicated to developing a greater understanding of the scientific side of sports and to training coaches in that approach. Known as "The Ice Hockey Professor," he became the leader in Czechoslovakia in the scientific study of hockey, publishing dozens of books and hundreds of scholarly articles on the subject. Kostka kept abreast of new developments in hockey theory and practice around the world and borrowed heavily from Anatoly Tarasov's thought and writing.[19] In the 1950s, Kostka began traveling with and advising Czechoslovakia's national hockey team. He formally took over as one of the coaches in the 1960s, a post he held off and on until he remained solidly in the position with Pitner after the 1967 World Championships.[20]

The players found Kostka to be dry, boring, and unfriendly. Unlike the gregarious Pitner, Kostka never smiled. His face usually wore a severe, no-nonsense expression, accentuated by his sharp cheekbones and receding brown hair. He appeared to have little interest in human connection, and his interactions with the men he coached usually consisted of blunt instructions.[21]

But working in tandem with Pitner, Kostka could afford to be aloof. Players respected Kostka because of his genius and willingness to live and breathe hockey, and Pitner supplied the human touch.[22] The Dukla coach seemed to know instinctively how to handle his players as individuals and let them know that he had their backs. In one tournament, when Soviet coach Tarasov ran into Jan Suchý smoking in front of the USSR locker room, he rushed in to see Pitner. "How is it possible that your player is smoking?!" Pitner calmly responded that Suchý was a smoker and that if he stopped the habit too abruptly, he would become unable to perform at his usual level.

Kostka and Pitner created an in-sync two-headed coaching model based on a division of labor. Kostka had never coached a league team and often skipped training and practices. Instead, he focused on developing strategy and plays, analyzing the opposing teams down to the tiniest details. Pitner applied Kostka's theories to the real-world ice and set the lineups. During games, Pitner acted as the lead coach, constantly moving between the players and the guardrail separating them from the ice, while Kostka simply stood quietly behind the bench, holding his chin as his computer mind contemplated changes to tactics. Between periods, the two coaches compared notes on what adjustments to make. In the locker room, Pitner spoke to the team as a whole, while Kostka gave specific suggestions to individual players.

Following the 1967 World Championships, Pitner and Kostka began to focus on the most frustrating issue facing the squad. In most years, Czechoslovakia did well in matches against nearly every team. However, that success was of limited value when it then got crushed by the USSR because of the Soviets' superior conditioning. When Pitner and Kostka realized that their players needed to both be in better shape and find a way to recuperate from the long Czechoslovak league season, they increased the length of the national team's training camp prior to the 1968 Olympics. They gave the players a heavy dose of conditioning, but included extra emphasis as well on a healthy diet, sleep, hot baths, and massage therapy. [23]

Kostka and Pitner also knew that they would need a new set of tactics if they were to have any chance of handling the overpowering USSR offense. Much of the problem, they concluded, was that most of Czechoslovakia's center forwards weren't good enough skaters—or sufficiently motivated defenders—to transition cleanly from offense to defense when the Soviets gained control of the puck. What if, the coaches pondered, we use our exceptional skaters, especially left-wing forwards like Jiří Holík and longtime star Josef Černý, as a central component of our defense? So was born the "left-wing lock" system in which, after a puck change, the left-wing forward immediately moves back and forms a line with the defense. Pitner first tried out the tactic with Dukla, where Jiří executed it to perfection. As a team player who diligently followed his coaches' instructions, Jiří didn't complain, especially as the system appeared to be the best chance to contain the Soviets' offensive firepower. But he often felt frustrated that it gave him less opportunity to be part of his team's offense. The system caught on quickly throughout Czechoslovakia, became common in international play, and ultimately turned out to be a staple for a number of top professional teams in North America. [24]

Despite Jaroslav Holík's absence, overall Czechoslovakia's national squad was now stronger than the year before in Vienna. Jan Suchý had become a massive star in the 1967–68 Czechoslovak league season. He had fully found his form on defense, successfully throwing his body in front of offensive players to block shots. And despite the fact that he was a defenseman, he had also become one of Czechoslovakia's top *offensive* players, finishing with the sixth most goals scored in the league that year.

The most important change from the 1967 roster was the return of Vladimír Dzurilla, a big goalie from Bratislava, Slovakia. Jaroslav Holík would never forget the day he met Dzurilla when, as seventeen-year-olds, they both joined the junior national team. As he first encountered his teammates, all seemingly big-city kids, Jaroslav felt like a small-town hick. But in the sea of macho teen posturing, Dzurilla exuded a sort of cuddly warmth. The two hit it off instantly, and from that day forward, Jaroslav openly adored the five-foot, ten-inch, 205-pound lovable bear cub of a man more than he did any other person in the hockey world.

In truth, *everyone* loved Dzurilla, and "Vlado" got along with the Czech players in a way that no other Slovak on the national team did. It was partly his natural friendliness. Dzurilla was easygoing and fairly quiet, his face always covered with a smile. But it was also his willingness to do whatever his team needed. Anytime anyone needed to practice his shots, Dzurilla happily strapped on his gear, working to the point of exhaustion and the loss of ten pounds of sweat. Laid-back and funny, Dzurilla loved to mock himself, laughing to his teammates that he couldn't drop down to the ice for low shots because he was too chubby to get back up again.

His teammates also knew that when it mattered, Dzurilla raised his game to another level. He seemed to prefer the big moments. He had been voted the top goaltender at the 1965 World Championships, and players around the world knew Dzurilla was the key for Czechoslovakia. He had been hurt in 1967, but was back now and ready for the 1968 Olympics.[25]

Czechoslovakia's team arrived at the Grenoble Olympics in the first week of February full of confidence that they were vastly improved, thanks to the return of Dzurilla and the new training provided by their two-headed coach. Opening the tournament, Czechoslovakia generally played well, winning its first four games, but the team wasn't consistent and lost to Canada in the fifth match. The radio crew broadcasting the games back to Czechoslovakia suggested that something was off, that the squad didn't appear to jell as a group.[26]

One person in particular agonized over Czechoslovakia's play. Jaroslav Holík's first child, a girl named Andrea, had been born in January, thus allaying some of his fury at being removed from the team, but he remained deeply upset. Hoping to calm him down, the army paid for Holík to go to Grenoble as a "tourist." Jaroslav watched every game from the stands, overwhelmed with the stress of being unable to do anything to help. [27]

Czechoslovakia's players could hardly be blamed for their lack of consistent focus in the early matches. They had been distracted for nearly a year by thoughts of their game six opponent: the USSR. The fight the previous year had fired them up, and now more than ever they wanted to take down the squad that had long dominated them. At home, many Czechs and Slovaks still believed that this dominance wasn't entirely real, that it was a result of orders from the Moscow political leadership. To these conspiracy theorists, the 1968 winter games offered a litmus test of just how genuine and far-reaching the political reforms in Czechoslovakia truly were.

The real problem remained: the Red Machine simply appeared to be better than everyone else. In Grenoble, the French crowds loved the intense effort put forward by the men from Czechoslovakia and openly rooted for them, [28] but few thought they could take the title. The defending champs had outscored their opponents 39–5 on their way to an undefeated record in five matches in Grenoble. Including Vienna, the Soviets had now won five consecutive World Championships and had not lost a match in World Championship play since 1963. In the pregame commentary, Czechoslovakia's radio announcers Vladimír Vácha and Oskar Mana told their listeners about the sad history of matches between the two countries. Their boys, the announcers underlined for listeners back home in Czechoslovakia, just didn't have much of a chance. [29]

Recognizing what it was up against, Czechoslovakia decided to try some gamesmanship. The Soviet skaters hated to get knocked off their routines, and Kostka and Pitner believed the key to defeating them was to break their rhythm. Viktor Konovalenko had been the USSR's top goaltender throughout the decade, but he was the team's weakest link, a tier below the world's best. Kostka and Pitner believed that it was possible to make Konovalenko lose his concentration. They would unleash their ploy right before game time.

On Thursday, February 15, the teams from the USSR and Czechoslovakia took to the ice, feeling the buzz of the sell-out French crowd. Just minutes before the match was to begin, Pitner sent Golonka, now the team's captain, to the referees to report an equipment infraction: seven Soviet players had no protective buffers on their steel skate blades, a violation of international rules. Insisting the Soviets fix the offending skates before play could begin, the officials halted the countdown to game time. As the match's scheduled start time came and went, the crowd grew impatient, showering angry whistles onto the ice. As the noise reverberated across the arena, the Soviets scrambled to address the infraction. After thirty minutes of ear-piercing whistling and a mad rush by the Soviets to fix their skates, the referees finally approved the defending champs' equipment and dropped the puck to begin play. When the Red Machine jumped out to a 1–0 lead within the first twenty-three seconds of the game, it looked like the gambit had backfired.

Pitner remained calm. He sent his players on all-out attacks, hoping to shake up the USSR netminder. Within minutes, Czechoslovakia evened the score. Now the Soviets really did appear off balance. Czechoslovakia scored again and then one more time to take a 3–1 lead after a single period.

In period two, even as the crowd roared its support for the underdogs, the Soviets blasted a shot past Dzurilla, cutting Czechoslovakia's lead to one. But then Jan Suchý made his presence felt. Throughout the Olympics, Suchý had continued his brilliant play from the Czechoslovak league season. Now, in the second period against the USSR, he skated like the wind, kept opposing players from getting solid shots at the net, and helped drive the offense. With just a minute and a half left in the period, Suchý got the puck and flipped it to Golonka, who smashed it past the Soviet goalie from twenty-five feet away to give Czechoslovakia a 4–2 lead.

As the third and final period began, the Czechoslovak players felt confident they could hold on. That confidence only grew as the minutes passed and no one scored. Dzurilla had been magnificent, stopping shot after shot by the swarming Soviet skaters. Suddenly, with just under four minutes left to play, Jaroslav Jiřík received a crisp pass from Golonka and knocked in a short-range shot to give Czechoslovakia what had to be an insurmountable three-goal lead!

As the puck went into the net, Golonka gave one of his classic celebratory performances. Despite constant pain in his thirty-year-old knees, Golonka played exceptionally well throughout the tournament, leading the team with ten combined goals and assists. After Jiřík's goal, Golonka dropped to his knees, sliding for fifty feet with his arms raised, before flopping down onto his stomach. Beaming, Golonka bounced his stick up and down, looking like a clapping seal, as an impassive Ragulin slowly skated by. Newspapers around Europe would run a photo of the moment with a caption suggesting that Golonka had placed his ear near the ice to better hear if the Soviets had decided to retaliate against his hockey team by closing the pipelines of oil and natural gas that ran to Czechoslovakia.

Czechoslovakia appeared to have the match as good as won—but then everything fell apart. As a huge celebration began on both the ice and in the stands, Team Czechoslovakia lost its concentration. The players kept looking up at both the jubilant fans and the now very slowly ticking clock. That was all it took to let the Red Machine back into the match. Within seconds, the Soviets snuck a close shot past Dzurilla. A minute later, they slapped in another. With a full two and a half minutes remaining the Soviets were now within a goal and seemed to be driving with impunity.

The Soviets picked up the pace, trying to avoid the powerful Czecho-slovak body checks. The puck appeared stuck at Dzurilla's end of the rink. Everyone on Czechoslovakia's bench was standing now, willing the puck to stay out of the net. With just a minute to go, the Soviets grew desperate and attacked in a frenzy. With twenty seconds left, the Soviets knocked the puck toward the big Slovak netminder. When the disk bounced out right in front of the goal, nearly every player on the ice dove into a scrum that formed on top of Dzurilla, knocking the big goalie onto his back and all the way into the back of the net. But no goal had been scored! The clock stopped as everyone on the ice reset. Exhausted and shaken up, it took Dzurilla a solid minute to get back to his feet. He skated slowly and gingerly in front of the goal to clear his head, while the Soviets pulled their own goalie out of the game and replaced him with one more possible scorer. Seventeen seconds left to play.

Six bright red Soviet jerseys now blanketed the ice, ready to attack Dzurilla once again. Golonka and USSR center Vyacheslav Starshinov set up for a face-off to the left of the goal. As the energy level and volume in the arena rose another notch, the Soviets controlled the puck and passed to their star defen-seman. Somehow, Czechoslovak television announcer Karol Polák managed to maintain a coherent commentary:

*RAGULIN! He shoots but only into Jiřík. Just ten . . . nine seconds until
the end. Eight! The whole arena is rooting for our lads. Four seconds!
Three! Two! One! THE END! We know so well what is happening
back home, dear viewers. We defeated the USSR team 5–4. The time for
happiness and joy is here. And I am sure you will fall asleep feeling pride
over the performance of our lads.* [30]

Suchý seemed to read the situation a split second ahead of everyone else. The
moment the clock hit zero, he leaped into the air with his arms raised, then
the rest of the team began celebrating as well. Golonka sprinted across the
ice and took flight, launching himself directly at Dzurilla's face. As Golonka
collided with his Slovak teammate, he wrapped his arms around the big man,
bringing the goalie facedown onto the ice. Within moments, the rest of Czechoslovakia's players rushed to join in. After a minute or so, they all composed
themselves and, without apparent thought, lined up to shake hands with the
Soviet team. As they did, Czechoslovakia's fans stormed the ice, awkwardly
slipping and falling as they went to embrace the players. [31]

Tarasov was furious with Golonka and Pitner. The move to call out his
players' equipment infraction left the mercurial Soviet coach in a fury. For
the next year, he told people, "Coach Pitner doesn't exist to me anymore.
What he and Golonka did to us before the game started was disgusting. . . .
Our friends . . . they ridiculed and embarrassed us at the Olympic Games
in front of the entire Western bourgeoisie." [32] Following the game, though,
Tarasov was the last thing that the men from Czechoslovakia were thinking
about. They had defeated their number one foe on the biggest of stages and
their joy overflowed.

Despite the victory, Pitner insisted that the players celebrate only modestly.
They had more work to do. They would need to be well rested when they played
their final game two days later. Pitner felt like the parent of giant hockey-playing
children, as he went from room to room in their hotel, putting the men to bed. [33]

Although nothing mattered as much to Czechoslovakia as defeating the
Soviets, the match two days later was among the most important in the country's
history. As TV announcer Polák finished the play-by-play of the match against
the Soviets, he reminded his audience: "Have a toast to [the players'] health, but
not too much! After all, our players must still face Sweden. And if we manage

to succeed on Saturday as well, then we will all celebrate properly."[34] With a victory in the final match of the tournament, Czechoslovakia would take home its first ever Olympic gold medal in hockey.

However, physically and mentally exhausted after the USSR match, the Czechoslovak players just couldn't repeat their heroics. With time running out in the final game, the score tied at two, and a number of chances theirs for the taking, Golonka tried to get the puck past the Swedish goaltender, but each attempt fell short. The game ended in a tie. The Soviets took their third Olympic hockey gold medal and, with it, their sixth consecutive world title. Czechoslovakia was left with the silver.[35]

The players were crushed. As they returned from France, they wondered how everyone at home was taking the loss. Then they arrived at Czechoslovakia's border. When the team beat the Soviets just a few days before, thousands had taken to the streets in Czechoslovakia to celebrate, with many painting "5:4"— the score of the victory over the USSR—on walls and sidewalks all over the country. Now, tens of thousands of people braved frigid February weather to cheer their returning heroes. The crowd packed in so tightly that it became difficult for the customs officials and border guards to process the players. Fans, including brass bands, bagpipers, and all sorts of other musicians, lined the road toward home. It took forever to get back to Prague because the players kept stopping to join revelers along the way.

The thrill of the victory over the Soviets energized the country. To millions of Czechs and Slovaks, the hockey win over the USSR fit perfectly into this time of change and the growing sense of freedom, adding to their conviction that the Soviets no longer had a stranglehold on them.[36] The celebration was not merely in support of a hockey team. It was also a celebration of a different feeling in the country. They had stood up to and defeated Big Brother! And there was more coming. As the people of Czechoslovakia looked ahead to warmer weather on the horizon, they sensed the emergence of what became known as the "Prague Spring."

The week following the hockey victory over the Soviets marked the twentieth anniversary of the Communists' takeover in Czechoslovakia, and Dubček used it as an opportunity to speak publicly of the changes he and the government would now pursue. He spoke of plans to develop an Action Program designed to reform and rescue the economy. Dubček believed, however, that this economic reform would succeed only if the country's politics changed first. He and his allies argued that power had become too centralized in the hands of a tiny number of Communist Party elites who were simply not equipped to address the complex issues facing them. By making information more widely available and opening up debate, Czechoslovakia could better tackle its myriad problems.[37] The program he launched in April looked nothing like the world Czechoslovakia had inhabited for the previous twenty years. Three democratic principles stood at its center: freedom of speech, freedom of the press, and freedom of movement.

Speaking through the media, Dubček described the importance of open discussion, and, indeed, open discussion soon became a reality. Farmers, workers, and students openly debated government policy with officials in public meetings. Press coverage, which had been carefully scripted and controlled by the government, abruptly became far freer. The media began to cover real news, even reporting on student protests in communist Poland.

The new openness especially washed over Czechoslovakia's capital. Perhaps the most visually dramatic expression was the Prague cafes, which became meeting places where people flocked to read the Western newspapers and magazines that were now flooding the country. Since 1948, people had risked losing their jobs or even being imprisoned if they said the wrong thing or spoke to a forbidden person. Now, in squares and on sidewalks, throngs of strangers talked openly with one another about the miraculous changes they were seeing and their opinions on them.[38]

The sense of freedom shaped popular culture. Continuing a trend that had begun over the previous few years, fashion and styles came to look more like the West. Men grew their beards and hair long, and young people clamored to get their own pairs of blue jeans. All around Prague, people listened to jazz and rock and roll music, and flocked to theaters showing previously banned plays.

It all created a sense of euphoria. Prague's beauty shone in the new light: the rolling green hills that looked down on the tree-lined Vltava River, the 650-year-old stone arch of the Charles Bridge that spanned the river, the stunning buildings from every major period of European architecture, including countless enchanting Baroque structures with white façades and red roofs. To many, the sights of the capital city sparkled with a crispness that had seemed absent for years.

Dubček had never been noted for his intelligence, his ability to inspire a crowd, or his political skill, but people praised him for his honesty, his willingness to listen, and his persuasiveness in small groups.[39] Following years of government repression and dissembling, these traits struck a deep chord of relief. As the reforms became increasingly tangible, popular support for the government grew. A public opinion survey conducted in Czechoslovakia at the time indicated that 87 percent of respondents were at least partially satisfied with the work of the government, and 89 percent wanted Czechoslovakia to remain communist.[40]

Then there was the most tangible freedom of all. In the past, travel to the West had been almost impossible for most people from Czechoslovakia, but now it became available to everyone. In 1968, half a million Czechs and Slovaks traveled abroad, including a thirty-one-year-old playwright named Václav Havel, who went to America to see his satirical work performed in New York. The freedom to travel went the other way as well, with hundreds of thousands of young people from the West coming to Czechoslovakia to bathe in the excitement and energy.

Many referred to the new system as "socialism with a human face," whereby the government sought to eliminate the most repressive elements of Communist rule. It denounced secret police investigations of people's personal beliefs and decried the Communist Party's abuses of the 1950s, which it went to pains to reveal. The wave of reform even touched many of the more conservative locales. Jihlava's local newspaper published articles that called for investigations into atrocities committed by the secret police in the 1950s.[41] As the 1968 Prague Spring moved to summer, the Supreme Court annulled—too late, of course—the horrible death penalty exacted in 1950 upon Milada Horáková, the social justice and women's rights activist. The government also set the record straight by "rehabilitating" numerous other innocent victims of its repression, including the 1950 national hockey team.

Despite the exhilaration, Dubček felt pulled in two directions, a feeling that only intensified as the summer progressed. Much of the public clamored for the government to move even faster with its reforms. But the Soviet Union increased its pressure on Dubček to undo the changes.

The Soviets had always meddled in policy making within all its satellites, but Dubček had put his Action Program together without the Soviets' input or permission. Soviet leaders worried that the Prague Spring posed a threat to their Eastern Bloc order. Time and again, leaders of other communist countries called Dubček to meet with him, gauge his plans, and caution against what he was doing. More than once, the Soviets called a meeting of the leaders (Dubček included) of its communist allies, the countries of the Warsaw Pact military alliance, to warn Czechoslovakia to rein in the new freedoms. Brezhnev himself pressed Dubček to meet in person multiple times to express his concerns.

Dubček found the in-person meetings with Brezhnev to be the most unpleasant. Following a variant on a Russian custom, the Soviet leader made it a habit to greet his counterparts from other Eastern Bloc countries with a kiss on the lips as a public relations show of solidarity. Dubček found the custom distasteful, particularly with Brezhnev, so he showed up at a major meeting with the Soviet leader in early August carrying flowers, which he used as a shield to avoid the otherwise inevitable meeting of the lips. Even more unpleasant for Dubček, Brezhnev made it clear that he expected Czechoslovakia to return to how things had been before 1968.[42]

Still, Dubček had every confidence that disagreements between the two countries would soon be overcome, especially because of the close friendship between them. He bent over backward to express his deep commitment to communism, the central role of the Communist Party in Czechoslovakia, and his country's undying loyalty to the USSR. He published an article in the Soviet newspaper *Pravda* that declared, "Friendship with the USSR is the foundation of our foreign policy." Nevertheless, the pressure took its toll on Dubček, who found himself able to sleep only three or four hours a night.[43]

Brezhnev continued to lean on him throughout the summer, but Czechoslovakia's leader felt he had a solid plan in place to push forward his agenda while simultaneously holding off USSR pressure. Dubček spent the early weeks of August ironing out the details. The Party Presidium, the policy-making body of Czechoslovakia's Communists, scheduled Tuesday, August 20 for a final meeting to plan the next Party congress. In that September congress, the Party would adopt new policies in line with the Action Program and, presumably, elect more pro-Dubček, pro-reform leaders.[44]

The 20th of August was a hazy, peaceful late summer day in Prague. Much of the city was away on vacation, but an influx of summer tourists and families strolled about, enjoying the warm air. Life was less pleasant for Dubček. Anna, his wife, had suffered throughout the previous night from a gallbladder problem, so he took her to the hospital that morning. It appeared treatable, but Anna needed to stay in the hospital overnight. Dubček reminded her that he would be working with the Presidium late that evening, so most likely he would return to see her the following morning.[45] It was a date he would be unable to keep.

# PART II

# THEY'RE HERE

*Jan Zábrana [was] a poet and professional translator who translated both American and Russian poetry. . . . On August 20, 1968, Zábrana was working late, as he tended to do. In the middle of the night, he heard the phone ringing. He didn't answer it. It rang again. He didn't answer. It rang one more time. He didn't answer it. He listened to airplanes circling the nearby airport in Kbely. There seemed to be a lot of airplanes, circling and circling without landing. There were so many planes that they couldn't land on the available runways. His wife was awake, and called to him from the corridor, just two words: "They're here."*

—Jonathan Bolton, *Worlds of Dissent*[1]

# CHAPTER 6

# Invasion

On the evening of Tuesday, August 20, Jaroslav's wife, Marie, had guests over to the Holík house in Jihlava. Jaroslav and his teammates were out of the country. Although hockey was considered a winter sport, Czechoslovakia's top hockey players actually played much of the year and often traveled to exhibitions during the summer. This August, the Dukla team had gone to a tournament in Fussen, West Germany. Because Marie was at home alone with the seven-month-old Andrea, she invited her school friend Jiřina to join her, along with Jiřina's husband, Jiří Pitner, the son of the Dukla coach. Jaroslav Holík owned an 8 mm camera and a projector, and the young Pitners brought a reel of film from their recent wedding that they wanted to view. The three friends stayed up late watching the footage and talking, and it was close to two o'clock in the morning before the Pitners left. Just a few hours later, at 6:30 A.M., the doorbell rang over and over, with increasing urgency. Marie's mother stood outside, looking disheveled. "We have been invaded! Quick, go to a store to buy groceries. I know how it is under an occupation. Go! I will watch Andrea!" Marie felt goosebumps rise and her heart pounded as the older woman went on: "It is the Russians. There are tanks everywhere."

Marie rushed to the phone to call her friend Evelína, and together the two young women raced to the store. There were not yet any Soviet tanks or soldiers in their town that morning, but the streets were already filled with Jihlavans trying to figure out what to do. It appeared that almost no one was going to work that day as the news cast a pall. Jihlava's older population remembered the Nazi occupation. They recognized the feeling of dread that accompanied the arrival

of an invading force. And like Marie's mother, they remembered the food shortages of the past occupation and set out first thing in the morning to tell their
adult children to buy as much as they could at the store. By the time Marie and
Evelína arrived at the market, there was almost nothing left on the shelves,
not even a cube of sugar. Marie could only buy a single slab of dried salami. [1]

Czechoslovakia's leaders were scarcely more prepared for the shocking news. As
Dubček expected, the 2 P.M. Tuesday meeting with the rest of the Presidium
in the Central Committee headquarters building extended well into the night.
As the proceedings wore on, Prime Minister Oldřich Černík began to receive
strange reports and left the room a number of times to speak by phone with
the minister of defense. Around 11:45 P.M., Černík returned to the Presidium
chamber looking grim-faced and pale. He walked to Dubček and whispered
something. Dubček's body gave an involuntary jerk, as if he had been physically
attacked. The man seen as the face of the Prague Spring leaned forward, steadied
himself on the conference table, and stood to interrupt the Presidium discussion: "The armies of the five parties have crossed the borders of our republic
and begun occupying the country." [2]

Operation Danube had begun in earnest at 10:30 P.M., when air traffic controllers at Prague's Ruzyně airport received an odd transmission from someone
claiming to be the pilot of a Soviet Aeroflot passenger plane that was running
out of fuel. Speaking in Russian, the pilot requested permission to land. The air
traffic controllers were suspicious. Commercial pilots were supposed to communicate with them in English. Not quite knowing what to make of the odd
exchange, the men at Ruzyně instructed the pilot to divert to a nearby military
airport. Within minutes, the air traffic controllers could do little more than
gawk as two enormous Soviet Antonov jets landed in front of them. On cue, a
group of "tourists" in the foreign departures lounge pulled out rifles to round
up airport workers, and another group in the airport charged into the control
tower to escort the airport staff out. More than fifty men in civilian clothes and
150 paratroopers wearing camouflage fatigues, steel helmets, and machine guns
exited the Antonovs. Two menacing tanks rolled down the ramp of one of the
planes, ready for their introduction to Czechoslovakia. [3]

Having secured the airport, Soviet military planes began landing as if in a convoy. At times one arrived nearly every minute, spewing tanks, military vehicles, fuel, supplies, and, of course, troops, then taking off to bring more. Over the next seven hours, 250 planes delivered an entire airborne division, the largest airlift the Soviets had ever conducted outside the USSR.[4] As the airlift continued throughout the night, a convoy of tanks followed the Lenin Highway, leading from the airport toward the heart of Czechoslovakia's capital. The tanks followed sinister-looking escorts in the form of the Soviet Embassy's black Volga limousines, the kind that had become infamous in Eastern Europe for abducting Moscow's enemies.[5]

Meanwhile, in a move that began at 11 P.M., well over 150,000 troops and 2,000 tanks, all under the control of the Soviet High Command, traversed some twenty crossing points into Czechoslovakia from the Soviet Union, Hungary, East Germany, and Poland. Some of the invading force had drawn from the militaries of Bulgaria, Hungary, and Poland. Throughout the invasion, it was widely believed that there were also East German troops. However, decades later, documents were uncovered indicating that, not long before go-time, Soviet leader Brezhnev canceled their participation. The Soviets feared that because of residual bitterness from Germany's previous occupation of the country, people in Czechoslovakia would be more likely to resist the invasion if the forces included East Germans. But to avoid humiliation, East German leaders' propaganda made it appear that East Germany fully participated.[6] Irrespective of the other countries involved, there was no confusion over who was in charge. This was the largest military operation in Europe since the end of World War II, and the USSR dominated the group in every way. Soviets had planned the venture, and out of a total of some 500,000 troops (and 5,000 tanks), as many as 400,000 hailed from the USSR.[7]

In Prague, in the Central Committee headquarters building, Dubček stood before his colleagues with tears in his eyes and an excruciating, almost violent pain that seemed to reach into his soul. He spoke softly, as though he was just wondering aloud, "That they should have done this to me, after I dedicated my whole life to cooperation with the Soviet Union, is the greatest tragedy of my life."[8]

Quickly composing themselves, Dubček and the leaders developed a plan. First, although Czechoslovakia maintained one of the most impressive militaries in the Warsaw Pact, the leaders rejected armed resistance. Their military was well integrated into the larger Warsaw Pact force and had no independent chain of command. At least as important, the invading force was overwhelming, and resistance would only produce a vast pool of Czechoslovak blood. Everyone remembered well the 1956 slaughter of Hungarian civilians killed for seeking freedom in the face of the all-powerful Soviet military. To Dubček and his colleagues, it was far better to show the world the picture of a peaceful Czechoslovakia that had come under the thumb of cruel Soviet invaders.[9] The Czechoslovak leaders put together a statement indicating that the invasion had occurred without their knowledge. It was an important point, since the Soviets had started announcing the bald-faced lie that the troops had moved in at the request of Czechoslovakia's Communist Party and state authorities. Fearing for the safety of the people, the statement added: "The Presidium appeals to all citizens of our Republic to keep calm and not to resist the armed forces moving in."[10]

The leaders sent the proclamation to Radio Prague, where the announcers began to read it: "Yesterday, 20 August 1968 at about 11 P.M.—" Midsentence, most radios in the area went dead. In concert with a group of upper-level members of the government and Communist Party who had decided to encourage and facilitate the Soviet invasion, the director of Czechoslovak communications had shut down the airwaves. However, radio technicians quickly found a different channel they could use. Everyone in the country soon understood what many looking into the streets already knew: they were occupied.[11]

Czechoslovakia's leaders briefly considered resigning to protest the actions of a fellow communist country against them, but they realized that by staying in their posts they would bolster their position as the true government of their own country.[12] Dubček and his compatriots remained in the Communist Party Central Committee building, unwilling to clear the way for Soviet collaborators to take their positions and give legitimacy to the invasion. Knowing full well that the Soviets would soon arrive to detain him, Dubček bided his time, pacing the halls of the expansive six-story building. As he walked, he couldn't miss the constant roar of the Soviet aircraft that, one after another, continued to deliver reinforcements.

When they learned of the invasion, hundreds of locals braved the night—and more—to meet on the Vltava riverfront where the tan neoclassical Central

Committee headquarters building sat. They carried Czechoslovak flags. Dubček heard them chanting his name and singing the national anthem. Looking out toward the river, he could see the Hlávka Bridge, just a stone's throw to the right. Finally, at 4 A.M. he saw the visitors he had been waiting for. A parade of tanks, with a black Volga limousine leading the way, rumbled south over the bridge across the river. With each second, they pushed closer to their target: Dubček and his team. In order to differentiate themselves from the identical tanks that Czechoslovakia used, the Soviets had painted theirs with two thick white stripes—one running lengthwise down the middle, and one in the center across the width—creating an easily visible cross. [13]

Dubček watched from the building in horror. The convoy turned right off the bridge road and reached the area where the crowd of Czechoslovak civilians parted too slowly to satisfy the invaders. Soviet machine guns fired, hitting a young man. [14] Soviet paratroopers, wearing military wine-colored berets and horizontally striped sailors' jerseys under their shirts, dropped from their vehicles and encircled the building, blocking off all entrances. [15] The soldiers spaced themselves twenty yards apart, tightly gripping their machine guns to make it clear no one would get in or out without their permission. [16] A journalist approached one of the soldiers and told him, "We are your brothers. In 1945, we welcomed Soviet soldiers in Prague." The soldier released the safety on his gun and shouted, "We will shoot." [17] As the paratroopers assumed their positions, all the telephones inside the building went dead.

As the morning sky turned to full daylight, a group of Soviet officers led a detachment that hurried into the Committee building. Dubček waited in his office, along with a group of his fellow Czechoslovak leaders. They felt as if they were watching a film, not real life. Nearly a dozen Soviet soldiers charged into Dubček's office and blocked the windows and doors. Forgetting that the lines had been cut, Dubček instinctively reached for his phone, leading one of the soldiers to point his Kalashnikov at Czechoslovakia's leader and rip the cable from the wall. On cue, the office's main door flew open and a group of Soviet KGB officers marched in, led by a very short colonel whose heavily decorated jacket indicated his importance. As Soviet paratroopers pointed machine guns at the back of each Czechoslovak leader's head, the little KGB man listed the names of the Czechs and Slovaks present. He then announced that he was taking them, Dubček included, under his "protection" and ordered them to follow him. They were led across the hallway to a windowless office, where a member of the Czechoslovak state security forces, speaking in a monotone, enunciated, "I am placing you in custody in the name of the Workers' and Peasants' Government." According to the security officer, this government was to be led by Alois Indra. Indra was a high-ranking member of Czechoslovakia's Communist Party who had helped bring down Novotný but, over time, had come to believe Dubček's reforms were too radical. "Within two hours, you will be brought before a revolutionary tribunal chaired by Comrade Indra."[18] The meaning was clear: death by firing squad.

No one inside the building appeared in a hurry to do anything more. Outside, hundreds more locals gathered. After about two hours passed, a pair of KGB officers escorted Dubček out of the building and ordered him into an armored carrier. Dubček knew full well that his life was in danger.[19] He complied with the order, and the vehicle, which contained no windows for passengers to see out, began to move. After riding for some time, Dubček decided that he had been in the dark—literally and figuratively—long enough and decided to try to learn more about his situation. Feigning difficulty breathing, he asked the guards to open the round manhole hatch above them to get air. The guards opened the door and Dubček sprang up to look out. The view around him made it clear—they were taking him to the airport! From that moment on, time moved at a strange pace for Dubček. As the hours—and even days—blended together, the Soviets kept changing their plans. They placed him in an airplane and then, after some time, moved him to a new one. They tried to confuse Dubček by putting dark glasses on him. They flew him to Poland. Then to Ukraine. And finally . . . to Moscow.[20] Liquidation, Dubček thought to himself, wasn't as easy as the Soviets had originally believed.[21] Things were clearly not going according to plan for the invaders. Earlier they had seemed ready to rub him out, but now they didn't know what to do with him.

The situation on the ground in Czechoslovakia was not what the Soviets had expected. On August 3, Indra and a group of co-conspirators who felt deep unease at the fast pace of reform had secretly sent Brezhnev a letter that asked the Soviets to intervene "with all the means that you have" to halt the changes occurring in Czechoslovakia. Over the following weeks, the conspirators had worked with the Soviets to formulate a plan: At the August 20 Presidium meeting, Indra and his partners would vote out Dubček, seize the reins of power, and formally request the "fraternal help" of the Soviet Union. Simultaneously, the Soviet-led Warsaw Pact forces would invade to keep Czechoslovakia's military from blocking Indra's moves. The planners were so confident of the outcome that East Germany's official newspaper ran a story *the night of the invasion* about the takedown of Dubček and how a new government had replaced him. [22]

The problem was that Indra and his mates had been unable to pull together enough Presidium members to unseat Dubček. The conspirators had not seized power. No call had gone out for "fraternal help." But hundreds of thousands of Warsaw Pact troops now pounded across Czechoslovakia.

The conspirators also had generally been too incompetent to block the Czechoslovak leaders' ability to communicate with the public, so government supporters continued to broadcast and massive crowds formed to show the invaders that they were not welcome. [23] The invasion began late Tuesday night, but by very early Wednesday morning Czechoslovakia's people were in the streets. Untold numbers had been awakened by the roar of the military planes landing in the capital city's airport. Many heard the government's proclamation over the radio, and thousands notified friends and family by telephone or pounded on each other's doors. Young people ran to their cars and spent the next hours leaning on their horns and calling for demonstrations in Prague's central squares. As the sun rose, the city swarmed with locals who refused to sit at home as occupiers patrolled their streets. [24]

What they saw was terrifying and bizarre. As they walked through the streets of Prague and other cities and towns around the country, countless people had similar experiences: The ground shook as a strange growl became audible. As the sound grew louder and louder, the locals took in the awful smell of grease and burnt rubber. From around the corner a massive olive metal contraption—a tank—rumbled toward them, followed by a succession of more tanks. The machines slowed to a halt, and the lid on the top of the first one opened. Slowly, a figure looking to observers like a spaceman invader in an old black-and-white film, covered with a black hood, goggles, fatigues, and gloves, emerged from the hole on the top of the machine. As he did, less bizarrely dressed soldiers stepped out from the other tanks. Very, very young looking, these soldiers wore khaki. Many never removed their fingers from the triggers of the guns they pointed around them. The spaceman looked down at a piece of paper, looked up and all around him, back down at the paper, and back up again. Within moments, the crowd realized that the spaceman and his group were lost, and that he was trying to make sense of a map and the reality around him. Unable to obtain assistance from the locals, the spaceman and soldiers soon climbed back down into their machines, pulled shut the lids, and drove on, leaving behind a residue of tank stench.[25] Over the coming days, residents removed, flipped over, and destroyed thousands of street signs, making it even more difficult for the spaceman and bands of young soldiers to figure out where to go. Some local citizens decided to leave a helpful set of placards in place for their invaders: signs that pointed the way back to Moscow.

Despite the awesome power of the invaders' tanks and weapons, across the country Czechs and Slovaks walked directly up to them: "This is a mistake! You are not supposed to be here!" They spat and threw garbage at the soldiers and their vehicles. Frustrated at having nothing else to use, some simply pounded on the tanks with their bare fists. Many of the soldiers were uneducated, poor teenage peasants, raised in a place that had given them little access to factual news about their country or any other. Because their commanders had told them that they were in Czechoslovakia to protect a brother country from a "counterrevolution," the soldiers could not understand the hostile response to their presence. Some of the soldiers were not even quite sure where they were.[26]

The Soviet soldiers were under orders to fire only if fired upon, but the invaders grew shaken by the hordes of angry locals all around them. Some soldiers lost their restraint, firing over the heads of the unarmed citizens or even occasionally at them. In one part of Prague, machine-gun fire left four Czech youths dead on the street, one with his head blown off.[27] Wild, aggressive, reckless, and at times even intentionally violent maneuvers by Soviet armored cars threatened and harmed the local population. Tanks smashed into buildings, crushing civilians in the rubble.[28]

Within hours of their arrival, the invaders had taken control of the entire capital city and leadership structure in Prague with one major exception: the radio. Even as the Soviets seized Czechoslovakia's leaders, Radio Prague continued to transmit not only the government's statements about the invasion, but also breaking news about the occupation and instructions for peacefully resisting the Warsaw Pact forces.[29] Thousands of people in the city began massing in the typical Prague spots, especially Old Town Square and Wenceslas Square, as well as outside the Central Committee headquarters. Wherever they found them, the occupied people confronted the invaders. The more succinct locals simply shouted "Russians, go home!" But others tried to engage them. "Why are you here? There was no provocation."[30] When the soldiers spoke, they regurgitated the words of their commanders: "We are here to halt the counterrevolution. We are here to maintain order."

Many in Prague responded with concrete action. Knowing that the radio was their main source of reliable information, thousands of locals moved quickly to physically defend the radio headquarters in central Prague. They derailed trams and grabbed empty vehicles of every size—even large passenger buses—which they used to create massive barricades.[31]

At 7 A.M., the Soviets decided to take the radio building, sending tanks through the streets to grab control by force. Radio Prague begged civilians to disperse and remove the barricades, all the while broadcasting what was occurring out on the street below it: "We appeal for calm. . . . Armed defense is out of the question. . . . Reports arrive that the first shots are being fired in front of the Prague building of the Czechoslovak radio, where six tanks are in position. . . . The troops fire tracer bullets—perhaps even live ammunition. . . . People . . . are trying to stop vehicles of the occupation troops with their bodies . . ." Soldiers fired on the building as Soviet planes roared overhead.[32]

The scene changed constantly. One moment, all appeared quiet. The next second everything looked like a war zone, with unspeakable noise and thick smoke obscuring any sort of clear view.[33] Thousands of young Prague citizens screamed, "Russians, go home!" as scores of armored vehicles circled the area. One youth stuck the pole of a Czechoslovak flag into the cannon of a tank on whose side others had scratched swastikas, while the people around them yelled, "Dirty fascists!" Another young man tried to reason with a soldier, offering a pamphlet demanding that the occupiers leave.[34]

As the invaders rumbled closer to the radio building, many in the crowd tried to argue with the soldiers, but some threw stones. Trying to intimidate the locals, the soldiers fired, usually over the people's heads and into the adjacent buildings. The armored vehicles charged full speed ahead, sending civilians flying apart to evade the death cars. Young men climbed onto tanks, punctured the fuel barrels, and set fire to the oil, producing a massive blaze. Determined to get to the radio building, the tanks pushed on, smashing through and rolling over the barricades, which burst into flames.[35] Enraged civilians tossed burning rags, large branches from fallen trees, mattresses, wooden crates, garbage cans, and even Molotov cocktails at the tanks.[36] Other locals collapsed, the victims of Soviet soldiers' lack of restraint. An overturned Prague bus, with a full tank of gas, exploded, with the reverberation shattering nearby shop windows.

Just a block away, where thousands more civilians now demonstrated at the top of Wenceslas Square, at least a dozen Soviet tanks appeared to mistake the neo-Renaissance National Museum building for something strategically important. Without clear provocation or reason—some suggested a tank's antenna had been shocked by a trolley wire—the tanks opened fire, shooting up the beautiful, ornate façade of the nearly hundred-year-old building that dominated the Square.[37] When the smoke cleared, the building's dark background had become pockmarked with hundreds of white dots, as if pecked by dozens of giant deranged birds who had decided to finish the job by repeatedly defecating on it as well.[38] Huge pieces of plaster fell from the building, injuring a collection of bystanders.[39]

Meanwhile, Soviet troops in full battle gear stormed the radio building and raced through the floors, machine guns cocked, looking for the broadcasting rooms. The announcers told their audience that they would hold out as long as they could, but "When you hear voices on the radio you are not familiar with, do not believe them!"[40] Those listening to the radio could hear gunfire and Czechoslovakia's national anthem playing. The Soviet soldiers shut down the first two floors of the building, but completely missed the fact that the radio continued to transmit for two more hours from studios on the third floor.[41] By 9:30 A.M., the soldiers found this final target, removed the staff at gunpoint, and shut down the broadcast.[42]

The residue of the battle over the radio building dotted the street and sidewalk. More than a dozen Czechoslovak civilians lay dead. Scores were seriously injured. The wreckage of an abandoned Soviet tank spewed bright orange flames and black smoke. Surrounding buildings burned. Countless locals continued to scream at the soldiers. Others simply wept.[43]

The Soviet invasion shook the lives of every person in the country. In Liberec, in northern Czechoslovakia, near both the East German and the Polish borders, a tank commander shot wildly into a crowd and tanks smashed through the arcades of the main square, crushing a group of people in the ensuing rubble.[44] In Košice, in southeast Czechoslovakia, tanks arrived and began crisscrossing the city's main streets. When residents came outside to watch, the tanks abruptly turned their cannons toward them. The crowd dropped to the ground to avoid the gunfire that might begin at any moment.

In Bratislava, the largest city in Slovakia, Soviet vehicles invaded from Hungary to the south and congregated in Šafárik Square, in front of Comenius University. Hundreds of locals descended on the area to confront their occupiers. Coeds distracted the soldiers with hiked-up miniskirts while young men smashed the Soviets' vehicles with rocks. The soldiers fired haphazardly at the surrounding buildings. But as the soldiers' patience grew thin and other Bratislavans tossed bricks at them, the invaders fired directly into the crowd of civilians, killing a group of students.[45] Kitty-corner from the university, Emil Gallo, a local plumber, marched with a fury directly to the mouth of a Soviet tank gun barrel. Bellowing "Shoot!" as he pulled open the top of his overalls, he made his torso the giant weapon's skin-toned target. A photographer, Ladislav Bielik, captured the moment, which he and his local newspaper splashed across the front page that day under the caption "The Bare-chested Man in Front of the Occupiers' Tank." The photo found its way to the German press and became a sensation in newspapers around the world.

With the invaders seemingly everywhere, simply getting around became complicated for Czechoslovakia's people. Hockey stars Jan Havel, Josef Horešovský, and their Sparta Prague team were staying in the tiny town of Litvínov for a training camp. Early in the morning, Mojmír Ujčík, the team manager responsible for the squad's daily logistics, began running from room to room in the hostel shouting, "Lads, get up! The Ruskies are here!" The team instantly packed, planning to rush back to Prague, but faced a problem. How would they get home? With the invasion, roadblocks halted traffic throughout the country. At least as important, to get to Prague, the Sparta players were likely to find themselves in the path of oncoming military forces. Soviet tanks had already crashed into morning commute buses, injuring and, in some cases, even killing local residents.

The Sparta team had already planned to charter a state-owned bus to get home. One was all set to go, but there was no one to drive it. All the married bus drivers with children wanted no part of the roads on this day, so the team begged the bus dispatchers to call around to see if anyone might be willing to take a chance with them. Finally, the company found a young, single driver who was willing to make the trip.

As the team headed toward Prague on the bus, now helmed by the brave driver, they passed columns of Soviet tanks and military vehicles full of soldiers, who aimed their guns at the Sparta men. Team manager Mojmír Ujčík went ballistic. Ujčík had run the pub where the fight and arrests of the 1950 national hockey team had occurred, and he got swept up in the trial that followed, leaving him imprisoned for the offense of "not reporting a crime." Seeing the Russian soldiers now, Ujčík climbed partway out of the window, screaming and shaking his fist. The Sparta players had to hold him back, fearing the soldiers would snap and shoot up the bus. Eventually, the team arrived at the Prague airport, where soldiers informed the driver he could go no farther or they would confiscate the bus. The driver cleverly moved on, taking backroads through the suburbs and finally halting at a paper mill, from which he could truly go no farther. The men began to lug their heavy hockey gear the half-mile back to the hockey arena. As they walked along one of the Vltava River's side-branches, they saw a man fishing. The men could see Russian planes flying overhead. In the not-so-far distance, they could hear gunfire. Ujčík spat at the fisherman, "You oaf! People are fighting for the freedom of our country, while you are fishing!" The fisherman replied coolly: "You know how this will all end. Those that are at the top will come down, and those that are at the bottom will rise up."[46]

Despite the battle outside the radio station and the gunfire that the Sparta men heard as they returned to Prague, peaceful resistance was usually the name of the game. Rather than try to fight their invaders—a hopeless proposition, given the soldiers' superior firepower—most Czechs and Slovaks confronted the occupiers with words, appealing to them with the simple truth that there was no counterrevolution. Untold numbers of civilians climbed aboard Soviet tanks and waved Czechoslovak flags. In central Prague, two young men standing amid a dozen other locals on top of one tank held high a sign that had clearly been designed for a different purpose but now seemed even more apt: "Entry forbidden to unauthorized personnel."[47] Countless youths marched through the city streets chanting "Russians, go home!" and repeating over and over, "Dubček! Dubček! Dubček!"[48] Late in the afternoon, thousands filled the wide streets near the radio station, forming a silent funeral procession led by a demonstrator carrying a Czechoslovak flag, one-third of which was covered in blood.[49] Throughout the country, the demonstrations continued into the night, bringing out millions in cities, towns, and village squares.

Many people had always loathed the Soviets and the communist system they had forced on the country, so the invasion was just one more reason to hate them. And it hurt all the more that it occurred just as the country had entered a joyful period of greater freedoms. But many others saw the Soviets as their brothers, their dearest friends, which only made this new occupation more devastating and bewildering. As the Soviet soldiers walked the streets of Czechoslovakia, a father told his little son to stay away from the evil occupiers. The boy had been taught in school about how the Soviets had liberated their country from the Nazis at the end of World War II. He asked, "Then why don't we call the Russians to chase them away?"[50]

The depth, vigor, and sheer numbers involved in Czechoslovakia's peaceful resistance took the Soviets by surprise, and the occupation forces soon turned their attention to trying to control Czechs and Slovaks on the ground. They imposed a nighttime curfew, prohibited public meetings, and banned work stoppages of any kind. All radio and television broadcasts and the distribution of printed matter were banned unless first given approval by the occupation authorities.[51] In various places, Soviet officers posted decrees that, in addition to all the other orders, prohibited locals from carrying firearms or "weapons that can be used for stabbing."[52] In the evenings, the Soviet military carried out thirty-minute exercises with live ammunition that lit the night sky and forced residents to move their beds far from their windows because no one could predict where the bullets would land.[53]

Despite the Soviets' edicts, civilians continued to fight back nonviolently. *Rudé právo*, the official newspaper of Czechoslovakia's Communist Party, told the people, "They have guns and rockets. Our weapons are chalk, pen, word, and consistently ignoring them."[54] Czechs and Slovaks left flowers to mark places where civilians had been killed, making it impossible to overlook deaths at the invaders' hands.[55] Shop windows became covered in posters with slogans and caricatures that mocked and railed against the Soviets. Each night, the occupying forces removed the posters; every morning new ones would appear.[56] Graffiti was everywhere. One said simply, "Who invited you here?" But others got more creative: "Ivan come home! Boris is going steady with Natasha. Love, Mother" and "With brothers like you, we beg Mother Russia to practice contraception." Clearly spelled out across a butcher's window were the words "Today: Russian Pigs." Protesters frequently posted the names of the

Czechoslovak leaders that the Soviets had abducted. Everywhere huge letters spelled out *DUBČEK*. Nearly as common was *SVOBODA*, the name of the president of the country and a word that translates into English as "freedom."[57]

No sooner had the invaders shut down the radio than Czechs and Slovaks across the country set up underground radio stations, which they housed in secret locations. Calling themselves "Legal and Free Radio Czechoslovakia," the new stations called out the lies in the Soviets' propaganda and helped mobilize public resistance to the occupation. Soon, successful efforts at underground television emerged as well.[58] The Soviets were also unable to stop the written press. If anything, the major newspapers and magazines increased their rate of production, printing daily underground editions. In a late edition published on August 21, *Svět v obrazech* put on its cover a photograph of the massive smoke and debris-filled aftermath of a bus explosion in Prague. Under the picture, which connoted nothing less than carnage in their streets, the editors had stamped in both Czech and Russian boldface type "Why?"[59]

Weekly magazines like *Svět v obrazech* began publishing on a daily basis to get word out about the occupiers' activities.[60] Miloslav Jenšík, who worked as a sports reporter at *Svět v obrazech* and had "discovered" Jaroslav Holík at the handball match years earlier, served as editor-in-chief of the magazine's daily two-page newsletter. At times the pamphlet provided information on what Czechoslovakia's government was actually doing, but mostly it helped direct Prague's resistance: "Don't talk to them, don't feed them, don't give them even a droplet of water." The words may have been simple, but the mere existence of a publication that continued to print and urge resistance to the invaders brought a sense of hope to the people who read it. The invasion devastated the population, but it also united the people who now stood up for their freedom, giving them a sense of purpose that had not previously existed.

Soon, Jenšík faced a logistical hurdle: The Soviets had created roadblocks on all of Prague's bridges that spanned the Vltava River, and the printing press for *Svět v obrazech* sat on the other side of the river from the office headquarters. Soviets on the bridges searched all cars and buses for printed matter, as well as anything of value—cameras, radios, watches, pens, even wedding rings—that a soldier might take for his own.[61] Jenšík and his graphic designer devised a strategy. As they drove together across the bridge, at each checkpoint they explained that they were in a hurry because one of their wives was giving birth.

The tactic worked until they reached the last checkpoint and came face-to-face with four machine-gun-toting soldiers and a hotshot twenty-year-old Soviet officer who refused to fall for their gambit. The officer searched the car. When he found the box of flyers, he slapped the forty-five-year-old graphic designer across the face and theatrically tossed the box into the river. Just as Jenšík and the designer returned, devastated, to the office, a miracle phone call came in. A fisherman had seen "some crazy Russian" toss the box of pamphlets into the river so he had fished out the still-floating container from the water. Where would they like to pick them up? [62]

So it went for the next few days. The occupiers continued to clamp down. The people continued to resist. Many who had been ashamed at how little their country had fought back against the German takeover in the 1930s now felt pride as they stood up to the Soviet might. [63] Yet the simple fact remained: one side had all the guns and tanks, and it had no plans to pack up and leave.

A relatively small town, Jihlava was hit less directly by the occupation. Nevertheless, the Soviet invasion shook the lives of everyone there. Fewer occupation soldiers came to Jihlava than to the big cities, and many of those who did just passed through during the night. But even these troop movements left their mark. On the evening of August 21, the first night after the occupation began, a group of Hungarian military vehicles passed through Jihlava. As they did, one of the vehicles ran over a local road maintenance man. [64]

In a practice seen in towns throughout the entire country, beginning that first evening—and then every night for the remainder of August—Marie and other Jihlavans came out into the streets. They turned around road signs. It ultimately didn't matter that few troops ever saw them. Messing with the street signs gave the people of the town a sense that they were doing something—anything—to fight back. And beginning that first night, untold numbers of Jihlavans, especially those in their twenties, thirties, and forties, came out to the main square to find some sense of comfort in the unity of their fellow townspeople. It was difficult for Marie, having to balance these trips with caring for baby Andrea, but it was important to her to be part of her community during the most terrifying time she could remember. The people rightly feared that the government would soon tighten the borders again, and in the coming weeks tens of thousands of people fled the country. A number of Jihlavans decided to leave as well. Before they did, they went to the evening Jihlava town square gathering, where Marie and hundreds of others came to say goodbye—even if they were complete strangers—and wish them well on their journey. [65]

With her husband's history of lashing out at the Communists and the Soviets, Marie worried Jaroslav would be locked up as soon as he crossed the border back into the country. She wanted to reach out to him, to beg him not to return. She would find a way to make life work for her and her little girl, and then the moment it was safe she would find a way—perhaps through the Red Cross or some other international organization—to escape and join Jaroslav. The problem, though, was that making phone calls out of the country—especially to a country in the West—just wasn't something people could do. Her older brother, Miras, and their dear friend, a clever engineer named Milan Novák, made a suggestion. Milan's nickname was *Guma* ("rubber"), and Guma was close to the entire Holík family, including Jaroslav. With Jaroslav's connections and fame, Miras and Milan believed that they could convince Radio Free Europe to send a message over its airwaves: "Jaroslav, don't come back, Guma sends his greetings." They thought Jaroslav would have to know that the message was for him. In the end, though, when it appeared that arrests of civilians were not widespread, Marie decided not to try it. She knew it wouldn't have mattered anyway. Jaroslav was too devoted to and dependent on his family ever to stay away from them if he could help it. [66]

Jaroslav was off in Fussen, near Munich in West Germany, with Jiří, Suchý, and the rest of the Dukla boys. The team had late-night games, so in the morning the players usually slept in. But on the morning of August 21, somebody raised a terrible ruckus in the hotel before 6 o'clock, yelling in Czech, "Holy crap! Get up, boys! The Russians invaded!"

The Dukla players rose in groggy shock. No one on the team had even considered that things were *that* tense between the two countries, and they found it inconceivable that the Soviets would do something so extreme. As the Dukla men rose and turned to the radio, it seemed every station was talking about the invasion. The broadcasters had few details, but the men got the core message: the streets of their home were overrun with Soviet tanks and soldiers. [67]

As they listened, alternating between numbness and fury, the Dukla men began to pack for the team's next game, in Davos, Switzerland. Before they left the hotel, the Fussen team's administrators stopped them. Feeling for the visitors—and also seeing an opportunity to raise the quality of hockey in West Germany—the Fussen administrators offered to provide any assistance that the Dukla men needed. They encouraged the Dukla squad to stay permanently in West Germany, where the players would be welcomed instantly into the top division in the German hockey league. [68]

On the way to Davos, the Dukla men listened obsessively to the radio, hoping for real news. They gleaned little. They did hear a plea from people back at home, however, urging fellow citizens to defend the radio broadcasting offices. By the time they arrived in Davos, the Dukla men were badly shaken. They were therefore deeply touched by the kindness of the local hockey organizers, who were heartbroken by the Soviet invasion. The locals asked the Dukla men what they needed. The Czechoslovak hockey players had brought only a few articles of clothing, and if they didn't return home, they would have to start from scratch. The Davos organizers brought the players to a clothing factory, where they gave the men their pick of items to tide them over in case they decided to remain in the West. The Davos hosts also opened a local hotel that had been closed for the season so the Dukla men could have a comfortable place to rest, eat, and collect their thoughts. Then the Swiss locals invited them to a march protesting the Soviets' invasion. A few hundred Davos residents joined in, even giving the hockey players Czechoslovak flags and signs to carry in support of their people back home. [69]

After their Davos matches were over, the Dukla men faced a dilemma: *Do we return home?* They boarded their bus and began riding northeast, unsure of what they would do. They eventually stopped near Vienna, just forty or so miles from Czechoslovakia's border, where they waited for more news. Was there all-out fighting in the streets? Were people being arrested? As they waited and listened to the radio reports, the only topic of conversation was whether they would take the final steps to cross back into their occupied homeland. [70] So it went for two days until, finally, the team administrators insisted it was time to return. As the men rode toward home on the bus, reality set in. The bus drove for a spell but stopped just across the border from Czechoslovakia.

The Dukla squad climbed off the bus, grabbed a stash of beers, and sat down on a collection of long logs. Staring at the wide-open area around the border in front of them, they tried to come to a decision. If they crossed the border and went back to Czechoslovakia, the Soviets might take everything from them. They might never be able to travel abroad again, even to play hockey. But what if they didn't go home? They were soldiers, and not returning—especially for those still in the basic military training stage—meant desertion and harsh punishments if they ever did try to come home later. About two-thirds of the team was made up of these young guys—only nineteen or twenty years old—who were fulfilling their basic military service. However, not yet married, they were excited by the possibility of living free in West Germany, and some of them didn't want to return.

The older men, though, the ones with families, simply couldn't bear the idea of leaving their loved ones behind. Jaroslav and Jiří thought about their parents. About how the government might punish Jaroslav Sr. and Věra for their boys' defection and how staying in the West might mean never seeing them again.

Most of all, Jaroslav couldn't stop thinking about Marie and Andrea. Were they okay? And if they were, but he didn't return home . . . to never see them again, to force his daughter to grow up without a father . . . it was unbearable. Jiří had just gotten engaged. He was freshly in love and might never see his fiancée again if he didn't cross the border now.

At last, the Dukla players heard the words they dreaded. "It is time." After a long pause, the men stood reluctantly, moving awkwardly out of sync with one another. Stiff from sitting on the logs, many of them stretched sluggishly and twisted to loosen up their backs. Ever so slowly, each man climbed back onto the bus and rode the remaining miles home.[71]

# CHAPTER 7

# On Fire

Just before 4 P.M. on Thursday, January 16, 1969, nearly five months after the start of the occupation, a twenty-year-old college student named Jan Palach entered Prague's bustling Wenceslas Square (*Václavské náměstí*) carrying a briefcase.

The space in front of Palach had been founded as a marketplace in the 14th century, but over time developed into a real city square. In the 19th century it received the name "Wenceslas" in honor of the patron saint of Bohemia. Wenceslas Square soon became the city's most important meeting place, where the newly founded Czechoslovakia celebrated its independence in 1918 and massive demonstrations were held during the Nazi occupation. The "Square" is actually more of a rectangle, nearly half a mile long and composed of the equivalent of multiple city blocks, with hotels, restaurants, and shops running down the sides. The length of the street slopes upward, so all eyes turn naturally to the top, where a statue of Saint Wenceslas, the grand façade of the National Museum, and an accompanying multilevel fountain all sit.

Palach walked to the fountain, took off his coat, and removed from his briefcase two bottles labeled "Ether." Using a small knife, he opened the bottles and took a whiff of their contents. He then doused his body with the bottles' liquid and lit himself on fire.

Engulfed in massive, vibrantly colored flames, Palach raced down the square, almost as if he could escape from the fire that engulfed him, nearly colliding with a passing tram. Turning toward a shop, the young man collapsed on the road. Bystanders rushed to his side, stamping out the fire with their coats. An ambulance rushed the still-conscious youth to a hospital and then to a nearby burn treatment center. Second- and third-degree burns covered more than 85 percent of Palach's body, but he was still able to speak. As he lay in his hospital bed, he repeated, over and over, "Please tell everyone why I did it."

Back in the early morning of August 21, when the Soviets had first seized Alexander Dubček, it had quickly become clear that the occupiers had no idea what to do with Czechoslovakia's leader. Seemingly winging it, they kidnapped him and brought him east. At 11 P.M. on Friday, August 23, 1968, three full days after the invasion began, Dubček found himself in the Kremlin, the Soviet leaders' headquarters in Moscow. Not that Dubček had any idea what time it was. His watch had stopped somewhere along the way. Now the Soviets did their best to keep him disoriented and gave him no time to clean up after the exhausting multiple days of travel.

Inside the Kremlin, Dubček's escorts took him through a tall door, into an anteroom, through another door, and then finally into a large office with a rectangular table. There stood Soviet leader Leonid Brezhnev and three other top Soviet officials. Given Brezhnev's stocky build and intimidating pose in photographs, people who met him were sometimes surprised that he was not especially tall, merely five feet, eight inches in height. Typically, he stood with his chin slightly lifted, wearing a default haughty expression. Brezhnev's head appeared exceptionally large and rectangular, covered on top with thick, combed-back hair. His most distinctive feature was his exceptionally thick eyebrows, which gave the impression that he was angry. Now, though, he attempted to create a relaxed atmosphere. Speaking in a fatherly tone, Brezhnev explained that the Soviets had needed to act because forces in Czechoslovakia were undermining the existing order. The Soviet Union needed to intervene to "safeguard socialism."

What Brezhnev didn't say was that the invasion had been a disaster. Back in Czechoslovakia, men loyal to Dubček remained in charge, the radio continued to broadcast freely, and hundreds of thousands, if not millions, of citizens had taken to the streets to show their opposition to the occupiers. Through their visible and overwhelming presence and their demands for their leader's return, Czechoslovakia's people had helped keep Dubček alive.[1] They also smuggled film footage out of the country that made the USSR look like a cruel bully and undercut the Soviets' claim that Czechoslovakia had invited them to put down a counterrevolution. Throughout the free world, the evening news broadcast scenes of young people in Czechoslovakia sitting bravely in front of a Soviet tank, which swiveled its gun turret trying to find just the right civilian target. Photos from the front pages of the world's newspapers and major magazines screamed out with images of unarmed Czechs and Slovaks waving bloody flags, throwing stones at Soviet armored vehicles, or simply pleading with Soviet soldiers to leave.[2]

Governments around the globe denounced the superpower for invading a peaceful European country under false pretenses. Communist Yugoslavia and Romania, both already on bad terms with the USSR, lashed out publicly at the Soviets. Only ten of the eighty-eight Communist parties in the world approved of the Soviets' action, and most offered sharp criticisms. Among democratic nations, France and Britain were among the first to condemn the invasion.[3]

Still, no one, least of all the people of Czechoslovakia, believed anyone would take concrete steps to help. The world did not intervene in 1938, and now nuclear weapons had changed the game completely. In August 1968, the United States was consumed by a disastrous war in Vietnam. In addition, American president Lyndon Johnson had become fixated on improving relations with the USSR. On August 20, just hours before the invasion, Johnson was looking forward to the following day, when he planned to announce the opening of arms control talks with the Soviets. He told aides that it might become "the greatest accomplishment of my administration."[4] Johnson had little desire to get involved in a crisis in Eastern Europe.[5] Upon learning of the invasion, he released a short public statement that the Soviets' justifications were "patently contrived" and called for a full withdrawal. Johnson and members of Congress also urged the United Nations to take action, calling the invasion a "flat violation" of the UN charter. But it was clear that the US government didn't have the stomach to do more. As he proposed that the UN take action, US Republican leader Gerald Ford stated that America "should not become involved in this communist family fight."[6]

It appeared that America's greatest concern was for the détente developing between the West and the USSR. Among the thousands of pieces of clever graffiti scrawled in Prague on the day of the invasion, one sophisticated writer penned: *MUNICH = YALTA*.[7] It meant that, just as the 1938 Munich

Agreement had delivered Czechoslovakia to the Nazis, the Yalta agreement among the world leaders at the end of World War II had divided Europe into spheres of influence and left Czechoslovakia to the Soviets. Czechoslovakia remained, just as Neville Chamberlain had said thirty years earlier, a "far-away country" populated by people of whom the world knew nothing. Once again, to keep the stable, peaceful global balance, the world sacrificed the little country to the whims of a superpower.

The USSR didn't have to contend with powerful military opposition from the West, but ironically it was stymied by the peaceful resistance inside Czechoslovakia.[8] To stabilize the situation, Brezhnev and his cohort needed to get Czechoslovakia's leaders to accept some sort of solution and so had brought Dubček to Moscow. Dubček told his "hosts" that, indeed, they desperately needed to work something out, but he pushed back on every Soviet argument about the legitimacy of the invasion. So it went for two hours, with the Soviets making odd and inaccurate claims about Czechoslovakia's reforms and leading reformers in the government, as well as sprinkling in antisemitic remarks intended to belittle specific Czechoslovak leaders.

As it became clear that nothing would be achieved that night, the Soviets led Dubček through another door into a large antechamber, where he found himself face-to-face with a number of other Czechoslovak officials who had come to negotiate with the Soviets. They had arrived many hours earlier and had been meeting with the Soviets without much progress.[9] Dubček felt buoyed by the presence of his countrymen, but soon his body betrayed him. Around 3 A.M., he began to suffer from what appeared to be heart and nerve problems. Becoming increasingly ill, he put himself to bed, where he remained for the next two days.

Discussions between the two delegations continued throughout Dubček's convalescence. The Soviet leaders hid their panic and presented an image of having all the time in the world, but they also made clear that they were more than willing to conduct an all-out attack on Prague if Czechoslovakia did not come to heel. In 1956, the Soviet crackdown in Hungary had led to the execution of the Hungarian liberalizing leader Imre Nagy. Now, though, the Soviets wanted no part of killing Dubček because doing so might draw even more support to his cause. Instead, they focused on imposing a plan of "normalization," which would destroy Dubček's reforms and return things to how they had been before the Prague Spring.

On Monday, August 26, Dubček rejoined the group. As Brezhnev opened the meeting with a series of clichés about his love for Czechoslovakia and the sorrow he felt when he decided to send in the tanks, Dubček felt nausea and rage rise in his throat. He stood and, speaking in Russian, defended his reforms and condemned the invasion, but also insisted that he wanted to continue to work with the Soviets. In response, Brezhnev berated Czechoslovakia's leaders, declaring that the USSR had saved them in World War II at the cost of millions of Soviet lives. That effort, he said, made Czechoslovakia part of the Soviet security zone, and the USSR wasn't going to let it go. He told the men before him that they had not properly asked his permission for any of their reforms and that he had been too patient with them. Dubček tried to express disagreement, but Brezhnev, face bright red and eyebrows crunched down over his eyes, shouted that he had had enough. The Soviet leader stood and walked slowly out of the meeting room, with his lieutenants in tow.

Dubček now knew for certain what he had always suspected: Brezhnev thought of Czechoslovakia as a colony. Dubček groaned that the Soviets were just going to do what they wanted, so why even negotiate with them? The other Czechoslovak leaders grew frantic and implored Dubček to change his mind: The hundreds of thousands of heavily armed Soviet troops in Czechoslovakia presented serious danger. At any moment, they might go on a rampage. Plus, the Soviet leaders were acting like "a bunch of gangsters" on the verge of snapping. There was no telling what they might do! The Czechoslovak men remembered the bloodbath in Hungary at Soviet hands in 1956. The Soviets might simply arrest all the reformist leaders and replace them with Soviet lackeys. The Soviets might partition the country and impose their will even more completely. By coming to some sort of agreement now, the Czechoslovak leaders might actually save some of their reforms and even themselves.

Dubček agreed to return to the negotiating table. After some soothing by part of the Czechoslovak contingent, Brezhnev and his team returned to the room and hammered out the details of a secret "Moscow Protocol" that would determine the future path of Czechoslovakia. Shortly after 8 P.M., Czechoslovakia's leaders signed the agreement. As they did, the entire Soviet group rose and, to the great dismay of the "guests," hugged the men from Czechoslovakia.

According to the Moscow Protocol, Czechoslovakia would need to reinstitute censorship, ban "unacceptable" clubs and organizations, and remove from office individuals whose reformist aims the Soviets found unacceptable. The occupying troops would not "meddle in internal affairs" of Czechoslovakia and would gradually withdraw once the "threat to socialism"—presumably as the Soviets defined it—was eliminated. Also, the Protocol stated that the details of the agreement were to be kept secret: Czechoslovakia's leaders could not tell their people exactly what they had promised to do.[10]

Unaware of the deal that had been signed, people in Czechoslovakia rejoiced on the morning of Tuesday, August 27, when the radio announced the leaders were on their way home. The negotiators landed at 6 A.M., and people stood along the road cheering as they traveled from the airport to central Prague. None of the public could get a good view inside the cars and therefore didn't know how exhausted and subdued—broken, even—their leaders truly were. However, as the hours passed, information trickled out about what the Moscow meetings had wrought, and it didn't sound good. Remembering too well his country's history, one local resident turned to a friend and said, "I wonder if, again, they've decided about us without us."[11] Yet, still feeling empowered by the week of resistance, the public prepared to continue the fight.

At 5:30 P.M., Dubček came on the radio to address his people. He opened with chilling words: "The life of our people will take place in a situation whose reality does not depend on our will alone." As he continued, clearly unsteady and weary beyond description, Dubček spoke with somewhat slurred speech, in part a result of holding off the sobs that rose in his throat. At times his voice trailed off. He paused for long periods to breathe, collect his thoughts, and compose himself. Listening at home, Czechs and Slovaks openly wept. Dubček went on, emphasizing that it was vital above all else to avoid bloodshed. He asked the country to accept an unacceptable arrangement: There was an agreement with the Soviets on the "phased departure of troops," but there was a catch. In exchange, Czechoslovakia would need to commence "normalization," a word he uttered multiple times in the speech. The people would need to keep their emotions in check. And they would need to accept "some temporary, exceptional measures restricting the degree of democracy and freedom of expression." He explained that if the country could work within these arrangements, he and the Czechoslovak leadership would continue the quest to achieve the aims they had set out in the Prague Spring.[12]

It wasn't clear which was more devastating to those listening, Dubček's words or the sheer anguish in his voice as he uttered them. Whatever the case, the idea of regressing to their long-held spot under the thumb of the Soviets, a world in which they had the barest of freedoms, cut like a knife. But Dubček had also made it clear that this was the only possible path forward. If weapons began firing, the people of Czechoslovakia could not possibly stand up to the Soviet Union's military might, and the unacceptable path that Dubček asked them to tread was the only way to get the troops out and return to the reform course. Following his speech, the general consensus was that the people overwhelmingly trusted and supported their leader and what he asked them to do.

Daily life appeared to return to something approaching normal. Czechs and Slovaks went back to work. Shops reopened. Public transportation restarted. The occupied people removed the anti-Soviet posters and graffiti adorning the walls, and within a couple of weeks the tanks moved to the countryside. As the people resumed their lives, they were able to take stock of what they had endured. On top of the sheer terror of half a million troops and thousands of armored vehicles running roughshod over their country, the occupying forces had harassed, detained, and raped innocent locals. By early September, the invaders had killed seventy-two civilians and physically harmed at least seven hundred more. The troops had looted and vandalized the buildings they had taken over. At the central television studio, the invading marauders had left the water running in the restrooms, thus flooding parts of the building. They demolished the toilets and, with a final touch of class, left their feces and urine everywhere they saw fit. [13]

Still, Czechoslovakia's people took seriously the task before them: in order to get the country back, they would not rock the boat. And with that, the drip, drip, drip of the rollback began. Almost immediately, the government established plans to reintroduce censorship, banned non-Communist political organizations, and removed from office high-level reformers who were especially repugnant to the Soviets. Before long, the government intimated that the borders would close soon.

The mood turned darker as capitulation became more tangible. On September 28, hundreds of young Czechs in Prague held a demonstration that police, led by a Soviet officer with armed paratroopers, quickly quashed. Even Dubček's language changed. On October 11, he went on television and warned that "democracy needs a certain discipline," and "everything is harmful that disrupts our alliance with the Socialist community."[14] Dubček and his allies hoped they could keep the rollbacks that the Soviets insisted upon from occurring too swiftly, but most of all they sought to create the conditions necessary to satisfy the USSR and bring about the withdrawal of troops.

However, as October progressed, Moscow expressed dissatisfaction with the pace of normalization and suddenly forced Czechoslovakia to sign a treaty establishing the "temporary" basing of Soviet troops in Czechoslovakia. The treaty did not set the number of Soviet troops or a withdrawal date. The Soviets threatened that if Czechoslovakia didn't agree, they would reoccupy its cities, carry out arrests, and impose a new pro-Soviet government. Czechoslovakia's National Assembly ratified the treaty on October 18. In effect, the Soviets had forced Czechoslovakia's leadership to accept troops on its soil forever.

Still, as hope crumbled, inspiration came from unlikely places.

In 1968, the most beloved woman in Czechoslovakia was twenty-six-year-old Věra Čáslavská, the country's greatest athlete. In the 1964 Tokyo Olympics, the five-foot, three-inch tall, blond-haired Čáslavská had become world famous and a national hero at home as she won three gold medals, including top honors in the women's all-around gymnastics competition. In 1968, she did much more.

In June 1968, two months before the invasion, Ludvík Vaculík, a well-known Czechoslovak writer, had published "The Two Thousand Words," a manifesto that called for dramatic reform. The piece blamed years of Communist Party corruption and incompetence for a multitude of problems. To save Czechoslovakia, Vaculík urged the country to support Dubček's proposed reforms and even greater liberalization and openness. Some seventy people, including prominent intellectuals and celebrities, openly attached their names to the document. Čáslavská's name was among them. Moscow expressed dismay at Vaculík's words and those who endorsed them and it was ultimately Soviet concerns over such strong pushes for reform that helped propel the invasion later in the summer.

It was no wonder then that within twenty-four hours of the August occupation, Čáslavská went into hiding in a small town in the mountains. With no standard equipment available to help her train for the upcoming Mexico City Olympics, she lifted sacks of potatoes to keep up her strength, shoveled coal to build calluses, practiced her floor exercise in a meadow, and solidified her other routines by swinging from and dancing across tree branches. In the end, no one ever came to arrest her, and in October Čáslavská flew to Mexico. She declared that she was prepared to "sweat blood" to defeat the representatives of Czechoslovakia's occupiers: "I'm not just fighting for myself, but for all of us." Victory would help lift the spirits of her people and also draw the world's attention to their plight. She felt buoyed as she marched in the opening ceremonies and heard the crowd jeer the Soviets and cheer her country.

During the first week of the Olympics, political protest entered the games. Seeking to call attention to racial discrimination in the United States, African American athletes Tommie Smith and John Carlos stood on the podium and raised black-gloved fists into the air as they received gold and bronze medals for their performances in the track 200-meter dash. Under pressure from the International Olympic Committee, the American Olympic Committee sent the two men home and banned them from future competition. Back in the US, many in the mainstream white public lambasted the runners for their "lack of decorum."

In the second week, eyes around the world turned toward Čáslavská, who won her second straight all-around women's gymnastics title and dominated the four individual gymnastics events. However, a controversial ruling in the balance beam—made by a panel that included judges from Bulgaria, East Germany, Poland, and the USSR—threw the gold medal to a Soviet gymnast, leaving Čáslavská with the silver. In the floor exercise, Čáslavská completed a routine that brought down the house, but a retroactive upgrade of a Soviet gymnast's score created a rare tie for first place.

Čáslavská wanted to do something audacious to push back against the Soviet Union and encourage people back in Czechoslovakia, but she had seen how Smith and Carlos had been punished for their protest. She decided to try a more subtle approach. Each time she stood on the medal podium as the USSR anthem played, Čáslavská turned her head away from the raised Soviet flag. The second time she took her stance, American television's sports analyst Jim McKay spoke excitedly to the viewers: "Now the Soviet anthem. And again she has turned her head to the right and down, just as she did at the last ceremony. This does not appear to be an accident."

Čáslavská became the star of the games. One poll at the time showed her to be the world's second most beloved woman, behind only Jackie Kennedy. In Czechoslovakia, the woman known simply as "Věra" reached legendary status.[15]

Ordinary Czechs and Slovaks wondered if there was still a way that they, too, could stand up to their occupiers. When it became clear that USSR troops were to stay permanently, people increasingly took to the streets. On October 28, the 50th anniversary of the founding of the country, most of Czechoslovakia's major cities faced protests and Prague was awash in anti-Soviet demonstrations. Marchers carrying Czechoslovak flags chanted "Down with Brezhnev!" "We want freedom!" and "Russian murderers out of Prague!" Police used truncheons to control the crowd. Men, women, and children went to Prague Castle, where the Communist Party met, and pushed against the gates demanding that the leadership speak to them. Elsewhere in Prague, they burned copies of the Soviet Communist Party newspaper and chanted "Russians, go home!"[16] Now feeling buoyed by the resistance, Dubček openly promised to continue his liberalization policies. In November, protesters tore Soviet flags from Prague buildings. On November 7, students and workers demonstrated in Wenceslas Square, where police used water-cannon trucks and tear gas to push back.

As the month continued, students, writers, and workers continued to speak out and demonstrate as the Czechoslovak leadership, under constant pressure from the Soviets, further rolled back the Prague Spring reforms. Czechoslovakia's Communist Party reshuffled the membership of its upper leadership. Dubček remained at the top, but the committee was now filled with "realists," who pushed the Soviet Union's dictates more aggressively.

Already facing an impossible task, Dubček found himself effectively neutered. In December, as his hair began to turn gray, he watched in despair as the realists, seeking approval from Moscow, forced out one of the Czechoslovak leadership's top reformers, Josef Smrkovský, who had widespread public support. Seeing Dubček respond with nothing except calls for "discipline and order," many in Czechoslovakia spoke of the leader of the Prague Spring as a spineless sell-out.

By January, the country had become like the proverbial frog in gradually boiling water. Back in August, by resisting the occupation, the people of Czechoslovakia had felt empowered and a part of something larger than their individual selves. Then their leaders asked them to show restraint. As Czechs and Slovaks refrained from acting, they also began to shrug helplessly with each new rollback.[17]

But Jan Palach had felt the temperature rising and the water boil over. Just prior to setting himself aflame on January 16, Palach sent out three copies of a letter he had composed. He carried a fourth copy in his briefcase. The letter expressed his dismay at the Soviet occupation, but what stood out most about his message was that it was less about the Soviets' actions than it was about the demoralization of a country. Everywhere he went, Palach saw occupied people who were giving up. His letter and his self-immolation were a call for political resistance, to not give in to the return of authoritarian control over their lives.

As the hours passed at the burn unit, Palach's breathing grew labored and he faded. On Sunday, January 19, he died, surrounded by thousands of flowers sent by supporters. The following day, tens of thousands of people in Prague participated in a remembrance march. Other cities across the country held similar events. On Saturday, January 25, hundreds of thousands silently walked the narrow Prague Old Town streets to pass by Palach's flower-surrounded coffin in the drizzling rain. The funeral procession morphed into a protest against the occupation. Over the following two days, hundreds of thousands of people met in Wenceslas Square and marched in further opposition to the Soviets, generating a feeling similar to August. But after the second day, under pressure from Brezhnev, authorities in Czechoslovakia began to send in police to break up protests forcefully.

Czechoslovakia's politicians feared that Soviet troops would intervene and desperately tried to convince the public not to respond further. In turn, the public grew more disenchanted with the country's leaders, even Dubček, who in the days following Palach's death lay in the hospital, overcome with the flu and possibly nervous exhaustion.

In February, though, Dubček began to heal and appeared galvanized by the people's renewed energy following Palach's death. In a February 10 speech, he spoke in a way that he hadn't since the invasion. If the country was to keep the reforms of the Prague Spring, he said, "they must be fought for."[18]

But what could the occupied people do? From big city to small town, they despised their occupiers, but they knew that it would be pointless to fight the Soviet forces directly. After months of their leaders telling them to hold back, the result, as Jan Palach had said, was a sense of hopelessness. It devastated Czechoslovakia's people not to be able to fight back at all.

An ice rink in Stockholm offered them a chance.

⁘

Back in August, the tension on the bus had been palpable for the Dukla men as they rode home from Austria to Czechoslovakia. They were terrified. The news reports they had heard provided little concrete information. They thought that they might be entering a war zone with shooting everywhere. Ultimately, they saw a smattering of field guns and tanks, but otherwise the ride across Czechoslovakia was quiet. They didn't fully exhale, though, until they arrived in Jihlava and saw that their families were safe. [19]

In Jihlava, residents had pushed back against the occupiers. Jihlava's politicians and the local newspaper openly condemned the invasion. Upon arriving, Soviet forces had snatched control of the Jihlava radio tower, the local newspaper, and the town's printing press. But somehow Jihlavans immediately found a way to put out a two-page newsletter that reported on the seizure of the printers. The city's Communist Party committee published news of the invading forces' activities in the area. Residents even managed to operate an illegal Jihlava radio station. But on August 31, Soviet army leaders informed local officials that the anti-Soviet activities needed to stop or the city would feel their wrath. Things quieted down in Jihlava. [20]

In the next months, the Dukla men didn't see many foreign soldiers, but it was obvious that they were there. The Holíks and Suchý all lived on the top floors of the same Jihlava apartment building. They could look out their living room windows and see tanks and cannons aimed at them. Because Jihlava housed Czechoslovak army units, in the event of military action the Soviets would take the town. [21]

The occupation left the Dukla men enraged. Jaroslav had always hated the Soviets, but the invasion added pools of fuel to the flame. Jiří returned his Communist Party identification card and resigned his membership. Jan Suchý had never joined the Party, but years earlier his father had. Following the invasion, František Suchy went in the evening, just as always, to his favorite pub. After a few rums, he walked out of the building and hammered his crimson Party ID card to a nearby fence. When he next saw Jan, he told his boy, "If you *ever* join those bastards, you're gonna get it!" [22]

Still, separated from the bigger cities, the people of Jihlava and the surrounding area were often able to forget what their country was experiencing, and hockey helped with that. The players decided to focus on what they could control. In the 1968–69 season, Dukla took its third straight league title.

The boys from Havlíčkův Brod reached a whole new level of stardom. Jaroslav finished second in the league in assists. Jiří had his greatest year yet, finishing with the third most points in the league. At the end of the season, *Gól* magazine, a Czechoslovak periodical devoted to soccer and hockey, began an annual poll of coaches, officials, and journalists to determine the country's top hockey player that season. In that first year of balloting for what became known as the "Golden Stick Award," Jaroslav finished third and Jiří fourth. But it was Jan Suchý who set the league on fire. By the end of the year, he would be widely viewed as the best defenseman in Europe.

As the season's end approached, however, it appeared that Suchý's personal antics had finally gone too far. On February 8, Dukla would play České Budějovice and a victory would give Jihlava the league crown. Suchý awakened that morning to the sound of men banging on his door, hollering for him to wake up. He wasn't sure where he was or why the men were screaming at him. Then he remembered. The night before, he had decided to go enjoy a few drinks and . . . it was now game day, and he had overslept! Rushing to the bus, he came face-to-face with his head coach. Coach Pitner sniffed hard. "You will either prove to me that you really are as great as they say, or I'll ship you off to the team in Košice." Feeling less than fully himself, Suchý didn't even try to eat anything and slept the entire two-hour ride to the game. But booze and lack of food never seemed to harm his play, and Souška proceeded to have one of the greatest individual performances in Czechoslovak hockey history. He scored five goals and assisted on another four, as Dukla won 14–3. Pitner fined Suchý more than a month's salary, but Jan felt relieved not to get sent away.[23] Perhaps he really shouldn't have been worried. He finished the season second in the league in goals scored and topped everyone in assists. All as a man whose principal job was to play defense. Suchý was the runaway winner of the inaugural Golden Stick award as the country's top player.

In truth, though, the league season was simply a distraction from the reality everyone faced. However, that didn't mean that hockey had become less important to people in Czechoslovakia. Far from it. More than ever before, in 1969 Czechs and Slovaks became completely obsessed with the World Ice Hockey Championships in Stockholm, Sweden.

The March World Championships had been scheduled to be played in Prague to celebrate the sixtieth anniversary of hockey in Czechoslovakia. But following the invasion, the Czechoslovak authorities announced the tournament should be moved because of "technical, economic and organizational conditions." Translated into plain language, Communist leaders feared the wrath of an uncontrollable, angry home crowd.

For the tournament, Pitner and Kostka made very few changes to the roster from Grenoble. The team included the usual stars like Jiří and Suchý, forwards Černý, Golonka, Jiřík, and Nedomanský, defensemen Machač and Pospíšil, and of course Dzurilla in the goal. The 1968 national team had welcomed the arrival of Josef Horešovský, a terrific twenty-one-year-old defenseman from Sparta Prague, who remained on the roster now. Only a small number of players joined the squad for the first time in 1969. The most critical addition to the team was a name well known to all. Without explanation, Pitner had added Jaroslav Holík back to the 1969 roster.

The 1968–69 team grew unusually close, inspired by their common hatred of the USSR and the team's role in offering the country a chance for revenge. The World Championship was no longer simply a sporting event. As the meaning of the games became clear, team captain Golonka bellowed, "Even if we have to die on the ice, we have to beat them!" To a man, the players shared the view.

And it wasn't just the players who felt this way. Even Czechoslovakia's leader saw the tournament as about much more than ice hockey. To Alexander Dubček, the World Championship matches against the Soviets offered Czechoslovakia's people "a replay of a lost war."[24]

For Czechoslovakia's team, the raised stakes weren't entirely helpful. Some of the players wanted to forgo the pleasantries of a hockey match and actually fight the Soviet players. Coaches Pitner and Kostka worried that their players' intense feelings would hurt the team. If players let their emotions take over, they would end up called for unnecessary fouls, sending them to the penalty box, thus giving the Red Machine a massive advantage.[25]

Kostka brought in world-renowned sports psychologist Miroslav Vaněk, his colleague at Charles University. Vaněk talked with the team about how to stay focused and avoid succumbing to emotions. He broke the players into small groups, where he guided them to a core conclusion: Wouldn't it be more effective to defeat the Soviets in hockey rather than in a battle of fists?[26]

In the end, though, it was probably the words of their fellow citizens that best locked in the players on their central task. Everywhere the players went, people implored them, "We don't care what else you do. Just beat the Russians!" At a meet-and-greet event for fans and the team just prior to the tournament, the entire auditorium shouted at the men: "No matter what place you finish in, if you beat the Russians, you will be the real heroes!"[27]

Even still, the players wanted to find a way to also display their hatred of their opponent. As the players met in Prague just prior to their departure for Stockholm, they made a decision. Despite the roughness of the sport, rules of decorum governed international hockey. The act of not shaking hands at the end of the 1967 World Championships after the fight in Vienna had been a significant breach, but at least that "oversight" could partly be blamed on the wild confusion of the moment. While still in training camp in March 1969, the players decided they needed to send a visual message that these games meant far more than just hockey. Aware that television cameras would be fixed on them, they decided that the best thing they could do would be to beat the Soviets and then not shake hands.

Not only was this plan against protocol—it risked the wrath of Czechoslovakia's authorities. Recognizing that the hockey federation could pick new players at any point during pre-tournament training, the players kept mum about their plans. Only after the entire team boarded the bus to head to Stockholm did the men hand their hockey federation officials a statement signed by all the players expressing their opposition to the occupation and their unwillingness to shake hands with the Soviets. The bureaucrats became apoplectic and kicked the group off the bus. As the players waited, the officials ran to the nearest phone to report the plot to their superiors and await instructions. After two hours, the federation officials returned and told them that they could all "figure it out later," ultimately leaving it in the players' hands. However, the risks remained. With increasing Soviet control of their country and more hard-line stances taken by the Czechoslovak leaders as a result, the players—especially those, like the Holíks and Suchy, who played for a military team—faced potential punishment upon their return home.[28]

Whatever the men planned to do after play ended, it would matter little if they couldn't beat the USSR, and Czechoslovakia's occupier still maintained the most dominant hockey team in the world. In fact, if anything, it would now be even tougher to defeat.

In 1969, the tournament would use a new format: only six teams, as opposed to the usual eight, would participate in the World Championships. Unlike the previous format, where each team played all the others once, now they would each play all the other teams twice. The team with the top record at the end of the tournament would be crowned champion. Soviet coach Tarasov saw the new system as an advantage for his squad. Having to play ten games in sixteen days would take a lot out of any team, but it would be far less difficult for the USSR, the best-conditioned squad in the world.[29]

The 1969 World Championships kicked off on March 15, and Czechoslovakia opened in dominating fashion against Canada. The Canadian team had traveled to Prague for a friendly match just before the tournament. The visitors had been filled with despair as they walked through Wenceslas Square and saw the bullet holes that pockmarked the front of the National Museum. They would root for Czechoslovakia throughout the tournament, but they wouldn't change their style when they played against them. The Canadians hit hard and often but were no match for the locked-in Czechoslovak team in the first match of the championships.[30] In the following two games, Czechoslovakia took down the United States and Finland as well.

However, Czechoslovakia confronted a much tougher test in game four. Jaroslav Jiřík had broken his wrist against Canada, and it was expected to take him at least four weeks to heal. His absence would be felt when the men from Czechoslovakia took on highly ranked Sweden. Swedish goalie Leif Holmqvist played inspired hockey and kept all Czechoslovak shots out of the net. Sweden won 2–0. Pitner left the game angry at the officiating, which he felt favored the home country, but it was obvious that another factor was at least as important in the loss: Just as they had been in Grenoble the previous year, the men from Czechoslovakia had been distracted. They were already looking ahead to their match two days later against the USSR.[31]

They would need to pull it together quickly; as good as the USSR had been before, it was more focused and better than ever. Czechoslovakia would not catch the Soviets by surprise as it had in Grenoble. When the men from the Soviet team had returned home after the 1968 Olympics, they had faced the same question, over and over: "How could you lose to Czechoslovakia?!"[32] It hadn't been enough to win the gold medal. Everyone in the USSR expected perfection.

The Soviet leadership placed immense pressure on the disciplined team. Even under ordinary circumstances, hockey had become central to the lives of millions in the Soviet Union. One Moscow resident commented on life in his country during the Brezhnev years: "Hockey, football [soccer], vodka, and love-making . . . That's all there was."[33] Soviet leader Brezhnev was fixated on hockey and meddled with not only the national team but also the very makeup of the Soviet league.[34] Moreover, following the previous year's invasion, 1969 was hardly an ordinary year. The pressure was greater than ever for the Red Machine to take down the Czechoslovak squad.[35] The Soviet players felt the constant presence of their country's leaders at the tournament. Noticeboards hung throughout the hallways of the hotels where they stayed, reminding them of the great victories of communism. Patriotic to the core, the Soviet players sought victory for the communist way of life.[36]

On top of the importance of the matches to the Soviets, and the fact that since 1963 it had lost just one match in major competition on the way to six world titles, the team came in with *seven* new players—and they weren't just additions around the margins. The new Soviet skaters made a dramatic mark on the 1969 World Championships. In the past, most Soviet players outside of Ragulin had not been particularly large physically. The new guys, though, were big. And fast. And skilled. They were a step up from most of the terrific players who were already on the top national hockey team in the world.[37]

Most notably, the Soviets added four rookie forwards—Valeri Kharlamov, Boris Mikhailov, Vladimir Petrov, and Alexander Maltsev—who would become the heart and soul of the national team for the next decade. They would win half of the Most Valuable Player awards in the Soviet hockey league in the 1970s. And they would all one day be named to the International Ice Hockey Federation Hall of Fame.

The USSR opened the 1969 tournament by sending a message that no one could even come close to touching it. Firsov was extraordinary as always, kicking things off with four goals in the first match. The USSR won its first four games with a combined score of 34–6 (most notably including a 17–2 win over the US). The four rookie forwards accounted for fourteen of the team's goals.

Now it was time for game number five: Czechoslovakia versus the Soviet Union.

On March 21—seven months to the day since the USSR had invaded their country—Czechoslovakia's players rode the bus from their hotel to the biggest hockey match of their lives. Some of the men focused on their tactics for the game, trying not to get overexcited. But others seemed on the verge of jumping out of their skins, saying to each other, "We need to do it for our people." Many of the players had been on the national team for years. Yet not one had ever felt quite the way he did on the ride to the arena that day.

Years later, Czechoslovakia's players felt sympathy for the Soviet men they faced in Stockholm. After all, their opponents were just hockey players. They had not driven the tanks that had stormed Czechoslovakia. They had not planned the invasion. They were simply young men with such great athletic ability that they had been selected to play in a series of games that month. But because of where they came from, the world hated them. And no one hated them more than the players from Czechoslovakia. Over the years, it had become common for the two teams to meet for social events. Or they just sat together in their hotel rooms, drinking and talking. Sometimes complaints about their lives slipped out.[38] When no handlers were there, occasionally the Soviet players talked about all the things they weren't allowed to do and how their bedrooms were bugged. The Czechoslovak men found the Soviet players arrogant as a group, and they disliked some of them personally, but a number of the players on each side had become friends with their counterparts on the other.

On March 21, 1969, in Stockholm, though, those friendships were dead. To the Czechoslovak players, the other side was made up of the "fucking Russians"—their sworn enemies. Team Czechoslovakia exulted as crowds in Sweden jeered the Soviets when they played. And the men from Czechoslovakia couldn't wait to do far more than just jeer.[39]

The locker room felt different that night. It was partly that most hockey changing rooms smelled like smoke and cleaning agents, but this one somehow had a fresh aroma. But the feeling had far more to do with the men themselves. Despite the best efforts of Dr. Vaněk to keep everyone calm, the atmosphere was thick with tension. The tight-knit Czechoslovak group fed off each other's energy. But there was also deep, personal anger and desire for revenge. *They invaded our peaceful country.*[40] Time crawled. The wait to take to the ice seemed interminable.

The coaches reminded the men to avoid getting too rough. Restraint was a tactic. They could not afford to become shorthanded because of plays that sent Czechoslovak players to the penalty box. The Soviets would eat them alive.

Then Coach Kostka surprised the men. Ordinarily, the robot-like hockey professor limited his comments to instructions about tactics, but on this night he added something more: "Remember, we have made a patriotic promise to our people that each and every one of us will do all that he can to defeat the Soviets tonight."[41]

Usually on game days, Jaroslav Holík focused on the pregame time as a moment to clear his head. When he played at home, he would lie down for a bit to settle himself, and he usually didn't pay attention to much in the locker room except his hockey stick. He'd just single-mindedly fix the tape on the blade of his stick until it was perfect.[42] But games against the USSR were different. As he prepared to play the Red Machine, Jaroslav thought back to his childhood, when the Communists had seized his parents' butcher shop. He recalled how he had listened along with his family to the broadcasts of the horrific Slánský show trial, and how his father and the men in Brod said that it was really Moscow pulling the strings.[43]

Finally, the coaches announced it was time.

As the players navigated the wide concrete moat separating the locker room and stands from the ice, they heard something remarkable: a roar of encouragement more akin to what they might have gotten back home in Prague. On average, most games at the tournament that didn't include the home team attracted only a relative smattering of about 4,500 spectators, but this March 21 match drew in nearly 8,000. Swedes made up the bulk of the audience, but on this evening it was as if they had been transformed. As the players looked around the stands, they saw signs written in Czech, supporting the team and condemning the invasion.[44] One otherwise unassuming young man stood holding his poster with hand-scrawled Czech writing (*Vy nám tanky, my vám branky*) for his hockey heroes to see:

*You Send Tanks, We Bring Goals*

# CHAPTER 8

# You Send Tanks, We Bring Goals

A group of eager spectators from the Canadian national team arrived at the arena for the 8 P.M. game, ready to see a high-quality match between Czechoslovakia and the Soviet Union. What they got was unlike anything they had ever witnessed in a hockey rink. From their seats near the ice the Canadians could practically see the emotion steaming from the pores of the Czechoslovak players. The intensity swirled through the arena and across the stands. Canadian defenseman Terry O'Malley would see pretty much everything during an international hockey career spanning sixteen years, four World Championships, and three Olympics, including the 1980 tournament that held the "Miracle on Ice" match between the US and the Soviet Union at the height of the Cold War. But none of those events felt remotely like 1969 in Stockholm. As he took his seat, O'Malley became engulfed by an atmosphere that looked to him "blue with hate" both on the ice and in the stands.[1]

Fresh off competing in the US National Collegiate Ice Hockey Championships for Cornell University, future NHL star and Hall of Fame goalie Ken Dryden had only just gotten to Stockholm. Exhausted from the trip across the Atlantic, the twenty-one-year-old Dryden decided at the last moment to attend the Czechoslovakia-USSR game.[2] Events at the match jolted him awake. Five days later, Dryden made his first start in the net for Canada, earning a 1–0 shutout over the US, but years later he said, "Even though this was my first and only World Championships, the only thing I or anyone else remembers about them were the Soviet-Czechoslovakian games."[3] People who were there called them the fiercest and most emotionally charged hockey matches they had ever seen.

By the end of that evening, the Czechoslovakia-USSR rivalry was all anyone at the tournament talked about. The front-page headlines in the Western press the next day described it aptly: *Hate Match.*[4]

Fans of Czechoslovakia in the stands held signs with slogans that expressed a desire for revenge. Words like, *Your tanks can't help you here* and *In August you, tonight us.*[5] The Soviet Youth newspaper *Komsomolskaya Pravda* would later lash out at the holders of the signs as "counterrevolutionary scum."[6] During the broadcast, Swedish television producers insisted on withholding camera shots of the banners,[7] but from time to time footage of them snuck through to Czechs and Slovaks watching back at home.[8] Swedes came to the game prepared to cheer on Czechoslovakia. Some even brought their children, who carried hand-drawn Czechoslovak flags and signs written in Czech and Slovak.[9] Watching on television, viewers could hear supporters in the stands chanting in Czech, *Revenge for August '68!*[10]

As they warmed up, the Czechoslovak players received a hyperboost of adrenaline from the cheers. Suchý drank it in and tried to keep any doubts in the back of his mind. *This is for our people. I hope we don't disappoint them.*[11] As the Soviets crossed the divide between locker room and ice, they felt something surprising—shocking, even—given that it was an ice rink in Stockholm: derisive, aggressive, almost violent, earsplitting whistles raining down upon them.

Unless the game involves the home team, audiences at a typical international ice hockey match tend to remain somewhat muted and restrained, but the invasion had turned the people of Sweden into supporters of Czechoslovakia. Despite the country's famed neutrality, the Swedish hockey federation had even briefly cut hockey ties with the USSR.[12] Given the strength of the feelings surrounding the game, the head of the local police had asked that the game be played without an audience present and in particular that no one from Czechoslovakia be admitted, because they might be especially raucous.[13] Ultimately, the request was rejected. Thousands of people entered the arena, including hundreds from Czechoslovakia and a literal boatload of Soviet fans. Police had to break up a fight in the stands as play began.[14]

The Soviets had brought roughly five hundred supporters.[15] The group, which was quartered on a liner in Stockholm harbor, came to the Soviet Union's games throughout the tournament, waving red flags and chanting in unison in support of the Red Machine. Their drab black coats and hats led one

Canadian sportswriter to suggest they resembled "a convention of professional pall-bearers."[16] On this night, every time the Soviet supporters began their coordinated chants, their efforts were buried under a wave of whistles from the rest of the crowd. Well before game time, the entire stadium was filled with rhythmic cheers and the blast of horns for the men from Czechoslovakia.

As the first Czechoslovak player flew out to the ice, the crowd roared. Within moments, the crowd began a chant in Czech that continued throughout the evening: "Let's go! Let's go!" (*Do toho! Do toho!*). The Czechoslovak players wore dark blue jerseys and pants, with white and red stripes around the neck, wrists, waist, and nearly knee-high socks. Each player's number popped out in bright white on the back and arms of his jersey. Displaying an energy usually reserved for the most crucial moments of the game, the men from Czechoslovakia raced around the pristine ice like bolts of blue chain lightning streaking across a white winter sky.

Despite the intensity, there was still time for a lighthearted moment before the game. The hockey team had become a favorite of numerous Czechoslovak actors, none more enthusiastic than famed actress Jiřina Bohdalova. Bohdalova was so devoted to the team that she had been allowed to sit on the bench with the players in the 1967 World Championships. After the team played poorly that year, some team administrators suggested that the actress was a distraction. But the players saw Bohdalova as a friend and good luck charm. They were thrilled when they learned that she would be visiting her sister in Stockholm in 1969 and planned to attend the championships. Before the warm-ups, team captain Golonka entered the arena with Bohdalova on his arm, alternately claiming that she was his wife and that she was a nurse. The ordinarily strict Swedish officials recognized Golonka's distinctively sleepy eyes and angular face and simply waved them to the bench, where Bohdalova performed a serious of critical functions: She began by sitting on a spare puck to "hatch a win," while squeezing together her thumbs, Czechoslovakia's version of crossing one's fingers for good luck. But it quickly became clear that she needed to do more. Dukla forward Josef Augusta, playing in his first World Championships, saw one of the giant buttons on his overcoat fall off. Knowing instantly that action was required or bad luck would befall the entire team, Augusta begged, "Jiřina, you've got to put the button somewhere so we don't lose!" With her thumbs squeezed together, Bohdalova couldn't hold it with her hand, so she jammed it into her mouth, where it stayed throughout the match. The button caused her anxiety. What if, in the excitement of Czechoslovakia scoring a goal, she swallowed it?! Even worse, she feared that if she did choke, the team doctor would be celebrating Czechoslovakia's goal so wildly that he wouldn't notice her plight.[17]

Two minutes before game time, the chanting stopped. In the quiet that ensued, fans might have noticed for the first time the large-lettered list of corporate advertisers—including Texaco, BP, and Telefunken—on the white boards that encircled the ice. Then music heavy with orchestral horns and bass drums announced the pageantry of the event, like the resounding processionals that accompany the entrance of royalty. The two teams faced each other, sixty feet apart, on opposite sides of the red center line; teammates stood side-by-side along the blue lines that extended across the nearly hundred-foot width of the ice. Czechoslovakia's players appeared fairly casual, almost like a group of teens waiting in line for school to begin. Some fussed with their sticks, which they held askew, pointing at different angles.

For those who wore helmets, individual preferences ruled the day. Golonka's and Suchý's white helmets matched the color of the ice. Jiří stood out in blue head gear that matched his jersey. Jaroslav, ironically, sported Russian red. Believing that it made him look like a scaredy cat, Jaroslav had refused to wear head protection until his hockey federation forced him.[18] Still, many of the Czechoslovak players stood bare-headed and remained that way throughout the game. The brown hair and movie-star good looks of Nedomanský, who was especially popular among female fans, remained noticeably unobscured by awkward-looking head protection.

The Soviet line offered a sharp contrast. The red "CCCP" lettering on the Soviet jerseys reinforced just who, and what, the team represented. Each player stood perfectly in sync with his teammates, red helmet on his head, stick facing out from his right hand, parallel to the sticks of his teammates. Except for some quick leg pumping, the Soviet players held totally still. USSR legend Vladimir Petrov, playing in his first World Championships in 1969, later described the team's attitude: "We're Soviet people. The mentality of the Soviet people . . . was all about discipline."[19]

Even before play began on this Friday night, it appeared to Czechoslovakia's players that Pitner and Kostka had displayed more gamesmanship. Ordinarily the Soviet team appeared in its traditional red uniforms, but not in Stockholm.

No longer the iconic, menacing Red Machine, the Soviets stood in white jerseys, with just a splash of red stripes, lettering, numbering, and pants to add contrast. The Czechoslovak players were convinced that Pitner and Kostka had somehow extracted an agreement over jersey colors to try to mess with the Russian players' heads.

As the teams broke from the blue lines and the crowd's cheering and horn-blowing recommenced, Golonka faced an uncomfortable situation: He and his teammates had vowed not to shake hands with the Soviets, but IIHF ground rules stated that prior to World Championship games each team's captain must shake the hand of his counterpart on the opposing squad while exchanging team pennants.[20] Fearing sanctions that might affect his side's chances that day, Golonka headed to the side of the rink where the referees stood. As the short but heavily muscled USSR center and captain Vyacheslav Starshinov approached him, Golonka ran through the process of exchanging the pennants at super speed. Never breaking his emotionless, dead-eyed expression, Golonka stared into the face of the multi-time Soviet goal-scoring champion, grabbed his hand, gave it a perfunctory pump, and skated briskly away.

The players on both teams skated back to their own nets, where the goaltenders were improving their footing by scratching up the ice with their skates and sticks. Czechoslovakia's Vladimír Dzurilla took to the ice that night in very good spirits. Back at the hotel, he had appeared totally relaxed, leaving his teammates in stitches as he pretended to be a troublemaking mouse.[21] The players marveled at Dzurilla's cool under pressure. Even on this day, as he settled in for the greatest battle of his life, "Little Mouse" (*Myšáček*) showed no signs of stress. But his goalie apparel painted a terrifying image. The cheerful twenty-six-year-old netminder looked like a massive Hannibal Lecter on skates. He wore no helmet over his ears and closely shorn dark brown hair, but simply a beige leather mask across his face. Two circular openings near the top of the contraption gave Dzurilla a clear view of everything in front of him and left no obstacles in the way of his peripheral vision. A series of straps wrapped across the front of his nose and mouth and created multiple holes through which he could breathe. In addition, enormous brown pads draped across his shins and knees. His left hand sat in what looked like an oversized baseball first baseman's mitt, while a glove resembling a giant foam waffle swallowed his other hand, which also gripped a hockey stick. The enormous white number "1" across his back and on his arms stood out brightly against the blue of the rest of his jersey. Dzurilla couldn't wait for the game to begin. He shifted back and forth in front of his net, his relaxed arms flapping with each movement.

As always, the Soviets appeared to be the stronger team at every position except the net. Throughout the entire decade, opposing players believed that the principal reason they couldn't score on the USSR was not the play in the goal but the genius of the Russian defensemen. The Soviet goalie in 1969, Viktor Zinger, had served largely as a backup during his four previous years on the national team, and the Czechoslovak players eagerly awaited the opportunity to see what he was made of. Blanketed in padding similar to Dzurilla's, Zinger spent the final moments before the start of play adjusting the straps on his equipment.

When the whistle blew to clear the ice, the crowd broke into wild, rhythmic, hard-to-decipher chants. Whistles pierced eardrums. Horns howled. Just as play appeared imminent, a single explosive *BOOM!* from the stands briefly drowned out all other sound, inspiring the crowd to yell even louder. The entire Czecho-slovak team encircled Dzurilla, offering encouragement and lightly tapping him with their sticks. After they did, a few players slid to the side and repeatedly smacked the posts of the goal as well.

The Soviet starting lineup readied for the opening of the game, but soon found itself confronting yet another of the Czechoslovak coaches' tricks. Pitner and Kostka decided to take every opportunity for delay, thus thwarting the Soviets' biggest advantage—their utterly superior conditioning. Even just a few seconds of extra rest allowed the Czechoslovak players to catch their breath. Plus, they had learned in Grenoble the previous year that halting play could throw the Soviets off rhythm. [22]

Soviet team captain Starshinov stood alone with the referee in the center ice circle, waiting to begin. All but his first-line teammates had skated off the ice, and the other four skaters in white stood near Starshinov, poised to start as well. But it soon became clear that they would need to stand and wait. And wait. And then wait some more. Even as the Soviet bench filled, Czechoslovakia simply wouldn't leave the ice. The men in blue continued to skate, driving toward the center red line, where the Soviet players stood, and then abruptly swerving away. Jiří pumped his stick sharply toward his twenty-two-year-old Dukla teammate Augusta, as if to say, "Let's take it to them!" Augusta hardly needed prodding. He pumped his fist back sharply. Next, it was Golonka who flew by the center circle in a seemingly never-ending warmup cycle. The referee motioned to the Czechoslovak players to begin, but the delay only continued.

On the Soviet bench, behind a sea of seated red-helmeted players, Coach Tarasov looked on impassively, a black notebook pinched between the thumb and forefinger of his left hand. He wore a thin dark tie and a winter jacket. To Czechs and Slovaks, Tarasov's pudgy cheeks and closely cropped hair embodied Russian arrogance. People in Czechoslovakia detested everything about him—his demeaner, the way he talked, even the way he scribbled notes on his clipboard. In post-1968 Czechoslovakia, he was probably the second most-despised Russian, trailing only Soviet leader Brezhnev.[23]

Watching Team Czechoslovakia's delays, Tarasov appeared unperturbed, but given his fury over Pitner's gamesmanship in Grenoble, the Soviet coach undoubtedly fumed inside. For now, all Tarasov could do was watch as the men from Czechoslovakia just wouldn't stop skating. No one had ever seen Jiří so pumped up. One of the top skaters in the hockey world, the blue-helmeted star left-winger continued to fly around the ice, suddenly driving directly toward Starshinov, who still stood in the very center of the rink. Only at the very last moment did the younger Holík brother tap the center red line and slide to the left to avoid running into the Soviet team captain. At last, Czechoslovakia's players started filling up their own bench. And then, abruptly, the entire group flew through the gate and over the boards to begin skating all over again.

After another minute of waiting, the referees blew the whistle and *finally* the Czechoslovak players slid off the ice. Coach Pitner, sporting a gray fedora and wearing a blue-gray tie and a white shirt under a dark navy overcoat, welcomed his team to the bench. Unlike the other men, who now moved with some speed to join Pitner, Jaroslav skated slowly, just rocking gently side to side. The emotional leader of the team took the seat closest to the gate that led back onto the ice, ready to pounce.

Golonka now skated to the center of the ice and pirouetted just before the red line in front of the unmoving Soviet captain. As he did, a deep voice from the stands yelled down in Czech, "Lads, let's go!" (*Hoši, do toho!*).

All of Czechoslovakia held its breath for what would happen next. In his column the following day, famed Czechoslovak sportswriter Václav Pacina wrote that the start of the game was "like a gate to happiness that we did not believe would come. . . . The game was like the center of the world, like the only path to eternal salvation."[24]

The referee dropped the puck between the two captains. Golonka won the face-off, tapped it back to a teammate, and they were off, as the noise level in the arena rose several decibels. Czechoslovakia went on the offensive, attacking Soviet goalie Zinger. The assault didn't net a score, but it immediately set the tone, sparking a Czech chant, seemingly from the entire crowd: "Fight them! Fight them!" (*Bijte je! Bijte je!*).

People in the stands went berserk, with frenzied, piercing, high-pitched whistles, when Soviet forward Yevgeni Zimin used his stick to trip Czechoslovakia's Černý. As Zimin took a seat in the penalty box and the jeering died down, the crowd began a boisterous Czech chant, "Let's go! Let's go!" (*Jedem! Do toho!*). Soviets in the crowd tried their own chant—"Good job!" (*Molodets!*)—but within seconds, whistles from the rest of the crowd drowned them out.

The vitriol in what should have been a neutral rink clearly affected the champions. Every time a Soviet man knocked a Czechoslovak player down, the crowd whistled furiously. Whenever a Czechoslovak player knocked down one from the USSR, the crowd went crazy with delight. And when a Soviet player raced up the ice with the puck, someone in the crowd often yelled out in Czech: "Hit him hard!" (*Do něj!*). Everyone could see the tentativeness on the faces and in the bodies of the Russian players. Usually models of cold confidence, the Soviets appeared stunned, even embarrassed, by the crowd's reaction. They lacked their usual intensity and precision, and uncharacteristically fanned on simple passes and shots. To the Czechoslovak players, the Soviets looked insecure, under enormous psychological pressure, and perhaps even scared.[25] The Soviet authorities undoubtedly feared negative treatment in the world press, and it was rumored that they had ordered their players to avoid responding to physical provocations.[26]

USSR officials forbade their players to talk to Czechoslovakia's men about the invasion, but when the two squads came together off the ice in future years, conversations sometimes veered to the forbidden topic. In these conversations, most of the Soviet men spoke fervently in support of the USSR's political and economic system. The men from the army team—a group that made up a majority of the national squad—insisted that the occupation was necessary to prevent the people in Czechoslovakia from killing each other in a counterrevolution.[27]

Yet looking at the Soviet players' reaction on the ice this night in 1969, the Czechoslovak team couldn't help but wonder if the USSR players were coming to realize that they might not be getting the full story from their government. [28]

To keep its own team's emotions in check and to throw off the Soviets' rhythm, Czechoslovakia's mantra became, "We must stop the Russian carousel!"[29] Whenever it was time for a new face-off, Pitner kept his players on the bench for as long as he could without aggravating the referees. Notorious for constantly negotiating with referees, Golonka grew even more talkative than usual, chatting up anyone who could possibly slow down the return to play. Czechoslovak skaters suddenly needed to go to the bench to swap out sticks, although they then came back to the ice with the same ones they had left with. At times, Czechoslovak players abruptly claimed that their skates had lost a screw, forcing them to hold off play for the sake of safety. Just before face-offs, Czechoslovak players begged off, claiming a need to check on their teammates' positioning.

Despite the best efforts of Professor Vaněk and the team's coaches, the Czechoslovak players vented at least some of their rage on the ice. There was little physical play in the Soviet hockey league, so the Czechoslovak men believed they could throw off the USSR players by hitting or even merely blocking them. Thanks in part to the hands-off approach of a pair of very tolerant referees, Czechoslovakia managed to pound the USSR men throughout the match. In general, in games between them, the members of the two teams chatted harmlessly throughout play, but today the Soviets were struck nearly mute. [30] At best, they answered Czechoslovakia's taunts with short responses—often simply retorting that the Czechoslovak players were "fascists"—and then skated away. Expecting to be the physically dominant team, they appeared shocked that anyone would go at them so hard. The new tactic had indeed thrown the Red Machine off its game. [31] The Soviet team tried to maintain its disciplined, machine-like approach, but at times Czechoslovakia's physicality achieved its aim and incited the Russian players to pay back their hits in kind.

If there was a fly in the ointment, it was that the Czechoslovak players were *too* hyped up. Czechoslovakia's offense didn't flow with its usual smoothness. In their excitement, the players missed on passes they would normally have connected on. They played somewhat out of control, out of sync with one another, and lacking their usual crispness. Over the course of the two games between the teams in the tournament, over-aggressiveness left Czechoslovakia a man down more times than it liked.

Yet on balance Czechoslovakia's emotional play paid dividends. Not only did it seem to disconcert the Soviets, it brought out something amazing from the team in blue. The players skated all-out at every moment and pounded their opponents at every opportunity. Even players who were usually more inclined to protect their bodies gave no regard to the pain they would inflict upon themselves. Man after man on the Czechoslovak side threw himself onto the ice trying to gain every inch possible to grab a loose puck.

Of course, no one was more maniacal than Jaroslav. Players from other countries expressed admiration for Holík's terrific play and the tough, straightforward way he went about his job.[32] The Soviet players, on the other hand, hated him for his attacks. Mocking the way his nose ran constantly on the ice, they called him "snotface."[33] On this Friday night in Stockholm, Jaroslav tapped into his fury and the surrounding atmosphere to summon an entirely new level of effort. He gave his opponents no peace, bellowing that they were "Communists!" "Whores!" "Sons of bitches!"[34]

Just minutes into the game, Petrov shoved Jaroslav to the ice from behind as the USSR drove toward the Czechoslovak goal. Even sprawled out on his belly, the Czechoslovak center swam desperately at the puck, reaching as far in front of him as he could to try to knock the puck away. With Holík temporarily down, the Soviet team drove ahead and knocked the puck to Soviet rookie forward Valeri Kharlamov on the right, just three feet from the goal with only Czechoslovakia's goalie to beat. As the Russian snapped the puck sharp and low, the Soviet team celebrated the first goal of the game . . . until it became clear that Dzurilla had stopped the shot! Flashing reflexes that should not have been possible in such a large man, he had dropped to the ice and swallowed up the puck. As he disentangled himself from the netting and his Czechoslovak teammates surrounded him, the crowd realized what had happened. The stadium roar reached new heights as Jaroslav patted his goalie's shoulder.

A number of players from Czechoslovakia raised their game. Jiří Holík flew all over the ice faster and more elegantly than anyone on either team and shaped play on both offense and defense. Nedomanský stood out in the middle of the action. He had taken to the ice that night overwhelmed by a desire to smash his stick over the head of every one of his opponents. Indeed, as play began, any Soviet player near the puck risked his wrath as Big Ned took every opportunity to crash into them. The big man also showed skating skill, repeatedly faking out his defenders and leaving the crowd gasping at his maneuvers. Throughout the game Nedomanský pounded the puck at USSR goalie Zinger, hoping that sooner or later it would find the back of the net. The big forward also repeatedly locked in battle with Soviet rookie Boris Mikhailov. Every time Big Ned emerged from these clashes with an edge over Mikhailov, the crowd roared lustily.

Perhaps most of all, though, it was Jan Suchý's brilliance that stood out. Multiple times, Europe's best defenseman grabbed the puck on his own end of the ice and led a fast break for his team. He seemed blessed with a sixth sense, knowing what other players would do even before they did. As a result, he always looked a step ahead of everyone.[35] Soon after Dzurilla's brilliant first-period save, Suchý grabbed the puck behind the Czechoslovakia net and looked to take off. Two Soviet players appeared set to block him, but he stopped on a dime and spun halfway around to distance himself from his opponents. Totally faking out the Soviets, Suchy continued the spin for the full 360 degrees, leaving him driving toward his intended goal while his defenders' momentum carried them off in the wrong direction. He then sprinted up the ice until he found a teammate to flash a pass to. At other moments, he dove to the ice, doing all he could to reach the puck before the men in white.

Repeatedly, the Soviets appeared to have good chances to score, but they constantly ran up against Dzurilla's spectacular glove work. Undaunted by the moment, Little Mouse joked with his teammates throughout. After beautifully nabbing one Russian shot, he leaned back and hung an arm across the goal behind him, as if lounging on a sofa. Following particularly good saves, Dzurilla spoke about himself in the third person, announcing to his teammates, "Vlado caught this one well!"

Still, the USSR looked set to take over the game. Late in the first period the referees called an infraction on Czechoslovakia, sending defenseman Josef Horešovský to the penalty box. As he sat down, the Soviet contingent in the crowd started a chant, "Shoot and score!" (*Shayba*; literally, "puck"), which was instantly drowned out by a Czechoslovakia-supporting wall of earsplitting whistling. Now down a man, the Czechoslovak team, led by Jaroslav, Jiří, and Suchý, fought back with all-out intensity. The crowd bellowed over and over, "Fight! Fight!" (*Bojovat! Bojovat!*). Powered by an emotional defense, the Czechoslovak team kept the USSR from scoring, leading to a stoppage of play.

During the Soviet offensive, Russian forward Vladimir Vikulov had appeared to throw an elbow near Dzurilla's face. As the whistle blew, Vikulov moved behind the Czechoslovak goal and started to skate slowly back toward the center line. As he passed by, Dzurilla began barking at him. Vikulov swerved slowly toward the area in front of the goal, intent on staring down the goalkeeper. Dzurilla moved to within two feet of the Soviet man and flicked his stick at him, as if to say, "Get the hell out of here!" The USSR supporters in the crowd tried their "Shoot and score!" (*Shayba!*) chant one more time, and yet again were deluged with whistles from the other parts of the stadium. The Soviets followed with multiple shots on goal, but no luck.

Now Czechoslovakia appeared to have a chance. As the crowd roared in support, Augusta skated down the left side with the puck and smacked it at the Soviet net. Zinger blocked the shot and it bounded back to Czechoslovakia's Klapáč, who hit it weakly toward the goal. The puck bounced back again. Czechoslovak defenseman František Pospíšil ran it down and swung it toward Suchý. With each prior attempt, the decibel level in the arena had risen. As Suchý reared back and took a mighty swing, the noise threatened to blow the roof off the stadium . . . until it became clear that the shot had missed its mark and ricocheted off Starshinov's face.

The Soviet captain crumpled to the ice and lay motionless on his belly. Play continued for several moments before the referees noticed the inert body and halted the action. As the Soviet men rushed to their fallen comrade, Starshinov slowly began to move his head. He rolled onto his side and stood up. With a teammate helping him, he skated gingerly toward the bench. It was impossible to miss the enormous gash by his right eye or the blood covering nearly a quarter of his face. Clearly loathing the Soviets, the people in the stands took no pity on the man. As Starshinov took a seat on the bench to receive medical treatment, the crowd again began to chant, "Fight them!" (*Bijte je!*), which soon morphed back into "Let's go! Let's go!" (*Do toho! Do toho!*).

The first period ended with the score knotted at zero.

Having a period under their belts and some time to rest, Czechoslovakia's players lost their early game jitters, but with a tie score the competitive tension mounted. The quality of the play improved as passing on each side more commonly hit its mark. Time and again, the Soviets got the puck near Czechoslovakia's goal, and time and again, swarming defense by Czechoslovakia held them off. About a third of the way into the second twenty-minute period, the referees called consecutive penalties on the Soviet team. The crowd erupted with whistles and cheers. The fans knew this was the opportunity they had been waiting for, as Czechoslovakia now held a massive advantage: five skaters on the ice to only three for the Soviets. Pitner and Kostka had planned for this moment, sending out a team of four forwards—Jaroslav, Jiří, Golonka, and Big Ned—along with Suchý, one of his country's greatest scorers.

Jaroslav had made a career out of setting himself up in front of the opposing net, where he wreaked havoc by surreptitiously slamming his body and stick against foes. Opponents' hearts sank when they saw him gain position there, as it guaranteed physical pain for them. Even goalies, more protected than other players, knew they were not safe when Jaroslav entered their crease.

Now, on cue as his team set up its power play, Jaroslav won a face-off in front of the Soviet goal and tapped the puck out to his teammates, who let fly a barrage of shots. The puck bounced out to Jiří, who stood ten feet directly to the left of the net. He passed to Suchý, who looked straight at the front of the net ten feet away, nearly on a line with the goal's left post. Suchý stared at the cluster of players between him and the goal. As usual, Jaroslav stood right there. The older Holík jostled the group, three feet in front of the goalie. An off-balance Soviet defender recoiled from a Jaroslav elbow shove, slipping and knocking the Soviet goalie Zinger to the ice within the net.

Never blessed with an overwhelmingly powerful shot, Suchý typically only made shot attempts when he was near the goal. From close in, he could hit the puck with accuracy. [36] As the Soviets in front of him fell, Suchý took a swing. But the area was clogged with players. The puck ran into Jaroslav, who tapped it gently back to his childhood friend. Angry with himself for missing a clear opportunity, Suchý quickly flipped the puck toward the net, allowing no time to set up or hit with his usual precision. Yet the disk flew higher than his previous effort. Right into the top of the net.

Bedlam. The crowd erupted. Team Czechoslovakia piled on top of Suchý and then stormed the net. Big Ned flew over the right side of the goal with his arms raised. He steadied himself and then came back around to the front of the net, where he ripped it off its right-side moorings. Jaroslav lifted his own arms and brought his stick down inches from the Russian goalie's face, screaming the greatest insult he could think of: "You fucking commie!!!"[37] Jaroslav smacked the top of the goal repeatedly with his stick and picked up the left side of the net. He raised the net, now fully off its moorings, and tossed the entire structure toward the boards separating the fans from the ice.

Sitting low in the stands, players from the other teams gasped at the over-the-top in-game celebration, which would never have occurred in any other hockey match.[38] Viewers from other countries took it for granted that there was a sense of appropriate behavior on the ice, and knowledgeable observers normally would have frowned on the extreme departure from hockey decorum. Yet on this night, nearly the entire hockey world cheered on Czechoslovakia's players and their show of emotion. Back in Prague, famed actor Jan Werich opened the window of his flat to yell "GOAL!!" but nobody was outside. Everyone was home watching the game.[39]

The goal pumped up the Czechoslovak players yet again. Just as they had skated at the beginning of the game, they flew all over the ice for the final ten minutes of the second period. When the period came to a close, the Soviet players skated slowly to the bench, looking exhausted and possibly even demoralized. In marked contrast, the men from Czechoslovakia seemed tired but also elated, joining together in groups to celebrate their lead.

But the margin was a tiny one. As the final twenty-minute period began, the world's greatest national hockey team needed only a single goal to tie things up. The crowd's rhythmic cheering and chants reached new heights. "Let's go, Czech team! Let's go! Let's go!" (*Cechy jedem! Do toho! Do toho!*). With time to compose themselves, the Soviets again looked like the offensive juggernaut that they were, skating and passing with skill and precision, but they were met by a Czechoslovak team that made the extra effort on every play. Acutely aware of the dwindling time that remained, both sides clawed desperately whenever the puck was in reach.

The fans grew increasingly tense, blurting out "Careful, careful! He's coming!" (*Bacha, bacha! Jede!*), as Soviet players drove toward Dzurilla. But most of all, the crowd urged the men from Czechoslovakia on, bellowing "Let's go!" in Czech (*Do toho!*) and "Czechoslovakia! Czechoslovakia!" in Swedish (*Tjecko! Tjecko!*).

As Jaroslav took to the ice in the third period, Pitner had reminded him to stay under control. So of course almost immediately the Dukla center met up with Ragulin near the Soviet-protected net as a well-hit shot caromed away from both men. When Jaroslav fought to get past the giant Soviet defender, Ragulin slammed him hard to the ice. Jaroslav hardly missed a beat. Focused solely on winning the play, he bounded to his feet and stole the puck.

Later in the period, Czechoslovakia knocked a puck down to the Soviet end of the ice. The goalie Zinger came way out of the net—forty feet away from the goal he was sworn to shield—to get the puck under control. Starting from his own end of the ice, Jaroslav took off on a mad dash from more than a hundred feet away, driving toward the puck . . . and the Russian goalie. Just as Zinger passed it off to a teammate, Jaroslav took flight. He became a missile flying directly at his opponent, smashing the netminder to the ice. Even with the cheering of the crowd, the crackling thud of the contact between the two men reverberated throughout the arena. Furious, Zinger shook off the man in blue and reared back with his own stick. At the very last moment he contained himself, merely staring down Czechoslovakia's emotional leader.

On the bench, Soviet coach Tarasov grew increasingly animated. He pumped his hands, exhorting his players to get the goal that would tie the game, but now it was Czechoslovakia that kept finding opportunities. Big Ned appeared to be everywhere, stealing passes and whipping shot after powerful shot at Zinger.

With each passing moment, the pressure on both sides became increasingly hard to bear. Throughout the game, Mikhailov had infuriated the Czechoslovak players with his painful elbow jabs.[40] Following a Soviet goal attempt, Mikhailov, whom the Czechoslovak players called a "Russian dog," flew into Suchý. After Suchý responded by shoving him back toward the boards, Mikhailov looked set to nail Czechoslovakia's star with an arm, or possibly even a stick, to the face. Only the referees' intervention prevented escalation as the spectators whistled bloody murder. But through it all, the champions couldn't get close to the net, and even when a player did have an open shot, Dzurilla moved with cat-like quickness to ensure it wouldn't get past him.

Suchý appeared to be playing on a different level from everyone else. On offense he kept faking out the opposition. On defense, he put on a clinic. Everyone around the rink winced as they watched Suchý and fellow defenseman Pospíšil courageously block shot after shot with their bodies.[41] Given the importance of the match, Pitner gave Suchý less rest than was the custom for most players on most teams. As a result, whenever there was a break in the action, the Dukla defenseman, who was also famous for his chain-smoking, could be found leaning up on the boards for support, panting heavily.

Six minutes into the final period, Suchý stole the puck, slickly skated between two Soviets, and, moving at nearly full speed at center ice, sent a perfect pass to his wide-open teammate Černý. Ordinarily, Černý would have in turn passed the puck off to the open Golonka on the right, but as he approached the Soviet goal the Czechoslovak left-winger saw an opportunity. Ragulin stood between him and the goalie, and the giant defenseman didn't stand a chance against the speedy Černý. With some nifty stickwork, Černý slid to the right, causing the Russian to fall flat on his face. Zinger flew out to block him, and Černý flipped the puck past the Soviet goaltender for Czechoslovakia's second goal.

In the arena, it was as if Czechoslovakia had just won the championship. The moment the puck flew into the net, the already cheering crowd reached a new level of frenzy. Nothing would calm the spectators as the entire team piled onto Černý. In Czechoslovakia's wins, Golonka had a history of pretending to play a sad violin on his stick to represent the death of the opposition's chances of victory.[42] On this day, Golonka's "concert" turned so wild that players on the Soviet side swore they saw him turn his violin around as if it were a rifle, which he fired at the USSR net.[43]

As play resumed, it became increasingly clear that the Soviets were not going to score on Dzurilla. With only a few minutes remaining, Soviet forward Kharlamov found himself with the puck just six feet from the net. Czechoslovakia's netminder gracefully kicked the shot attempt away with his left foot. Moments later, Firsov slapped a shot Dzurilla's way. With a snap, the big goalie thrust his right arm and leg out to the side, popping the puck away. Less than sixty seconds later, he snatched another USSR effort out of the air with his glove. With each spectacular save, the crowd's admiration for him grew. As he casually dropped the puck from his glove onto the ice, the fans began to pound, "Dzu-ri-LA! Dzu-ri-LA!" With under two minutes left to play, Dzurilla dove to protect the goal, injuring his nose. The Czechoslovak team held its collective breath as the training staff brought him to the bench to inspect his wounds—and then exhaled as he quickly skated back to his post, wearing a broad grin across his happy-go-lucky face. Within thirty seconds, Dzurilla showed he was more than fine when he stepped to the left to nab yet another Russian try with his glove. The big Slovak had faced twenty-four shots on goal and turned them all away for the first World Championship tournament shutout of the Soviet team since 1955. [44]

As the final seconds ticked away, the men on Czechoslovakia's bench cheered and raised the tools of their trade in triumph. When the clock showed zero, the clearly exhausted Suchý started to wobble uncertainly on his skates as he raised his stick straight up into the air. Skating out from the net to join his teammates, Dzurilla pulled off his mask. Jiří got to the goalie first, wrapping his right arm across the big man's shoulders. Moments later, the entire team engulfed the two men, with Jaroslav and his signature red helmet jumping on top of the pile. Some players kissed the ice. Completely ignoring the Soviet team, a gaggle of photographers surrounded Czechoslovakia's hockey players, capturing their every move. The men continued to celebrate, and the entire crowd made clear just what the victory truly represented, as thousands of voices chanted "Dubček! Dubček!"

Once Czechoslovakia's players regained some measure of composure, they and the Soviet players lined up on the ice. When the music representing their small, occupied country played, the Czechoslovak players, many still out of breath, sang their hearts out as they watched the raising of their giant blue, white, and red flag. When the anthem concluded, the crowd let loose with a deafening roar.

The Soviet players were overwhelmed by everything going on around them. They didn't like or even approve of how the Czechoslovak players had treated them. But they didn't see the men from Czechoslovakia as enemies. The Soviets understood that on this night they had been involved in something that was far more than just a hockey match. [45]

As the anthem concluded, the Czechoslovak players cheered mightily, raised their sticks in the air, and embraced one another. The crowd continued to roar as the players skated off the ice, still hugging, now with arms and sticks lifted high, waving wildly with joy. Isolated in the net all evening, Dzurilla now flew alongside his teammates as they passed under the Czechoslovak flag, that had been unfurled, for the winning team, over the exit. As they left the ice, the Czechoslovak players conspicuously avoided shaking hands with their Soviet counterparts. Meanwhile, the Soviets continued to look bewildered, uncertain how to handle their opponents' enmity.[46] The men in blue appeared unaware that their opponents were even there . . . except that they made sure to get off the ice before the Soviets did. With the USSR team well behind them, the Czechoslovak players were unable to see Soviet defenseman Vitaly Davydov trailing them off the ice, flipping his hand dramatically underneath his chin as if to say, "Fuck you, too."

Among the last to leave the arena were a few flag-waving fans of the victorious team. One young man slid joyfully around the ice, flapping his own blue, white, and red Czechoslovak flag. Another supporter gripped a sign hanging down from his neck written in Czech: "We are not afraid of the Russians, we will beat them in hockey, and we will pay them back for August."

Czechoslovakia's players rushed to the locker room, where they cheered incoherently and embraced one another with the jubilation of men who had won a two-decade war, not a hockey match in the middle of a two-week tournament. Equipment flew every which way across the room. The coaches made a half-hearted attempt to calm their forces, gently pointing out that they still had nine days to go, in which they would play five more games.

But nothing could contain the players' rapture. To them, this was as joyous a moment as they had ever experienced. It was a victory that belonged not to any one person. And it belonged not just to a team, but to an entire country, whose people desperately wanted to fight back against the Soviets themselves.

Looking around, Pitner thought to himself, "This is not a locker room. This is an insane asylum."[47] He gleefully strode out of the room, locking the inmates in to enjoy their madness.

# CHAPTER 9

# Blacked Out Stars

As Pitner left his players in the locker room, Sweden's coach Arne Stromberg rushed over to congratulate him: "This is something only you people from Czechoslovakia can do. You nearly drove the Soviets crazy!"[1]

Stromberg's words brought a smile to Pitner's face, but Czechoslovakia's coach could not entirely enjoy the moment, because he had to deal with the residue of the players' end-of-game protest. Pitner and Kostka were displeased by what they saw as a reckless act.[2] Everyone associated with the World Championships knew that skipping the post-game handshake was way outside hockey protocol and could only serve to heighten tensions between the two teams—and the two countries.[3] The message had clearly been directed not just at the Soviet hockey squad, but at the USSR itself. The Czechoslovak players, on the other hand, felt dismayed when they learned later that no one at home saw what they had done. Czechoslovakia's television producers had cut the feed at the moment any handshake would have occurred.[4]

With their rush to get off the ice, the players didn't see USSR defenseman Vitaly Davydov flipping his hand underneath his chin at them. When they heard about it later, it perplexed them. Probably the most popular of the Soviet players with his Czechoslovak counterparts, Davydov often spent time with Jiří and especially Suchý off the ice. Unlike most of the Soviet players, who played much of the year for the army squad, Davydov hailed from Dynamo Moscow, the state security intelligence team. The army team players commonly regurgitated state propaganda and openly celebrated the invasion. But in talking privately to his friends from Czechoslovakia, Davydov stood out as the only member of the Red Machine to condemn the occupation. Jiří and Suchý would never learn what inspired Davydov's gesture, but they felt pretty sure it had something to do with their handshake protest.[5]

At the post-match press conference, surrounded by more than a hundred journalists, Pitner had to address his players' breach of protocol. Fortunately for him, USSR coach Tarasov did not attend. The Czechoslovak players' behavior on the Stockholm ice had turned Tarasov's anger from Grenoble into pure enmity. To Tarasov, it was despicable how Team Czechoslovakia that night had treated his players, who were but innocent victims in the middle of something that had nothing to do with them. From this day forward, Tarasov loathed the men from Czechoslovakia and yearned to embarrass them on the ice.[6] However, Pitner wouldn't need to deal with his counterpart's fury until another day. The Soviet coach was consulting with doctors at a Stockholm hospital after suffering mild heart problems during the game.[7] Pitner let out a sigh of relief, fearing the two men might have come to blows.[8]

As he stood before the press, Pitner first tried to explain the absence of a handshake from his players as an oversight, born out of the joy of the moment, but then slyly, and disingenuously, added that back in Czechoslovakia it was the job of the losing team to reach out to the winner.[9] Soviet head coach Arkady Chernyshev also attended the press conference. Unlike his tempestuous colleague, Tarasov, Chernyshev tended to remain calm and diplomatic—especially when meeting with journalists.[10] He stayed on good terms with Pitner and chose not to raise a stink about the handshake slight at that time.[11]

The people back in Czechoslovakia may not have known about their team's protest, but the rest of the world certainly did. Article after article in the Western press would highlight the Czechoslovak players' action. With the great importance that the host country placed on fairness and sportsmanship, many Swedish editorials expressed disappointment at the "unsportsmanlike" end-of-game behavior of the Czechoslovak players.[12] The players understood the Swedish press's reaction, but also felt it missed the point: this was no mere sporting event.

Nevertheless, the handshake incident aside, the Western press hailed Czechoslovakia's victory. In Sweden the next day, reporters praised Czechoslovakia's win.[13] In Canada, the *Montreal Gazette* wrote that Czechoslovakia's players "obviously were out to play the game of their lives."[14] Even in the less hockey-mad United States, the victory in the "hate match" made page one news.[15] Toronto's *Globe and Mail* went a step further, not only putting the story on the front page, but adding a subtle dig at Czechoslovakia's occupiers in the headline: "Czechs win hate match, refuse to shake with Russian losers."[16] A kicker above the main headline referenced the sharpest of the crowd's signs, "Tonight, Even Tanks Won't Help."

Some clever phrasing even allowed thinly veiled sentiments to get past the censors in Czechoslovakia. Both Czechoslovak coaches had lived for years as loyal Communists. Nevertheless, in the days that followed the match, the Czechoslovak periodical *Lidová demokracie* (People's Democracy) quoted Coach Kostka as exclaiming, "The victory was a sports triumph . . . and something more."[17]

However, all that was to come later, and on the night of March 21, the Czechoslovak players' celebration continued even after they left the stadium. They crammed every possible supporter onto the team bus to travel back to the hotel with them and broke into joyful singing of "Škoda lásky" ("The Beer Barrel Polka").[18] The bus arrived at the hockey players' home in Stockholm, the Hotel Bromma. As the Czechoslovak players disembarked, the American hockey squad, which was staying in the same hotel, stood waiting for them with congratulatory bottles of whiskey.[19]

Meanwhile, back home, thousands spontaneously took to the streets of Prague to celebrate, causing traffic jams. People sprayed the ground and walls with "2:0," memorializing the score of the game. Marchers carried signs such as "No tanks were there, so they lost."[20]

The Czechoslovak players awoke the next day to learn of all the excitement at home through 830 telegrams that arrived in Stockholm.[21] The team assigned the masseur, the doctor, and anyone else who was not busy to sort through them and pick out the best to share with the club.[22] The telegrams included funny poems and heartfelt messages of thanks, including:

> *They were strong last August, but the small ones won today.*[23]

> *You prove that if fair play is the norm, the spirit always defeats the sword.*[24]

> *Thank you for this small band-aid for August, and for the moral slap in the face in front of the entire world.*[25]

The people of Sweden showed no less support. Czechoslovak sports reporter Miloslav Jenšík, who had set up the special editions of the *Svět v obrazech* magazine in the days after the invasion, came to Stockholm to cover the tournament. After the first game against the Soviets, he and a group of journalists drove back to their motel in a car emblazoned with the Czechoslovak flag. All along the drive, drunken, dancing Swedes toasted them with their beers.[26] The same Swedes also found their own Czechoslovak flags in all shapes and sizes, which they waved at the foreign journalists. For the next few days, locals constantly rushed up to the writers from Czechoslovakia to slap them on their backs, congratulating them as if they, the men with pens, had just won the gold medal. Throughout his stay in Sweden, whenever it came out that Jenšík hailed from Czechoslovakia, complete strangers treated him like a long-lost friend. The Swedes repeated over and again that if anyone from Czechoslovakia wished to stay in Sweden, they would make it happen. They promised stipends to Czechoslovak émigrés so they could spend their first six months just learning Swedish.[27]

People in the host country even encouraged Czechoslovakia's players not to return home. Stockholm's leading hockey team offered Suchý a big contract and a house next door to a gas station, where he would be given secure employment as the manager once he retired. The Swedish hockey team assured him that it would work with the Red Cross to deliver his wife and two young sons safely to him, but Suchý didn't want to risk becoming separated from his family or, far worse, putting them in danger. If he couldn't make the move with the legal blessing of the Czechoslovak government, he just wouldn't do it. Plus, with his serious smoking habit, living next to a gas station might prove problematic.[28]

In such a supportive, safe place, the men from Czechoslovakia felt able to express themselves freely . . . up to a point. The players talked of their admiration for Alexander Dubček. Many even gave interviews to Karel Drážďanský for Radio Free Europe, which had been established by the US government to promote anti-communist communication and ideas. The players spoke so candidly of their anger at the occupation that Drážďanský began to fear for them. A soccer stadium next door to the ice rink housed the press center for the tournament. In between the two stadiums sat a heated tent, where Czechoslovak journalists chatted with one another about what the hockey games meant to their people. In past years, their government had punished Czechs and Slovaks who, when visiting other countries, dared to consort with defectors from

Czechoslovakia. But now the reporters took the opportunity to meet with emigrants from Czechoslovakia's 1948 coup and 1968 invasion.

Nevertheless, Czechoslovakia's Communist machine still found its way to Sweden. The Czechoslovak journalists spoke elatedly about how the hockey victory helped exact revenge upon the Soviets. But they stopped short when Czechoslovak Communist hardliner Gustav Vlk, the editor of one of the country's leading sports magazines, overheard them and asked with disgust, "How long are we going to keep 'paying them back' for August?" The group became silent. Václav Pacina, the Czechoslovak sportswriter who had been moved to poetry by the start of the match against the Soviets, desperately wanted to retort, "Forever ... Forever!" But he dared say nothing in the face of the frowning editor.[29]

Still, the hockey tournament continued. Neither Czechoslovakia nor the USSR played the day after their battle, but off-days were not the norm. Two days after their big game, the USSR and Czechoslovakia returned to the ice against other teams. The Soviets immediately reasserted their dominant ways and won the next three matches.

Czechoslovakia, on the other hand, faced an emotional hangover following its huge win. Knowing how flat the players were likely to be, team psychologist Dr. Vaněk offered Jaroslav something to give him "a bit of an edge." Jaroslav didn't know much about performance-enhancing drugs, but it felt weird to take something to pump himself up. He refused the offer.[30]

International Hockey Federation officials actually *did* drug test Jan Suchý at the tournament. Unlike 1965, when Suchý *had* taken something illicit, by 1969 the Hockey Federation instituted random checks, in which they pulled three players into a controlled space, where they were asked to urinate into a cup. In one of the first matches of the 1969 tournament, this proved to be a problem when the authorities wanted to test Suchý, who refused to drink water during games, believing that by not hydrating he remained light and fast on his feet. Plus, water took up valuable stomach space needed for his post-game beers. The testers gave Suchý lemonade, and when that didn't produce the desired result, they allowed him a beer. After time passed, it became clear that Suchý required more liquid, so they permitted him another beer. After three hours and six beers, Suchý *finally* completed his part in the process.[31]

Had the Czechoslovak players known the difficulty they would face in the coming days, they might have been more receptive to Vaněk's pharmacological offerings. The players were flat and barely got it together to defeat Canada and Finland in their next two matches.

The Finland game marked the return of offensive star Jaroslav Jiřík, whose injury early in the tournament had been expected to require four weeks of recuperation. With his team playing to lift the entire country, and with a chance to win the world title, Jiřík decided to suit up, even though he could barely dress himself.[32] Ignoring throbbing pain and playing with his broken wrist immobilized in a cast, Jiřík saved the day against Finland, scoring two goals.[33] Just one day later, Czechoslovakia took down the United States 6–2.

The stage was now set for the matchup everyone wanted. On Friday, March 28—exactly one week after their first meeting in the tournament—Czechoslovakia would take on the Soviets on the ice again. This time, however, with the two teams tied atop the standings with seven wins apiece and only two games remaining, it appeared all but certain that the winner would take the world championship crown.

Unlike the previous week, this time the Red Machine would be ready. The Soviets would not be surprised again by the energy and physicality of their opponent, and would steel themselves against the wrath of the crowd. This match truly mattered to the Soviets, and according to the Stockholm rumor mill, Moscow had now ordered its team to crush Czechoslovakia.[34] To Leonid Brezhnev, hockey uber-fan and the leader of the Soviet Union, after winning the previous six World Championships, anything less than another title in 1969 was unthinkable. It also could not have been far from his thoughts that a Soviet victory in this game might quiet the forces of resistance back in Czechoslovakia.

Czechoslovakia's team, meanwhile, faced a serious problem. Up 5–1 late in the game against the US, Suchý made one of his patented shot blocks, in this case sticking his hand in the path of a flying puck. In the process, he broke his index finger. He didn't notice the problem at first and finished the game. Then his hand started swelling, and the team rushed him to a local doctor. Suchý learned that the bone had snapped in half. Speaking through an interpreter, Suchý begged the physician to set the finger in a way that would permit him to still place it in his hockey glove and grip his stick. Cursing Suchý and his translator out in Swedish for what he saw as an imbecilic request, the doctor told him that such a move would make it impossible to ever straighten the finger again. Knowing that it meant the end of his ability to play in the tournament,

Suchý watched, completely crushed, as the doctor set the finger straight.[35] Czechoslovakia would be without its star defenseman for its final battle against the greatest team in international hockey.

On March 28, 1969, reportedly 93 percent of all households with televisions in Czechoslovakia flipped on their sets to view the final matchup between their boys and their occupier, the Soviet Union.[36] Under Czechoslovak communism, with its notions of a disciplined society, children were expected to go to bed early. On this night, though, parents didn't hesitate to let their little ones stay up to watch the game. The previous summer, a twelve-year-old Czechoslovak girl named Martina had bravely thrown rocks and an apple at an invading Russian tank. Now she huddled with her family, the Navrátils, watching the game on their little TV, their bodies tensed as if their own physical strain might help will their team to victory. At Czechoslovakia's most successful moments during both matches against the Soviets, Martina and the rest of the Navrátils shouted at the television, "This is what happens when it's a fair fight! This is revenge for what you have done to us!"[37]

Tens, if not hundreds, of thousands of people who had never before watched a hockey game suddenly cleared their calendars to ensure they could see this one on their tiny black-and-white screens. Years later an American visitor to the country asked a woman named Líba, who was born in Czechoslovakia in 1943, to talk about her life during the 1960s. Líba's face fell when she learned that the visitor wanted to hear about hockey in Czechoslovakia. "I'm so sorry. I just don't have any interest in hockey," she said. "That's okay," the visitor replied. "Just talk about your life. What do you remember about 1969?" Líba didn't hesitate. "That was the year our hockey team fought the Russians! They were such incredible games. I watched them on TV!"

To some people, it may have felt like déjà vu. Friday night world championship hockey in Stockholm. Same two teams. Same two referees. But to the keen-eyed observer, something looked different. Given the magnitude of the Soviets' transgressions against them and their country, many on Czechoslovakia's side felt that simply beating the USSR once and withholding a handshake was *not* enough. "We have to think of something for those bitches," Jaroslav told his teammates. And sure enough, they did.

In the center of the front of Czechoslovakia's jerseys sat the country's coat of arms. For much of its existence, Czechoslovakia's crest had contained a lion with a crown on its head (representing Czech lands) and a shield fronted by a double cross (representing Slovakia). After the USSR formed in 1922, the Soviets adopted socialist heraldry, using emblems that symbolized the country's socialist principles, and many communist states followed suit after World War II. Czechoslovakia continued to use its traditional coat of arms until 1960 when the country's leaders changed the crest, removing the cross from the Slovak shield and replacing the lion's crown with a five-pointed red star, the symbol of communism.

The hockey players hated the star on the jersey. [38] As they complained with one another, Jaroslav Jiřík talked about how his family had always told him that the national symbol was the Czech lion with a *crown*. [39] Another player, Jan Havel, chimed in: "The Czech lion has a crown on his head, not a star that oppresses him!" [40] They decided to do something about it.

When they took to the ice for their rematch against the Soviet team, a number of Czechoslovak players wore jerseys with black tape conspicuously slapped over the star. The act became legendary in Czechoslovakia, taking on almost mythical status. But even after decades of probing, and after myriad variations on the story, there is no consistent account of precisely who all the conspirators were, when they came up with the plan, or who the original ringleader was. [41] There is total agreement, however, on one thing: on March 28, 1969, Vladimír Dzurilla, Jan Havel, Jaroslav Jiřík, and Jaroslav Holík all came out to battle the Soviets wearing jerseys they had altered to show their derision for the international symbol of communism. They sent a clear message to the Soviets: *You and your system are dead to us.*

Everyone who knew anything about Jaroslav Holík could only nod with understanding: *Of course he stood at the center of the incendiary act!* It would have been shocking if Holík, who had screamed "You fucking commie!" at the Soviet goaltender in game one against the USSR that year, *hadn't* done it. Brash, outrageously provocative gestures were his modus operandi. [42] When Jaroslav's wife Marie learned about the players' amateur tailoring, she knew instantly, "Only my husband could do something like that!" [43]

There were various reasons that more of the men didn't take part. A small number were genuine Party members who would never vandalize the star. Some, like Jiří Holík, were so focused on beating the Soviets that they didn't even notice what their teammates had done. [44] And some were unimpressed with the plot, thinking that the star was too small to notice, and the tape kept falling off anyway.[45]

But a small group of others agonized over what to do. František Ševčík, a twenty-seven-year-old forward for Brno, initially joined in the protest and then started to worry about retribution. The government could pull him from his privileged place at a university or, worse, might punish his family. He reluctantly removed the tape before the match.[46]

Young defenseman Vladimír Bednář had precisely the opposite reaction. Just twenty years old and a member of Dukla with the Holíks and Suchý, Bednář was playing in his first World Championships. The youngest player on the team, he worshipped the veterans and was astonished that the federation had chosen him to play with them on the world's biggest hockey stage. He knew nothing about the tape until he got out onto the ice and saw it. A wave of anxiety followed: "Oh God, what did I do? I did something wrong. I should have taped my star over as well!" Not wanting to bother his heroes at such a moment, only after the game did he ask them about it.

In truth, the protest was a *huge* deal. Not merely decorative, the coat of arms served as a national symbol, and in the past the state had punished dissidents who defiled that symbol.[47] According to law, citizens could be imprisoned for three years for defaming the Czechoslovak republic or another communist state, or speaking in a way that damaged the interests of Czechoslovakia abroad. It was therefore not surprising that, during a practice in the week leading up to the second game against the USSR, Jenšík, the Czechoslovak journalist, was astonished when he saw Jaroslav wearing a team jersey with a taped-over star. Jenšík took a picture and had it developed in Stockholm, knowing no one would handle the order in Czechoslovakia. He then sent it home, where it ran as a full-page picture in the *Svět v obrazech* magazine.[48] When the Czechoslovak skaters took to the ice with their altered jerseys, sportswriter Václav Pacina turned to one of his fellow journalists and asked incredulously, "What's with their lion?" Scarcely believing his eyes, his stunned compatriot could only answer "They taped over the stars."[49]

Tape or no tape, on March 28 Czechoslovakia's players arrived at the arena hyped up, and there was an electricity in the locker room that outstripped even the feeling prior to the first game against the Soviets. But they also felt an urgency, a deep-seated tension greater than before. As they took to the ice, they saw they weren't the only ones feeling it. Golonka noticed something unusual. Two Soviet players sat in front of their own locker room, just staring out in silence. As Czechoslovakia's captain began to skate, something on the Soviet bench caught his eye: defenseman Viktor Kuzkin was sitting, his eyes completely unfocused, not paying attention to anything. It seemed to Golonka that the pressure was getting to the Soviets.[50]

As with the earlier match, in Stockholm the second Czechoslovakia-USSR game seemed to be all anyone was interested in. A boisterous crowd of 10,000 roared in support of the underdogs, recording even greater attendance than the games involving the host team. Signs of support in Czech again dotted the crowd: *We were not born to lose our country* and *Your tanks can't help you here.*[51] With a constant deafening roar, the crowd raised its own game. Throughout the match and throughout the arena, nearly everyone in the mostly Swedish crowd yelled as loudly as they could: In Czech, they chanted "Let's Go!" (*Do toho!*), and "Fight them!" (*Bijte je!*). In Swedish, they yelled "Czechoslovakia!" (*Tjeckien*). Just as in game one, every time the pro-Soviet contingent tried to get a cheer going, the rest of the stadium drowned it out with whistles.

The players turned the energy up another notch as well. Both sides seemed to skate even faster than they had one week before. Czechoslovakia's skaters remained intense, but the Soviets were a changed bunch. They looked more like their old selves. Unlike in the previous game, when they'd seemed in a trance, they now played with their usual confidence and speed. They were, again, the greatest national hockey team in the world.

The Soviets opened the match with a fast-paced swarming offensive that never quite bore fruit. Both teams hit hard and looked as close to fighting one another as on the previous Friday. Many of the Czechoslovak players felt that the Russians were playing dirty, calling out Mikhailov in particular for constantly throwing elbows.[52]

Suchý felt pure agony as he stood in civilian clothes, watching helplessly from the bench. He had been playing the best hockey of his life, in this, the most important tournament of his country's life. Despite missing the final two games, he would be named the tournament's top defenseman. That mattered little to him now. In earlier matches, he, too, had worn black tape over the Communist star. Now all he could do was cheer his teammates on. And even yelling in support wasn't much help. The arena was so loud that his teammates couldn't hear him.[53] Able to do little else, Suchý took his aggression out violently on the gum in his mouth. Sitting in the stands, the journalist Jenšík periodically ached at the miserable sight of Czechoslovakia's greatest player pacing back and forth in a black jacket and white sling, wearing a white cast on his right hand with the damaged finger jutting out pointedly in a permanent number one sign.

Suchý may not have been able to play, but the Holíks put on a show. Jiří looked like he was trying to make up for the absence of his longtime buddy all by himself. The famously laid-back younger Holík brother shifted into a higher gear, consistently outskating even the most talented of the opponents. Back home in Czechoslovakia, millions, including Martina and the Navrátils, marveled at his speed and fearlessness. He also hit more and with greater force than usual. Jiří ended up in the penalty box twelve minutes into the first period after he hooked one of the Soviet players with his stick, inspiring a wave of crowd whistles aimed at the referees.

Down a man, and facing potential disaster, Team Czechoslovakia ramped up the effort level. In the previous game against the Soviets, it was the brilliant glove work of Dzurilla that repeatedly saved the day. Now the defense clamped down, refusing to allow lanes for the Russians to shoot through. Over and over, Czechoslovakia's players on defense slapped the puck back to the other end of the ice, trying to keep the USSR from setting up its power play offense.

When his two-minute penalty time expired, Jiří flew out of the box. He sprinted with a laser-like focus right into the middle of the action, as the crowd roared "Let's go! Let's go!" (*Do toho! Do toho!*). The volume increased, leaving no doubt that the thousands of Swedes in the building were going all in urging Czechoslovakia on.

Jiří and his brother bolted straight at two Soviets who tried to control the puck, forcing a turnover that put the Holíks and their teammates on the offensive. Moments later, after a series of frantic moves by both sides, Czechoslovak defenseman Oldřich Machač collected the puck deep in his own end and flew up the right side of the ice. He smoked it along the boards around to the back of the goal and then beat a Soviet to the disk. Machač flipped it toward Jaroslav, who outraced another Soviet player to the puck on the left side of the goal. Jaroslav flicked it farther away from the net toward Jiří and then applied an American football-style block into a Soviet player, who might otherwise have been able to get to his brother. Jiří drove to his left, moving farther from the middle of the ice to control the puck, which was some thirty feet away on a forty-five-degree angle from the goal. With a USSR defender collapsing in on him, Jiří lunged. Starting with his back to the net, the younger Holík spun his body around and hit the puck without much force.

Always self-critical, Jiří was sure he had botched the shot. He had driven his brother mad over the years with this kind of pessimism.[54] The shot did indeed deserve low marks for presentation—out of character for the usually elegant Holík boy—but the degree of difficulty was high: it had begun with the puck nearly out of reach, and his body facing away from the intended target.

As though it had an intelligent steering system, the puck threaded through the sea of players and into the net just to the right of the goalie Zinger. The crowd's deafening roar muted the wild cheers of the Czechoslovak players, who mobbed the two Holíks. Jiří bellowed with joy as his brother and teammates grabbed at his shoulders, his jersey, his neck, celebrating wildly.

Jiří wasn't alone in channeling his anger at the USSR into superb play. Famed for his extraordinary power, Václav Nedomanský stood out as one of the strongest of the Czechoslovak players, and ordinarily was also among the most sportsmanlike men on the team. But this was no normal game. Big Ned and Mikhailov had been going at it throughout the tournament. Earlier in the game, Big Ned had smashed Mikhailov to the ice, leading to time in the penalty box for the Czechoslovak forward. Soon after Jiří's goal, Mikhailov got sent off the ice for elbowing.

Now, despite being down a man, the USSR went on the offensive, taking the puck all the way up to the Czechoslovak goal. Dzurilla made a beautiful catch of a shot at his face and sent the puck up the ice toward his teammates. But the nearest skater to the puck was the giant Alexander Ragulin, around the midway point on the ice. Starting nearly twenty feet behind him, Jiří sprinted up, causing the Soviet defenseman to fly past the puck. Ragulin still managed to collect the disk and turned to try to pass it to a teammate, but Jaroslav smashed into his old nemesis, forcing the pass to go awry and end up in Jiří's possession, a slapshot distance from the goal. Czechoslovakia moved the puck around, drawing in closer and closer to the net. Jiří grabbed it not far from where he had scored his goal just five minutes earlier and skated forward until he stood with the disk fifteen feet directly to the left of the goal. Without warning, he centered it to Big Ned, who had floated in and now stood a mere ten feet from the Soviet goalie. Without even waiting to collect himself, Nedomanský smashed the puck with such force that he dropped to the ice on his left knee. The shot blazed to the right of the Soviet goalie, who could do nothing but reach his left gloved hand out after the puck had already flown into the net.

Back in Czechoslovakia, Martina and the Navrátils went bonkers. Martina Navrátilová stood out as a brilliant athlete, often the only girl playing hockey on the ice. Sometimes, as she slapped at the puck on the pond, she pretended to be Big Ned scoring a big goal. Now her imaginary game took on a new reality as she watched Nedomanský's feat.

In Stockholm, the crowd's roaring reached epic levels, and the blue-clad men on the ice appeared to lose all control. Jiří flew around the ice with his teammates, fist pumping, face pointed upward in a perma-grin. To his left, Big Ned tried to skate around in exultation, but he couldn't get anywhere because Jaroslav swallowed him up in a bear hug from behind, while the rest of the team engulfed him from the front. After congratulating the goal scorer, the men took turns hugging Jiří for his brilliant pass. When the referees tried to restore order, Jiří had to go on a rescue mission to find his equipment—his helmet, stick, and gloves—which had all disappeared in the revelry.

The Czechoslovak players believed that the champs would fall apart when they faced a deficit, because they were so rarely in a losing position, but the Soviets took over in the second period. The swirling USSR offense took twelve shots in the period, while Czechoslovakia could only get off six.[55] Future two-time USSR league MVP Kharlamov knocked in a powerful shot from the blue line, some sixty feet away, for the Soviets' first goal on Dzurilla in the tournament. As the Soviet players briskly hugged their young teammate and the USSR supporters in the crowd began to cheer vigorously, more than a hint of worry crept into the Czechoslovak faithful.

Ten minutes later, Golonka incurred a penalty for slashing, leaving his team down a man.[56] The Soviets quickly capitalized. After controlling the puck, they sent it to Firsov, the incumbent MVP of the Soviet hockey league and the leading goal scorer in the tournament, who stood with the puck some ten feet in front and slightly to the left of the spot where Kharlamov had slapped it in. Firsov feinted a move toward the goal, completely spinning a Czechoslovak defender around. Even with multiple blue shirts between him and the goal, Firsov collected himself and crushed the puck past them all, and beyond

Dzurilla's gloved left hand. In one of the most impressive goals of the tournament, the disk came to rest in the back of the goal behind Czechoslovakia's
netminder almost before he even saw it. Just like that, the USSR side looked
refreshed. The Russian players celebrated with real energy, as Coach Tarasov
kissed Firsov full on the lips and the pro-Soviet contingent's noise level rose. [57]

The Red Machine offensive wave left Team Czechoslovakia feeling bereft. [58]
The lead had disappeared and the players sensed their fuel tanks approaching
empty with nearly thirty minutes still left to play. The unusually long tournament had taken its toll, leaving them more tired than usual. As exhaustion
threatened to overcome them, the players dug deep, mining their desire to show
the people at home that they could push through anything to fight—and maybe
even beat—the Soviets once more. [59]

The squads began the third period tied at two, and the arena grew quieter.
The players seemed more tentative, no longer flying about the ice at the same
speed as at the start of the game. The crowd became lively when scoring opportunities appeared, and the whistling picked up whenever a Soviet player did
something objectionable. But otherwise those watching in the stadium appeared
too nervous to even breathe.

Early in the period, it looked like Czechoslovakia's energy and luck had
finally run out as the USSR unleashed a storm of sizzling shots at Dzurilla.
The screaming from the stands grew louder, the crowd begging Czechoslovakia
to do something to halt the terrifying assault from the swarming Soviets. A
Russian player got the puck on the right wing, ready to finish the assault, when
seemingly out of nowhere Jiří appeared, after traversing more than fifty feet of
ice, and threw himself down to block the shot. Moments later the crowd erupted
as he drove toward the Soviet goal with the puck in tow. Under pressure, Jiří
centered the puck to his brother, who had outraced Ragulin toward the goal.
Just before Jaroslav could shoot, the big man brought the Czechoslovak forward
down. Ragulin went to the penalty box, and the crowd came alive.

Looking very much in charge, Soviet coach Tarasov instructed his forces on
the bench. But now a man up, Czechoslovakia went on the offensive, launching
shot after shot at Zinger as the cheering grew. When the Holík brothers drove
swiftly toward the Russian goal, moving in unison and passing the puck back
and forth, Czechoslovakia appeared set to score. But they missed the try just
as Ragulin returned to the ice.

The entire stadium flew into a frenzy. Each side now had the same number of players. Mikhailov grabbed the puck, sprinted up the ice, and drove straight toward Dzurilla, who waited patiently for the Soviet wunderkind. Nearly close enough to touch the big goalie, Mikhailov let his shot fly, only to have Dzurilla swat it away while the fans applauded Little Mouse's agility. Still the USSR continued on the offensive, pounding shot after shot at the Czechoslovak goal with the crowd going wild. In Czechoslovakia, the entire country held its breath. To Martina, the Navrátils, and everyone else who was watching, Dzurilla was playing out of his mind. Viewers everywhere froze with each shot that flew in his direction and exhaled in relief as he made save after save. On the bench, Pitner calmly congratulated his group for its tough work holding off the Soviets.

As the well-conditioned USSR team's effort mounted, Czechoslovakia's defenseman Josef Horešovský found himself increasingly in the middle of the action. Just twenty-two years old, Horešovský stood out as among the youngest but also the biggest and brightest players on the team. He had graduated from high school at sixteen and enrolled in Prague's Charles University at seventeen. He had a temperament that took no pleasure in hurting his opponents, but standing over six feet tall and weighing more than two hundred pounds, he had the physical attributes to play a rough brand of hockey. He was as wide as a couch, and when opponents entered his zone, they came away feeling like they had been hit by a truck.[60] He also smacked the puck as powerfully as anyone. In one league match, he had helped Sparta crush Dukla Jihlava by scoring four separate blistering shots sixty feet from the goal.[61] Now, in the opening minutes of the final period of the most important game in Czechoslovakia's existence, it was Horešovský, with no helmet to protect his head, who anchored the defense in front of Dzurilla and regularly came away with the puck to end Red Machine sets that appeared destined for success.

As the seconds ticked away, the crowd grew louder and more animated. "Czechoslovakia, let's go! Czechoslovakia, let's go!" (*Tjeckien, do toho! Tjeckien, do toho!*). With thirteen minutes remaining in the game, Big Ned got the puck near his own goal. The crowd grew suddenly quiet. Nedomanský skated briefly before slamming a powerful but wild shot from just beyond the red midline. The puck went wide right and bounced off the board to a Soviet player, but Czechoslovakia's Richard Farda snatched the puck away and tapped it cleanly back to Horešovský. The crowd's roar washed over the stadium like a wave. Horešovský gathered the puck just inches in front of the blue line on the right wing, about fifty feet from the Soviet goalie and with an open alley to shoot through. He had practiced shots like this thousands of times. In training, he always aimed for specific spots and could hit them with accuracy, but he knew that in any game there was always an element of luck.

Horešovský reared back and slapped the puck hard, aiming low on the left side of the net. As Zinger threw out his right leg to block the shot, the tiny triangle of space underneath his stick hand shrank, but never completely closed, and the puck snuck through to break the 2–2 tie.

Horešovský would never attempt a bigger shot in his life, but the feeling that came over him was oddly familiar. It was exactly the same as with every winning goal he had ever scored: a weird tingling sensation washed over his entire body, followed by a wave of relaxation and pleasure, as every ounce of stress flowed out of him.[62] When he realized what he had done, Horešovský began to skip—not skate, but actually skip!—across the ice with his stick raised high in his right hand. His teammates tackled him from every direction, all falling onto the surface together as the crowd went ballistic. It took a full minute to pull the players off the big defenseman.

When the game resumed, the players were exuberant, knowing they were up on the Soviets, but they still faced an eternity against a great hockey team. As they switched ends of the ice for the final ten minutes of play, Dzurilla's extraordinary calm reassured them. Nothing could shake the big goalie. When he took to the ice for the final minutes, his teammates patted him on the back, urging him on: "Let's go, Little Mouse!"[63] Yet as well as Dzurilla had performed, the team knew a one-goal lead wasn't enough against the Red Machine. Czechoslovakia's skaters needed to bring something more.

Jaroslav Holík had made a reputation for himself as the greatest fighter in Czechoslovak hockey history. His legend had grown partly as a result of constant fisticuffs. But more than that, it was that in every game he went all-out, like a wild man, to the very last second. In moments like the one he found himself in now, he always wanted to do something more, something that would keep the other side off balance.[64] After his removal from the 1968 national team, Stockholm provided him with a venue to show what he could truly do. When the games ended, he would be tied across the leaderboard for the most points in the tournament, and his ten assists led all players. Yet that would mean nothing if he couldn't do something to help pull his team to victory over the Soviets.

Jaroslav saw his chance as the final ten minutes of play opened and the crowd continued to cheer for Czechoslovakia, chanting "Fight them! Fight them!" (*Bijte je! Bijte je!*). The puck flew to the left boards, around the center line. Jaroslav and Jiří sped over and entered into a vicious battle with a pair of Soviet players. Twisting his body to fend off Petrov, Jiří, now with a bloody gash on the bridge of his nose, gained control and flipped the puck to Jaroslav. The older Holík charged toward the USSR goal with just one defender and the goalie to beat. Driving from the left wing, he leaned to his left and then abruptly cut to the center, leaving the defender lying in a heap on his face. As Jaroslav continued moving right, Zinger stepped out toward him, and Firsov, trailing behind, tried to get to Czechoslovakia's center. But they were too late. Jaroslav tossed in the goal. The roar of the crowd reached its loudest level yet, as the team yet again mobbed a Holík boy. Even Dzurilla, weighed down with mounds of heavy goalie gear, flew over to celebrate his buddy.

Czechoslovakia now led 4–2, but nine very, very long minutes still remained. Because of the physicality of the match, the seemingly spent Czechoslovak players hung on just by a thread.[65] Propelled by boisterous chants of "Fight them!" (*Bijte je!*) from the crowd, both teams continued to attack. The Soviets couldn't get a close, clean shot, but fatigue was clearly starting to overtake Dzurilla. To stymie a desperate attempt by the Soviets from the center line, the goalie dropped to his knees. As he sat on the ice scarcely moving, it was clear that he was nearly out of gas. Ever so slowly, he got to his feet, hoping to make it through the final minutes of the game without disaster striking.

The Soviets went on another blistering offensive, doggedly attacking, while on the bench Suchý paced, urging his teammates on. With two and a half minutes left, the Soviets grabbed the puck and moved it to Ragulin, who stood dead center forty feet in front of the goal. The defenseman uncoiled his big body and slammed a shot low on a line past the collapsing Dzurilla. 4–3! The Soviet faithful came alive, roaring with a volume that belied their small numbers, able for once to outcheer the deflated thousands rooting on Czechoslovakia.

Back in Czechoslovakia, all air seemed to have been sucked out of the country. In Stockholm, the Czechoslovak players became deeply uneasy, sweating through their uniforms. Clearly frustrated and physically and emotionally spent, Dzurilla rose slowly to gird himself for the final two-plus minutes.

As play resumed, the crowd implored Dzurilla and his teammates to hold it together just a bit longer. "Let's go! Let's go!" (*Do toho! Do toho!*). Czechoslovakia had but a one-goal lead. Even as the puck moved back and forth across the ice, for Czechoslovakia's players, and indeed for the entire country, the clock ticked away at a painfully slow pace.[66] But still it *did* move. Meanwhile, the players kept waiting for the Soviet coaches to pull the goalie and replace him with one more skater who might score, but they never did.[67]

With just about a minute left to play, as the crowd began to chant the Czechoslovak goalie's name, Jaroslav lined up for the last major face-off at the center line. Following the battle for control, the puck slid toward Dzurilla. Horešovský rushed back to grab it and Czechoslovakia looked to bring the disk forward. Scrums broke out along the boards as both Jaroslav and Big Ned fought the Soviets for control, but the USSR nabbed the puck and pushed toward Dzurilla. With the seconds dripping away, the Russians attempted a weak shot, which Dzurilla easily stopped with his stick. As the two teams continued to battle, the puck moved back and forth across the ice, rapidly changing possession time and again, but with no one able to get it too close to either net.

Calling the game for Czechoslovak Television, announcer Vladimír Vácha despaired as he looked at the Red Machine, which threatened to tie the game at any moment. But then he looked up and saw Team Czechoslovakia's greatest ally: the clock. As Vácha continued to describe the action, he silently began to count down in his head.[68] Half a minute left. Twenty-five seconds. Twenty. The Russians gain possession and attack. Fifteen. Jaroslav stops the Soviet drive. Ten! The puck gets loose! Czechoslovak players surround it! END!!! Final score: Czechoslovakia–4, USSR–3!

Czechoslovakia's players on the ice threw their hands in the air, tossing their sticks and helmets without regard for gravity, as the men on the bench sprinted to celebrate with them. Knowing Dzurilla's performance had been the key, the Czechoslovak players mobbed their goalie, knocking over their net and again hurling their sticks and helmets into the air. The only one with his helmet still on, Jaroslav rushed through the group, rubbed his head on Dzurilla's chest, and gave the big man's head a giant smooch. From behind, Golonka grabbed Dzurilla's face, pulling his head way back so it looked like it might snap off his neck.

Again, the crowd chanted "Dubček! Dubček!" as young Czechoslovak men from the stands rushed to the ice to hug the players. Feeling like a schoolkid, Golonka slid across the ice on his knees, while booming celebratory explosions pounded in the stands.

Eventually the players collected themselves and—with Suchý joining them—lined up for the playing of Czechoslovakia's national anthem. Vácha, the Czechoslovak announcer, found himself singing out of tune because of the emotion overwhelming him.[69] Even foreign observers like Jim Coleman, the veteran Canadian hockey columnist attending the tournament, were overcome. As Coleman watched a young Czechoslovak woman singing her country's national anthem so loudly that he became convinced that he saw her breath muss the hair of Soviet coach Tarasov in front of her, and as he heard the profoundly moved voices of the Czechoslovak writers who sang behind him, Coleman felt a tightening of his own throat.[70] After the anthem, the Czechoslovak players escaped the ice yet again without shaking the hands of the Soviet players.

When the live broadcast ended in Stockholm, Czechoslovakia state television returned to its studio news coverage. Bursting with joy, TV announcer Milena Vostřáková exuded, "Normally, I drink herbal tea, but today I will toast our hockey players with wine." Downing the glass before her, she added, "Because this is not only a victory in sports, but also a moral one."[71]

News of Czechoslovakia's victory would reverberate around the world. Headlines included "A Great Moment for Czech Pride"[72] and "Czechs stage own overthrow, tip Russians."[73] The *Montreal Gazette* would declare, "All the pent-up Czech emotions were let loose once more as the Czechs beat the Russians for the second time in eight days. There was much more than hockey involved in the show of Czech nationalistic fervor. . . . The reminders of the bitter Czech feelings toward the Russians since the Soviet-led invasion of Czechoslovakia last August always were there."[74]

Back in Czechoslovakia in the moments following the team's victory over the Soviets, there was simply joy. In Jihlava, Jaroslav's wife Marie stayed home to watch one-year-old Andrea, but crowds of boisterous people bounced giddily all over the town, knocking on the doors of the players' houses to applaud them. They soon arrived at Marie's doorstep to cheer her. In Havlíčkův Brod, Jaroslav Sr. slipped out of the house, only to be surrounded by jubilant residents who insisted he should be president of the country, or at least mayor of the town![75] In cities all over the country, parents dropped their kids off with the grandparents and went outside to revel with friends and strangers.

In Prague, Líba, the non-hockey fan who watched the two games against the Soviets as if her life depended upon their outcome, was pregnant with her first child. Her mother feared that the excitement would cause her to go into labor. However, filled with emotion, Líba took to the streets the moment the second game ended to march with well over a hundred thousand others in celebration. Kenneth Skoug, an American diplomat watching the Prague throng that stretched for miles, saw something extraordinary:

> That cheering, marching, tumultuous vortex required no explanation or interpretation. Their transport had only the minimum to do with the love of sport that always had characterized the Czech people. . . . For a small, humiliated nation, deprived of the last vestige of free expression . . . it was a moment of truth. The night air throbbed with the sound of national redemption. I had never seen Czechs so happy. Clearly, the city had not experienced such joy since the defeat of the Nazis in 1945. It was as if their self-respect had been recaptured on that rink in Sweden.[76]

# PART III

## THE RETURN TO WINTER

*Why are people in fact behaving in the way they do? Why do they do all these things that, taken together, form the impressive image of a totally united society giving total support to its government? . . . They are driven to it by fear. . . . Everyone has something to lose and so everyone has reason to be afraid. . . .*

*Order has been established . . . a bureaucratic order of gray monotony that stifles all individuality; of mechanical precision that suppresses everything of unique quality. . . . What prevails is order without life.*

—Václav Havel, "Dear Dr. Husák"[1]

# CHAPTER 10

# Quashed

A s soon as the broadcast of the match ended around 10 P.M., in Czecho-slovakia hundreds of thousands of people turned off their televisions and took to the streets. Traffic from the suburbs overwhelmed the roads to Prague.[1] Within the capital city, a parade of cars drove about, honking horns in celebration. Before long, 150,000 people on foot were in Wenceslas Square, nearly filling the ten-plus acres. Students played trumpets and set off firecrackers. Even in the cold rain, young people climbed the Saint Wenceslas statue waving Czechoslovakia's flag and singing the national anthem. The scores of the two matches against the Soviets, "2:0 4:3," appeared on surfaces all around the square. And it wasn't just in Prague. In dozens of towns and cities, more than 500,000 people marched jubilantly.

It felt like a return to the week of August 21 when, as a united force, Czechs and Slovaks had resisted their invaders. After that momentous summer week, most people in Czechoslovakia had willingly sat on their hands after warnings from their leaders that action could only make things worse. But now they felt empowered again.

Many people carried signs. Some were now old hat. "There were no tanks, so they lost." But others were new. "BREZHNEV 3, DUBČEK 4," echoing the score of that night's match. People chanted. "Russians, go home!" "Today Tarasov, tomorrow Brezhnev!"

Enraged by the presence of some 70,000 troops still on their soil, countless Czechs and Slovaks began to do far more than just celebrate across some two dozen locales where USSR forces were based. In town after town, thousands of Czechs and Slovaks rushed to the buildings that housed the Soviet military, and alternately bellowed out the scores of the hockey matches and "Ivans, go home!" As they did, locals set Soviet flags aflame and belted out Czechoslovakia's national anthem. They threw bricks through barracks' windows and flipped over Soviet military vehicles, which they then set on fire. The demonstrators hurled stones and flaming torches made of newspaper at local security forces who then pounded the protesters with truncheons and tear gas.

The greatest fury was reserved for Prague. Late in the evening, a group of four hundred celebrants left Wenceslas Square, apparently headed to the Soviet Embassy. Only the actions of security forces halted it. Another group of nearly 4,000 headed to the Wenceslas Square office of the Soviet airline Aeroflot. Abruptly, someone threw a brick through the office's front plate-glass window. Someone else began to smash the office's neon sign. Others rushed inside and grabbed everything that they could carry—heavy furniture, filing cabinets, posters, models of Soviet airplanes, even pictures of Vladimir Lenin— and tossed it all into the street. The crowd stomped on the items and then created a bonfire out of them. Only after busloads of riot police in full gear arrived did the crowd finally disperse. [2]

The following morning, Czechs and Slovaks woke up still elated from the hockey victory, but now also feeling a sense of foreboding. Would there be consequences for the actions of that night in Czechoslovakia?

They also faced a surreal fact. There was still more hockey to be played in Stockholm.

Team Czechoslovakia had one more hockey match to play, and it was against the home team. As long as they didn't lose, the Czechoslovak players would bring home their country's first World Championship since 1949, the year before the imprisonment of the national hockey team. On Sunday, March 30, Czechoslovakia took on Sweden in both teams' final game of the tournament. As play began, something seemed off. In part because they knew that they merely needed to tie, the Czechoslovak players seemed less focused on winning than on trying not to lose. Their play looked tentative. Even more important, after their matches against the Soviet Union, the men from Czechoslovakia were physically, mentally, and emotionally spent. [3]

Late in the first period, Dzurilla deflected a shot, but the rebound got stuck between his pads and he accidentally let the puck slip in for a goal that put Sweden up 1–0. [4] From there, it became vital for the men from Czechoslovakia to find a way to score. Multiple times, they smacked shots from point-blank range, but terrific play by Holmqvist, the Swedish netminder, kept everything out of the net. At one point, Jiří Holík found the puck sitting on his stick right in front of Holmqvist, who had fallen to the ice. All he had to do was lift it over the goalie's stick . . . but the try was no good. Sweden took the match and the missed goal chance would haunt Jiří for the rest of his life.[5]

In the locker room afterward, Czechoslovakia's players sat quietly, seemingly unable to change out of their hockey gear. Between exhaustion and grief, some of the men couldn't even bring themselves to move at all. Sweden, Czechoslovakia, and the USSR all finished with identical records, each having won eight matches and lost two. The Soviets took the gold medal because, in the tournament as a whole, they had scored many more goals than they had allowed. Sweden took the silver. Czechoslovakia, the bronze.[6]

Then one of the Czechoslovak players finally said it: "We beat them twice! We beat the fucking Russians twice!" From the beginning, all that their people had asked of them was to defeat their country's enemy, their occupier. They had done that for their people and they had done it twice![7] By the time that they were flying home, the players celebrated with beer and champagne. Not everyone joined them in raising a glass. Officials from Czechoslovakia's embassy chastised the players. It was public knowledge that the players had refused to shake hands with the Soviets. Worst of all, they had taped over the stars on their jerseys. Czechoslovakia's authorities were furious. "You put on quite a show, didn't you!? What an embarrassment!"[8]

When the players landed in Prague, they saw a sea of people waiting around the airport for them. The crowd engulfed the men, treating them as if they *had* won the World Championships. The fans held dozens of signs, but one stood out: "It doesn't matter you didn't win the gold, those two Fridays were worth it all."[9]

What happened next suggested that in the short time the players had been away something big had changed in Czechoslovakia.

The players were sent to an old terminal at the airport, where a member of the country's Athletic Federation greeted them. He thanked them for their service and then informed them that there would be no celebration in Prague. Instead, the federation would take them individually to bus or train stations, where they could each make arrangements to get themselves home. The events of the night of March 28 in Czechoslovakia had shown that if anything could still bring out the passions of the people, it was their hockey team. The authorities were now making sure that nothing like that night would happen again. The first step was to prevent any more celebrations of the team's Stockholm victories. [10]

The "Hockey Riots," and the Czechoslovak government's inability or unwillingness to halt it, provided the excuse the Soviets needed to remove Czechoslovakia's recalcitrant reformers once and for all. In fact, the event seemed so tailor-made to the Soviets' purposes that countless Czechs and Slovaks—including even Dubček himself—insisted that StB agents must have been behind the Aeroflot attack as a false flag operation, even though there was no conclusive evidence to support such a view. Whatever the case, on March 30, as Czechoslovakia's hockey team took on Sweden in its final match, the USSR leadership, in an emergency meeting, decided to use the riots as the impetus to push a change. The Soviets openly condemned "rightist extremists" and "counterrevolutionaries" for the organized "mass hooligan attacks" on Soviet installations in Czechoslovakia on March 28. On April 1, Soviet defense minister Andrei Grechko and deputy foreign minister Vladimir Semenov descended upon Prague to hand deliver a note warning the Czechoslovak government that the Soviets would intervene if it could not maintain peace. [11]

Czechoslovakia's leadership immediately responded with a statement making clear that it would now move in lockstep with the Soviets. Czechoslovak leaders declared that, far from a spontaneous burst of national joy, the Hockey Riots had been planned in advance by "rightist and anti-socialist forces" as well as the media, and that the government would hunt down and punish the perpetrators. On April 2, the government formally passed a series of measures "to secure peace and order." In addition to formally instituting new forms of censorship, it planned to use the army to aid the police in future cases of unrest. [12]

When the hockey players first came home from Stockholm, much of daily life obscured what the country was facing. This was particularly the case for Jiří Holík. For Jiří, life had already changed dramatically a couple of years earlier, before the Soviet invasion, when he had become smitten with Marie Rosendorf, a young nurse he'd seen around town in Jihlava. Just as Marie Prchalová had been with Jaroslav, Miss Rosendorf was skeptical of the intentions of a Dukla hockey player. By now, though, Jiří had outgrown his youthful shyness, and asked that she at least get to know him before she drew any conclusions about what he was like. It helped that Jiří had grown up to be exceptionally good looking, not unlike a stocky Steve McQueen, but with less sharp facial features. Even better, he also had a way about him that made people feel comfortable. There was something about Jiří's deep, gentle voice that made others feel like he was really listening and genuinely cared about what they had to say. Most of all, though, his warm, irresistible smile made them feel that he was truly happy to see them. Eventually, the young woman gave Jiří a chance and, after dating for some time, they got engaged. The wedding took place soon after the players' return from Stockholm and offered a reprieve from the darkness overtaking Czechoslovakia.

The escape, though, was only temporary; there was no avoiding the new reality that Czechs and Slovaks confronted in the weeks after the Hockey Riots. On April 4, just after the Dukla hockey players returned to Jihlava, tragedy hit their hometown. At 6 P.M., at a fair in the town's Peace Square, a man in a long cloak suddenly appeared and rushed toward the square's fountain. He was on fire. Jihlava now had its own Jan Palach. Someone tried throwing a blanket on the man, but the flames burned right through. The adults quickly evacuated the children as the man, Evžen Plocek, who had been severely burned all over, gasped for air.

Nearly forty years of age, Plocek was a manager at Motorpal, an automotive parts company and the biggest factory in Jihlava. Plocek had been a strong believer in communism—grateful for a system in which workers didn't have to worry about losing their jobs or beg for food—but over time he became dismayed by the disconnect between communist values and the reality in Czechoslovakia. The 1968 reforms, therefore, were like a breath of fresh air to Plocek, a chance for communism to work for people as it should. The Soviet invasion and then the quashing of Czechs' and Slovaks' resistance efforts left him devastated and angry.

Between January and April of 1969, there were twenty-nine reports of people in Czechoslovakia self-immolating. Most who did appeared to suffer from severe mental illness, but Palach, Jan Zajíc (another young man in Prague), and Plocek all seemed to act principally out of a selfless desire to protest the crushing weight of the Soviet-imposed normalization. Plocek died on April 9. Three days later, the local cemetery overflowed when 5,000 people gathered to celebrate him and to demonstrate against the occupation.[13]

Plocek's funeral marked the end of public unity against the occupation in Jihlava. In the coming months, the local branch of the Communist Party, on orders from higher up, began investigating the anti-occupation actions of countless Jihlavans. The branch ousted from their positions a number of high-ranking politicians, the editor of the local newspaper, and employees of the local library and museum.[14]

Meanwhile, the national authorities started to deal more aggressively with those who had not properly accepted the presence of the Soviets on their soil. An investigation began into the hockey team's behavior in Stockholm. Coach Pitner had to confront the matter of his players' refusal to shake hands with the Soviets. On four separate occasions, his army superiors questioned him. Eventually, they accepted his explanation that it was the responsibility of the losing team to initiate the handshake, but a coterie in Czechoslovakia continued to attack him. Pitner received letters that slammed him and the entire team as a gang of counterrevolutionaries who did not appreciate their Russian "liberators."[15]

The taped-over stars were a bigger deal. The authorities called in the team's massage therapist Miroslav Martínek, who had been tasked with tracking and maintaining the team's uniforms. Prior to the meeting, Martínek grabbed the relevant jerseys and ripped them right at the star. He showed the authorities the ripped jerseys and explained that the tape had been used to keep them from tearing more.[16]

But when Jaroslav Holík got called in, he played it straight. He told the review board that, yes, he had taped over his star. The investigators labeled him the main instigator in this act of "tomfoolery" and sent him to the executive board of the Ice Hockey Federation. Clearly hoping that the matter would blow over, the board did not take immediate action. Nevertheless, when the authorities later discovered photographs of Jaroslav with tape covering the star on his jersey, they made sure to confiscate them, even going so far as to seize hundreds, if not thousands, of copies of unsold magazines with the picture.[17]

Some in Czechoslovakia blamed the national hockey team for inflaming passions at home. An article in the local Jihlava paper stated that the players should be punished for inciting the riots.[18] The authorities were reluctant to do much against the wildly popular squad, which provided such great propaganda, but they soon made an example out of others.

Claiming that the media was partly responsible for the Hockey Riots, the authorities launched a special commission to investigate the television broadcast. As the second match against the Soviets had concluded, Vladimír Vácha, who had announced the game on Czechoslovak Television, had exclaimed,

"Enjoy this jubilation well." Those investigating claimed that Vácha said, "Celebrate it well at home, you know how," suggesting that people in Czechoslovakia should riot. Vácha went to the investigators and listened with them to the audio, and nowhere could they find the offending sentence. Even still, he suddenly found himself out of a job, ending his career in television. A similar fate befell Milena Vostřáková, the television announcer in Czechoslovakia who, after the end of the game broadcast, had come on the screen and raised a toast to the players, "Because this is not only a victory in sports, but also a moral one." The investigators informed Vostřáková that her words had sparked the anti-Soviet riots and sacked her, thus ending her television career as well. [19]

Ultimately, Czechoslovakia's new hard-line leaders went after countless opponents of the Soviet invasion, but they were particularly quick to punish writers whose ink had been spilled in the service of fighting the invaders. The Communists purged nearly half of the 4,000 members of the Union of Journalists and fired forty-five of the eighty editors employed at *Rudé právo*, the Communist Party's official newspaper. [20] Sportswriter Miloslav Jenšík, who led the efforts of *Svět v obrazech* in August 1968 to publish daily issues that helped support resistance to the occupation, found himself in trouble after his return from Stockholm. The authorities assigned *Svět v obrazech* a new set of administrators, who informed many of the staff at the magazine that they "no longer had the faith of the working people." Jenšík and his colleagues were flabbergasted and grew even more so when they then were forced to sign a document in which they "requested" dismissal. One of Jenšík's colleagues conferred with a lawyer, who told the man, "Don't be crazy. Sign it or they'll crush you and your whole family."

Of course, the single person the Soviets and the Czechoslovak Communist hardliners most wanted to fire was none other than Alexander Dubček. The Hockey Riots finally provided the excuse they needed to remove the face of the Prague Spring and finalize the coronation of a new leader, Gustáv Husák ["HU-saakh"].

Born on January 10, 1913, Husák had become a member of Czechoslovakia's Communist Party when he was just sixteen years old. During World War II, he moved his way up to become one of the leading Communists in Slovakia. At the end of the war he helped lead the fight to free Slovakia from fascist forces and then was part of a group of Communists who negotiated the political future of Czechoslovakia. He did so while also arguing for Slovakia to receive significant autonomy. After the war, Husák quickly rose in power within the Communist Party and played a major part in crushing democratic opposition to the Communists in Slovakia.[21]

During the final years leading up to the 1948 coup, the Czech Communist leaders undercut previous promises to grant Slovakia greater independence and warned Slovak Communists to stop talking about divisions between the Czech and Slovak regions of the country. In 1951, the Communist Party purges targeted prominent Slovak Communists for the crime of "bourgeois nationalism," meaning they had placed the cause of Slovakia over the interests of the Party. The leading Slovak implicated was Vladimír Clementis, the country's foreign minister. Clementis was included among the accused in the Rudolf Slánský show trial and, like Slánský, he was found guilty and then executed in 1952.

Husák found himself implicated in the "bourgeois nationalist" witch hunt as well. In 1951, he was arrested for "treason and sabotage." In an effort to force a "confession," Husák's jailers tortured him, but his resolute unwillingness to claim any guilt probably saved him from being put to death. In 1954, Husák received his sentence: life imprisonment.[22]

In the growing openness of the 1960s, government commissions investigated the purges of the 1950s and determined that the charge of "bourgeois nationalism" had been bogus.[23] In 1963, the charges against Husák were overturned, and over time he rose back up within the Party ranks. As Dubček came to power, Husák publicly urged support for the changes just beginning to emerge. He spoke of "ardently" welcoming and supporting Dubček's call for reform and the election of Dubček as head of the Party. In February, Husák even expressed a desire to hasten the pace of reform.[24]

There was reason to remain cautious about Husák's sincerity. To be sure, during his imprisonment by the Communists he had courageously withstood three years of brutal interrogations. But he also showed a willingness to give up his principles for the sake of his self-preservation. In the 1940s and leading up to his arrest in 1951, he had agreed to halt any behavior that displeased the authorities and even criticize his previous positions if it meant avoiding detention.

When the Soviets kidnapped Dubček at the start of the 1968 invasion, Husák went to Moscow to join in the negotiations. He initially stood up to the Soviets, but he also impressed Brezhnev and company with his pragmatism.

He struck many people at home as someone who simply wanted to help the country move forward by restoring calm and fixing the economy. In the weeks and months that followed, Husák moved away from his previous reform stance to more of a "realist" position. He increasingly hewed to the Soviet line, pushed to roll back the Prague Spring reforms, and found the Soviets more and more fulsome in their praise of his actions. By April 1969, he had gained the support of the bulk of Czechoslovakia's leadership, in part because of his personal history of persecution, which led others to believe that he would never permit Czechoslovakia to return to its repressive 1950s ways. [25]

Dubček did not trust Husák, believing his Slovak compatriot had long demonstrated "serious character flaws and unscrupulous ways." Dubček feared that Husák would abandon the country's reforms in the name of satisfying the Soviets' and his own ambitions. The Soviet officials who visited following the Hockey Riots met with Czechoslovakia's leaders to lobby for Dubček's ouster. Dubček himself saw the writing on the wall and proposed as his replacement Prime Minister Oldřich Černík, who had been a major supporter of the Prague Spring reforms. Černík refused. With no other options, Dubček resigned on April 17 and, in his place, nominated Husák, who had garnered Brezhnev's support. Dubček was permitted to stay in the government as chairman of the Federal Assembly. [26]

Husák's reign did not begin with all-out repression, but he would eventually ramp up the normalization process and undercut nearly all the Prague Spring reforms. When Husák took power in April 1969, he reinstituted strict censorship, which included banning several periodicals. Knowing that demonstrations were likely on the first anniversary of the Soviet invasion, a government team led by the former reformer Černík prepared its forces to "handle" protesters.

The change in just one year was stark. In August 1968, Czechoslovakia's demonstrators had confronted Soviet and other Warsaw Pact soldiers. But, on August 21, 1969, when crowds took to the streets to demonstrate in thirty cities around the country, they were met now by thousands of Czechoslovakia's own police and soldiers and a tank regiment. Hundreds of citizens were injured, five were killed, and nearly 2,500 arrested. There would be no more major public protests against the occupation.

The following day, the government enacted legislation that established jail sentences for anything that didn't fit with the regime's sense of public order. The legislation also gave officials wide latitude to hear criminal court cases and pass down convictions, allowed employees to be fired for a "lack of confidence," and permitted the government to dissolve any organization it chose. On August 29, Husák openly praised the 1968 invasion, explaining that it had saved the country from a "counterrevolution." The USSR and Czechoslovakia soon began drawing up a new treaty of friendship. [27] As they did, people in Czechoslovakia quietly began to circulate a joke: "Did you hear that Husák has the biggest car in the world? The seat is in Prague, but the steering wheel is in Moscow." [28]

In the fall of 1969, the Czechoslovak leadership began a series of purges, inspired in part by a dossier that Brezhnev sent over to show, step-by-step, how to remove undesirables from the Communist Party. Panelists began the process of interviewing each person in Czechoslovakia's Communist Party to determine whose membership might be renewed. Those interviewed had to assert their support for the Party, renounce the Prague Spring reforms and anything that they might have done in support of the reforms, and express thanks for the Warsaw Pact troops' "fraternal assistance" that "saved" the country in August 1968. In some cases, those screened were even required to provide written denunciations of friends and coworkers who had supported the reforms. Even then, people with an actual history of supporting the reforms or opposing the invasion typically did not receive new Party membership cards. Between the logistics and the fact that over a million and a half people needed to be screened, the process took many months.

But after a bit more than a year, Czechoslovakia's Communists had purged as many as half a million Party members. Those purged were typically demoted at work or even fired. Their children found it hard to get into a university, and even their spouses faced the threat of punishment. [29] In September 1969, the government had also initiated a campaign to fire university instructors who had supported the Prague Spring reforms and forced them to shift to manual labor. The regime shut down twenty-one different academic institutions and fired hundreds of their staff. The normalizers also hit reform-minded trade unions, dismissing one-fifth of all union members for their "transgressions."

The hardliners also came down on celebrities who had used their fame to push back against the occupation. Marta Kubišová, one of the country's most popular singers, had recorded a song that became the peace anthem of the occupied people at the time of the invasion. For her efforts, the authorities eventually brought Kubišová up on false charges of making "pornographic" photographs and banned her from the music industry. With no other employment options, she was forced to work in a factory that made polythene bags.[30]

The crackdown also hit the formerly untouchable Emil Zátopek. Even in 1968, at the age of forty-six, Zátopek remained perhaps Czechoslovakia's most adored athletic icon. Though he had sided with the Party in the past, in June 1968, Zátopek signed the pro-reform "Two Thousand Words" manifesto. In August, he verbally confronted the invading Soviet soldiers and, in the months that followed, denounced the occupation. In response, in 1969 the army and Communist Party both expelled Zátopek, who suddenly found himself unemployed. With no other options, eventually he got a job at a company that searched for underground resources and was willing to hire people who had run afoul of the state. Zátopek left his home and wife in Prague for the wilderness, where his new job required him to dig from dawn to dusk. Under pressure from the regime, he eventually recanted his support for the 1968 reforms as well as his opposition to the invasion and the normalization that ensued.[31]

In fact, many who had supported the Prague Spring reforms did an about-face once normalization kicked in, but it was usually too late. Prime Minister Černík completely walked back his previous reform positions and even his condemnation of the invasion. For some time, he was able to retain his government post. But in January 1970 Černík was forced out as prime minister, and in June he was expelled from the Party. He couldn't glaze over what he had done: "I have shat away my position and my honor."[32]

The big fish, though, was Dubček, who had no chance of escaping the normalizers' nets. Dubček pledged to support the new regime, but he refused to disavow the Prague Spring reforms. By the end of 1969, he had been removed from his position in the Federal Assembly. Some hardliners even wanted to put him on trial for treason, but the Czechoslovak leaders simply wanted to get him out of the public eye. They began to discuss potential ambassadorships with Dubček. The initial offers included Ghana, Mongolia, and North Korea, which were all so far away that Czechs and Slovaks just might forget that he existed. In January 1970, the hardliners sent Dubček to serve as ambassador to Turkey. Yet, even there, they continued to undercut him, even sending a commission to investigate Dubček and the embassy. It was clear that Czechoslovakia's leadership was pushing him to defect. Dubček refused to abandon his country, feeling that his dissenting voice was still needed. However, in June, he found himself expelled from the Party and forced to find employment in a manual labor position in Slovakia.[33]

Following the events in Stockholm, the players from the national hockey team wondered if the regime would crack down on them as well. The initial response had not looked good. Upon returning, Jan Havel, one of the men who had taped over the star on his jersey, went to meet with Antonín Kapek, a high-ranking and hard-line member of the Communist Party and the director general of the state-owned company that ran Havel's Sparta Prague team. As Havel walked into the Kapek's office, the director general placed a glass of champagne and a bag of money in front of him. Havel was eager to celebrate and to receive what looked to be a bonus. Then Kapek pulled out a picture of Havel wearing the tape over the star on his jersey and asked, "So, what happens when you tear your jersey?" Havel stormed out, terrified that his career and possibly his freedom were in jeopardy. Kapek called Havel back the following day and apologized for "overreacting." He added, "You can remain captain of the Sparta squad, but you are off the national team."[34] However, Havel's case appeared to have more to do with the feelings of the man who controlled the Sparta Prague team than those of the actual Czechoslovak Hockey Federation. The federation didn't suspend anyone, so in March 1970 everything appeared set for the squad to head off to the next world championship tournament.

Except for Golonka, who had retired, the entire top group from 1969 returned, but they didn't seem ready to compete again. Both Suchý and Nedomanský performed terrifically in the World Championships, but on the whole 1970 was a lackluster tournament for Czechoslovakia, which finished with five wins (and one tie) in ten matches for a third-place finish. Worst of all, the team lost handily twice to the Soviets, who took their *eighth* consecutive world title. Czechoslovakia's authorities didn't appear terribly concerned about their team's poor showing, but instead seemed focused on keeping everyone in line. Upon the team's return home, the government denounced the behavior of its own fans, who had jeered the Soviets mercilessly.[35]

By then, there was relatively little public misbehavior in Czechoslovakia to upset the regime. With each passing month, government repression grew more all-encompassing and deflating, and most Czechs and Slovaks gave up. They stopped resisting and many even willingly attended events *in support of* the regime and the USSR. Over the course of 1969, more than a million Czechs and Slovaks had attended events organized by the Union for Czechoslovak-Soviet Friendship. In 1970, people grew even more quiescent. No major protests marked the second anniversary of the invasion, and some local Party activists even held ceremonies of *thanks* to the Soviets for "liberating" Czechoslovakia in 1968. [36]

As word spread of each new punishment the government imposed, Jiří Holík grew increasingly worried. On the ice, Jiří had always driven his brother crazy with his pessimism whenever their team fell behind, and now his tendency to fear the worst cropped up in a realm with greater consequences. Throughout his life, Jiří had generally avoided politics and lived in a world where he could focus on hockey and his family. Now, though, he grew deeply concerned that one of his few forays out of that world might have been costly. He had been so angered by the Soviet invasion that he hadn't hesitated to quit the Communist Party, but now he feared that it might have been a big mistake. Under the new hard-line regime, his position as a hockey star might not provide him with protection. Far more than worrying about what could happen to himself, Jiří found unbearable the idea that his daughter, who had been born in 1970, might suffer. Perhaps she would never be admitted into the university or . . . who knows what the government could do?

Jaroslav, though, didn't worry that much about such things. In general, he just acted in whatever way felt natural, usually with a furious level of effort. When the action was done, it was done. Regret was not really part of Jaroslav Holík's psyche. Not for a moment did he look back wishing that he had done anything differently in Stockholm in 1969, least of all his move to tape over the star on his jersey.

But it all came back to bite him.

Following the 1969 World Championships, Czechoslovakia's press began to write about the "unhealthy currents" developing in the country's hockey program. After the 1970 World Championships, the rumblings got louder. One day Jaroslav received word that he was off the national team and would not be invited to attend the 1971 World Championships. Coach Pitner told others that Jaroslav had been removed because of his "lack of discipline." The Czechoslovakia Hockey Federation, meanwhile, informed Jaroslav that he would not be on the team because he was not playing well, which felt like nonsense given that he clearly remained one of the best center forwards in the country. No one ever told Jaroslav officially that his removal was for political reasons . . . but one day, deep within the records kept by Czechoslovakia's secret police, there would be a section devoted to "hidden enemies," which included a file with the name "Jaroslav Holík" printed on the first page. The file included a picture of Jaroslav in Stockholm with tape covering the star on his jersey. A typewritten memo noted that, "This picture was a source of much trouble [for Holík]. . . . He was penalized for his transgression by being removed from the national team."

Jaroslav had lived his life according to the principle that, as long as he was good enough in hockey, the Communists would not dare touch him. But for the second time, he found that there was in fact a line and, yet again, he had crossed it. [37]

## CHAPTER 11

# Crossing the Line

D espite everything shaking the country, daily life continued. And with it, so did hockey.

Even without Jaroslav, Team Czechoslovakia felt confident going into the 1971 World Championships played in March and April in Bern, Switzerland. The core of the squad from the past few years remained. The defense was led by a group of players in their prime, most notably the twenty-six-year-old Suchý, new Golden Stick winner František Pospíšil, Josef Horešovský, and Oldřich Machač. On offense, veterans like Nedomanský, Jiří Holík, Josef Černý, Richard Farda, and Jiří Kochta continued to lead the way.

Much of the excitement surrounding the team involved new additions. Two outstanding twenty-one-year-olds had raised the ceiling on the team's potential. The short but stocky right-winger Vladimír Martinec of Pardubice had taken Czechoslovakia's league by storm with wily, creative, improvisational play. Meanwhile, big, strong center Ivan Hlinka of Litvínov made his presence felt through his innate sense of strategy, natural charisma, and ease at creating scores. Despite his youth, Hlinka's intelligence and magnetic poise made him one of the national team leaders almost instantly. Martinec and Hlinka were joined by other youngsters like defenseman Jiří Bubla and wingers Bohuslav Šťastný and Eduard Novák.

But one addition above all others gave the team a reason to think that it might be ready to step up a notch and, surprisingly, it was at a position where the squad already had a well-known figure. In 1963, when he was nineteen years old, Prague-born goalie Jiří Holeček had joined Dukla Jihlava in order to complete his military service. Coach Pitner saw that Holeček had potential but was not ready to supplant the team's incumbent goaltender, so he sent the newcomer to Dukla Košice in Slovakia on a one-year loaner deal. Holeček performed so well that Košice never allowed him to return.[1] In sharp contrast to the 200-plus-pound Dzurilla, Holeček stood a lean 160 pounds in a five-foot, eleven-inch frame. Like most top-notch goalies, Holeček had lightning-quick reflexes in both his hands and feet. But unlike more conventional players like Dzurilla, Holeček resembled an acrobat, throwing his body onto the ice and all around the crease in front of the net to block shots. In the 1970–71 season, he supplanted the popular Dzurilla as Czechoslovakia's top netminder. It was Holeček who would anchor Czechoslovakia's defense in the 1971 World Championships.

The tournament opened *terribly* for Czechoslovakia, which lost its first two matches. Not knowing what else to do, the coaches brought in each player to discuss how to improve. When Suchý walked in, the defenseman offered a simple explanation. "I am playing like total shit, I know, but you can't expect anything amazing from me when I don't have any beer or cigarettes." The coaches took action. The next day Suchý received a delivery of four cartons of cigarettes and several crates of imported Pilsner beer.[2] In the following match, Czechoslovakia crushed West Germany 9–1 and then eagerly awaited its next opponent: the USSR.

Despite the two and a half years that had elapsed since the invasion, in matches involving the USSR the Swiss crowd let the Soviets have it, jeering and whistling constantly. During the playing of the Soviet anthem after the USSR's defeat of the US in the tournament, the crowd yelled so loudly that the music couldn't even be heard.[3] But that derision was nothing compared to that felt by Czechoslovakia's players, including Holeček.

Unlike the Holíks, Holeček didn't have a strong personal reason to dislike the Communists. His family had little before 1948, and it still had little once the Communists came to power. However, the occupation did something to him. He was living in Košice on August 21, 1968, and went outside to see what was going on. Abruptly, a tank turned its gun toward him, forcing Holeček and a group of other residents to drop to the ground. From that moment on, he hated the Soviets.

He also felt irritation over the attention a member of the Soviet team received. For years, the biggest weakness on the Soviet team had been at goaltender, but after 1969 the Soviets began playing a teenager named Vladislav Tretiak in the net. Born in 1952, Tretiak performed exceptionally well in the 1970 World Championships, giving up an average of just over one goal per match. As observers gushed over the Soviet wunderkind, Holeček bristled. He believed he was a better goalie than Tretiak, who he felt only found so much success because the players surrounding him were so talented. Holeček would bring his loathing of the Soviets and his frustration over Tretiak's acclaim with him onto the ice any time Czechoslovakia played the USSR.

Holeček's first big chance came on March 24 in the first of two times Czechoslovakia would play the Soviets in the 1971 tournament. He was fired up and set the tone for his team. Right after blocking a Soviet attempt on goal, he yelled at his opponents, "It's not your day, and it won't be next time, either!"[4] It was a thrilling contest. Each time one side scored, the other soon matched. When the horn sounded, the two sides had tied 3–3. From there, Czechoslovakia went on a roll, winning all its remaining matches, including a 5–2 victory over the Soviets. Suchý was again named the tournament's top defenseman and Holeček was named the best goaltender.

The USSR took its ninth consecutive world title, but the event had also served as that year's European championship. In matches only involving teams from Europe, Czechoslovakia had compiled the best record in the tournament, and was therefore named European champion, ahead of the USSR.

The following year, Czechoslovakia would have the chance to do more. The year 1972 would include separate Olympic and World Championship tournaments, the latter to be hosted in Prague. Czechoslovakia's team had terrific up-and-coming players, and its veterans were superb and solidly still in their prime. The country might, at long last, win its first world title since 1949 and possibly even the first hockey Olympic gold medal in its history!

But Czechoslovakia would have to do so without Europe's best defenseman.

In September, just a few months before the team was to fly to Japan for the Winter Olympics, Jan Suchý took Dukla teammate Ladislav Šmíd and Ota Morávek, the manager of a local pub, roe deer hunting. On the way back, the group stopped at the pub for a beer and a shot, and then began the drive home. The men were in a great mood, chatting animatedly, and Suchý, the driver, stopped focusing on the road. Suddenly, he found himself too close to the edge and panicked. He tried downshifting and hit the gas, which caused them to go into a sharp slide. The car smashed directly into a tree. Morávek was an exceptionally heavy man and the seat belt wouldn't fit around him, so he never used one. With nothing to restrain him, the impact of the collision threw Morávek out of the car. He did not survive.

The police took Suchý to Jihlava, where he registered a blood alcohol level of 0.038 percent, below what is usually considered high risk. They then took him to jail in Brno, where a prosecutor explained the situation. "Comrade Suchý, if you join the Party, we could let you off with probation. After all, there was not that much alcohol in your blood." Suchý refused. He was sickened by the corruption of it all. It seemed wrong to him that simply by joining the Communist Party, the rules didn't apply to you. He told the prosecutor, "I did what I did and I should be punished." He received a prison sentence of eighteen months.

Once the sentence was handed down in November, after he had already been jailed for two months, the authorities told Suchý that he could serve the rest of his time the following summer, after the hockey season was over. On November 23, he returned to play. From the moment he went back to the ice, opposing crowds showered him with insults, calling him a criminal. The heckling never really bothered Suchý,[5] but there was the question of how the entire experience would affect his hockey. The answer came quickly. On November 30, Dukla Jihlava took on Dukla Košice, which had the league's best goalie in Holeček. Within a forty-seven-second span in the first period, Suchý scored three goals. Whatever his problems on solid land, Jan Suchý remained a genius on ice.

The 1972 Olympics were scheduled for early February. After the September accident, Suchý had been removed from the national team. Despite his November release from prison, for the authorities it was far too soon to consider reinstating the defenseman. Suchý would not be part of Czechoslovakia's Olympic team in Japan.

However, a different star suddenly found himself with a surprise invitation to join the squad.

After the Stockholm tape incident, it had seemed that Jaroslav Holík's brash, outrageous behavior had finally caught up with him, but in 1972 it became clear yet again that Czechoslovakia's authorities were willing to overlook a lot for those whom they deemed essential. When a position on the national team suddenly opened up, the coaches jumped at the excuse to add Jaroslav to the roster. He was overjoyed. For the first time in Jaroslav Holík's career, the twenty-nine-year-old heartbeat of Czechoslovakia's national team would get to compete in the Olympics.

Team Czechoslovakia arrived in Japan in late January for the Sapporo winter games. If the US had felt like another world to the Czechoslovak players, then Japan felt like a totally different universe. The players walked around Tokyo, mouths agape at the luxury hotels, the palm trees in hotel hallways, the koi ponds, and especially the electronics sold in the shops. Then they headed north to Sapporo. Jiří had attended the Olympics in Innsbruck and Grenoble, but for the first time in his career, the surrounding area *looked* like the winter games should: five feet of snow everywhere and surrounded by mountains.

Expectations for Team Czechoslovakia jumped when it opened with a 14–1 blowout of Poland, but next, out of nowhere, the usually lowly American team upset Czechoslovakia 5–1. The following day, the US squad ran into Soviet coach Tarasov, who in his inimitably dramatic way dropped to one knee and put his hand over his heart to express his appreciation for what the Americans had done to his team's top foe.[6] Czechoslovakia would need to be perfect the rest of the way. In the next match, both Jaroslav and Jiří scored in an easy 7–1 win over Finland. Then, in a tough match against Sweden, Jaroslav scored the first goal and fought to control the puck in a set that led to Horešovský scoring what turned out to be the winner. Czechoslovakia would face the Soviet Union in the tournament's final match for the Olympic gold medal.

Then something crazy happened.

On Saturday, February 12, the day before the deciding game, Czechoslovakia's sports authorities brought an indecent proposal to Coach Pitner, who in turn sent longtime star Josef Černý, the captain of the squad, to speak to his teammates about how to proceed. Černý had been known for years as the source of much of the fun on the national team, especially through the tall tales that he loved to tell. He raised carrier pigeons and he entertained his teammates with stories of how he had trained the birds to become marathon runners.[7] Now, though, he showed zero mirth. "Our team's leadership has just come to me with a proposal that it says was brought to it by the Soviet management. We have been asked to rig this match so that we tie." Presumably, the idea was that a tie score would allow the Eastern Bloc to finish with the gold (Soviets) and silver (Czechoslovakia).

Most of the team expressed disgust. They felt that intentionally throwing any match was repellant. And to do so against the USSR was unimaginable.

The players overwhelmingly voted down the proposal. But Černý was so disturbed by the fact that the squad had even been asked to consider it that he quit the team. His match the next day against the Soviet Union was the last he ever played for Czechoslovakia's national team. Most of the rest of the team was badly shaken up as well. For years it had bothered the players that people at home thought they *had* thrown matches against the Soviets. To actually be asked to do so now was beyond the pale.

Team Czechoslovakia had the opportunity now for its first ever Olympic gold in hockey, but by game time a number of the players felt off balance, even unnerved, as a result of the request to rig the match. Maybe the players' discomfort had no effect on how well the teams performed, but the game was a bloodbath, with Soviets taking an easy 5–2 victory and their third straight Olympic gold. Czechoslovakia finished with the bronze, behind the silver-medal-winning US.[8]

However, even before the match ended, there was time for the enmity between the two teams to rear its ugly head again. Tarasov had never gotten over his anger from the matches against Czechoslovakia in 1968 and 1969. As the Soviets pulled away toward the end of the game in Sapporo, Tarasov launched a stream of obscenities at the Czechoslovak players. Skating by, Nedomanský heard Tarasov's screed. Already loathing the Soviets, and frustrated by yet another lost opportunity for gold, Big Ned snapped. After getting the puck, he turned up the ice, pivoted toward the Soviet bench, and fired! Some claimed that the shot nailed Coach Chernyshev, but fortunately there were no serious injuries.

The moment proved to be pivotal—and not because of Nedomanský. Over the years, Tarasov's superiors had lost patience with the face of Soviet hockey as he engaged in serious acts of insolence and insubordination. Perhaps the most egregious case had occurred when, in a Soviet league match in which USSR chief Leonid Brezhnev was in attendance, Tarasov had pulled his army team from the ice because of his displeasure with the referees. Eventually, he agreed to send his players back out to finish play, but only after the minister of defense entered the locker room and ordered him to do so. Now, Tarasov's behavior in Japan in February 1972 only worsened his position as it undercut an important piece of government propaganda. The invasion of Czechoslovakia had harmed the USSR's public standing in the world, and the Soviet leaders were eager to mend at least the image of their close friendship with their satellite.

Sports Committee chairman Sergey Pavlov decided that he had had enough. Over the years, Tarasov and Chernyshev had made a regular practice of threatening to resign from the national team in order to force the Sports Committee to lure them back with extra compensation. After their return from Japan in February 1972, the coaches attempted their usual ploy. Pavlov had counted on them doing so. "I understand. As bitter as it is to see you go, you deserve your rest." And with that, Tarasov and Chernyshev "retired" from the national team. They were replaced by new head coach Vsevolod Bobrov, one of the greatest athletes and hockey players in Soviet history.[9] Bobrov would lead the Soviet team in the World Championships that was to take place in Prague less than two months after the end of the Olympics.

Eager to put together their best possible roster for the World Championships, Czechoslovakia's coaches nominated Suchý to the national team and brought him to the squad's training camp, even though they had not yet received permission to do so. New team captain Pospíšil led a delegation of players who spoke directly to Communist Party leader Husák to plead Suchý's case, explaining that to succeed they needed the great defenseman. Husák responded that the decision ultimately belonged to Antonín Himl, the head of Czechoslovakia's Physical Education Union. Himl rejected the team's request, stating that Suchý's crime made him a poor example for Czechoslovakia's youth. Upon receiving the news, Suchý instantly packed up his things, called a taxi, and grabbed the first train home.[10]

Even knowing that its star defenseman would be absent, Czechoslovakia buzzed with excitement over the World Championships, but in a way that was clearly different from Stockholm in 1969. The upcoming games still felt political, and for Czechs and Slovaks the desire for revenge hadn't gone away. But the feelings weren't as powerful as they had been three years earlier. Normalization had worn everyone down. To Czechoslovakia's players, the April 1972 World Ice Hockey Championships were first and foremost a sporting event now—but one that still had the power to shape the mood of an entire country.

Team Czechoslovakia stayed in a hotel just a few miles outside the city so players had space to stay focused. But somehow it seemed everyone in Prague always knew precisely when the team bus, led by a police escort, would rush the men to the arena to play. As the bus approached, people stuck their arms and heads out of buildings, lined the streets, jumped up and down, and cheered madly for the players.[11]

The authorities went to extremes to avoid a replay of the 1969 Hockey Riots. They called in Czechoslovak writers covering the tournament to explicitly lay out what they could and could not write or say. Officials made clear that journalists would immediately lose their jobs if they expressed anything that might be interpreted as political, incendiary, or critical of either Czechoslovakia's government or the USSR, or that might potentially inspire anyone to engage in political resistance. [12]

The government set up a special operations team to monitor and, if necessary, contain any suspicious behavior in the streets of Prague. As part of the plan, an unusually large number of regular Prague police went on patrol. The greatest concern was over what might happen during and after the matches against the USSR. The Ministry of Interior, which controlled state security, therefore scheduled an additional 860 plainclothes officers carrying guns, ammunition, and tear gas to go out into the streets precisely at the start time for the two matches between the communist rivals. [13]

Most of all, state forces set up unprecedented levels of security in the arena where the matches were to be played. Officials installed cameras high above the playing surface to observe everyone sitting in the stands. The images were transmitted to more than a dozen television screens in a room above the seating area. Secret police monitored the screens and radioed down to security forces if anything looked off. [14]

The action in the stadium stands showed in no uncertain terms that Czechoslovakia had become a police state. Before every game, even matches that didn't involve Czechoslovakia or the Soviet Union, riot police with big white helmets and batons lined up throughout the building. If anyone in the stands made a commotion or did something that looked suspicious, a group of helmeted men pulled the offenders from the stadium. The first row of seats, right in front of the ice, sat empty until just before each game. Then, abruptly, a line of secret police "watchers" in identical dark coats, hats, and ties paraded in and filled them. During each break, the watchers marched off in unison to purchase hot dogs. Then they marched back together to their seats by the time play resumed. [15]

The players occasionally noticed the squads of white-helmeted men patrolling the stands as they warmed up between matches or took a break during games, but for the most part the skaters from Czechoslovakia focused on the task before them: defeat the Soviets on the ice and win the country's first title in twenty-three years![16]

Adding Holeček in the goal and the new youngsters to a team stacked with first-rate veterans, Team Czechoslovakia opened the tournament with a vengeance: three strong victories and then a tie against the Soviets. In the next four matches, Czechoslovakia and the USSR continued to skate all over the other teams, leading to a big showdown on April 20.

Both Czechoslovakia and the USSR were undefeated, and the only blemish on the record of each was their earlier 3–3 standoff. The winner of this next game would almost certainly take the tournament gold medal.

Aside from the battles against the USSR in Stockholm in 1969, no match had ever meant so much in Czechoslovakia. With the advent of normalization, it seemed that every public act was about complying with the edicts of the state. There was no safe way to openly vent about the grip that the USSR had over their country. But international sports offered a loophole. There was nothing wrong with rooting openly and enthusiastically for Czechoslovakia against the Soviets in a sporting event. There was also one other thing: Czechoslovakia had beaten the USSR in major competition four times since 1968, but, somehow, these individual match victories had never produced a major championship. It was yet one more way that the world felt tilted against Czechoslovakia and in the Soviet Union's favor.

Just as had been the case in 1969, nearly every television in the country turned on the match, and the arena was filled to capacity with some 14,500 people in attendance. As play commenced, Czechoslovakia came out of the gates strong. Nedomanský, Martinec, Farda, and Holeček made a series of terrific plays, and the home team led 2–0 after twenty minutes.

In the second period, the Prague crowd, smelling blood, became more involved, chanting wildly as the Jaroslav-Holík-Force-of-Will Show took center stage. Jaroslav adored the most high-pressure matches and somehow never feared that he would make an error. Yet, midway through the second quarter, Jaroslav made a doozy. He got the puck on Holeček's end of the rink and carelessly looked to pass to a teammate across the width of the ice. Right away he knew that he had made a major mistake. He had completely missed Soviet wing Vladimir Vikulov in the space right in front of him. Vikulov slid in, easily intercepted the pass, sprinted up the ice, and flipped the puck to superstar center Alexander Maltsev, who drove up to the net and smacked it in. Had one of his teammates made a similar gaffe, Jaroslav would have lit into the man, but the other players knew better than to do the same with Holík.

Again, Jaroslav's unique psychology took over. He simply *knew* he would redeem himself. Within one minute, he got his chance. Pospíšil intercepted the puck on his end of the ice and, as he did so often, dished out a perfect pass to Jaroslav sprinting down the center toward the Soviet goal. A USSR man in red appeared to nab the puck from Jaroslav, but Holík muscled it away and drove toward the goal just slightly left of center with another Czechoslovak player flying forward on his right. Everyone on both teams knew Jaroslav was a mediocre shooter but one of Czechoslovakia's best passers. And in that split second, Jaroslav realized everyone therefore expected him to set someone else up for a shot.[17] Indeed, with his slow-moving push, Holík looked like he really was about to send the puck to his teammate. The Soviet defender tried to cover against both men and only at the last moment dove toward Jaroslav. Too late, as Holík flipped the puck past Tretiak. Goal!!!! 3–1 Czechoslovakia! Jiří got to his brother first, just before the rest of the team piled on top of Jaroslav.

Just minutes later, though, Jaroslav committed a penalty and, now up a player, the Soviets scored an easy goal, leaving them down just 3–2. A full twenty-seven minutes remained, plenty of time for the world's greatest hockey team, but Czechoslovakia's players buckled down, didn't allow any more damage in the second period, and entered the final frame clinging to a one-goal lead.

In the third period, the USSR attack mounted and with nine minutes remaining the Soviets went full throttle, knocking the puck violently and repeatedly at the goal. A gaggle of Czechoslovak players dove to the ice to try to prevent anything from getting to the net, and Holeček nabbed anything that got by them. The Soviet offensives gained greater urgency, but Czechoslovakia kept snatching the puck away and counterattacking. With five and a half minutes to go, the arena was in a full frenzy. When play halted, the Czechoslovak players looked spent, gliding with their shoulders lowered and hands on their knees. Play resumed and the Soviets slammed shot after shot at Holeček, as the crowd bellowed to hold off the Red Machine.

With three minutes left, the Czechoslovak faithful began to get a sense that their sporting dreams could come true as their team gained control of the puck and headed up the ice. Two and a half minutes to go! Czechoslovakia kept holding off the Soviets, and the clock kept ticking. One minute to go! Jiří Holík raced about, grabbing the puck and keeping it away from the Soviets!

With twenty-five seconds left, the USSR pulled Tretiak for one additional skater as the chanting grew louder still. Jaroslav went for a face-off against Petrov on the same end of the ice as the goal into which the Soviets were trying to score. The Soviets tried to drive, but Czechoslovakia's defense wouldn't let the Red Machine get a good look. Jiří continued to follow the puck everywhere, refusing to let any Soviet get it with open space. As the final seconds ticked away, the men from Czechoslovakia knew they were finishing strong, and all but those in the middle of the action felt the tension ooze away.[18] Jiří and Pospíšil converged on the final Soviet puck handlers, and the horn sounded.

For a moment, Jaroslav stood still in the middle of the rink. Just a year earlier, he had been left off the team, and now he was the hero. His fifteen combined goals and assists had tied for the team lead in the tournament. At least as important, he had been the squad's undisputed emotional heart and soul, constantly pumping up his teammates. And just as it had been in game two against the Soviets in Stockholm in 1969, his final goal was the difference maker in the match. After briefly taking in the moment, he raced across half the ice and was the first man to get to Holeček. Seconds later, the rest of the squad threw their sticks into the air and charged at their goalie, the team's skinniest man, piling onto him as the roar from the crowd became deafening.

The players had only been little kids—or not even born—the last time Czechoslovakia's national hockey team had achieved something of this magnitude, so they knew their victory meant the most to their parents' generation, which had endured so much over the years. Ordinarily, it is the younger generation that goes crazy in celebrations, but now the players could see countless older Czechs and Slovaks exulting wildly.

While the rest of the team rejoiced on the ice, Jiří and Jaroslav found each other. For perhaps the first time ever, the two brothers embraced over and over, massive grins etched across their faces. They knew what it would mean to their parents to see them like this. Sitting above them in the stands, their mother, Věra, couldn't believe it. She had seen her boys fight, seemingly from birth. And there they were, skating together, arms around each other's shoulders. "Look! Our boys are hugging!" Even beyond the hockey victory, this was among the most joyous moments of her life. A photograph of Jiří and Jaroslav in that very moment became one of the most famous in Czechoslovak sporting history and one of Věra's most prized possessions. [19]

Meanwhile, the regime's greatest fears didn't materialize anywhere in the country. There were no meaningful demonstrations. In an internal memo, the Interior Ministry complimented itself: "Attempts of insignificant groups of politically irresponsible elements to make use of the enthusiasm after the match . . . for an anti-socialist riot were thwarted by a well-timed and organized action of the riot police." [20] In reality, though, the regime's work had been done well before the tournament: after three years of normalization pressure, most Czechs and Slovaks had been worn down, and didn't even consider challenging the authorities.

But full-blown celebrations materialized in the streets everywhere in Czechoslovakia. As the players rode back to their hotel, cars honked and flashed their lights, people jumped up and down and waved wildly all along the streets, and complete strangers hugged. Ordinary people lived for the national hockey team, so the victory this night felt as if everyone in the country had actually won. [21]

When the players got back to the hotel, they began chanting for Coach Pitner to make good on a promise he had made to them: he abided, jumping into the freezing-cold hotel pool fully clothed. [22] The players busted out the champagne, and the revelry began in earnest.

Still, to Jaroslav and Jiří, there was something missing. After all they had gone through together and after everything that Jan Suchý had meant to the team . . . he should have been on the ice with them . . .

Then their parents arrived and the brothers began to think about everything that Věra and Jaroslav Sr. had done for them throughout their lives. Jaroslav Sr. had always believed that praise could kill an athlete's motivation and therefore had been careful to keep his kids' egos in check. Nearly twenty years earlier, when eleven-year-old Jaroslav had gotten his picture in the paper for a goal he had scored, his father had told him "Only when you win a World Championship can you say that you know how to play hockey." [23] But on this night, as the Holík parents made their way to the hotel to celebrate with their sons, Jaroslav Sr. thought back to the work he had put into the boys' hockey and how it had all been for this moment. It had been his dream as much as it had been theirs. He arrived at the hotel and locked eyes with Jiří and Jaroslav. "Now, as world champions," he told them, "you can finally tell me something about hockey!" [24]

# CHAPTER 12

# Up, Up, and . . . Away

With the victory, the entire country rejoiced in a wave of national pride. Jaroslav's 1972 winning goal became part of Czechoslovak lore. When the post office produced special stamps to commemorate the title, one portrayed him scoring.[1]

In the decade that followed, Czechoslovakia's people would have more opportunities to celebrate their national hockey team, but there was little else that truly unified them. Under the repressive government regime, public life turned dark and, over the course of the 1970s, this darkness would touch everything. Even sports. As it did, it became reasonable to wonder whether the darkness would eventually drive away the country's heroes, especially its star athletes.

In the early 1970s, government officials warned the country that it was in "mortal danger" of a "counterrevolution" and they would therefore punish anyone who stepped even slightly out of line from what the regime demanded. Indeed, between late 1971 and early 1972, the government arrested hundreds of people for acts of political expression that mocked or openly called out the regime. One set of arrests followed the November 1971 election, when a group of citizens handed out leaflets reminding voters that they had the right to vote for whomever they wanted and even had the right not to vote. In response, in January 1972 the regime imposed lengthy jail time on a number of the protesters for "anti-state subversion." One of the leafleteers found himself sentenced to six and a half years of prison.[2]

Between 1969 and 1974, the authorities tried more than 3,000 people for similar "actions against the republic."[3]

No one was safe from the regime. In 1971, Věra Čáslavská reached out to officials at her sports club about the possibility of becoming a coach. Instead of hiring her, the club expelled her for her earlier political stances. The following year, Czechoslovakia's leader, Gustáv Husák, himself called Čáslavská in to recant her support for "The Two Thousand Words" manifesto. When she refused, her career in the gymnastics world was over. To support herself, she took a job cleaning homes. Eventually, a club permitted her to begin coaching children, but she had to hide when anyone of note appeared.[4]

Despite these dynamics and widespread disdain for the hard-line Communist leadership, a delicate but stable balance developed in the country. Communist leader Husák asked the people to go to work and follow the regime's basic instructions. In exchange, he offered them employment and basic economic well-being.

Czechoslovakia's economy lagged behind the West, but in the coming years improved and produced one of the highest standards of living behind the Iron Curtain. The cost of housing was relatively low. There were often shortages of simple desirable goods, but eventually Czechs and Slovaks could afford items like televisions and automobiles. Medical care was below Western quality and involved long waits to see a doctor, who expected to receive bribes in exchange for certain treatments. But—officially—the care was free.[5]

Czechs and Slovaks had economic security and a measure of comfort, but public life in Czechoslovakia became a dull, routinized farce, based on feigned support for a regime that at any moment might punish those who didn't play their scripted role. In the 1950s, many in the country had supported communist ideology, believing that it would create a better society, but in the 1970s, few seemed to believe in that ideal anymore. Under normalization, the system appeared geared toward maintaining public obedience and personal advantage for those with access to power. The government had eliminated the hierarchy of class differences, but replaced it with a system that placed Party members over other citizens. Communist Party members had the opportunity to get better housing, jobs, and basic goods. Their children were more likely to be accepted into better schools and had better chances for advancement. Many Czechs and Slovaks saw little to aspire to since rising professionally had more to do with connections and place in the Party than with merit or even competence.

In public, Czechs and Slovaks went through the motions to avoid triggering the regime's displeasure. Simply criticizing the government within earshot of the wrong person could lead to severe punishment. Elections were held in which all citizens were expected to participate and vote for regime-approved candidates (the only ones on the ballot). All citizens were expected to participate in events like May Day parades, which celebrated the Party and the USSR and played the anthems of both countries. The authorities compiled lists of people who skipped such events and punished them by withholding benefits. Attached to countless buildings were *two* flag holders, in which people were expected to prominently display, next to one another, the blue, white, and red Czechoslovak flag and the red Soviet flag. Everywhere, banners, billboards, and even shop windows proclaimed, "Friendship with the Soviet Union Forever!"[6] Czechs and Slovaks increasingly turned inward, focusing on their own private lives and personal well-being.[7]

Partly in response to the shortage of decent housing in towns and cities and partly to maintain quiescence, the regime permitted people to build country homes where they could relax and quietly garden. During the first decade of normalization, roughly 100,000 new cottages (*chata*) were built, adding to the more than 100,000 that already existed. Countless families spent their weekends off in their safe country homes, far from public life and the constant sense that someone was keeping track of everything that they did. And the social and political order in Czechoslovakia remained undisturbed.[8]

Culture also took on a more private spin. When the regime banned particular artists' work, small groups organized private exhibitions in the countryside where hundreds might attend. When the state banned new music for being "nonconformist," a black market emerged for records, and the offending acts appeared in venues that the authorities would be less likely to catch. *Samizdat* publishing became the way to share new writing: writers typed up their work and passed it around within small networks of friends.

To many in the West, life in Czechoslovakia in the 1970s may have looked something like a prison, with its heavy limits on personal freedoms and sharp restrictions on travel beyond the country's boundaries. To Jan Suchý, beginning in July 1972, life looked *exactly* like a prison, as he began serving his sentence at the Oráčov facility, which mostly held people who had been convicted of nonviolent crimes like tax evasion.

Inmates were expected to work, and Suchý was given the job of leading Squad 8, a group of twelve men incarcerated at Oráčov. Most commonly, Squad 8 went to nearby farms to harvest and weed hops fields. Being a famous hockey player paid dividends. While Squad 8 worked, the director of the farm inevitably invited Jan to sit with him to have a shot, a cigarette, and some coffee. At the end of the day, the farm director would write up a report that included a note of commendation for Suchý and his men.

Every month, Suchý negotiated a visit home. "If you let me out on Thursday, I will be back by 10 P.M. on Sunday!" The warden always permitted it but insisted upon compensation. Each time Suchý left, he came back with "gifts" for the man: badges, pennants, and pins from the World Championships and Olympics. On one such visit, he learned that, while he was gone, only one person had offered to help his wife, Marie, with money or anything else that she might need: Jaroslav Holík. Suchý thought to himself, "Jaroslav can sure be loud and a bit bone-headed, but he is truly a caring, stand-up man."[9]

Each morning in prison began with the men lining up to be counted and reporting their work performance. Squad 8 always came in with the top score. As a reward, eventually each member of the squad had his sentence reduced. After seven months in Oráčov, Suchý was released.[10] Coach Pitner personally came to the prison to pick him up. "So, are you ready to play?"

He was indeed. In prison, Suchý had cut back on smoking. He ran and lifted weights. During the winter he skated each night. On January 23, 1973, Jan Suchý played his first match in nearly a year, contributing a goal and an assist in a Dukla Jihlava win.[11]

Despite Suchý only having been gone for a short time, Czechoslovak hockey appeared different from when he had last played on the national squad in 1971. It was now in a period of transition. Young stars like Martinec and Hlinka had risen to another level and become team leaders. But the national team was still emotionally hungover from the 1972 title and wasn't firing on all cylinders.[12]

Meanwhile, the Soviets were hungry. Tarasov and other leading USSR hockey officials had always desperately wanted to see how their team would fare against Canada's great professional hockey players. In 1972, negotiators from the USSR and Canada finalized an agreement to play eight matches against each other in September of that year, with no amateur rules limiting eligibility. Superstar Canadian center forward Phil Esposito described the upcoming series as a war, "Our way of life against theirs."[13] The Canadians entered the "Summit Series" expecting to dominate, but after five games the USSR had won three and Canada just one, along with one tie. The Canadians turned to overwhelmingly physical, at times even violent, play, and intentionally incapacitated Soviet star forward Kharlamov. Canada narrowly took the final three matches to finish with four wins against three losses and a tie. Many in North America talked of the need to incorporate elements of the Soviets' emphasis on conditioning, skating, and passing. The Soviets talked of continuing to improve their beautiful style of hockey. In the April 1973 World Championships, the USSR went undefeated for the gold. Czechoslovakia finished third.

After the 1973 tournament and six years together, Pitner and Kostka handed the reins of the national team over to Karel Gut, a former player and coach for Sparta Prague, and Ján Starší, who had previously starred on and coached Slovan Bratislava. Jaroslav had remained among the country's top players, but he didn't get along with the hyperstrict Gut. Jaroslav thought Gut blathered unendingly and Gut had no patience for Jaroslav's blunt outspokenness. Holík found himself off the national team, this time permanently.[14]

After three years away, Suchý returned to the national team for the April 1974 World Championships, where Czechoslovakia lost three times and finished second behind the USSR. Jan led all defensemen in assists and points, but, at the Golden Stick award ceremony later that spring, Coach Gut told Suchý that the national team coaches wanted to bring in younger players and therefore would not invite him back the following year. Suchý, who had been drinking, snapped, "If you can fire one of the two best defensemen in the tournament, then clearly you don't understand hockey! Karel, if I am not good enough, then shove the national jersey up your ass." And with that, Suchý, like Jaroslav, would never again be a member of Czechoslovakia's national team.[15]

Despite the team's inconsistent play in the most recent World Championships, there continued to be bright spots. With goalie Jiří Holeček, Czechoslovakia always had a chance. Vladimír Martinec and Ivan Hlinka were now world stars. The team was still stacked with elite veteran players, including Jiří Holík, who seemed to be as good as ever.

Perhaps most noteworthy, Václav Nedomanský had become the best hockey forward in Europe. And that was going to turn out to be a problem.

Nedomanský had been born on March 14, 1944. He dominated youth hockey and at eighteen joined the Slovan Bratislava team, just across the border into Slovakia, fifty-five miles from his hometown, Hodonín. At the age of twenty, during the 1964–65 season, he became one of the top scorers in the league and made the national team for the first time. In the years that followed, he cemented his position as the dominant offensive force in Czechoslovak hockey. In 1968–73, he was always near the top of the league's scoring list, and in international play led Czechoslovakia every year in goals scored.

Czechs and Slovaks treated him like a rock star. Big Ned was a Czech playing in Slovakia and therefore wildly popular everywhere. Despite his naturally shy disposition, he played with charismatic power. With his forceful skating and accurate thunderclap shot, there was an expectation of something thrilling whenever he neared the puck. His big, muscular physique and handsome face meant girls constantly asked his teammates about him. He was also especially intriguing to another group that resided far beyond the borders of the Iron Curtain.

As the quality of Soviet and Czechoslovak players' hockey skill rose in the 1960s, NHL coaches, scouts, and executives grew interested. In 1968, representatives of the Detroit Red Wings met with Jiří Holík and Jan Suchý fully prepared with plane tickets and travel documents for the Jihlava men if they would come to the NHL.[16] Over the next year, the St. Louis Blues tried the same thing with Jan Havel and Josef Horešovský of Sparta Prague, even bringing suitcases of cash as further inducement.[17]

None of the men chose to go. Under Czechoslovak law, it was a criminal offense to defect to another country, and families of those who left illegally could be treated as accessories. Nonetheless, in the first two years after the Soviet invasion, some 170,000 people escaped from Czechoslovakia. Fearing large-scale defections, the government reimposed strict restrictions on travel to the West and punished émigrés' families who remained behind.[18]

Nedomanský dreamed of going to the West legally and playing in the NHL. As a member of Czechoslovakia's junior national team, he had first traveled across the Atlantic when he was a teenager and had been left awestruck. Unlike at home, it seemed to him that in North America colors popped and people actually smiled as they walked down the street or greeted you. Then he began to notice the myriad options available. All the different things you could buy, but also all the freedoms to do, say, or go as you liked. It was wonderful.

Big Ned reached the peak of his powers in 1974. His forty-six goals in forty-three games set the league record for most scores by one player in a season. At the 1974 World Championships, he led all players in goals scored and was named the best forward in the tournament.

North American scouts had long known that Big Ned was special. Since 1965, NHL teams had reached out to Czechoslovakia's authorities, eventually offering both Nedomanský and Czechoslovak hockey administrators hundreds of thousands of dollars to bring him west. In 1972, the World Hockey Association (WHA) had debuted as a new North American league and, in an attempt to challenge the supremacy of the NHL, offered big money to stars, including some of Europe's best. In 1974, the WHA's Toronto Toros got word to Nedomanský that, if he could get out from behind the Iron Curtain, they would sign him to a five-year $750,000 contract.

During the Prague Spring, the authorities had worked out arrangements to allow a small number of coaches and players over the age of thirty to play in Western Europe and, in 1969, even permitted Jaroslav Jiřík to spend part of a season in the NHL. But by 1974, as full normalization settled in, Czechoslovakia had ended this practice.

Desperate to play in the West, Nedomanský, now thirty years old, decided he'd had enough of Czechoslovakia's regime telling him what he could and could not do.

Along with his wife and young son, Big Ned arranged for a special travel visa for a "vacation" to Switzerland, where they caught an international flight out of Zurich. On Wednesday, July 17, 1974, the Nedomanskýs disembarked from the plane in Montreal. It was among the most high-profile escapes ever by a citizen from the Eastern Bloc. The story appeared on the front page of the *Toronto Sun*. Above the fold, the headline screamed out "CZECH HOCKEY STAR DEFECTS TO CANADA." Less than three weeks earlier, Soviet ballet great Mikhail Baryshnikov had also sought asylum in Toronto. The defection of the two cultural icons was a major embarrassment for the Soviet bloc.

The Nedomanskýs got an apartment in Toronto and soon found themselves receiving phone calls and notes in Czech informing them they could still come home with no repercussions. They received warnings that their family members would be punished if they didn't return. Nedomanský also faced challenges in North America. Fans and players, even some teammates, screamed that he was a "commie!" Players, angry with him for "stealing" North American jobs, pounded him on the ice. Toughest still, Nedomanský's North American agent took advantage of the hockey player's inexperience with the English language and Western customs, and worked out contracts that ultimately cost Big Ned hundreds of thousands, if not millions, of dollars in potential earnings. Through it all, though, one thing remained as before: Big Ned was a hockey scoring machine in North America just as he had been in Europe.[19]

Back in Czechoslovakia, there was no easy way to explain what had happened. One of the country's greatest heroes had simply disappeared. The Communists labeled Big Ned a traitor. His name was removed from team pictures and league record books. People in Czechoslovakia understood that they were not to speak his name, lest an informer might report them.

Nedomanský's escape highlighted just how suffocating many found life to be in Czechoslovakia in the 1970s. In the two decades after the Soviet invasion, nearly a quarter of a million (out of a total population of roughly just fifteen million) Czechs and Slovaks would leave the country for good, including well-known writer Milan Kundera and film director Milos Forman.[20] Following Nedomanský's departure, the government grew worried that more of the country's top athletes might follow suit.

On this front, the authorities' greatest fear centered not on an established male hockey star, but, rather, an eighteen-year-old girl.

Martina Šubertová was born in Prague on October 18, 1956. Her parents divorced when she was three, and her mother, Jana, moved with the little girl to the village of Řevnice. When she was nearly five, her mother married a man named Miroslav Navrátil, and with that Martina Šubertová became Martina Navrátilová, the little girl who would cheer wildly with her family as they watched the 1969 hockey matches on their tiny black-and-white television.

(In Czech and Slovak, males and females do not have identical surnames. In most cases, "ová" is added onto the last names of girls and women. In this way, the daughter or wife of a man with the family name of "Navrátil" would be "Navrátilová.") Even as a young child, Martina easily picked up any sport that she tried, but with her natural foot speed and hand-eye coordination, she was perfect for tennis. She began to dream about winning Wimbledon. And she fantasized about leading Czechoslovakia to its first ever women's world team title in the Federation Cup tournament.

On August 21, 1968, when she was eleven years old, Martina was in a tennis tournament in Pilsen and woke early to the loud ringing of the phone. When someone finally picked it up, the instructions were clear. "Don't go outside. There are tanks out there." Eventually, she headed to the tennis club. The local crowd pelted the Soviet tanks with stones, so Martina did too.

Over the next six months, there was little more that Martina and her parents could do to vent their fury. That's what made the March 1969 hockey matches so important. With every hit on the Soviets, and every goal that Czechoslovakia scored, Martina felt as if she herself was fighting back. She had worshipped players like Big Ned and Jaroslav Jiřík, imagining herself as them when she played hockey. But now they were much more than just athletes to her. She couldn't articulate it at the time, but she realized later what those matches had meant: the victories gave Martina and everyone around her hope and a sense that the Soviets hadn't taken everything. The hockey team showed that they still had the freedom to fight back in sport. That they still had the freedom to win. As long as they had that, it meant their occupiers didn't own them.

Martina took this feeling with her as she began playing tennis more seriously. "The Russians" had more tanks, guns, and soldiers, and they could seemingly influence scores in a sport like gymnastics, where judges had more subjective latitude. But the Soviets didn't look so tough when the playing field was level. Not long after the hockey matches in Stockholm, Martina and a partner defeated a pair of Soviets in a doubles match in Prague. One of the Soviet girls refused to shake hands properly, leading Martina to snap, "You can beat us with tanks, but you can't beat us on the tennis court."

In the years that followed, Martina's tennis game improved by leaps and bounds. Before she even turned sixteen, she won Czechoslovakia's national championships for female players of any age. She became the second-ranked women's player in Czechoslovakia and began playing on the world tour, including professional tournaments in the United States.

To Martina, the experience of *being* in America was a glorious shock. The visuals blew her mind. Americans wore bright, lively colors, in contrast to Czechs and Slovaks who, in Martina's mind's eye, appeared to live in muted tones and wore mostly black and gray clothing. It was more than visual though. She was taken by the openness of Americans, who, it seemed, instantly sought to create a human connection, sharing their own experiences and thoughts freely. From that first visit, she felt that for the first time in her life she had found a place where she could truly be herself.

By May 1974, she was ranked in the top ten in the world. She performed well in multiple tournaments, but saved her best for the end of the year. In late December, she entered the Australian Open, her first major tournament after turning eighteen, and took second place. In May 1975, Czechoslovakia's Tennis Federation asked Martina and Renáta Tomanová to represent it in the Federation Cup tournament in France. In the Fed Cup, pairs of countries compete directly against one another in rounds of best-of-three matches (two singles and one doubles). In each pairing, the first country to win two matches moves on to the next round. Martina didn't lose any of her singles matches or her doubles pairings with Tomanová on the way to achieving her childhood dream of leading Czechoslovakia to the Fed Cup title.

Then her problems began. After the 1975 Fed Cup win, Czechoslovakia's Tennis Federation told Martina's father that she had become "too Americanized." When Martina asked what that meant, officials told her that she appeared too fond of the United States and too friendly with American players. The federation warned her to distance herself from all things US and then threatened to pull her out of tournaments in the West. Eventually, Antonín Himl, the head of Czechoslovakia's Physical Education Union, reluctantly permitted her to go to the 1975 US Open in New York, with the understanding that she would return immediately after its conclusion.

Martina felt Czechoslovakia's repressive grip crushing the will of her country's people, and she feared that the federation might never allow her to leave again. She advanced as the third seed to the semifinals of the tournament on September 5 before losing a close match to top-ranked Chris

Evert. Right after the match, she headed to the US Immigration and Naturalization Service. "I would like apply for political asylum in the United States." With that, Martina Navrátilová began the process of defecting from Czechoslovakia.

Martina's departure dealt a big blow to Czechoslovakia's regime, but just months later the country's people gave it little thought as they became fixated yet again on the exploits of their national hockey team. In February, the 1976 Winter Olympics would commence in Innsbruck, Austria, and Czechoslovakia had real reason to believe that, at long last, it was the team to beat for the gold medal in hockey.[21]

It was probably the best roster Czechoslovakia had ever put together. It had experienced players in their prime like Martinec and Hlinka, as well as twenty-four-year-old scoring machine Milan Nový from Kladno. Veterans like Pospíšil, Machač, and Holeček remained at the top of their game. And, a far cry from the timid teen that he had been at the 1964 games, Jiří Holík was now a confident thirty-one-year-old world champion and his team's elder statesman as he prepared for his *fourth* Olympic Games. Somehow Jiří had actually seemed to get better with age. In the previous league season, he had finished third in Golden Stick balloting. If Czechoslovakia's hockey team was ever going to win Olympic gold, it was going to be in 1976.[22]

On Friday, February 6, Czechoslovakia defeated Finland in its opening game, but Hlinka took ill and had to leave the match early. Two days later, Jiří Holík rose in the morning fired up for his match that day against the Americans, but with each passing minute, his body crumbled. His head pounded. His temperature climbed to 104 degrees. By noon he could hardly move. Soon he became overwhelmed by violent coughing. And he wasn't the only one. That day, 124 cases of the flu were reported in the Olympic Village. Czechoslovakia seemed to be the only hockey team affected, but the bug hit it with full force. That night, Jiří and one of his teammates couldn't even get out of bed. At least a half dozen other Czechoslovak players were also horribly ill but just barely well enough to suit up. Fortunately, the Americans were not particularly skilled and Czechoslovakia nabbed a victory.

From there, things only got worse. Fearing their athletes might get sick, Czechoslovak administrators had given their hockey players flu shots just before the games. Eventually, though, with the exception of two men who had *not* received the shots, every single Czechoslovak hockey player became terribly ill. Despite having only part of its roster available, on Tuesday, February 10, Czechoslovakia took on Poland, the worst team in the tournament. Czechoslovakia pulled out a 7–1 victory.

After the match, a news bombshell dropped: Czechoslovakia's captain František Pospíšil had tested positive for a banned substance. Like the rest of the squad, Pospíšil was overcome by a severe dry cough and struggling to play, so the team physician prescribed him medication that included codeine. The International Ice Hockey Federation did not list codeine as a banned substance, but the International Olympic Committee did. When the IOC had informed teams of which medications were prohibited, Czechoslovakia's doctor had been needed at the hockey team's practice and therefore had not received the list. After the positive drug test, International Ice Hockey Federation leaders begged the committee to overlook the infraction, arguing that IIHF rules were different and that codeine was *the opposite* of a performance enhancing drug. But the IOC wasn't having any of it. Pospíšil was not punished, but Czechoslovakia's doctor was banned from the Olympics for life and Czechoslovakia had to forfeit the Poland match.

Despite the setback, however, after winning its next game Czechoslovakia still had a chance. On February 14, it would face the undefeated Soviets for the Olympic gold medal the players and, indeed, the entire nation yearned for.

Given how ill the Czechoslovak players were, few observers expected much from them—but they came out blazing and led 2–0 after one period. By the second period, though, Czechoslovakia was running on fumes. The USSR scored twice and the teams entered the final period tied at two.

With twenty minutes to go, the Czechoslovak men willed themselves to squeeze out one more ounce of strength. For the first ten minutes of the third period, both sides tried to attack, but neither could score. The short intermission at the midway point in the period gave Czechoslovakia's players a welcome break. But when it was time for play to resume, it seemed to take a massive effort to even get them off the bench to finish the match.

Everyone double-checked the scoreboard. Ten minutes to go. The score still tied. The crowd, which had cheered wildly throughout, became strangely silent.

The USSR, wearing all red, displayed little urgency. As long as no one scored, and the game finished as a tie, the Soviet Union would finish with a superior overall record in the tournament and win the gold medal. Meanwhile, the white-clad Czechoslovak players were desperate. They needed to score, needed *to win* the game, to take the gold.

Pospíšil controlled the puck from behind his own goal and calmly skated up the ice. He abruptly stopped mid-ice, pivoted, and sent the puck to teammate Eduard Novák on the left. Without slowing down, Novák flew forward and, surrounded by Soviet red jerseys, suddenly thrust his stick. The action seemed to surprise Soviet goalie Tretiak, who sank to his knees as the disk flew to the back of the net. 3–2 Czechoslovakia! Nine minutes to Olympic gold!

With Czechoslovakia now up by one, for three and a half minutes the two squads went back and forth. Jiří Holík nearly scored. The Soviets nearly scored. And then, with five and a half minutes remaining in the match, an infraction that a Canadian writer later described as "a very, very cheap cross-checking penalty" was called on Novák. Czechoslovakia was forced to play with only four skaters against the Soviet five. The crowd whistled its vehement disapproval. Czechoslovakia put in a lineup designed to halt the Soviets' offense. Jiří flew around, desperate to keep his body between the Soviet players, who grabbed the puck, and the net they were trying to score into. But he was exhausted, and it was all he could do to keep going. The Soviets charged toward Holeček. Suddenly, Soviet Alexander Yakushev got past Czechoslovakia's defense and tied the score.

Now, with four and a half minutes left, the pressure was back on Czechoslovakia to find some offense. The Czechoslovak men in white went on the attack, but the Soviets quickly got the puck back and drove again toward Holeček. Just twenty-four seconds after Yakushev's game-tying goal, the Soviets ended Czechoslovakia's dreams as Kharlamov sent the puck into the net for a 4–3 USSR lead. One could almost see the Czechoslovak players' emotional life leave their bodies. Yet again, Czechoslovakia's hockey team had just missed in the Olympics. And yet again, it was the Soviets who came away with the gold.

Nobody knew the pain better than Jiří, who *three straight times* now had gone into the final match with a chance for Olympic gold and three straight times had come up short. He knew this had been his last opportunity, and his best one. But this time, it didn't even feel like they had lost to another team. This time it was as if some invisible force had aligned everything against them. It was as if the gods themselves had decided that for Czechoslovakia the Olympic hockey gold just wasn't meant to be.[23]

Just two months later, Czechoslovakia dominated the April 1976 World Championships in Katowice, Poland. Jiří couldn't recall a single Czechoslovak hockey squad that had ever played better.[24] The team went undefeated in its first nine matches, including a 3–2 win over the Soviets, and would easily take the gold medal. Following the victory, as Czechoslovakia's leader, Gustáv Husák, bestowed upon him a special "Workers' Order" in honor of his service, Jiří thought to himself, "Perhaps my kids and I won't suffer after all from my decision to leave the Party," and finally let go of the fears that had haunted him for nearly eight years.

The hockey team then showed that it could do more. Czechoslovakia was invited to the 1976 Canada Cup, where it would compete with Canada, the US, the USSR, Sweden, and Finland. Each roster was composed of any player from the country, irrespective of his amateur or professional status. Czechoslovakia performed magnificently, defeating Canada in an early-round match, and then narrowly lost in overtime to the hosts in the tournament's final game. Canada took the title of "world's best team," but Czechoslovakia finished second, ahead of the USSR (which sent an "experimental" team that excluded many of its best players).[25]

The following year, in the April–May 1977 World Championships held in Vienna, the IIHF finally fully permitted professional players, so Canada, which hadn't played in the Championships since 1969, returned to the tournament. In one of the final matches, NHL Canadian star Phil Esposito skated by Czechoslovakia's bench and punched Coach Ján Starší in the face on the way to an 8–2 Canada victory. But Czechoslovakia still took the tournament title, its second in a row. Sweden nabbed the silver, which gave the USSR the bronze, the worst result by the Soviets since 1961.[26]

Despite Team Czechoslovakia's incredible run, when the tournament ended Jiří was done with the national team. He had first been named to the squad in 1963. In the years that followed, he played in four Olympics and twelve World Championships. Physically he remained in top form, but he was exhausted mentally. Every year, he spent much of the summer in training camps. Then, after the fall league season, nearly every year at Christmas he flew off to America for a tournament. He had gotten married in 1969 and had begun having children. It was painful to be away from his wife and kids so much. Each year, after his annual Christmas trip to the West, the league hockey season picked back up. In leap years, there would be the Olympics, early in the calendar. Every spring he headed to the World Championships. Soon thereafter, summer training camp would begin once more, away from his family again.

In 1971, Jiří told his brother and Suchý that he just couldn't bear it anymore and planned to quit the national team, but somehow he kept returning even as his patience ran thin. The worst was in 1976. Jiří had to attend special training for the Canada Cup, so he was absent for most of the summer when his wife was pregnant with their second child. He was in Canada, playing in the tournament, when his son was born. He had to learn about the birth from the editor of a Czechoslovak sports magazine who was traveling with the team.

Jiří retired from Czechoslovakia's national team as the iron man of international hockey. He had played 319 international matches, more than anyone from any country in hockey history. Even nearly fifty years later, he remained in the top ten for most career points in World Championship play. He concluded his Czechoslovakia career for Dukla Jihlava with his brother and Suchý in the 1977–78 season.

Despite losing Jiří, the national team remained strong but was hamstrung by injuries as it began the 1978 World Championships. Even still, it came out in dominating fashion, winning its first nine matches. In the finale, Czechoslovakia played for the title once more against the Soviet team, which had undergone a major change. After the 1977 bronze medal, the sports authorities cleaned house, bringing in Viktor Tikhonov, an established coach with a dictatorial style, to take over both the army team and the national squad. Under Tikhonov, the Soviets placed all the country's best players on the army team and forced the men to live together, without their families, in a tightly controlled compound eleven months per year. Facing a renewed Soviet squad and with its own players at less than full strength, Czechoslovakia lost 3–1, ending its streak of two straight world titles. [27]

The year 1978 marked a watershed for Team Czechoslovakia. The regime would never let the players leave while still in their prime, but after the 1978 tournament it decided to take advantage of an opportunity. Many of the players were over thirty and on the downswing of their careers, but they were still a big draw throughout Europe. The national team no longer needed them, but Czechoslovakia's government could take a large share of the ample salaries offered to Czechoslovak players when they played in other countries' leagues. The Communist leaders wouldn't allow them to go to the NHL, but they now permitted a group of elite players—most notably, Jiří Holík, Holeček, Dzurilla, Pospíšil, Machač, and Černý, all thirty-two years of age and older—to join teams in West Germany and Austria.[28]

There was concern that with so many of the top veterans gone, the window for Czechoslovakia's hockey success had closed, but, in fact, a terrific core remained. There was Hlinka, the new team captain. There was Martinec. There was Nový, who had set a league record with fifty-nine goals in forty-four games in 1976–77.

But there was even more. There were three young men who shared a last name and whose presence created optimism about the future of the national team. In the coming years, one of those young men would directly take on the hard-line authorities who sought to control him. The conflict that ensued would shake up hockey in Czechoslovakia.

In 1970s Slovakia, the name "Šťastný" was legendary.

Like most Slovaks, the Šťastnýs were devoutly Catholic, which created risks. In the first decade following the 1948 coup, the Communists had cracked down on religion and imprisoned—and in some cases even executed—many priests and nuns. But there were too many Catholics in the general population in Slovakia for the state to go after everyone, so most families there were able to continue to practice their faith.[29]

But it wasn't for their religion that the Šťastnýs were most famous. It was the fact that their boys were incredible hockey players. And they would embody yet one more way in which the people of Czechoslovakia had grown apart since normalization.

The 1968 Soviet invasion had produced an unprecedented level of unity in Czechoslovakia, as people across the country united to resist their occupiers, but before long divisions reemerged and in some ways grew more severe. Normalization had produced derision toward the country's Communist leaders, but also weakened social ties. Human connection was harder for people who had to constantly watch what they did and said outside of the family.

The invasion had also quelled the long-held tensions between Czechs and Slovaks, but soon both sides returned to old resentments and even found new ones. With the rise of Slovaks like Dubček and Husák, as well as Vasiľ Biľak, who took over major roles in both the government and Party, there was reason to think that Slovakia's position in the power structure had improved. Indeed, Husák placed a number of Slovaks in important posts. In addition, the only Prague Spring reform to survive the rise of Husák was an increase in federalism, which allowed Slovakia a greater say in the country's overall policy making. With the changes, however, many Czechs came to feel that Slovaks now had disproportionate power and that the leaders overwhelmingly favored Slovakia in political positions and economic subsidies. Meanwhile, most Slovaks were hardly satisfied, believing that their people who had moved into important positions in Prague had simply become "Czechs" and forgotten where they came from. [30]

As ever, the schism between Czechs and Slovaks carried over to the ice and the Šťastnýs fought passionately for their side. The Šťastný family had six kids and the first to gain glory was the third oldest, Marián, who in 1970, at just seventeen years of age, made the Slovan Bratislava professional squad. Just three years later, sixteen-year-old Peter began to play with the team as well. By the 1976 World Championships, twenty-three-year-old Marián and nineteen-year-old Peter were easily two of the best players in Czechoslovakia and became central figures on the national team. They also felt resentment, believing that Czechoslovakia remained biased in favor of Czechs, even in hockey. The country had not included a single Slovak skater on the 1976 Olympic hockey squad, not even Marián, who had performed well on the national team the previous year.

The Šťastnýs seethed and longed to show the Czechs what they were missing. No Slovak team had ever won Czechoslovakia's league championship. But, if ever a team had a shot, it was one filled with Šťastnýs. In 1977, younger brother Anton joined Marián and Peter on the club. They were a striking group, all with brown hair, fair skin, chiseled features, and sharp green-blue eyes. And they made a brilliant line together, with Anton on the left, Marián on the right, and Peter in the middle. All three were great skaters and passers. They were smart and had an exceptional sense of timing with one another. [31]

Their rise coincided with the final Dukla season of Jaroslav Holík and Jan Suchý. Marián had always told his younger brothers about players who impressed him and, years before, he had given Peter a heads up: "Hey, check out Jaroslav Holík. What a player!" Marián was right. Peter was blown away by how Jaroslav wouldn't back down from anyone. He looked like a pitbull on the ice! When Peter made the league, he found it surreal to play against Holík, but the Jaroslav playing in the late 1970s was not the one of previous years. By 1977, Jaroslav knew that he was done as a professional hockey player. His body wouldn't let him do what he wanted anymore. Thanks to his strength, never-say-die attitude, and experience, he played two more seasons, but he viewed his own play as terrible. During the 1978–79 season, he broke a bone in his hand. As the doctor set the cast, Jaroslav felt emotionally and physically drained from his years of unhinged training and thought that it really might be time to quit. That summer, he made one more go of it at training camp until he broke his jawbone, and that was it. Meanwhile, throughout the 1970s, as Jan Suchý aged and hockey got rougher and faster, the star Jihlava defenseman also figured out that his days in the league were numbered. After the 1978–79 season ended, Suchý left Dukla and the authorities allowed him to join a team in Austria.[32]

The 1978–79 Czechoslovakia hockey season, though, belonged to the Slovan Bratislava team and its stars, the Šťastný brothers. All three Šťastnýs finished among the top five scorers in the league, and Marián finished second in player of the year balloting. When Slovan took the league crown, Bratislavans flooded onto the ice in elation. Marián and Peter had previously won World Championships, but to finally show the whole country that Slovaks were at least the equal of—and, in this moment, better than—the Czechs was the most precious hockey victory of their lives.

All three Šťastnýs made the national team that took the silver behind the rejuvenated and undefeated Soviet team at the 1979 World Championships. Anton, Marián, and Peter continued their outstanding play during the following year, and all three made the Olympic team that would compete in February 1980 in Lake Placid, New York.

The 1980 winter games were among the most politically charged in Olympic history. On December 24, 1979, just weeks before the Olympics' opening ceremonies, the Soviet Union had invaded Afghanistan, ratcheting up Cold War tensions between the world's two superpowers to a level not felt in years. Home-country Americans saw the Lake Placid games as a proxy war between themselves and the USSR, and desperately sought to defeat the Soviets in any event in which they went head-to-head. Most of all, Americans dreamed, delusionally, of taking down the Soviets' hockey team, the most prominent representative of the USSR in Lake Placid.

As usual, the Soviets came in as clear favorites, and Czechoslovakia was the obvious next best squad. Hlinka was out with an injury, but players like Nový, Martinec, and the Šťastnýs would be there. No other team especially impressed the international hockey analysts. The US squad, made up of amateurs and a tiny smattering of minor league players, was, at best, an afterthought.

However, one person had high expectations for the Americans. After his retirement from coaching the national hockey team, Professor Vladimír Kostka had become dean of the Charles University Faculty of Physical Education and Sport and eventually chairman of the Czechoslovakia Hockey Federation. In December 1979, he attended a pre-Olympic tournament in Lake Placid and returned home with some outlandish impressions. "It is the strongest team the US has ever built! It is the favorite in the winter Olympic Games. I've never seen Americans with so much motivation, with such discipline."[33] Few took Kostka's words seriously.

Czechoslovakia arrived in Lake Placid, easily took its first match, and then prepared to play the US in game two. As Czechoslovakia practiced one day, a blond woman called assistant coach Luděk Bukač over to her. She spoke to him in Czech and suddenly he realized who she was: Ivana Zelníčková. Nearly thirty-one years old now, she had once been a terrific downhill skier in Czechoslovakia and Bukač had helped her out with her schooling more than a decade earlier. Since then, she had moved to the West and was now at the Olympics with her husband, whom she wanted to introduce. Bukač moved to where a tall man stood in an enormous white chinchilla coat and hat. "This is Doníček! My husband. He is a *visionary*." The three chatted briefly before Bukač went back to his team. Before he left, he wished her well. "It is very nice to see you again, Ivana Zelníčková. Oh, wait, you're married. What is your name now?" The woman broke into a big grin. "Trump," she said. "I'm now Ivana Trump."[34]

The Thursday, February 14, match against the Americans turned out to be nothing like what the Czechoslovak team had expected. With the departure of the veterans in 1977–78, Czechoslovakia's team chemistry had fallen apart and the US thrashed the visitors 7–3.[35] From there, the remainder of the tournament was a disappointment for Czechoslovakia. After losing a match to Sweden, it beat Canada in a 1:30 P.M. game on February 22 to finish in fifth place.

Within an hour after the Czechoslovakia-Canada game, the Americans and Soviets took to the ice in what became the most famous hockey match in Olympic history. The two squads finished the first period tied 2–2, before the Soviets scored once, to take the lead in the second period. In the third period, as the crowd went wild with "U-S-A!" chants, the US team scored twice to improbably beat the Soviets 4–3 in what became known as the "Miracle on Ice." The Americans went on to beat Finland 4–2 in their final match for the gold medal. In Czechoslovakia, it stung that the US—which didn't even seem to particularly care about hockey—had now won two Olympic gold medals (in 1960 and 1980) and Czechoslovakia, where people worshipped the sport, had won none.

Despite the poor outcome of its team in the Olympics, the fine performances of a number of its players, including the boys from Bratislava, gave Czechoslovakia hope going forward. Indeed, as a group, the Šťastnýs scored 40 percent of Czechoslovakia's goals in Lake Placid, and the following league season continued to excel. Each of the Šťastnýs finished in the top ten in points, and Peter became a full-fledged superstar. Just twenty-three years old, he became the first Slovak ever to win the Golden Stick award as the league's best player.

And then, at the end of the season, he found himself in hot water.

Even growing up in an authoritarian system that punished people who didn't play by the rules, Peter Šťastný never seemed to recognize the authority of the Communists. Because of his position as a hockey superstar, he had never gotten into any trouble, even as he openly flaunted his Catholic faith and called out police who tried to intimidate Slovak civilians. However, he finally crossed an invisible line in the months after the Olympics when the Bratislava players revolted against the Slovan team's head coach, Ladislav Horský. Horský showed up late for games; he missed practices; and he traded away six of the team's best players, seemingly just as a cash grab. Peter helped lead the squad in formulating and signing a petition to remove the coach and refused to practice until management did so. It was quite a move—players in a communist country refusing to play. And Czechoslovakia's leaders had no patience for those who pushed back against their dictates.

To be sure, not everyone in Czechoslovakia agreed to follow the rules. The most prominent of these "dissidents" was playwright and philosopher Václav Havel. Born into a wealthy family in Prague on October 5, 1936, Havel found the path to his preferred schools blocked by the Communists in the 1950s because of his bourgeois background. In the 1960s, he began to work as a stagehand in Prague theater but turned increasingly to writing his own plays. His first full-length work was staged in Prague in 1963, followed by others over the next five years. In 1968, one of his plays was performed in New York City.

The year 1968 marked Havel's move to serious opposition. During the Soviet invasion, he took to the radio airwaves to broadcast about events on the ground. As he saw the shift that occurred under Husák in the years that followed, he grew deeply concerned. On the first anniversary of the invasion, Ludvík Vaculík, the author of "The Two Thousand Words" manifesto, crafted an open petition, signed by Havel and eight others, that condemned normalization.

The authorities charged the petition's signatories with the crime of subverting the republic, and in the years that followed found other ways of punishing dissidents like Havel and Vaculík. The police followed, harassed, and interrogated them, tore apart their homes, tapped their phones, banned them from organizations, fired them from their jobs, and threatened them with prison.

These actions hardly dissuaded Havel, who sent an open letter to Husák in 1975 in which he decried the meaninglessness of life in Czechoslovakia. Husák and the Communists, he said, had created a system of "political apartheid," in which the regime had no real aim except the protection of its own power and therefore used fear of punishment to force everyone else to act and speak precisely as it dictated.

In 1976, the Czechoslovak regime took its repression a step further, which elicited an even sharper response from the country's dissidents. In the early

1970s, the government had announced that only musical groups that it licensed could perform and refused to authorize some 3,000 musical acts.[36] In 1976, the authorities forcefully asserted their power on this issue, arresting nineteen people associated with the country's underground music industry for "disturbing the peace." What that really meant was that the detained were "nonconformists" who wore their hair long and performed unconventional music.[37]

On January 1, 1977, an unlikely union of former reform Communists, Catholics, other religious advocates, and intellectuals, including Havel, formed an organization named Charter 77. The group put together a manifesto, with more than 240 signatures, that criticized the government for eliminating people's freedoms and violating their civil rights. The chartists decried the way that the regime controlled every aspect of public life. Life couldn't just be about the narrow range of things approved by the regime. People had to be free to control their own fates. Eventually, more than 1,500 people signed the document.

The regime decided to show what would happen to people who criticized it. When Havel, Vaculík, and fellow Charter 77 member Pavel Landovský attempted to deliver the manifesto to official government bodies, they were immediately detained and subjected to further harassment. Landovský was banned from working in theater, beaten severely by a government agent, and ultimately chose to emigrate to Vienna for his own safety. In the past when the government had tried to pressure Vaculík to halt his opposition activities or to leave the country for good, he refused. But following the release of the Charter 77 document, the authorities pushed harder. They knew that several years earlier, Vaculík had posed for nude photographs with a woman with whom he was having an extramarital affair. Now the regime published the photographs and even broadcast them on television. In 1978, Havel helped found a new dissident group that focused on uncovering and revealing specific cases of government injustice in Czechoslovakia. For their actions in this area, in 1979 the government took six people, including Havel, to trial for subversion. All six were convicted and Havel was sentenced to four and a half years in prison.[38]

The authorities had no interest in cracking down so forcefully on their star athletes, but officials would do what was necessary to maintain control. When confronted with the Slovan Bratislava player revolt in 1980, they started off more gently than they had with the country's dissidents. The Slovan front office began to pressure the players and, before long, most of the squad agreed to return to the ice. But not Peter Šťastný.

In late spring 1980, the team management abruptly reached out to Peter, informing him that a limousine was on its way to pick him up. The car delivered him to a group of men that included a high-level official from Slovan, other high-ranking Communists, and a military colonel. The group had grown tired of Peter's "independence" and informed him, "If you don't do what we tell you, you will never again play for Czechoslovakia's national team." The words stabbed Peter like a knife to the heart. The prospect of losing hockey was unbearable. He returned to Slovan, but the authorities had forced his hand.

The weeks passed all the way from spring into late summer. At 2 P.M. on Thursday, August 21, Gilles Lèger, the director of player development for the NHL's Quebec Nordiques, was sitting in his office when the club's receptionist buzzed him. "A Peter Stastny" was on the line for him. The Canadian man nearly fell out of his chair. Lèger had scouted the Šťastnýs for years, and the Quebec team owner, Marcel Aubut, told people that he had heard about "a mother in Czechoslovakia who gave birth to three hockey stars." Aubut and Lèger had vowed to find a way to get them out from behind the Iron Curtain.

After the Slovan officials had threatened Peter with the end of his hockey career, he had gone to see Anton. "We need to get out of here." They looked ahead and saw a chance. Each year, the IIHF held the European Cup, and Slovan Bratislava had qualified to be one of the Cup's final four teams in Innsbruck in August of 1980. Moreover, because the Cup was such a big honor, Czechoslovakia's hockey authorities permitted Peter's eight-month pregnant wife, Darina, to attend the tournament as well.

In late August, the Bratislava squad headed to Innsbruck. After settling into their hotel, Peter and Anton walked to a public pay phone and dialed the number they had found in an NHL media guide. Peter had been studying English and haltingly told the Canadian man that he and Anton were in Austria. "Do you have interest? We are prepared. We only come in pairs. But hurry. The tournament ends on August 24." Lèger had *a lot* of interest. He told Peter to sit tight. Just before noon the next day, Peter received a phone call. It was Lèger. "Peter, we're at the Europa Tyrol Hotel, two blocks away from you." Following

Slovan's match that evening, Peter and Anton came to the hotel and worked out contracts with the Nordiques.

As they finalized the contracts, they finally told their brother Marián. There had never been any chance that the authorities would permit Marián's wife and three children to join him in Innsbruck. To even make the request would have raised suspicions. And without his wife and kids, there was no way Marián would even consider leaving with his brothers. But Innsbruck was Peter and Anton's best chance to go, and they told their brother their plan. It was the worst moment of Marián's life. "What? You're not coming back?" He saw it all in front of him. Life as he had known it in Bratislava would be over.

Around midnight after the final match was played on the evening of Sunday, August 24, the Slovan team bus idled, waiting for the final passengers. Peter and Anton were not there, and it soon became clear that the two younger Šťastnýs would not be coming. When the despised Slovan coach Horský boarded, Marián snapped: "It's your fault!" The bus grew silent and began the long drive home. [39]

Meanwhile, Aubut provided a red Mercedes to transport the other Šťastnýs. After driving through the night, Anton, Peter, and Darina arrived at the Intercontinental Hotel in Vienna, where they discerned that Czechoslovak agents hiding behind tinted car windows and dark sunglasses had them staked out. Austrian police officers, including commandos, swung into action. The heavily armed forces, looking ready to shoot at a moment's notice, cleared the hotel—the hallway from the hotel room, the elevator, the lobby, and the sidewalk—to create a corridor for the Šťastnýs. No one could get within fifty feet. As they walked through, Lèger and Aubut handed out $100 bills to the men protecting them. To avoid being tailed to the Canadian Embassy, they all jumped into a car that received a full police escort. With sirens blaring, the group charged ahead, racing onto sidewalks, park lawns, and even the wrong direction down one-way streets. After the three Šťastnýs got visas at the embassy, the escorts continued with the group to the airport and then stayed with them until the flight was ready for takeoff.

The group arrived in Montreal on the evening of Monday, August 25. Within hours, the news in Canada was all about Peter and Anton. When they then flew to Quebec, thousands of Nordique hockey fans came to greet them at the airport. The hockey super-brothers had come to the right place, and they rewarded their Quebec supporters with terrific hockey play. Peter, in particular, quickly became recognized as an NHL superstar as he set the single season record for scoring by a rookie.

But Anton and Peter suffered over the plight of their brother. Although he was just twenty-seven and in the prime of his career, in Czechoslovakia Marián had become toxic. No one could safely speak to him. Anyone who tried might be brought to police headquarters for questioning. The Slovan team management instructed Marián to collect his belongings and never again set foot inside the team locker room. Other authorities let him know that his children would not be permitted to attend the university. He was under heavy surveillance and required to report twice a week to his local police station.

Marián focused on finding a way out. As the months passed, he got the chance he was looking for when he learned that the authorities were no longer monitoring him full-time. On Tuesday, June 2, 1981, a little more than nine months after Anton and Peter had left, Marián and his wife, Eva, piled the three kids into their car's back seat and took off for a "holiday." Just days later, Marián, Eva, and the kids boarded a flight in Austria. When they landed, they were in Montreal. [40]

Not just one, but all three brothers had made it to Canada. They proceeded to form a potent, terrifying Quebec offensive line that took the NHL by storm.

But there was no forgetting where they had come from and what the regime there was willing to do to those who crossed it. Even after he had settled safely in Quebec, Peter would wake up in the middle of the night drenched in sweat from a nightmare. In his dream, he was playing a match against the Soviets in Prague when suddenly he realized that he had to get away because otherwise they were going to lock him up. [41]

# PART IV

## CHILDREN OF THE OCCUPATION

*It was hell. It was a war . . . . If you're going to play against Russians, you had to give it back 110 percent. Even if you have to die out there, you wanted to beat them. You wanted to kill them on the ice, pay them back for what happened to us, the whole country, in 1968.*
—Miroslav Frycer, Czechoslovak hockey player[1]

# CHAPTER 13

# Training to Go

E ven as he remained in Czechoslovakia, Jaroslav Holík didn't worry about getting locked up. In fact, it seemed that there was little—outside of ski jumping and flying in an airplane—that scared the man. On the ice, he mixed it up with the largest, most vicious opponents. Off the ice, he constantly criticized everyone, even the Communists, who could squash him like a bug. But one thing did terrify Jaroslav: that something might happen to his family.

Sometimes acquaintances would, very timidly, ask Marie how she could live with such a beast. But the wild man actually had a softer side, which came out more as he got older. To be sure, he never held back his natural abrasiveness. Sometimes Marie had to kick him under the table to stop him from blurting out his irritation with dinner guests. But over the years, he began to show other parts to his personality as well. He developed an appreciation for classical paintings and art. He grew bonsai trees. And at times, he even displayed charming sweetness. Female cashiers from the local markets glowed to Marie about her husband's gentlemanly flirting: "My dearie, can I buy a few slices of bacon? But don't tell. I'll have to eat it in the car so my wife doesn't punish me for eating it all!" This side of Jaroslav emerged in countless little ways at home. Marie felt that he was transformed when he came in the front door. He had little interest in music, but knew that Marie loved classical. When he came across an arrangement on the radio that he thought that she would like, he rushed to share it with her. He brought Marie flowers regularly. And he told her every day that she was his "everything."[1]

Most of all, Jaroslav's insides were mush when it came to his kids. He didn't let anyone see, but like any parent, he worried constantly about their safety.

And living under the Communists, he felt unbridled terror at the possibility that the regime might one day decide to ruin the lives of the two young people at the center of his universe. So even before Big Ned, Martina, and the Šťastný brothers took their big leaps overseas, Jaroslav developed an ambitious plan to help his children escape.

It seemed almost surprising that anyone on Dukla, especially players who were also on the national team, even had kids. Between matches, tournaments, and training camps, the players traveled *a lot*. Lacking subtlety, Jaroslav was fond of telling people that, because of this schedule, he and Marie were rarely in the same place except for March and that their kids, therefore, were born in January.

Jaroslav and Marie's first child arrived on January 15, 1968, nine months after Jaroslav's return from the 1967 World Championships that had first caused him so much trouble. With the uber-masculine Jaroslav as the father, Marie fully expected a son who would carry on the family's hockey name. "Jesus Christ, it's a girl," she exclaimed in shock when she met her daughter. Jaroslav and Marie named her Andrea after a popular Czechoslovak actress at the time. Jaroslav immediately built the little girl into his training. Passersby soon saw the mad hockey player on his daily runs to the local pond, pushing a baby carriage with Andrea in it . . . and Marie sitting on his shoulders.[2] On January 1, 1971, Jaroslav and Marie got their baby boy. They named him Robert after Jaroslav's kind maternal grandfather, Horák.[3] As Jaroslav found himself sitting out the 1971 World Championships for his actions in Stockholm, a leading hockey magazine put on its cover a photo of the beaming Jaroslav and Marie, along with a blond preschooler and a new baby, under the headline, "Has a new hockey star been born?"

Jaroslav Holík loved his life in Czechoslovakia. He loved the beauty that surrounded him. He loved living in a town where his children were surrounded by the values of hard work and family. And he loved how in Jihlava the athletic facilities were so close to home that he could constantly be there to oversee the children's training.

He also wanted to help his kids get the hell out of there.

He despised the Communists for taking away his family's butcher shop. He loathed the leaders who dominated the country and, all the while, served as Moscow's puppet. He hated how the government kept people locked within the country's borders and regulated every aspect of their lives. And he abhorred the system that could remove him so arbitrarily from the national team. Jaroslav knew that his prominent position while he was still playing inoculated him to some degree, but he feared for his children, who might not be equally protected as they grew up in what he called the "commie morass."

As the kids got older, Jaroslav told them, "Living an average life isn't worth it." He meant the sentiment partly as a life philosophy. But given the Czechoslovakia he lived in, he especially meant it as a roadmap. Only through athletic greatness, made possible by *his* training, could Andrea and Robert escape. Jaroslav determined everything—their diet, their daily training, and more. Ája and Bobby, as their parents called them, couldn't even choose their own sports. Before they were born, Jaroslav had determined that the girl would play tennis and the boy would play hockey. Each began with Jaroslav as coach.

Marie thought Jaroslav had gone overboard, that he was *too* fixated on the kids, but she agreed with his logic. As the family of a star athlete, the Holíks lived a good life. They had a good income from a job that Jaroslav adored. While others couldn't afford or get access to many even marginally desirable goods, the Holíks always got first crack at everything. For the average person in Czechoslovakia, it was a rare treat, occurring maybe once a year, to purchase bananas. Communist Party members could usually get them first, but exceptions were also made for the families of stars like Jaroslav.

However, the invasion made clear to Marie how quickly and completely things could change. Given Jaroslav's prominence and his big mouth, he might be imprisoned if he wasn't careful. Marie wanted to defect, probably to Sweden, where Jaroslav could make a living playing hockey. But he simply didn't want to leave. As frightened as she was about what could happen to her husband, Marie's greatest concern was for the kids. What could happen to them under a regime that controlled the lives of everyone, had no constraints on its power, and felt no limits on its willingness to act vengefully? Marie, too, became dedicated to pushing her children into careers that they could use in the outside world. Part of that dedication involved making sure that the kids stuck precisely to Jaroslav's training plan. But part of it was recognizing how hard they were working and making sure that they had enough support, love, and food (!) from her to sustain them when they were at home. [4]

By the early 1970s, Czechoslovakia had become a great place for youngsters, especially girls, who wanted to develop as tennis players. The country had an ambivalent relationship with the sport. The Communists and even Czechoslovakia's sports organization looked down upon tennis as a "bourgeois" game.[5] Yet decades earlier the authorities had also celebrated the tennis brilliance of Jaroslav Drobný. But after Drobný defected to the West in 1949, the government did not permit Czechoslovakia's tennis players to travel outside the Eastern Bloc for the next five years.[6] Still, many of the country's top athletes flocked to the sport, and over time the tennis program developed. By 1974, Martina Navrátilová had become one of the world's best female players, and even after her defection in 1975, Czechoslovak tennis continued to thrive.

Andrea was five years old, with short honey-blond hair and delicate facial features, when Jaroslav first thrust a racket into her hands and began training her. Andrea was skinny, but also fast and agile, with terrific hand-eye coordination. Although not especially big for her age, she was the best natural athlete in the Holík house. Sports were simply *easy* for her. Jaroslav filled Andrea's days with long runs, strengthening exercises, and hours on the tennis court. As soon as little Bobby could run, he joined her, but not as a player. The tiny towheaded boy ran all over the court picking up errant balls, which he stored in a large laundry detergent bottle.

After a few simple words of instruction from her father, Andrea marched dutifully out to a wall where she might smack balls for two hours without supervision. When he felt that her effort level or performance were not up to snuff, Jaroslav nailed her with a tennis ball, once even leaving a bruise. He hired additional coaches to provide greater expertise. Whenever he learned that one of his hockey teammates played tennis, Jaroslav insisted that the man hit balls with his daughter. He spent huge sums of money on a West German machine that fired powerful shots all around the court for her to try to return. Even when the family went on vacation to Yugoslavia, Jaroslav hired a local to practice with Andrea. Beach time began only after the day's training had been completed.[7]

It soon became clear that Andrea was something special on the tennis court. In 1976, when she was just eight years old, she received her first trophy as the winner of a major youth tournament in the town of Třinec, nearly 200 miles away from home.[8] Andrea hardly cherished the brutal training, but when she started to beat other kids, she figured out what she loved about tennis: winning.

She wanted to be better than everyone else. As this fact dawned on her, she worked harder.[9] By the time she was ten, she had become one of the country's most promising young players. Jaroslav felt so proud of her that he introduced her to her greatest challenge yet: a tennis match against Jan Suchý, one of the best *adult* athletes in the country. So confident was Jaroslav in Andrea that he bet a case of champagne on the outcome.

It was an odd pairing. On one side of the net stood the stocky, dark-haired thirty-three-year-old defenseman, whose default serious expression couldn't help but intimidate the little girl. On the other side stood Andrea, who looked like a typical ten-year-old, with her lanky frame, generally sweet expression, and straight blond hair that was just a step away from a traditional bowl cut. However, someone looking closer would have also noticed sharply defined muscles in the girl's arms and legs and flawless coordination as she strode across the court. Play quickly turned intense as the two traded points. Andrea's strokes looked smooth and she could seemingly hit the ball anywhere that she chose. She concentrated so hard that she didn't notice her own funny habit on forehand shots of holding her non-racket thumb and index finger apart, as if trying to show how long an inch-and-a-half was. Her skinny arms belied the great power of her strokes, especially on the backhand side. Ultimately, though, Suchý's speed and especially his strength proved too much for Andrea, leaving Jaroslav openly frustrated with his daughter's performance.[10]

Over the 1970s, as he moved past thirty years of age and Andrea's tennis skill developed, Jaroslav watched his own hockey game start to unravel—but not before he kickstarted his son's career. Big, strong, and with the genes of an athlete, Bobby learned to walk at ten months old and then turned to trying to skate.[11] By 1974, Jaroslav began to bring three-year-old Bobby to Dukla practices with him. So little that he couldn't even see over the boards onto the ice, throughout practice Bobby waited impatiently for his turn. During a break in training, Jaroslav helped Bobby put on his skates, tied the laces, and sent him out to the ice, where the littlest Holík would start with an unsteady grip on the boards, let go, and fall.

Soon, though, Bobby gained his balance and glided confidently around the rink. Before long, he found himself skating with a hockey stick, smacking a puck into a net. The local Modeta Jihlava club invited him to join a competitive traveling team that was otherwise entirely populated by kids a year or two older than the five-year-old Holík boy. There was a downside to this success. Bobby was named team captain and ran home in tears. As captain, he was required to sign the team's scorecard, but he hadn't started school yet and didn't know how to write.[12]

Jaroslav pushed his kids hard, so that as small children they cried over the difficulty of the workouts. Long before high-tech athletic footwear was popular, Jaroslav sent Andrea and Bobby out for long runs in the fields wearing specially made shoes to reduce the stress on their joints.[13] When they saw factory workers walking straight to the pub after a long, grueling day, Jaroslav told his kids, "That's how you'll end up if you don't work hard."[14] Rather than get a job, Marie stayed home with Andrea and Bobby and focused on the kids' non-sports side. The division of labor between the two parents was so sharp, and Jaroslav so fixated on athletics, that at times he wasn't quite sure what grade in school they were in.[15]

Bobby took after his father in his training. Neither had the natural athleticism of Andrea or Uncle Jiří, so both Bobby and Jaroslav had to push their bodies to absurd limits. Every day at 11 A.M., Jaroslav dropped Bobby off at the rink to practice his skating for an hour. One day, Jaroslav got hung up with an errand. When he returned to the rink after three hours, he found little Bobby, who couldn't tell time, sobbing—but still pushing himself all-out on his drills around the ice. At its core, though, Bobby *loved* to play hockey. It was always fun, but he got particular joy out of putting every effort into succeeding at the highest level that *he* could, and he therefore followed his father's instructions carefully. Bobby never got upset by his father's overbearing training. He thought that it was simply part of the process of becoming great. Jaroslav told him about North America's hockey stars and brought the boy copies of the English-language *The Hockey News* from the West. To someone in the middle of Czechoslovakia, behind the Iron Curtain, playing hockey in the great North American National Hockey League was all but an impossibility, but even at that very young age Bobby decided he would find a way to play in the NHL. In school, he wrote an essay explaining that he would become a hockey player—but only after he worked exceptionally hard for many years.

Surrounded by big personalities, especially his father's, Bobby developed into a shy, quiet child, especially around his older teammates. He became noted for his stoicism, almost totally unwilling to let anyone know when he felt physical discomfort. It was alarming therefore when, at nine years of age, he began to complain of pain stabbing him at the roof of his mouth. After finding no luck with the local dentist—who pulled the boy's tooth without even using anesthesia—the Holíks took him to a specialist, who informed the family that Bobby had tumors in his jawbone. Surgery was needed, but Bobby insisted that they wait until the end of hockey season so that he wouldn't miss any time on the ice. Six months after the procedure, which left Bobby in the hospital for a month, the tumors grew back and Jaroslav and Marie were broken-hearted when told that their little boy might need radiation treatment. With tears streaming down their faces, Bobby's parents explained the situation to their son. Incredibly, in response, it was Bobby who consoled them. "Radiation doesn't hurt. It'll help me." After more surgeries, a substantial portion of Bobby's jawbone and his rear teeth were gone and he had little feeling in his face. But the tumors stopped appearing.[16]

Despite the central place sports held in their lives, Jaroslav also talked about compartmentalizing: when you do sports, you give it everything, but for the rest of the day you need to live the other parts of your life. For the Holíks, time with the grandparents was top priority. Bobby had friends in Jihlava and he spent time with all his grandparents, but his maternal grandfather was the single person in the world he was closest to.

Born Josef Chmelař in 1918, Marie's dad never knew his own father, who for unexplained reasons was out of the picture by the time Josef's mother died in 1924. Prior to her death, Josef's mother married another man who didn't raise Josef but gave him the last name Prchal. Raised by his older sister in a small village near Jihlava, Josef Prchal largely kept to himself as a child. Unlike others in the village, when he grew up, he eschewed the drinking and card-playing social life at the pub and instead spent his time reading. Although very bright, Josef never had a chance to attend school beyond the most basic levels. Ordinarily the village church provided orphans with academic scholarships. However, since Josef had a living stepfather, the church did not view him as qualifying for funding. For the rest of his life, he remained disappointed that he never received a proper education, and he never forgave the church for turning its back on him. When he grew up, Josef became an office clerk. He eventually met Marie's mother, who first dated him because she felt sorry for the lonely orphan. Over time, though, Josef won her over with his quiet intelligence and kindness. When the Communists came to power in 1948, the Prchals, who had little money or hope for upward mobility, embraced the new government and became members of the Party.[17]

Many years later, Josef would show an even deeper commitment to something nearer to his heart: his grandchildren. Josef had chain-smoked throughout his life, but he wanted to keep the kids healthy. The moment Andrea was born, and long before most people were concerned about tobacco, he quit smoking.

However, it was with Bobby that he most bonded. People would say that Bobby was like Jaroslav in hockey, but in everything else he was like Marie's dad. Josef had always loved nature, and in Bobby he found a soulmate to join him in the outdoors. Beginning when Bobby was little, the boy and his mother's parents regularly hopped into Josef's East German Trabant automobile and headed to a little cottage in the woods. When it rained, the car sometimes got stuck. Bobby and his grandmother tried to push the car as Josef yelled instructions while spinning the wheels. Long before they got the car moving again, Bobby and Grandma would be covered in mud. At the cabin Josef taught Bobby how to hunt all year round, but otherwise each season was different. In the spring, Bobby and Josef worked together on a garden, which by summer produced wonderful peppers, tomatoes, and carrots. In the winter, they took long walks around the outside of the cabin, snow up to their waists. In the summer, they hiked in search of natural water sources. During one summer hike, they even saw lightning hit a tree right beside them, leaving Bobby terrified of thunder for years afterward.

It wasn't just the outdoors that drew them together. Grandfather and grandson both craved knowledge. Josef constantly read about history and geography and then taught Bobby. The two also loved to just sit together reading silently. The young boy, trying to learn everything about the world past and present. The older man next to him, with reading glasses, a newspaper, and a pen in his chest pocket to systematically mark off each article that he read. Bobby became known as a walking encyclopedia, and future teammates would refer to him as "professor."

But much of the time that Bobby and his grandfather spent together they just talked. Usually about books, life, and the world around them.[18]

Sometimes Bobby heard his father and grandfather argue about the Communists. Josef believed in the ideals of communism, which promoted equality even for those like himself, who had grown up with little education and few opportunities for advancement. Over time, though, as it appeared obvious that Communist Party officials benefited much more than everyone else in Czechoslovakia, Bobby watched his grandfather become increasingly hesitant, half-hearted even, when he pushed back against Jaroslav's declarations that the regime was corrupt. At times, Grandpa simply drifted into lugubrious silence, possibly agreeing but not wanting to admit it.

As she approached middle-school age, Andrea became so busy with tennis that she had much less time to spend with the grandparents, but Jaroslav's father insisted on also coaching her. When she was born, Jaroslav Sr. announced, "She will be a skier!" When Ája was just a few years old, he began to train her to become a downhill racer. Throughout the winter he took her up to the mountains, trips that required massive effort on his part. No more than five feet, nine inches tall but well over 250 pounds, the out-of-shape man trudged up the hills to the starting gates. Before he could catch his breath, the little girl would be done, waiting for him at the bottom. When Andrea tired of the sport, her grandfather remained dogged: "You just have to stick through it. The old ones will soon stop and then you will be the best!"

As Andrea developed in both tennis and skiing, the Holíks entered a transition period. In 1977, even though he knew that it was time to hang up his skates, Jaroslav stayed on for two more years because he believed that it was his relatively flexible schedule as a player that allowed him to spend so much time with his family. It was essential that he have time to train the kids, but there was also more to it. To Jaroslav, it was important just to see them.

Even when he returned home late at night from a trip out of the country, the next morning Andrea and Bobby found their father waiting for them in a chair by the dining area, in his pajamas, or a bathrobe if it was cold. He chatted with them while they ate their breakfast before heading off to school.[19] He told them stories of what he saw outside their little bubble. The extreme poverty of people in the Soviet Union. The amazing products sold by stores in the West. How, in the West, governments didn't control people's lives so much, thus creating much more opportunity for those who worked hard.

As Jaroslav moved toward retirement, he saw his ten-year-old tennis prodigy reaching new heights. Jaroslav and Marie decided that it was time for their girl to train her outstanding left-handed tennis strokes year round, even in the winter when her grandfather insisted on taking her up to the ski slopes. But they weren't sure how to break the news to the old butcher.

Fate intervened. Jaroslav Sr. had never treated his body with care, eating and drinking to excess and chain-smoking, following a pattern that wreaked havoc on the health of his family. His sister, brother, and father all died at the age of fifty-six. Sure enough, Jaroslav Sr. had his first heart attack in 1964, at the age of forty-two. He tried to cut at least some of the excess weight, but never fully committed. He had no such trouble, though, putting his all into caring for his grandchildren. Every week, he looked forward to taking them fishing. And every year he couldn't wait for the weather to turn warm so that he could take Andrea and Bobby to a nearby lake to frolic. One such lovely day in 1978, the two Holík kids and their grandfather, looking much older than his fifty-six years, headed to their favorite spot. Andrea and Bobby sprinted into the water to swim, but they soon noticed a commotion on the beach. As they ran to get a closer look, they saw a group of adults surrounding their grandfather, trying to give him nitroglycerine. Paramedics rushed him to the hospital, but there was nothing anyone could do. Bobby would never forget that his grandfather had died caring for him. [20]

As the Holíks grieved, the country's tennis centers took an interest in Andrea. The elite state-run Přerov tennis academy invited Andrea to join its Youngsters Program. Each week, mother and daughter traveled the hundred miles east to Přerov, where they stayed for three days while Andrea trained. When Andrea turned twelve, the training grew more intense, and she moved full-time into a dormitory in Přerov. Despite the difficulty of being away from her family, she found comfort in the care of her coach and his wife, who all but adopted the young phenom. Her tennis improved sharply. Andrea had always been a huge fan of Swedish star Bjorn Borg and modeled her game accordingly, developing a terrific two-handed backhand and a strong forehand. Andrea never quite perfected the art of playing at the net, but with her speed, agility, and instincts, she could reach and return balls hit seemingly anywhere on the court. She moved rapidly up the junior rankings. [21]

In the summer of 1979, as Andrea's game jumped up a level, Jaroslav decided to retire from playing in Czechoslovakia's hockey league. The obvious next move was to follow the same path as his brother and Suchý, among others, and play professionally in the West. But, to Jaroslav, moving to the West looked miserable, and leaving the top tier of hockey in Czechoslovakia looked just as awful.

In 1978, Jiří had gone to play for a professional squad in West Germany and would later join teams in Austria. Even giving the Czechoslovak government 30 percent of what he took in, Jiří would make more money playing briefly in the West than in his entire time with Dukla and the national team combined. However, players couldn't bring their families with them to the West and Jiří missed his horribly. After just a few years, he fully retired from playing hockey and stayed in Czechoslovakia for good.

In 1979, Jan Suchý joined a team in Vienna, but his pay was nothing close to Jiří's. To subsidize his income, Suchý smuggled in champagne and Hungarian salami, which he then sold to his Austrian teammates. The biggest highlight of his time in Vienna was off the ice as he brought his mother-in-law for a visit. Having consumed a steady diet of anti-Western propaganda, the woman couldn't believe how different everything was from what she had been told back home. People behaved politely. The streets looked beautiful. And the shops . . . they contained products that one could only imagine in Czechoslovakia. She began to cry, feeling stupid for believing the Communists' lies. Suchý didn't remain in the West for long. He moved to a West German team, where he dominated the competition not only on the ice, but also in organized beer-drinking competitions, but after a couple of years found that no one could pay him enough to merit staying any longer.

As they returned home, Jiří and Suchý learned firsthand how quickly Czechoslovakia's leaders forgot those who were no longer of any use to them. Late in Jiří's career in Czechoslovakia, President Husák had told him and the other hockey players, "Don't worry, comrades, after you retire, we will take care of you." Yet, when Jiří returned from the West, the authorities informed him that by law he had one month to find a job. After years of being paid well below Western salaries, Jiří thought ruefully: *the comrades really "took care of" me, didn't they?* Fortunately, during off-seasons he had studied education at a university in Brno. He could have made more money as a professional hockey coach, but the idea of spending one more day in a training camp away from his family made his heart hurt. So, in 1985, international hockey legend Jiří Holík began his new career as a geography and physical education teacher for students eleven to fifteen years of age.[22] Suchý, meanwhile, signed to play in one of Czechoslovakia's lower hockey leagues, where a smattering of fans attended simply to heckle him: "You criminal!" "Retire, grandpa!" It wasn't great money, so Suchý had to rely upon a day job as a dispatcher for a recycling center.[23]

Even in 1979, as he contemplated his own retirement, Jaroslav could see the direction in which Jiří and Suchý were headed and wanted something different. Moving to the West without his family was a nonstarter. But it was also unimaginable to him to leave high-level hockey.

Jaroslav prepared himself for a job that would allow him to remain in hockey and stay with his family. He would become a coach. At the invitation of Professor Kostka, he studied physical education and sport at Charles University. In classic Jaroslav fashion, Holík dove into his studies. Often, he put his kids to bed at 9 o'clock in the evening and then stayed up all night doing his schoolwork.

Knowing what he had in Jaroslav, Coach Pitner brought in Holík to serve as his second assistant coach behind Neveselý. From the moment Jaroslav traded his hockey jersey for a coach's civies, he brought his usual intensity to the position. He only lauded players in private, believing public praise killed their drive. He channeled the theories introduced to him at the university into new drills and in-game sets. He even consulted with top track and field trainers to develop new off-ice training approaches. When Pitner stepped down in 1982, Neveselý moved up to the head coach position and Jaroslav became the official assistant coach. Neveselý and Jaroslav shared a manic obsession with the sport and talked about nothing but hockey all day, constantly strategizing over how to take the Dukla team to another level. In each of their first three seasons together, they led Dukla to Czechoslovakia's league championship.[24]

Jaroslav's boosters warned him that he would never have the opportunity to become head coach of Dukla if he didn't join the Communist Party, so beginning in 1984 Holík agreed to let Neveselý make appeals to admit him into the Party. When the Party leaders took up the case of Coach and Lieutenant Colonel Holík, they dispatched the secret police to investigate him further. What they learned didn't look good. Much of the intel wasn't *so* bad, especially for a person who had brought so much glory to Czechoslovakia. He had socialized with known defectors and illegally acquired and attempted to exchange foreign currency.

However, the investigators also found detailed evidence of his disdain for the Czechoslovak state. Jaroslav had openly expressed his view that the regime cared simply about maintaining its own power and bestowing favors upon those who joined the Party, independent of whether they had any talent or even put in effort. Jaroslav was openly disgusted by what he saw as a corrupt system in Czechoslovakia that encouraged widespread laziness. The secret police gleaned that at a meet-and-greet event between Dukla Jihlava and members of an agricultural cooperative Jaroslav ripped into the farmers, telling them, "I would never do your job no matter how much I got paid. You oafs, you do nothing, you get everything from the government for free!"

Investigators had no difficulty finding other expressions of Jaroslav's contempt for the state. Informants told story after story of Holík badmouthing the Czechoslovak system and the Communist Party as responsible for everything wrong in the country, as well as speaking favorably about the West. Jaroslav had complained about how much better the supply of consumer goods was abroad. He also talked about how much better Andrea's opportunities were in the West and how terrible it was that she had to give up so much of her prize money to Czechoslovakia's government.[25] The final report pulled no punches:

> It was discovered that [Holík] likes to evaluate life in [Czechoslovakia] negatively; has constant reservations toward events in our country; and is overly critical toward the faults of his superiors, army officials, and other state officials. [Holík] is unduly critical of various problems in our state, is very vulgar, and creates a negative atmosphere wherever he talks about these issues. . . . [Holík] frequently contrasts life in Czechoslovakia with life in the West, and this comparison is presented generally in favor of the West. . . . I recommend that his investigation is conducted under the codename "REBEL," and to deepen, confirm, and document further observations. The file will be located in the section "hidden enemies."[26]

With all that, the Party refused to consider further the matter of Jaroslav's admission.

For the most part, Jaroslav couldn't have cared less about the Party's decision. As a hockey star, he was well connected. He knew people in the capital's active black market who could acquire nearly anything he wanted from the West.

When he visited Prague, he often ran into the country's prime minister walking his dog. The prime minister feared that the giant German Shepherd would attack Jaroslav, but the Communist also always made a point of offering to help Holík and other athletes with whatever they needed.

Most of all, Jaroslav was happy with his role with Dukla, which worked perfectly with his greatest obsession. With Neveselý handling the bulk of team responsibilities, Jaroslav could dedicate himself to his family and to his kids' athletic development. [27]

He never considered, though, that at times he could have helped his kids most simply by keeping his mouth shut.

One evening, Jaroslav took Andrea to practice on a Jihlava tennis court at a time that he had reserved. He found the space taken by the Communist Party's regional secretary. When the Holíks' reservation time arrived, Jaroslav yelled for the official to move on, but the man refused, declaring, "I'm gonna play here and you'll be in line until I allow you to play." Jaroslav lost his mind, screaming "You shit face!" prompting a massive public shouting match.

The next day, the local Party committee ordered Jaroslav to report to a hearing, where it reprimanded him for his behavior and then referred him to a higher-level committee in Prague for further investigation. The Prague group ordered him to report to the political section of the highest levels of Czechoslovakia's military leadership, which dressed him down in the harshest terms. The group threatened to fire him from the military and from his position with the Dukla team. Then they uttered the words he most feared. "Comrade Holík, if you're going to continue to put on such a show, your children will pay for it." Staring into the face of his superiors, Jaroslav could hear the roar inside his own head, *I don't give a fuck! My kids are going to run away, anyway!* But for once, he held his tongue. Jaroslav deeply admired those who spat in the face of the Communists, even at the cost of their own families, but he would never be one of them. He submissively apologized and walked out of the meeting, completely broken. Feeling like a whipped dog, all the way home he thought how utterly powerless *everyone* was under the Communists, who could carry out any order, no matter how arbitrary or extreme, with the snap of a finger. But at least his kids were still safe.

With Andrea off at the tennis academy and Bobby getting older, Jaroslav sharply ramped up the boy's training. He started attending and helping coach Bobby's youth practices. Jaroslav actually enjoyed working with youngsters, especially because he could see the boys tangibly improve every day. Surprising no one who knew him, he didn't change his style for the kids. He drilled them mercilessly and no mistake went unpunished. He screamed at the boys in the locker room. On the bench. On the ice. As long as it was part of the hockey training, no space was safe from Jaroslav's ire. Years later, one of the stars of that peewee team told his own sons, when he didn't like how they were behaving, "Shut up or I'll beat you up like Mr. Holík!"[28]

Most of all, training Bobby to get out of the Eastern Bloc became Jaroslav's top priority. As Bobby got older, the cherubic, blond little boy turned into a dark-haired, square-jawed young man who was physically and mentally solid as a rock. To anyone who saw what Jaroslav had Bobby do every day, it was evident why the kid was getting so strong. It began when Bobby was six years old and Jaroslav suggested that the little boy start setting his morning alarm a bit earlier so that he could work out before breakfast. "How about you get up and do 100 push-ups, 100 pull-ups, 100 sit-ups, and 100 squats?" Bobby dutifully got up early the next day and did the workout. From then on, on his own, Bobby did the same workout every day until it got easier, at which point he would increase the number of repetitions.

By the time Bobby was a teenager, his training was akin to a montage in a *Rocky* film. Basic hockey preparation. Endless hours of skating. Joining multiple teams and playing different positions to learn every facet of the game. Drills. The Holíks' wall at home was made of concrete. "Practice shooting 1,000 pucks a day at specific spots on the wall."

The conditioning, though, was at a whole other level. Based on the science Jaroslav had learned in his physical education training, during the summer he took Bobby to a ski hill just outside of Jihlava. "Run to the top of this hill. Do pushups and situps for two minutes. Then come back down the hill. Do the whole set six times." Fridays meant two workouts, one that included sixty miles of bicycle riding over hilly terrain. Jaroslav incorporated training into leisure time. "You would like to go swimming at the lake today? Run the six miles there and have fun in the lake. When you're done, run back." To help the boy gain muscle weight, the son of a butcher fed him a heavy diet of protein, offering regular treats of steak tartare.

And, somehow, Bobby embraced it all. Jaroslav's genetic code had imprinted itself on the boy. He knew his father's reputation for hard work and decided to make it his own. *I will never let him down. I will outwork even him! I will be even greater than him!*

Jaroslav recommended that Bobby go for a lengthy run every day after hockey practice. One winter day, Bobby noticed that it was snowing unusually hard with massive gusts of wind. Without pausing, he put on his tracksuit and headed out. A family friend dropped by the house and asked where Bobby was. "Out for a run." The friend's jaw dropped. "Jaroslav, it's a blizzard out there." Responding to his friend's concern, Jaroslav took his car out and followed Bobby's usual route. Through the wall of falling snow, Jaroslav could barely make out a faint shape that appeared to be running in front of him. The father pulled up, rolled down the window. "You okay?" Bobby grunted, "Yeah, I'm good." Jaroslav nodded, gave a quick "Okay," and drove home. The wind blew so hard that by the time Bobby got back to the house he had an ear infection, but he could still skate, which was all that mattered. He was so ill at his next tournament that he could scarcely concentrate on what he was doing. Powered by instinct, he took home the event's best-player honors.

Still, Bobby *never* refused Jaroslav's orders. Only once did he even really hesitate to follow his dad's dictates. When Bobby was a teenager, Jaroslav had the boy handle the outdoor chore of leaf cleanup. One gray, damp day, he handed his son a gasoline can. "Pour it on." Bobby poured the gas on the leaves. Jaroslav then tossed the boy a set of matches. "No, Dad. No. It's going to explode." Jaroslav raised his eyebrows. Bobby threw the match. As the explosion knocked them back, Bobby screamed out, "That was fucking stupid!" Jaroslav bellowed back: "Did you just call me stupid?!" Bobby shut his mouth and refused to say more. But Jaroslav wouldn't let him forget it, forever reminding Bobby of that time he had talked back to his dad.

Through it all, Jaroslav never lost sight of the ultimate aim, which was to prepare the kids to move to the world on the other side of the Iron Curtain. He hired a private English-language tutor for them and even had a family friend share year-old *Time* magazines to help them practice English-language reading. Jaroslav installed satellite English-language television, which was fun because they could watch Western shows like *Magnum P.I.* or NHL hockey. [29]

Over time, Bobby started to get a sense of just why his parents wanted him to escape. When he first began school, Bobby mostly just accepted that the world was the way his teachers described, but as he got older he started to find it more difficult to reconcile what he learned at school with what his father told him. He attended a school where the vice principal was a dead ringer for Vladimir Lenin, the Communist hero of the Russian Revolution. Resplendent in a beige polyester suit and a pointed goatee, the vice principal also taught the school's geography classes. He stood over the children, quick to mete out punishments to anyone who was out of line as he spoke passionately: "Over here on the map is America, which plans nothing less than to spread its imperialism all over the world, scheming to go so far as to take control over the very land on which we live." The words just didn't jibe with what Bobby heard at home.

Every year for the big International Workers Day celebration held on May 1, the country's schools shut down so that the kids could play a central part in the festivities. Bobby marched with his classmates, all carrying Soviet flags and pictures of Stalin, Lenin, and Klement Gottwald, the first Communist president of Czechoslovakia. A man with a megaphone would chant out slogans that the children all dutifully repeated in unison. Even as they did so, Bobby and his friends recognized the absurdity of being instructed in how to express adoration for the regime and the puppet master that pulled the strings. Once away from the event, the boys openly laughed at it all.[30]

Bobby mostly didn't worry about such things, though, because it was training that dominated his life, his dad at the center of all of it. Hockey teammates, opponents, and parents alike shuddered when they watched Jaroslav treat his son—a star—like the worst, most gaffe-prone player on the ice, bellowing brutally harsh criticisms, with spit flying about as he screamed nonstop for hours at Bobby. Jiří tried to town down his brother's coaching and parenting style. "You're working them too hard!" Jaroslav pushed back. "But maybe they'll handle it and become something!"[31] Actually, on the sports side, the result of the training was hard to dispute. Bobby loved hockey, and from his earliest childhood he wanted to be great. As long as it would get him to the NHL, *any* training was fine with him.

Never the ideal child psychologist, Jaroslav feared that Andrea was too sensitive. Because she was typically well-behaved on the court, Jaroslav worried she might become unnerved by the words of her opponents. After he lambasted her for losing a winnable match, Andrea replied in tears, "But, Dad, she called me a bitch during the game!"[32] However, in worrying about Andrea, Jaroslav overlooked the influence he'd had on her. After years of her father's drilling, she constantly heard a voice in her head screaming to never quit on the court.[33]

In fact, as good as Bobby was in youth hockey, it appeared Andrea had become an even bigger star. Between her natural athleticism, intense training, and drive, Andrea found stunning success. At eleven years old, she began to play tournaments abroad, with Marie traveling with her. But each trip they made to the West created potential coordination problems: fearing defections, Czechoslovakia's government would not permit both parents to visit the West at the same time, so Jaroslav was limited in his hockey travel when Andrea was out of the country. The sacrifice was well worth it. Within five years, Andrea became one of Czechoslovakia's top junior players. At fifteen, she joined one of the country's oldest and most prestigious tennis clubs, the Czechoslovakia Lawn and Tennis Club in Prague. Jaroslav bought her a three-room apartment in Prague so she could train full-time there, with Marie coming to stay with her each weekend.[34] At sixteen, she began to play regularly on the women's professional tour.[35]

By 1985, Andrea had been transformed. Her hair was now darker, with blond streaks, and she had traded the no-nonsense haircut of her childhood for an up-to-date style with curly flipped bangs. More important, her physique was clearly that of a sturdy, muscular adult female athlete. As her game progressed and she found more and more success on the court, the Communists allowed her to travel widely for her tennis events. In January, just days before her seventeenth birthday, Andrea headed to Florida, where she won a pro tournament in Key Biscayne.

The year turned into a whirlwind of tour events and preparation for the major tournaments. Andrea arrived in Paris in May for the French Open with a head of steam, having just reached the semifinals of the Spanish Open. She instantly connected with the glorious, vibrant city, and found the Roland Garros clay courts lovely.[36] The vibe clearly worked for her. She played terrific tennis, making the second round of the women's singles, the finals of the junior girls' doubles event, and even the women's doubles' quarterfinals.

A couple of weeks later, she headed to London to compete at Wimbledon, the world's oldest and most hallowed tennis event. Although Andrea was excited by the history and tradition of the place, she found herself thrown off by the hectic pace of the tournament, the wild media coverage, and the rain that constantly interrupted matches. Despite the distractions, Andrea stayed focused and won the girls' junior championship! Jaroslav was beside himself with pride. All the hard work was paying off!

In August, Andrea traveled to New York for the US Open, where she finished second in the junior girls' singles, made the third round of the women's singles event, and won the girls' doubles.[37] For good measure, in October, she played doubles in Japan for Czechoslovakia's Federation Cup team, which won the entire tournament for the third consecutive year. She finished the year as the third-ranked junior female tennis player in the world, stood among the greatest female players of any age in Czechoslovakia, and was poised to move quickly up the ranks of the women's professional tour.

# CHAPTER 14

# Homebound

I n the following year, 1986, Jaroslav found his well-laid plans uprooted after a young hockey player named František Musil came to town.

Musil had been born on December 17, 1964, in the industrial city of Pardubice, fifty-five miles north of Jihlava, but it was easy to imagine him as a Kansas-bred homecoming king and star quarterback. With an easygoing manner, handsome square-jawed face, and quick, warm smile, people were instantly drawn to him. He was also clearly a jock, eventually expanding to an athletic 215 pounds packed into a six foot, three inch frame, and had massive paws—when you shook his hand you remembered it afterward.

"Franta" was exceptionally close with his family, especially his father, who was a locksmith in a chemical company. The boy didn't really take to the ice until the age of six, geriatric by Czechoslovakia's standards, and never became a great skater. But his dad adored hockey, so Franta took up the sport and became a defenseman, where his skating deficiencies would be less of a liability. The two Musils regularly went to see Czechoslovak league matches. The games when Dukla Jihlava came to town were a special thrill because they could watch Jan Suchý show Franta how to play his position and Jiří Holík move on the ice in ways that seemed impossible.

Given his personal charm, Franta probably would have been terrifically popular no matter what, but thanks to his hockey prowess he was something of a high school celebrity. He and his buddy Dominik Hašek had been in the same class together since they were little kids, and they were both hockey stars, always on teams with kids at least a year older than they were. Big, strong, tenacious, emotionally intense, and tough, Musil got promoted when he was seventeen years old to the Pardubice professional team, one of the country's best. Eighteen-year-olds Musil and Hašek were then selected to the national team for the 1983 World Championships.

They joined a national team that was in a period of transition after the Šťastnýs' escape and the aging and retirements of the stars from the 1970s. In contrast, the USSR still had the exceptional Tretiak in the net and a new set of young superstar skaters. The new USSR group would form the core of possibly the greatest roster in the country's hockey history. Over 1981–83, Czechoslovakia took, in order, third, second, and second at the World Championships, as the Soviets didn't lose a single match and nabbed all three gold medals. [1]

As he moved his way up in the hockey world, Musil's eyes gradually turned toward Jihlava. In the Holíks' and Suchý's prime, Dukla Jihlava had taken seven titles in eight years: 1967–74. After 1974, Jihlava's fortunes dipped, but in the 1981–82 season, Pitner's last, the team won its eighth championship. When the Neveselý–Jaroslav Holík tandem took over in 1982, Dukla Jihlava continued to surge and many young players chose to fulfill their mandatory military service under the coaches' rigid conditioning and discipline-focused hockey program.

In 1984, Musil began his military service and joined Dukla Jihlava where, thanks in part to the squad's exceptional coaching, his skills developed rapidly. [2] But, in Jihlava, he also found teammates who shared his love of hijinks. He got caught being out after curfew so many times that Neveselý sent him to a regular military unit that rose daily at 5 A.M. for long days of construction work. [3] Far worse, for his repeated transgressions, Neveselý also removed Musil from the 1984 Olympic squad. Franta could only watch in agony from home as his teammates, undefeated in the tournament, took on the also undefeated Soviets in the final for the Olympic gold medal. Perhaps predictably, the USSR took the final match and the top spot on the medal podium yet again.

By September 1984, Musil was back in his coaches' good graces and reinstated to the national team that competed in the Canada Cup. Playing against professionals from Canada and the US, as well as the usual Soviet squad, Czechoslovakia did terribly. But the experience of traveling to North America was mesmerizing for Musil, who felt like Alice gawking at all the strange things in Wonderland. The tall skyscrapers. The big beautiful cars. The modern jet planes and airports. And most of all, the shopping malls filled with perfectly packaged, mint-condition items that didn't exist at home. It was the first time Franta had ever seen real jeans.

Returning home, Musil became integral to two of the greatest teams in Czechoslovakia's hockey history. He starred on the 1984–85 Dukla squad, which lost only seven out of forty-four games, en route to its fourth straight championship. Then, nine Dukla players, including Franta, were selected to the national team that hosted the World Championships in Prague in the spring of 1985. Drawing energy from the home crowd, Czechoslovakia took the gold medal.

Celebrating with youthful enthusiasm, Franta hardly noticed the state police monitoring the movements of a number of the team's players. In fact, the authorities were giving twenty-year-old Musil especially close attention. It was common knowledge that Franta loved languages and was one of the few players who had learned English. Everyone knew that the young man adored the NHL and Canadian hockey. And two of his biggest sports idols were defectors Martina Navrátilová and Peter Šťastný. Starting in 1980, Franta had gone out of his way to listen to Radio Free Europe and Voice of America to get news of Šťastný, whose exploits in the NHL were an inspiration to young hockey players in Czechoslovakia.

The Šťastnýs' departure, the model they provided for Czechoslovak players, and the way NHL interest in those players intensified all terrified Czechoslovakia's authorities. The NHL and Czechoslovakia had already begun working out arrangements to let past-their-prime Czechoslovak players head to North America. In 1981, Czechoslovakia permitted older superstars Ivan Hlinka and Jiří Bubla, both thirty-one years old, to play for the NHL's Vancouver Canucks. The following year, the authorities allowed Milan Nový and Miroslav Dvořák, also both thirty-one, to play in the NHL as well. Czechoslovakia would not agree to such moves for its younger players, but NHL teams still held out hope of somehow nabbing the next Šťastný.

Every year, the NHL holds a draft in which each team has the opportunity to select new players. Once a team drafts a given player, within the NHL only that team can sign him. The process didn't necessarily work, though, for NHL teams that selected players from Czechoslovakia. Early in the 1981 draft, the Buffalo Sabres selected nineteen-year-old Czechoslovak Jiří Dudáček, but they should have done their homework first. Dudáček's father was a prominent Communist Party member, and the young man never made any moves to head west. Nevertheless, the allure of Czechoslovakia's deep talent pool proved too much to resist. In 1982, NHL teams drafted thirteen Czechoslovak players.[4]

In 1983, as NHL teams took another nine players from Czechoslovakia, the Minnesota North Stars drafted Musil. Lou Nanne, the general manager of the North Stars, had seen Franta play at the World Championships in West Germany. Taken by the young man's talent, Nanne had even gone to Musil's hotel room to let him know the North Stars would try to acquire his services. Opening the door just a crack for the Minnesota general manager, Musil was terrified that the secret police might find out and punish him for even that brief meeting, but soon he couldn't stop thinking about the idea of playing in the NHL.

Many Czechoslovak players didn't even learn at the time that they had been drafted, and they often didn't know what it meant when they did hear. In early August 1983, two months after the draft, Musil and his Pardubice buddy Hašek had gone with their team to play a series of games in France. During their off time, they went to a news stand. As Hašek perused a photo-filled magazine that was geared to male audiences, Franta picked up *The Hockey News* and suddenly exclaimed, "Dom! I was drafted! Damn! You were drafted too!" Hašek had no idea what his pal was talking about, so he returned to his magazine, but Musil knew full well what this meant. The greatest hockey league in the world wanted him. Czechoslovakia's authorities knew what this meant as well, and by 1985 they were watching their star hockey players extremely closely.[5]

After winning the 1985 World Championships Musil began to seriously consider defecting, but his personal life complicated the situation. Jihlava is a small city and Jaroslav Holík was his coach, so Musil inevitably saw Andrea around town. He found her extremely attractive. Then he saw her play tennis, and witnessing her impressive athletic display sealed the deal. Musil began to tease Jaroslav, suggesting that he was going to marry the coach's daughter. Knowing how wild Musil was, and fearing that a serious relationship might derail Andrea's career, Jaroslav blew a gasket. "You ass! I'm going to kick your balls so hard that you will forget all about such nonsense."

In reality, Jaroslav wasn't sure that Andrea would like Musil. The old-school hockey man had begun to hear that many female tennis players were lesbians. When Andrea turned eighteen in early 1986, Jaroslav gathered up his courage to ask her if she was attracted to women. She quickly retorted, "Dad, don't worry. I like boys." Jaroslav soon learned that she meant one in particular.

Each year, the Jihlava team held, of all things, a ball, and the March 1986 Dukla Ball changed the lives of Musil and the entire Holík family. As a member of the hockey team, Franta attended the event. As the daughter of the assistant coach, Andrea was there as well. She had previously noticed the handsome and charismatic Musil, but the two had never had much chance to talk. At the ball, they bumped into each other at the bar and got to chatting. Sparks flew. Total chemistry. One drink turned to another as they talked for hours. Finally, at 2 A.M., Jaroslav asked his friend Petr to let Andrea know that it was time to go home. After a spell, Petr returned to Jaroslav with a message that made the man's blood boil. "Andrea is sitting in the ballroom with Franta Musil and does not plan to leave. She says that she is 18 and will go home when she wants." It was the first time that Andrea had ever disobeyed one of Jaroslav's directives, and it left her father in shock. Marie made Jaroslav go home, where he stood at the window fuming until Ája finally arrived in the morning.

The relationship between Andrea and Franta that grew out of the evening was hardly conventional. Soon after the Dukla Ball, Andrea left for a series of tour events in the US, and Franta rejoined the national hockey team, which was preparing for the 1986 World Championships. As a result, much of their early time together was spent on the phone, getting to know each other from a distance. They soon fell in love, but decided to hide the relationship rather than risk Jaroslav's wrath. Marie eventually figured it out and told Jaroslav, who needed a couple of shots of hard liquor to calm down.

Jaroslav's fury overflowed when he thought about how an Andrea-Musil relationship might upend all of his planning. In the previous couple of years, young Czechoslovak hockey players Petr Svoboda and Petr Klíma had invited Franta to defect to the West with them. Even as the two Petrs headed off to play in the NHL, Musil wasn't ready to pull the trigger, but it was obvious that it was only a matter of time until he went as well. As Franta grew close to Andrea in 1986, Jaroslav grabbed the young man and exploded, "Look, if my daughter defects with you, they'll throw me out of the army and I'll kick your ass so hard you couldn't even imagine!" Musil just stared at Jaroslav and said: "I love her and you can do whatever you want."[6]

The couple ignored Jaroslav's rage and grew closer, but then suddenly an even more powerful force threatened to separate them.

In April 1986, Czechoslovakia's national team—the defending champion—had been embarrassed at the World Championships, finishing fifth. Between the team's poor showing and the threat that its best players might defect, the Czechoslovakia Hockey Federation feared the collapse of its hockey program. It decided to take a dramatic step to halt the exodus of players.

Ironically, the government actually *wanted* many of its other citizens to emigrate.

Throughout the 1980s, dissidents had continued to speak out against the regime, which in turn made them pay. The authorities came down hard on those they deemed most threatening to the political order. One example was Pavel Bratinka, who distributed information to the public about the Charter 77 dissident movement. As punishment for his "crime," Bratinka was dismissed from his position as a high-ranking physicist and relegated to work as a stoker for the Prague rail system. Another was Rudolf Batěk, a successful sociologist who was removed from the academy of sciences for demanding that the regime investigate the 1968 invasion, found himself repeatedly jailed, but still spoke out and attempted to educate others about how to stand up to the state.

Believing that it would produce order at home and reduce pressure from abroad, the regime offered prominent imprisoned dissidents like Václav Benda and Jiří Dienstbier an immediate end to their jail time if they would just leave the country. Dozens took the authorities up on their offer,[7] but many were reluctant to do so. Dissidents knew that their martyrdom helped attract worldwide attention to their cause and defecting would undercut their message. They also saw what happened to those who went abroad. Famed Czechoslovak writer Pavel Kohout, who had been an active part of the public push for reform, received permission in 1978 to travel to Austria. While there, he found his Czechoslovak citizenship revoked and couldn't return home.

Of all of Czechoslovakia's dissidents, Václav Havel was probably the person the authorities most wished would depart. In fact, in 1979 Havel had received an invitation to serve as a playwright-in-residence at the Public Theater in New

York as an alternative to prison in Czechoslovakia,[8] but leaving would sharply weaken his ability to bring about change at home. He refused the offer and, through his imprisonment, became a thorn in the side of Czechoslovakia's Communists. Following his 1979 jailing, the world gave Havel, Czechoslovakia's most famous playwright, unprecedented amounts of attention. Not only were Havel's plays put on in cities like Paris and Warsaw, but theaters in other countries performed a dramatic reconstruction of his trial. Around the globe, universities bestowed honorary degrees upon him and organizations awarded him prizes for his writing and his push for human rights. Prominent groups in other countries, as well as the European parliament, pressed for the release of political prisoners in Czechoslovakia, and called special attention to Havel. Early in his prison sentence, Havel had been transferred to a facility in a part of Czechoslovakia beset with dangerously high levels of air pollution. He grew ill and needed to be hospitalized. Even after being moved to a new camp, Havel's health problems continued. During his fourth year in prison, he returned to the hospital with severe pneumonia. In February 1983, fearing a global backlash if he died in their custody, Czechoslovakia's authorities released him.[9]

However, when it came to the rest of the country, especially elite athletes, the Czechoslovak leadership did whatever it could to stamp out even the thought of emigration. In early July 1986, the Czechoslovakia Hockey Federation called a meeting with its top players. The organization forced the young men to agree to contracts that bound them to never play for another country. One player refused: Musil. The federation officials kicked the defenseman out of the conference room, told him that he was no longer a member of the national team, and confiscated his passport.

As Franta's world collapsed before his eyes, Andrea was in the midst of preparing for the biggest event of her career. She had been named again to Czechoslovakia's Fed Cup team, which was now the three-time defending champion in the event. Later that July in Prague, Czechoslovakia would become the first communist country to host the tournament, which was regarded as the world championship of women's team tennis. As Musil left the meeting with the hockey officials, he couldn't even wrap his mind around the excitement in

Andrea's life. Andrea drove him directly to the train station. His head filled with dark thoughts, Musil rode the rail home to Pardubice.

Unwilling to accept a life without hockey, he set in motion a plan that would allow him to continue to play the game he adored. He had another passport and, miraculously, a travel permit to holiday for fourteen days in Yugoslavia. Knowing he might never get another chance, Musil told his parents he was going on vacation, and on July 8 he headed to a Yugoslav resort town on the Adriatic Sea. In reality, though, he was determined to make his way to the NHL. Ever the twenty-one-year-old, he felt bulletproof. He thought to himself, *If they shoot at me, I will outrun them. And if they send the dogs after me, I will outrun them too.*

Through a hockey contact, Musil had the name of an agent, Ritch Winter, in Canada. Even as Andrea prepared for her tournament, she and the contact worked with Winter to lay the groundwork and then, in the week before the Fed Cup, Winter received a phone call. It was Franta. "I now want defect. I must now. Understand?" Just twenty-nine years old, Winter was in his early days as an agent and had no experience with anything quite like this. He called Lou Nanne, the general manager of the Minnesota North Stars, to let him know that the Czechoslovak defenseman he had drafted was ready to come. Winter and Nanne each flew to Europe. The problem they faced was how to get Musil out of Yugoslavia without proper documentation. They considered renting a private plane, sticking him in the trunk of a car and driving through a checkpoint to Italy, or even possibly sprinting through the forest in the middle of the night.

It began to appear that such extreme tactics might actually be necessary. Winter, who flew separately from Nanne, arrived in Belgrade, Yugoslavia, first and tracked down Musil. They headed to the US diplomatic authorities, who offered little help, suggesting he might be sent to a refugee camp, where it could take two years to process his application. Unsure of what to do, Musil and Winter checked into a hotel, where the stress finally became too much. Franta lay despondently on the bed, his giant hands covering his face. His visa would expire soon, and then . . .

It was at that moment that Nanne's savvy saved the day. Local Minnesota Twin Cities sports anchor Bob Bruce and a cameraman had come with the general manager to chronicle Musil's move to the West. When Nanne heard that US officials in Yugoslavia had become an obstacle, he threatened to film the consulate's unwillingness to help a young man escape to freedom. Just like that, the office began processing the needed documents. Nanne used his connection to US Senator David Durenberger to get Musil a working visa, and the next morning they rushed to the airport. As they waited to depart, Musil and the rest of the group kept an eye on the space around them, which was crawling with police. Would the local authorities allow them to leave? Franta was sure that the plan would collapse . . . until the plane began to move and took off. They finally exhaled and opened a bottle of wine to celebrate.

At 10:45 P.M. on July 18, 1986, at the end of an incredibly long day, Musil, Winter, and Nanne held a press conference at the Minnesota Twin Cities airport to introduce the North Stars' new defenseman. Franta explained things simply. "I don't want to forget my country or my parents, but I want to play in the NHL."[10]

Just hours after Musil introduced himself to his new home, Martina Navrátilová nervously returned to her old one. Following her move to the West in 1975, Navrátilová's tennis career had skyrocketed. In 1978, she won Wimbledon for her first major singles title and the world number one ranking. In 1981, she became an American citizen. By 1982, she was the dominant force in women's tennis, but back in Czechoslovakia Martina had become a "non-person." The posters of her displayed at her Prague tennis club were gone. As she won major championship after championship around the world, the Czechoslovak news refused to report her victories or that she even existed at all. In early July 1986, Czechoslovak TV did show Navrátilová winning her seventh Wimbledon tennis title (and fifth in a row), but only because she was playing Czechoslovakia's top player, Hana Mandlíková. Still, even at twenty-nine years old, Martina was not welcome in the place of her birth. In 1985 she had tried to get a visa to visit, but the Czechoslovak authorities denied her entry. However, that all changed in 1986, in the most important tournament of Andrea Holíková's life.

Czechoslovakia's tennis officials had desperately wanted to host the Federation Cup. They, and the country's Communist leaders, wanted the international community to see Prague as a place to hold major world events. They built a stunning new tennis complex and pitched tennis's bigtime sponsors, including Coca-Cola and Nike, that Czechoslovakia was a perfect place for such a tournament. The 1986 Fed Cup was, aside from the 1984 Sarajevo Olympics in

Yugoslavia, the most significant athletic event ever held in a communist nation where all the world's top sporting countries would attend. The Communist leaders could scarcely wait to show off the beautiful city of Prague, the impressive new stadium, and the lovely country that was Czechoslovakia.

But there was a catch.

Those very same leaders would also have to let into Czechoslovakia the Western free press and one Martina Navrátilová, the top player in the world, the headliner for the US team, and the favorite in the competition. It had been her childhood dream to win the Fed Cup for Czechoslovakia and she had done that eleven years earlier, just four months before she had emigrated to the US. Now, it was that very same tournament that made it possible for her to come back to the land where she had been born, with the bittersweet hope of taking the Fed Cup title away from Czechoslovakia and bringing it to her adopted home.

As the Cold War raged and Navrátilová stood out as possibly the most famous Eastern Bloc athlete to defect to the West, there was huge interest in her first return to her birthplace. When she arrived at Prague's airport on July 19, she was met by her family—including her father, who gave her a corsage—as well as more than two hundred Czechoslovak citizens and a tidal wave of reporters and photographers. This would be no typical tournament.

The following day, several thousand people rhythmically clapped as the teams entered the stadium. The applause intensified when a smiling Navrátilová walked in. Czechoslovakia's top player, Hana Mandlíková, spoke to the crowd, and despite the Czechoslovak leadership's desire to avoid mention of the defector, she twice referred to Navrátilová by name. When it was time to play the host country's national anthem, a wave of emotion overcame Martina. As the military band struck up "Where My Home Is," she told herself, "Don't cry!" But tears filled her eyes as she sang the Czech words that she had been unable to forget.

> *Among the Czechs is my home!*
> *Among the Czechs, my home!*

The host leaders did what they could to make the attendees forget the world's number one player. Around the stadium, fans were able to purchase photos of all the top players, except Martina. The ploy seemed silly. Navrátilová's matches were usually the hottest ticket in the place. On day one of play, only a smattering of fans—many openly rooting against the Soviets—attended the USSR–Bulgaria match held in the stadium's grand 7,500-seat Central Court, while simultaneously the US and Martina were placed in a smaller, less visible court with only enough seats for 800 attendees. Hearing that Navrátilová was there, hundreds more fans rushed to the outer court to stand and watch four-deep from behind the seats. Playing China, Navrátilová received almost continuous applause from the fans and had to pause at length before beginning new points because the crowd wasn't done clapping for the previous one. As the match went on, she seemed to grow more at ease with the support, at first waving politely, later moving on to a thumbs-up sign. After easily dispatching her opponent, she blew a kiss to the crowd, drawing even louder cheers. Despite the apparent popularity of Navrátilová's return tour, Czechoslovak Television avoided broadcasting her matches, and the local newspapers barely wrote anything about them. It didn't matter. Word of mouth spread news of what was transpiring at the tennis arena. One local doctor told the foreign press, "Martina has freedom, and we do not, so I must cheer for her. How else can I ever let the bastards know?"

When Navrátilová walked out for her quarterfinal match against Italy, the chair umpire—apparently under orders not to say the defector's name—announced that "Raffaella Reggi from Italy" would be playing "the woman from the United States." The crowd grew boisterous. *Say her name! Say her name!* Louder and louder. Reggi grew upset, thinking that the crowd was booing her. Martina waved her to the net to explain what the crowd was saying, leading the Italian woman to chuckle. Finally, the umpire gave the people what they wanted, announcing that for the US the player was "Miss Navrátilová." Following a mighty roar, the stands quieted and play began.

Throughout, Andrea was fairly oblivious to the fanfare surrounding Navrátilová. Musil's defection was a big distraction, but also this was the biggest moment of her career. Winning junior events was one thing, but she had been named to her country's team in what was essentially the world championship of the sport. The US team, with Martina and the world's number two player Chris Evert Lloyd, was the clear favorite. But Czechoslovakia was outstanding as well, led by Mandlíková and Helena Suková, who were respectively ranked fourth and seventh in the world. Mandlíková and Suková handled singles play and destroyed everything in their path through the semifinals. Andrea and her good friend Regina Maršíková represented Czechoslovakia in doubles for most of the tournament. The pair went undefeated through the first three rounds and only lost a three-set match to a terrific Argentine pair in the semis, but Mandlíková's and Suková's singles victories pushed the team into the finals.

Focused as they were on the task at hand, Andrea and her teammates were kept largely bubbled and therefore missed most of the hubbub surrounding Navrátilová, but they had their own bombshell to deal with. On Friday, July 25, an off day just prior to Saturday's semifinals, Mandlíková abruptly got married to a Czech expatriate who now called Australia home. It was clear to Andrea and her teammates that the wedding was hardly an act of passion. Painfully aware of the difficulties that defectors like Martina faced, Mandlíková found a work-around. By marrying a foreign citizen, she could retain her status in Czechoslovakia, but also freely travel the world without repercussions.

Whatever the case, both the US and Czechoslovakia won their semifinals on Saturday, producing the showdown everyone, except Czechoslovakia's Communist leaders, wanted to see on Sunday: Martina and the American squad against the defending champion hosts.

It had been one of the greatest weeks of Navrátilová's tennis career. US fans had never fully embraced Navrátilová at home, as she continually defeated America's sweetheart Evert Lloyd. But now, back in Prague, where the fans openly adored her, Martina felt like she was on the home team for one of the few times in her life. Relishing the moment, she turned to her good friend Evert Lloyd and half-jokingly quipped, "I want to play you here!"

Even before finals play began, the crowd, which included Jaroslav, Marie, and Bobby Holík, was raucous and excited. A significant group sat courtside this day: Czechoslovakia's prime minister and six other leading Czechoslovak Communists. Evert Lloyd defeated Suková in a close match and, knowing how much a victory would mean to her friend, showed uncharacteristic emotion in her celebration afterward, jubilantly tossing her racquet and thrusting both arms up into the air. Then it was time for the main card. Navrátilová and Mandlíková took the court to great applause. A funny moment came as warm-ups ended and the chair umpire introduced Martina as "Martina Navrátilová from Czechoslovakia . . . er, the United States." As play began, it became clear that, as much as the crowd loved Martina, it wanted the woman representing Czechoslovakia to win. Navrátilová received big cheers, but rhythmic applause, much like what one would hear at a team sporting event, filled the stadium prior to Mandlíková's serves and roars of approval followed her successful points. With the crowd urging on the leader of Team Czechoslovakia, both players played well early, but a brief lapse in concentration led Mandlíková to double fault at a key moment. First set, Navrátilová.

In the second set, Martina demonstrated why she was the world's top player. As the Communist leaders quietly seethed, Navrátilová shone. Constantly on the attack, she repeatedly wrong-footed the usually spectacularly coordinated Mandlíková. Navrátilová, one of the most athletic tennis players of either gender ever to play the game, seemed to run down every shot. She made one spectacular volley after another and literally threw herself across the court to save points. As the match went on, she became more tenacious and her game more brilliant. In the course of the set, the crowd shifted from hometown support for Mandlíková to awe at the genius that was Navrátilová's game. With each remarkable play, the stands grew louder and more appreciative of the woman who had returned home, and the fans' roars of approval continued longer. Mandlíková had no answer for what she now faced. When Martina hit a powerful winning backhand to take the match, the stadium erupted and thousands took to their feet to support their long-lost daughter. As they did, Czechoslovakia's seven Communist leaders who had been sitting courtside rose and, without acknowledging either player, strode out of the arena.

Even as disappointed as they were to lose the championship, Andrea and her teammates marveled at the extraordinary response around them. After the doubles team of Navrátilová and Pam Shriver finished the sweep of Czechoslovakia, the award ceremony began. Receiving the trophy for the US, Evert Lloyd told the packed stadium that the team dedicated the victory to Martina, to whom she then handed the microphone. Navrátilová spoke briefly in English and then captured the attention of everyone as she transitioned to Czech, eliciting more cheers from the crowd. The fans slipped into a sharp silence with each of her words, but then roared in support of her with each pause. Finally, she closed. "I hope it will not be another eleven years until I can play with you again." Next to her on the court, the usually unflappable Evert Lloyd dabbed at her eye. Sitting courtside, tears streamed down the face of Martina's mother. As the cheering turned to rhythmic in-unison clapping, Navrátilová wiped her own eyes and leaned into Shriver, her longtime doubles partner, who hugged her. The applause grew louder, still in sync across the 7,500 people filling the stadium. It grew more intense. For minutes on end. It. Just. Wouldn't. Stop.

For once, the Czechoslovak public could cheer for a defector in front of its repressive government and get away with it. Asked about the cheers for Navrátilová, Mandlíková said: "When Martina came back, it was the only way the people could express themselves towards the government: to cheer. I didn't feel bad because I know what they feel. She represents something to them that's important: freedom." Thanks to her clever use of marital vows, Mandlíková had that freedom now as well. But it would soon be clear just how little Andrea Holíková had. [11]

In a piece about Navrátilová's return to Czechoslovakia published the following week in *Sports Illustrated*, famed sportswriter Frank Deford casually mentioned in passing that a hockey player from Czechoslovakia had defected to the US in the week prior to the Fed Cup. But no one seemed to comment on, or was even aware of, a deeper connection—that the defector, Musil, was involved with Andrea, a player on Czechoslovakia's Fed Cup tennis team. Still, Andrea had no plans to emigrate. Musil was only twenty-one years old. She was eighteen. And they would be able to see each other when she played tournaments in the US.

The initial transition to the US was difficult for Musil. To be sure, it had more than its share of positives. He soon visited his buddy Petr Klíma, who had defected to the US in 1985 and had already figured out how to spend his money, getting a house with a pool and a set of sports cars. Even more heartening for Musil was the knowledge that he was free to do what he wanted, most of all to play hockey. But he missed his friends and family. His first call to his parents when he landed in the US was horrible. They were, quite simply, crushed by his leaving. Because he was so close to his family, he felt he had betrayed them by keeping his plans hidden. He would never muster the courage to ask what the government did to them in response to his defection, but he felt certain that the authorities had carried out some form of retribution. The government soon accused Musil of the crime of remaining outside the country illegally, noting that the offense was especially reprehensible because he was a well-known top athlete who represented the country abroad. Franta knew that the Communists would never let him back in the country without severe punishment so, as far as his family was concerned, it was goodbye forever. [12]

He also missed Andrea. Fortunately, she came to New York that August to compete in the US Open. Andrea and Franta were able to see each other throughout her trip to Flushing Meadows, which was wonderful. On the other hand, she was really worried about the tournament. For her first-round match, she was placed on center court against none other than Martina Navrátilová. It would be an evening match with the eyes of all tennis fans on it, and Andrea was terrified that Martina would annihilate her. Mustering all her courage, and the mental game her father had helped her develop, Andrea refused to psych herself out. Ultimately, Navrátilová beat her, but in a competitive match. Things were looking up. As she headed back to Europe after the tournament, Andrea was delighted with how she had played against the world's greatest player. And she knew that she and Franta would find a way to see each other regularly as she traveled to tournaments in the US.

Then everything fell apart.

At the end of October, Andrea flew back to the US for matches in Indianapolis and Puerto Rico. In between the two, she visited Musil in Minneapolis. When she did, somehow word got to the authorities in Czechoslovakia. Not only did they figure out what Andrea was doing in Minnesota, but someone had already let them know that she had seen Franta in New York in the summer. Interacting with a defector was a cardinal sin. Andrea's doubles partner Regina Maršíková warned the Holíks that when Andrea got home, officials would take her passport and ban her from leaving the Eastern Bloc. Jaroslav and Marie wasted little time getting in touch with their daughter to let her know. If she returned to Czechoslovakia, she wouldn't be able to see Musil anymore—and her career as a tennis player would largely be over. Andrea was aghast, but it appeared her government had given her no choice. She called her parents early in the morning of November 17, right before she was scheduled to return home. "Dad, what would you say if I didn't come back?" Andrea worried about what would happen to her parents and to Bobby. Jaroslav responded through clenched teeth, "Bobby will be fine. They will certainly throw me out of the army. But we didn't raise you to live in this hell hole! I brought you up to play tennis and travel all over the world." And with that, and a little help from the North Stars and Senator Durenberger of Minnesota, on November 20, 1986, Andrea formally applied for political asylum in the United States.

When the Czechoslovak authorities learned of Andrea's decision, they first tried the "good cop" role to get her back. The head of Czechoslovakia's sports union called Jaroslav, claiming that Musil was actually running away with a different girl, but Andrea quickly put that lie to rest, telling her father that Franta was living with *her*, Andrea, in Minneapolis. Meanwhile, Cyril Suk, Helena Suková's father and the head of Czechoslovakia tennis, bombarded Jaroslav with calls. He finally came to Jihlava to talk to Holík. "If she returns, I promise you that the Minister of Interior will ensure that nothing will happen to her." "Great," Jaroslav replied, "just give that to me in writing." Naturally, the government was unwilling to make such promises and promptly transitioned to the "bad cop" role. Knowing full well what was to come, the Holíks rushed to Andrea's apartment in Prague to move out all her belongings—just before government officials confiscated the property.

Then pressure came to bear directly on Jaroslav's position in the army. He received anonymous letters stating that, with a daughter like his, he had no business training hockey players. More serious, Jaroslav's superiors started pressuring him to resign his post. One day, General Tvaroška, the chief of political management, who controlled the lives of all army athletes in Czechoslovakia, charged into Jaroslav's office. "You are no longer welcome in the army! Pack your things!" As usual, Jaroslav had little ability to hold his tongue, even when faced with a superior, but he did manage to keep his composure. The general's own daughter had emigrated to Italy twenty years earlier, and Tvaroška had been demoted as a result. Jaroslav quietly asked the general what had happened to him when his own daughter had left. The general flinched. "Don't ask me about her. I will dismember all of you!" he boomed, and stormed out of the room, slamming the door behind him. Jaroslav was forced to resign from the army. But because of his status as one of the country's greatest hockey legends, he received a severance payment and an invitation to stay on as a civilian assistant coach of the team.

The authorities unleashed their wrath on Bobby as well. Prior to Andrea's defection, the fifteen-year-old Holík boy had been named to a junior national team and was invited to training camp before heading out with the squad to Sweden for a series of matches against the best young players in Europe. Jaroslav contacted the Czechoslovak team's coach to make sure that, despite Andrea's defection, Bobby would in fact be allowed to travel with the squad. The coach reassured Jaroslav. "Don't worry. He has special permission." Wanting to do nothing with his life but play hockey, Bobby was thrilled. Not long after Andrea's departure, he headed to the training camp. But the night before the team was set to leave for Sweden, the coach called Bobby into his office. As the boy walked through the door, he knew what was waiting for him. "I can't go to the tournament, can I?" The sports authorities had informed the coach that Bobby was a flight risk and not permitted to travel abroad. The regime had decided to make an example of him.

Jaroslav's and Marie's hearts broke when they received the phone call from Bobby and heard him sob as he explained that he would be returning home. The next morning Bobby watched his teammates board the bus and depart for the airport. Grief stricken, Bobby carried his clothes and heavy hockey sticks and gear to the local transit station, where he climbed on a public bus to get home. Like his father and the Dukla players eighteen years earlier, when they returned in 1968 to Soviet-occupied Czechoslovakia, Bobby began the long bus ride back to Jihlava, hating the Communists.[13]

# CHAPTER 15

# Inspiration for a Generation

B obby was hardly alone in his feelings toward the Communists. Countless people in Czechoslovakia despised their government. But there was no way to safely express their fury toward the regime.

The Soviets, though—the puppeteers who pulled the strings—they presented a different kind of target. Coming of age in the wake of 1968, Bobby's generation grew up openly loathing "the Russians." It was a generation of Czechs and Slovaks who were born after the invasion or were too young to remember it, but their parents made sure they knew how Soviet tanks and troops had stormed their streets and continued to occupy their country. It was also a generation of hockey lovers who grew up on stories of how Czechoslovakia's national team had fought back in 1969 in Stockholm. With few other opportunities for upward mobility, during the 1970s and 1980s young boys all over Czechoslovakia threw themselves into hockey. And knowing what their people had endured since 1968, they yearned to fight the Red Machine on the ice. It was ironic, really. The Soviet occupation had provided the inspiration for the greatest generation of hockey players in Czechoslovakia's history.

Bobby had been among the better junior players in the country for years, but getting sent home by the authorities pushed him harder. The morning after he returned to Jihlava, he got up early to hit the ice, driven to become so great that he could escape the regime.

Jaroslav was more than ready to double down on Bobby's training.

In the months that followed in 1987, Coach Neveselý left Dukla Jihlava. In his place, the authorities named as head coach Josef Augusta, yet another boy born and raised in Havlíčkův Brod, and who for years had starred for Dukla and the national team. Jaroslav took Augusta's hiring poorly. In reality, after Andrea left, Holík was lucky to still have his job as assistant coach, but he didn't see it that way. Jaroslav believed *he* had earned the head coaching position. And if they weren't going to give it to him officially, at least they should make Augusta, who was four years younger, more of a figurehead. But the Augusta and the Holík families had been friends for many years, and Augusta didn't see a reason to defer to the older legend. Jaroslav grew angry and lost much of his interest in engaging with the team.

Instead, Jaroslav put even more of his energy into coaching Bobby. When he and Marie saw how the regime had ripped their son from his traveling team, they grew worried about what the authorities might do to him in the future. It became essential to them to raise Bobby's game substantially. Bobby was big, already six feet, three inches tall and 185 pounds, but there were others his age who could skate and control the puck better. He would need to do more if he was to make it to the West.[1]

As the 1987–88 hockey season approached, the new coaching combination of Jaroslav and Augusta had its first big conflict. And it was over Bobby. As training began for the Dukla team in the summer of 1987, Jaroslav became convinced that his boy was ready to join the professional ranks, but the new head coach was more cautious about the idea of calling up a sixteen-year-old. Jaroslav blew up, believing this was just Augusta's ego getting in the way and screwing over both Holíks in the process. However, Augusta, who had a great relationship with Bobby, kept an open mind. When he saw the success that a different sixteen-year-old was having that season with another team in the league, he gave the Holík boy his shot.

Jaroslav concealed from Bobby two feelings he had about his son's promotion to the professional team. Jaroslav didn't let Bobby know how well he thought the boy was doing, but he told everyone else. "Bobby is really going to be something!" But that wasn't all. Czechoslovakia's iconic hockey tough guy was also terrified of what the bigger players, fully grown men, might do to the teen. In classic Jaroslav fashion, he swallowed his fear and overcompensated. Throughout practice, Jaroslav screamed at his son, lobbed the most vicious expletives at him, and smacked him across the back with a hockey stick for minor errors. Witnessing the assault, even Bobby's big, professional, league-hardened teammates winced.

But the Dukla players also grew frustrated by the younger Holík. Jaroslav had taught his son to harass opponents constantly. Bobby followed his father's practice of poking, hitting, and pounding the men on the opposing team throughout every second of play. He did so even in practice as he scrimmaged against his own, now much older, teammates. One day, a six-foot, two-inch, two-hundred-pound Dukla veteran snapped. He slashed Bobby with his stick, breaking the boy's hand. For the rest of practice, young Holík performed poorly, unable to hold his stick properly. Irate at his son's low-quality play and unaware of what the teammate had done to his hand, Jaroslav bellowed, "If you keep playing like that, I'll punch your mouth!" The teen just silently stared at his father.[2] Incredibly, what looked like abuse to outsiders never seemed to bother Bobby. With his father's genes and his own thick skin, he handled each haranguing simply as an indication that he needed to do a better job.

With a dream of playing in the NHL and the maniacal training methods of his father both driving him, Bobby rapidly improved, but he was hardly Czechoslovakia's only teenage hockey star. Four other boys his age formed the basis of a junior hockey powerhouse in the little town of Litvínov.

Although just sixty miles northwest of Prague, Litvínov, population 20,000, appeared to be in the middle of nowhere. A trip by train from the country's capital could take over two hours to reach the town, which sat just eight miles southeast of the East German border. Along the route, a number of the stops appeared to be little more than wilderness. The surrounding region included beautiful villages and small farms, but also swathes of undeveloped land.

Coming by tram, it was hard to miss the local Chemopetrol plant's giant ceramic vase-shaped smokestacks, which looked terrifyingly like America's Three Mile Island nuclear plant. Throughout the 1970s and 1980s, Czechoslovakia's central government had built up state-owned plants in the area, working to ensure an ample supply of petrochemical factories, oil refineries, and coal mines, often over the complaints of local officials and residents who suffered from the effects. At times during the winter, the plant's emissions, along with those of a neighboring power station's sulfur, created a cloud layer that left a thick haze in the sky over Litvínov. The plant dominated not just the region's environment but also the community itself. It was understood that the city would not meddle with the company, especially with respect to its emissions. In exchange, Chemopetrol offered ample jobs to locals, built apartment buildings for its workers, and provided them with subsidized meals. It also did something that meant just as much to the people of Litvínov. It sponsored the town's beloved hockey team, whose official name was the "Physical Education Union of the Litvínov Chemical Plant."

Since 1959, Litvínov had been the smallest town to consistently maintain a team in Czechoslovakia's top hockey league, but thanks to a steady stream of talented young players, it kept up with the big boys. With little else to do and nowhere else to go, hockey was central to town life, but love of the hockey team became all-consuming in the 1970s. Born one day apart from each other in late January 1950, Ivan Hlinka and Jiří Bubla transformed the sport in Litvínov. A charismatic, big center forward, Hlinka could seemingly score at will. Bubla was a brilliant defenseman who also was among the top passers in the country. Both joined the team in the late 1960s, and at points in the 1970s raised Litvínov to the league's top tier. Both men served as stars on the national team, and Hlinka was voted the country's top player in 1978.

With them, life in Litvínov became hockey, hockey, and more hockey. Residents kept their noses down, performed their jobs, and then looked forward to the two or three days a week that they could watch the sport. Nearly a quarter of the town's population crammed itself into the local stadium for every game. The locker room sat so close to the crowd that the players could smell the famous sausages sold in the arena. Inspired by the energy radiating from Hlinka, an amazing team spirit engulfed both the town and the team. Across the country, people couldn't miss the way that hockey seemed different in Litvínov. Litvínov players showed no stress but instead exuded joy on the ice. They seemed to play simply for the love of the game. In years to come, coaches of Czechoslovakia's national team exhorted their men to play like they were from Litvínov.

The town became a hatchery for hockey players, and the world took notice.[3] When Czechoslovakia began to allow some of its players who were past their prime to play for a period in the NHL, the first to go, in 1981, were Hlinka and Bubla. The two instantly made a mark as contributors to the Vancouver

Canucks team, which made the Stanley Cup finals (the NHL championship). From then on, as NHL teams looked to convince more young Czechoslovak players to come west, Litvínov players were often their target. Beginning in 1983, NHL scouts and executives went wild over the play of Franta Musil's friend Petr Svoboda, a young Litvínov defenseman. Following his final game in the European junior championship tournament, held in West Germany in April 1984, the eighteen-year-old Petr showered in his team's locker room. After drying off, Svoboda defected to the West, carrying nothing but the clothes on his back. Less than two months later, the Montreal Canadiens made him the fifth player picked in the NHL draft. Because of their son's actions, Svoboda's parents were fired from their jobs and left unemployed for two and a half years. [4]

Throughout the 1980s, one of Czechoslovakia's greatest players was Litvínov's Vladimír Růžička, another big—six-foot, three-inch, over 210 pounds—center forward, whom the NHL's Toronto Maple Leafs drafted in 1982, when he was nineteen years old. The Communist authorities kept a close eye on Růžička, ensuring that he remained in Czechoslovakia, where he regularly led the country's top league in scoring.

However, Litvínov had never seen as great a collection of teens as emerged in the town in the 1980s. The new core was made up of four boys—Robert Lang, Robert Reichel, Martin Ručinský, and Jiří Šlégr—who had all been born within six months of Bobby Holík's January 1, 1971 delivery. As kids, the four became inseparable. They played together. They attended school together. In the winter, they skied together. In the summer, they rafted together. They got into trouble together in all the innocent ways that young kids do.

They also played hockey in a way that no one else in the country could. In a sport where it was unusual for a single team to score in the double digits, the Litvínov boys sometimes defeated their opponents by twenty goals. It was more than skill. Litvínovans insisted that it wasn't just a hockey team. It was a lifestyle! An attacking, go-for-the-goal, *joyful* lifestyle! [5] They flew around the ice with an aura of fun that seemed utterly impossible for players like the intense Bobby Holík. Everyone watching Litvínov play wanted to have that kind of fun on the ice, too! The junior Dukla Jihlava team often played Litvínov, and Bobby looked with envy at the creative flair and genuine ebullience of the Litvínov boys. Bobby daydreamed about what it would be like to play like that and then realized that, if he did play with them, the

Litvínov boys would mock his do-or-die approach to hockey and tell him to chill out.

The Litvínov kids played with a lightness unlike anyone else in the country, but they also saw darkness. The 1968 Soviet invasion had been a wake-up call to their families that they would always be under someone's thumb. The years that followed were a constant reminder. In private, the Litvínov boys' parents complained about how corrupt and all-controlling the regime was, but even in their little town they feared informants. When the boys spoke disparagingly at home about the Communists, their parents reprimanded them. "Don't say that outside of the house!" People were far more open, though, with their feelings about the Soviets and the fact that everyone still burned over the 1968 invasion. Even as little kids, the boys all knew about the 1969 games in Stockholm where their heroes stuck it to the Soviet team. The Litvínov boys yearned to exact a similar form of revenge.

The problem with trying to get revenge on the Soviets was that, by the late 1980s, the quality of Czechoslovakia's national team had dropped off. At the 1986 World Championships, Czechoslovakia finished a disappointing fifth place. In 1987, it improved a bit to third place. And in the 1988 Olympics, the squad took sixth, one of the country's worst finishes ever. This was not a squad that could compete with the Red Machine. Czechoslovakia's hockey program clearly needed an injection of new talent. It got it in three superstar teens who had the skill and the motivation to take on the Soviet skaters.

The first of the three teens was Litvínov's Robert Reichel. Even as a child, everyone knew that Reichel was special. In 1987, he made the local professional team, when he was sixteen years old, under new head coach Hlinka. A few months later, Reichel turned in a stunning performance at the World Junior Championships, producing more points than any other sixteen-year-old in history except for Canadian Wayne Gretzky, the consensus greatest hockey player of all time.

The second teen star was a boy who one day would literally wear his hatred of the Soviet Union on his sleeve. Born in 1972 in a suburb of the small industrial city of Kladno, roughly fifteen miles from Prague, Jaromír Jágr was a year younger than Bobby Holík and the four Litvínov boys, but by the time he hit his teen years Jágr had reached legendary status. At one big tournament when Jágr was eleven, Kladno faced the four Litvínov boys and Bobby. First, Kladno defeated Litvínov, as Jaromír netted six goals. Next, Kladno squared off against Dukla for the tournament title, with talk of a battle between Jágr and Holík. Jaroslav boasted that Dukla would teach Kladno a lesson. Despite Jaroslav's never-ending screaming throughout the match, Kladno won, with Jágr scoring four goals. Even Bobby was mesmerized by the young boy's size and ability to move as if his skates were on rails.

Jágr's father raised the kid to love hockey, but the boy's grandmother brought him up to hate the Communists. Jaromír's grandfathers had been farmers and both had been imprisoned for resisting the government's collective farming orders. As a result, their children, including Jaromír's parents, were prohibited from attending college. Jaromír's paternal grandmother, Jarmila, told the boy of his family's misfortunes under communism and about the Soviet invasion in 1968. As a reminder, Jágr would later scratch the number "68" on the back of his helmet, along with the initials "DA"—Alexander Dubček's initials backward.[6] Drawing from his grandmother's lessons, in the 1980s Jágr began carrying a picture of Ronald Reagan in his schoolbook because he admired the way the US president, who called the Soviet Union the "evil empire," stood up to the Communists. His teacher kept finding the picture and, fearing that the boy could be severely punished, insisted that he throw it away. But somehow the picture always ended up back in Jágr's possession.

Bobby Holík had never been as naturally talented as Reichel and Jágr. Bobby was smart and strong. He fought for everything on the ice and knew how to contribute to his teams in little ways. But he didn't fill up a stat sheet with large numbers of goals and assists. When he was younger, he would dissolve into tears because he felt that no one noticed his performance on the ice. Jaroslav reminded the boy that hockey was a team sport and that the point was to notice the team, not the individual player.[7] As Reichel, Jágr, and Bobby became teenagers, the young Holík boy didn't receive the fanfare that the other two did, but before long the training that his father pushed on him began to pay dividends. In the years following his sister's defection, Bobby became an intimidating, dominant force on the ice because of his enormous size, spectacular conditioning, and willingness to do anything to control the game. By 1989, when he turned eighteen, Bobby stood with Reichel and Jágr at the top of Czechoslovakia junior hockey.

Playing hockey internationally meant something extra to youths from Czechoslovakia. When they showed up at an international junior tournament, they saw teens from Canada, the US, and the USSR and wondered what on earth they—kids from a tiny, unknown country—were even doing there. When they saw the other boys get off their buses and walk around the lobby of the hotel, Bobby and his teammates were sometimes intimidated simply by the size of the countries whose teams they were to face. But as soon as the puck dropped, the boys from Czechoslovakia knew they belonged. Playing together against the world's best gave the Czechoslovak teens a sense that they mattered and that the world had to respect them.[8]

Of course, these were not just hockey players; they were also teenaged boys, and like teens throughout the Western world in the 1980s, young hockey players in Czechoslovakia were crazy about heavy metal music. Throughout the second half of the decade, Czechoslovak boys used music by bands like Def Leppard and especially Metallica as the soundtrack for their lives. Like teens in North America, Czechoslovak kids blared the music in their locker rooms and especially on the bus to tournaments. For the junior national teams, it was the metalhead hockey players from České Budějovice, in tight jeans and rocker big hair, who usually brought the boom box. The rocker boys might not have been as skilled as other players, but they provided the pounding loud guitar sounds that pumped up the rest of the team.

So it was at the European Under-18 Junior Championships held in Kyiv in April 1989 that Bobby, Reichel, and Jágr played on a major international squad together for the first time. Before the matches, the boys rocked out, thanks to sounds provided by the České Budějovice players. But they also found themselves expressing feelings they had rarely talked about before. Kids growing up in the 1970s and '80s, in the shadow of the 1968 Soviet invasion of Czechoslovakia, had a sense of how their parents felt about their invaders. But as the young hockey players became teenagers and directly confronted people on the ice who came from the country that occupied them, they began to speak in a new tone, filled with hatred. As they approached play against the Soviets in Kyiv, the boys felt it rise out of their throats. "*Fuck* the Russians! This is for 1968!"

TOP LEFT: Jaroslav Sr. and Věra's newlywed photo (1942). *Courtesy of Memory of Nations and family archive of Jiří Holík.* TOP RIGHT: Věra, Jaroslav Jr. (left), and Jiří (around 1948). *Courtesy of Memory of Nations and family archive of Jiří Holík.* BOTTOM LEFT: Jaroslav Sr. (in later years at the fast-food shop he ran). *Copyright © Jiří Pekárek.*

ABOVE: Havlíčkův Brod teens: Jiří Holík (3rd from left), Jan Suchý (2nd from right), Jaroslav Holík (1st from right). *Courtesy of the Jaroslav Holík Archives.* BELOW: Jiří (left) and Jaroslav Holík as kids. *Courtesy of the Jaroslav Holík Archives.*

ABOVE: In the army, meeting a general: (from left) Jaroslav Holík, Jiří Holík, Jan Klapáč, and Jan Suchý. *From the photo archive of HC Dukla Jihlava.* BOTTOM LEFT: Jiří (left) and Jaroslav Holík in Dukla uniforms. *From ČTK / Karas Jiří.* BOTTOM RIGHT: Jan Suchý (wearing a national team jersey). *From ČTK / Karas Jiří.*

ABOVE: Czechoslovakia team captain Jozef Golonka celebrates a goal against the USSR in the 1968 Olympics, as Alexander Ragulin, Jaroslav Holík's nemesis, skates by. Moments later, Golonka lay down on the ice, prompting the Western press to joke that he was trying to hear if the Soviets retaliated by closing the pipelines of oil and natural gas that ran to Czechoslovakia. *From the SOŠV photo archive, Slovak Olympic and Sports Museum.* BELOW: Alexander Dubček, the face of Czechoslovakia's 1968 Prague Spring. *From Sovfoto/UIG/Bridgeman Images.*

ABOVE: Dubček meets with Soviet leader Leonid Brezhnev in 1968. Brezhnev was deeply concerned about Czechoslovakia's liberalizing reforms. *From ČTK / Krejčí Bedřich.* RIGHT: Line of Soviet T–55 tanks in the streets of Prague as part of the August 1968 invasion. *From akg-images / Interfoto.* BELOW: Unarmed Czechoslovak citizens jeer at invading Soviet military forces, shouting, "Fascists!" and "Russians, go home!" *From RBM Vintage Images / Alamy Stock Photo.*

ABOVE: Prague demonstrators surround an invading Soviet tank. *From akg-images / Universal Images Group / Sovfoto / UIG.* BELOW: In Bratislava, Emil Gallo, a local plumber, bellows "Shoot!" as he confronts an invading tank. *From akg-images / Ladislav Bielik.*

ABOVE: 1969 Czechoslovak national team. Front row, seated from the left: Jaroslav Jiřík, Miroslav Termer, Jozef Golonka, Vladimír Kostka (coach), Zdeněk Andršt (Czechoslovakia hockey federation), Jaroslav Pitner (coach), Josef Černý, Vladimír Dzurilla, and Jan Suchý. Middle row from left: Otto Trefný, Richard Farda, Vladimír Bednář, Václav Nedomanský, Miroslav Lacký, Josef Horešovský, Jaroslav Holík, Jiří Holík, and Harry Martínek (masseur). Top row from left: Oldřich Machač, František Ševčík, Jan Havel, Josef Augusta, Jan Hrbatý, Jan Klapáč, Rudolf Tajcnár, and František Pospíšil. *From ČTK / Havelka Zdeněk.* BELOW: Various Czechoslovakia supporters brought signs to the 1969 tournament. One (right) showed a tank firing at a hockey net. Another (left) said, "We are not afraid of the Russians, we will beat them in hockey, and we will pay them back for August." *From ČTK / Havelka Zdeněk.*

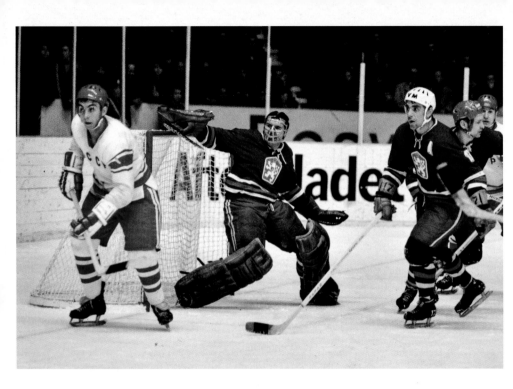

ABOVE: Vladimír Dzurilla (looking like "Hannibal Lecter on skates") and Jan Suchý (right) try to keep the Soviets from scoring in their first matchup in 1969. *From Imago Images/Jan Collsiöö/TT.* BELOW: Jiří (far left), Jaroslav (#5, center), and Nedomanský (#14, right) celebrate Jan Suchý's goal in 1969 Game 1 against the USSR. Moments later, Jaroslav shakes his stick in Soviet goalie Zinger's face, screaming, "You fucking commie!!!" *From Imago Images/Jan Delden/TT.*

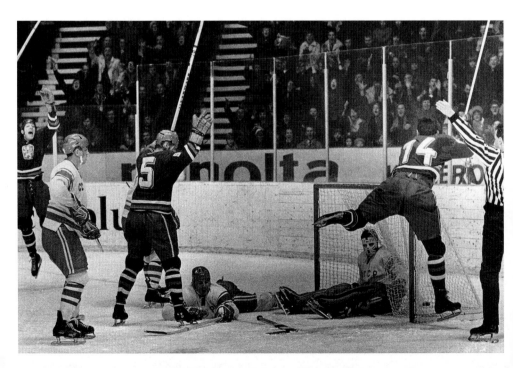

ABOVE: 1969 Game 2: bareheaded Václav "Big Ned" Nedomanský and Soviet Boris Mikhailov pounded each other repeatedly throughout their two matches. *From ČTK / Havelka Zdeněk.* RIGHT: (from left) Jan Hrbatý, Jaroslav Holík, and Jiří Holík at the 1969 World Championships. Jaroslav has taped over the star on his jersey. *From ČTK / Havelka Zdeněk.* BELOW: Celebration in Prague's Wenceslas Square following Game 2 against the Soviets in 1969. "4:3" sign announces the score of the match. *From ČTK.*

ABOVE: Cover of the secret police file on Jaroslav Holík—refers to him as codename "REBEL." *From the Czech Archive of Security Forces: Collection "Central administration of military counterintelligence SNB, personal file," archival file no. KR-18188 VKR.* BELOW: Jiří (left) and Jaroslav after the second match against the Soviets at the 1972 World Championships. It is believed to have been the first time the brothers ever hugged. *Copyright © Jiří Pekárek.*

ABOVE: Marie (left), Andrea, and Jaroslav Holík. *From ČTK / Havelka Zdeněk.* RIGHT: Jaroslav helps Bobby get his hockey gear on. *Copyright © Jiří Pekárek.*

Dukla player Bobby Holík (left) with Dukla coach Jaroslav Holík. *From Jiří Koliš.*

ABOVE: Franta Musil (middle row: 5th from left/6th from right) and Coach Jaroslav Holík (front row: 4th from right) and the 1984-85 Czechoslovakia champion Dukla Jihlava team. Jaroslav would grow enraged when he learned of Musil's interest in Andrea. *From the photo archive of HC Dukla Jihlava.* BELOW LEFT: Martina Navrátilová thanks the crowd at the conclusion of the July 1986 Federation Cup tennis tournament in Prague. *From ČTK / Khol Pavel.* BELOW RIGHT: Andrea Holíková practices in preparation for the 1986 Fed Cup. *From ČTK / Hajský Libor.*

TOP: In 1990, the future of Czecho-slovak hockey looked bright, with the presence of three teenage super-stars (from left): Jaromír Jágr, Robert Reichel, and Bobby Holík. *From Jiří Koliš.* RIGHT: Jan "Cicero" Reindl took to the ice to voice his support for the revolution in the streets and then helped lead Sparta Prague to the 1990 league championship. *From Jiří Koliš.*

ABOVE: November 1989: in his first public appearance in Prague in two decades, Alexander Dubček waves to a crowd of hundreds of thousands of demonstrators in Wenceslas Square. *From Sovfoto/UIG/Bridgeman Images.* BELOW: November 24, 1989: Václav Havel (right) and Dubček (center) toast "To a free Czechoslovakia!" *From ČTK / AP / Vranic.*

ABOVE: Czech Republic goalie Dominik Hašek looks to block a shot against Russia in "The Tournament of the Century," the 1998 Olympics. *From ČTK / Jiji Press Photo / Yasushi Arishima.* BELOW: Hašek, with a brace on his dislocated left thumb, following the epic match against Canada in the 1998 Olympics. *From ČTK / AP / Paquin Denis.*

ABOVE: Petr Svoboda (left) after scoring against Russia in the 1998 Olympics. *From ČTK / Profimedia / Stephen Jaffe / AFP.* BELOW: The 1998 Czech Republic Olympic hockey team. *From ČTK / imago sportfotodienst.*

The USSR and Czechoslovakia, both undefeated, faced off in the final. The Soviet team was led by forward Pavel Bure, yet another boy born within just a few months of Bobby. Bobby and Reichel had faced off against Bure since they had all been just fifteen years old, and they knew what they were in for: one of the fastest-skating hockey players in the world. At sixteen, he had begun playing for the top Soviet professional squad. And despite the stacked Czechoslovakia team, the Bure-led squad narrowly took the match and the tournament title. The Soviets had come out ahead yet again, and the Czechoslovak boys returned to their locker room in tears.[9]

The Czechoslovak teens had played magnificently, but it hadn't been enough against the Soviet junior team in Kyiv. And it certainly wouldn't be enough to defeat the adult national team, the Red Machine. To do that, Czechoslovakia would need more. At a minimum, it would need someone who had not been in Kyiv: a skinny young man in giant pads who held the key to the future of Czechoslovak hockey.

From the time they were kids, one of Franta Musil's best friends was the boy named Dominik Hašek ["HA-shekh"], born in January 1965 in Pardubice, just a month after Musil. Compared to the big, strong, rugged Franta, "Dom" was a beanpole, drawn to skills where direct contact was less important. As long as he could remember, Hašek didn't try to score goals in any game. Even as a four-year-old, facing off in his living room doorway against tennis balls hit by a family member, or out in front of the giant nets on the soccer pitch, young Dominik insisted on playing the position of goalie, where he could try to block the best efforts of his opponents.

By 1982, when he was seventeen years old, Hašek was the full-time starting goaltender for Pardubice's professional squad and took the league by storm. Not especially tall at five feet, eleven inches, but wiry and under 170 pounds, he was blessed with stunning flexibility—he could do the splits!—and spectacular reflexes. Hašek played in an utterly unconventional fashion, spending much of his time flopping around on the ice like a fish and contorting his body into bizarre positions to block the puck. In his first full year as the Pardubice team's goalie, he became a national star, despite turning just eighteen partway through the season. It was during that summer of 1983 that Hašek and Musil found themselves at a magazine stand in France. The young netminder, partly distracted by his reading material but also largely clueless as to the meaning of Musil's words, hardly noticed when his buddy informed him that the NHL's Chicago Blackhawks had drafted him. Leaving Czechoslovakia just wasn't something he thought about.

As a kid, he had received some basic lessons about his country's relationship with the Soviets. In 1976, when Dominik was eleven years old, he could not wait to turn on the television to watch the final hockey match of that year's Olympics. The Hašek house whooped with joy as Czechoslovakia took a quick 2–0 lead after one period. Finally! Finally, they might win that cherished Olympic gold! And then the family television stopped working. It was late, anyway, and Dominik needed to get up the next day for school, so his parents put him to bed and headed off to the grandparents' home to finish watching. The next morning Dom learned what had happened in the horrible flu game. The lesson was a terrible one: when it came to the most important matches, when it came to the Olympics, there just was no beating the Russians.

In the 1980s, as Dominik grew older and started playing on national teams against other countries, he noticed a pattern to how he and his teammates talked about matches against their occupier. "The Russians can beat us with tanks, but those fucking commies are not going to beat us on the ice." He started to see the strangeness of it all: *But wait . . . We're commies too . . .* But then he worked out an answer. *They're the BAD commies!*[10] Nevertheless, as the 1980s continued, Czechoslovakia's victories over the bad commies were few and far between.

By 1987 Hašek had become not only the best goalie in Czechoslovakia, but was also voted the best player at any position in his country's top hockey league. The Chicago Blackhawks offered him a five-year, $1.2 million contract. Hašek seriously considered the offer, but decided he was happy with his life in Czechoslovakia and couldn't risk what might happen to his family if he left.[11] The Blackhawks' loss was Czechoslovakia's gain.

By the fall of 1989, between the extraordinary Hašek in the goal and the three teenage superstar forwards, the future of Czechoslovakia's hockey program looked bright. Indeed, it just might have a chance at once again challenging the Soviets on the ice . . . unless there was a significant exodus of players . . .

·:⁙:·

In 1989, the Holík name was a major topic among NHL executives. Scouts who knew international hockey believed that, if available to join the NHL, Bobby and young Soviet superstar Pavel Bure would be the first two players picked in the annual draft in June. One scout said about Bobby, "He's a top-five player, no question of that. He's big and strong and really has no flaws. He's tough and has tremendous skills." The Quebec Nordiques had the first pick in the draft. At the 1989 World Junior Championships in Anchorage, Alaska, a Quebec scout, Pierre Gauthier, met Bobby in secret. Gauthier informed young Holík that the Nordiques would select him as the first overall pick if he defected right then. Bobby told Gauthier that he wasn't ready to emigrate, but rumors began to fly. As the June draft approached, the *Los Angeles Times* even published a piece about Bobby with the headline "Czech Hockey Star, 18, May Have Defected." This supposed move would have been news to the young Holík boy, who was busy training in Jihlava, unaware of the discussions swirling about him in North America.

Ordinarily, Bobby's unwillingness to go would have tamped down interest in him, but the intervention of a Czechoslovak legend—a tennis player—produced an unexpected outcome. Ivan Lendl was born in 1960 to a pair of highly ranked Czechoslovak tennis players. In the 1980s he became the greatest men's tennis player in the country's history. When he won seven professional tennis tour titles in 1980, Lendl became a national hero, and then proceeded to get better. By early 1983, he was the world's top-ranked men's player and would spend half the decade at number one. Over time, though, he refused to accept the regime's control over his life in Czechoslovakia, and in 1984 he bought a home in Greenwich, Connecticut. Unlike Martina Navrátilová, he never formally announced that he was defecting, but he refused to play for the Czechoslovak men's tennis team and stopped returning to his birth country. In 1986, the Czechoslovak authorities labeled him an "illegal defector." Between his athletic success and his willingness to buck the wishes of the regime, many Czechoslovak athletes, Bobby included, hailed Lendl—along with Peter Šťastný and Martina Navrátilová—as among their biggest heroes.

As a kid growing up, Lendl had been a huge hockey fan and had gone out of his way to watch Jaroslav Holík play, even crawling out onto the rafters at arenas to get a better view. Now, in 1989, having become a major athletic figure in Connecticut, Lendl found himself serving on the board of advisors for the local NHL team, the Hartford Whalers. Hearing about Bobby's prowess on the ice, Lendl told the Whalers' brass: "If this Holík kid is half as good as his dad, he's going to be great."

Since the draft that year was held in Minnesota, where Franta Musil and Andrea lived, many people suspected that Bobby had already defected and that the Minnesota North Stars had hidden him away, planning to pull him out at the last second as they drafted him. It was therefore a surprise when, with the tenth pick in the June 17, 1989 draft, the Hartford Whalers selected Bobby. Given the risk that he would never be able to come, it was a stunning move to pick a player from behind the Iron Curtain with an early first-round pick. Surmising that Bobby might be chosen, Andrea attended the event and stood in for her brother, posing for photos wearing a green Hartford jersey.[12]

As was typical for him in June, Bobby had been in Czechoslovakia training all day, cycling for hours to build up his conditioning. As he walked through the door of his home, about to pound water after the long workout, the phone rang. It was Andrea with the news. He was thrilled, but could only mutter, "Great . . . now what . . . ?" Planning to defect, but also recognizing how hard the government could come down on those who escaped before completing their military service, Bobby had enlisted in the army a year earlier than required. For the time being, getting drafted had changed nothing. He would serve his two years and then look for his way out.

Little could he anticipate how, just a few short months later, his plans would be completely upended. And the most powerful move on Czechoslovakia's ice that year would be made not by Bobby, Hašek, or any of the country's hockey elite, but by an oft-forgotten Prague defenseman whose nickname portended a different sort of greatness.

# CHAPTER 16

# 89 is 68 Turned Upside Down and Backwards

I t was obvious when Jan Reindl was a child that he was never going to be a hockey superstar. He was a good but not great athlete. He didn't have an obsessed sports parent who trained him mercilessly from a young age. He was solidly built but not enormous like Bobby Holík. He didn't have great natural speed or skills like Jágr or Reichel. And he certainly didn't have reflexes like Dominik Hašek's. No, young Jan Reindl was never going to be a hockey superstar. However, one day he would do something so extraordinary on the ice that even the greatest of the sport's superstars hadn't ever dreamt of it.

In retrospect, it seems obvious that Reindl, born on November 8, 1960 in Prague's Holešovice district, was destined to play for Czechoslovakia's most famous hockey team, Sparta Prague. Holešovice was home to the Sportovní hala stadium, where Sparta played. Jan learned to skate on ponds in Stromovka, a huge park near the Holešovice. And he loved both hockey and Sparta. As he walked home from Stromovka one day in the fall of 1967, Jan saw a poster on the arena wall advertising tryouts for Sparta's youth team, so he made his grandmother take him. The tryout didn't include any serious tests of skill. The coaches simply told the boys to skate. And skate. And skate some more. Intermittently, coaches would point at a boy who had shown something on the ice. "You! Come!" So it went until they filled a roster of twenty-five. Jan grew exhausted from the never-ending skating and, as he watched other boys get picked, became convinced that they would never choose him, until abruptly one of the coaches finally came his way.

Jan began practicing with the team two days later. He didn't have great talent, but he was extremely likable. He also had a knack for getting the others to stay on task, and no one outworked him. During his second year with Sparta, he was named captain of his squad of eight-year-olds.

Part of the decision to name Jan captain undoubtedly stemmed from his moxie, something that only grew as he got older. He spoke directly, telling others what he really thought, and showed no timidness in approaching authority. Reindl played defense and idolized Sparta star defenseman Josef Horešovský, the man who had scored the big goal that gave Czechoslovakia the third period lead in the final 1969 match against the Soviets. When Reindl was twelve and a member of Sparta's youth team, the boy was often around the stadium when the professional squad practiced and one day marched up to Horešovský. "Pepík! Can I have your stick?" "Pepík" in Czech is like the nickname "Joey" in English and, although normally among the nicest of the professionals, Horešovský felt irritated that some little kid would act so casually with him. "Don't you dare call me 'Pepík'!"

As Jan got older, he made his way up to Sparta's junior squad, where he was again named captain, but he didn't appear to be a good enough player to make it on a topflight team at the adult level. So, in 1980, as he aged out of junior play, Reindl's hockey career appeared to be over. However, as a nineteen-year-old, he was required to fulfill his compulsory military service. Reindl went to serve in Jihlava where, although he wasn't good enough to play for the team, he practiced with the squad and honed his hockey skills for the next two years.

Upon completing his military service in 1982, Jan had offers to join a couple of teams, but there was only one that he truly wanted to play for. Reindl got himself a tryout with Sparta and was given until the end of the preseason to prove himself. But the team's head coach seemed uninterested. Sparta played a series of preseason matches as it winnowed down its roster. Through the first eleven, the coaches kept Jan on the bench. But in the eleventh, two defensemen got hurt, and Reindl finally had his shot. In game number twelve, he collected a goal and an assist and played his usual suffocating defense. Following the match, it became official: Jan Reindl had achieved his life dream of making Sparta Prague's professional hockey team.

At the beginning of his professional career, Jan hardly ever scored or assisted on goals, but he contributed to the team in other ways. No one listened more attentively to the coaches or worked harder than Reindl, inspiring his team-mates through his example. He performed the role of the classic defenseman, terrifying opposing forwards with his rough play. Jan also had no concern for his own safety and became beloved by his team for constantly jumping into shots to block them.

However, it wasn't through his play that Reindl most stood out. His mother had wanted him to go to college and get a job that used his mind more than his body. Jan disappointed her on that front, but her influence on him was clear. Everywhere he went, he carried books, especially about history, and read in every spare moment. In this way, despite receiving relatively little formal schooling, Jan gave himself a rich education. When he went into the locker room for the first time to collect his professional team jersey, he heard two players exchanging "facts" about the world that struck him as absurd. Reindl interrupted to correct the men, who immediately put the rookie in his place. "Shut up, Cicero," they said, comparing him to the great Roman statesman, scholar, and orator. The nickname "Cicero" stuck.

Despite making fun of him, Jan's teammates soon came to adore him. Reindl himself wished that he were more elegant and skilled, able to skate beautifully and put the puck into the net, but his teammates appreciated him for what he was: a player with massive heart, always the first to give up his body to get the puck or respond if anyone attacked one of his teammates. They also fed off his natural leadership. No one cheered louder on the bench. And he was the single player who knew just what to say and how to say it to pump up the men. The Sparta professional squad named Jan Reindl captain.

Jan had grown up hating Czechoslovakia's Communists. Jan's maternal grandfather owned a renowned butcher shop and a lovely house with a small fishpond in Prague. In 1949, the regime took it all and, when Reindl's grand-father refused to go along with the plan, imprisoned him for ten years. As a result, Jan's mother didn't really get to know her father. Jan's paternal grandfa-ther was a larger-than-life figure who, it was said, once wrestled and defeated a bear at a local fair. The future Grandpa Reindl resided in southern Bohemia, where he ran a farm with fields, trees, cows, and horses. He used the horses to run a transportation business. Over the summer, they transported milk. In the winter, it was lumber. Grandpa Reindl claimed he had the horses so well trained that they had the whole milk delivery route memorized. He just snoozed all the way, waking only when he arrived at the pub at the end of the line. When Communists grabbed power, they took everything from Grandpa Reindl except the horses.

With their property gone, Grandpa Reindl told his son to move to Prague, where the young man met and married Jan's mother. Because their own parents had bucked the Communists, neither of Jan's parents could attend college. Jan's father worked as a machinist and a technician in a factory, and Jan's mother ran the municipal telephone operator switchboard. The entire family was beside itself when the Soviets invaded in 1968. Jan never forgot how his maternal grandmother looked out over the columns of tanks when they arrived: "Here they are, those swine."

As he grew up, Jan openly expressed his contempt for the people who were responsible for his family's plight. Seemingly unaware of what he was saying, he often spoke disdainfully of the regime in public, blurting out phrases like "those shitty Communists." In 1986, Sparta Prague developed a two-headed coaching staff with Pavel Wohl, a great motivator of players, and Horešovský, the terrifically smart former national team star whom Reindl had annoyed by calling "Pepík" years earlier. Natural-born psychologists who introduced Soviet-style training methods to the team, the two raised the quality of Sparta's play. They were also fond of their team captain and worried that his outspokenness would land him in trouble. They knew team officials wouldn't kick Jan off the squad—if Sparta fans learned that the popular Reindl had been booted for speaking out, there would be hell to pay. But Horešovský and Wohl feared what would happen if the wrong person heard his rantings and reported him to the secret police.

As the 1989–90 season opened, Prague fans had decent hopes for their team. They had finished in the top four in the playoffs in each of the previous three seasons and had acquired Petr Bříza, Czechoslovakia's best goalie not named Hašek. On November 17, 1989, Sparta stood with a respectable record of eleven wins, seven losses, and two ties. However, that didn't hold a candle to the top team. Dominik Hašek had been forced that year to move to Jihlava to complete his military service. Now with Czechoslovakia's greatest goaltender, Dukla had lost its first game but not a single match after then, winning fifteen and finishing with a draw in four others. On Saturday, November 18, Sparta learned just how good Dukla was when Reindl and his teammates traveled to play in Jihlava. The home team came away with an easy 5–0 victory.

Listening to the radio on the bus as they rode back to Prague, the men from Sparta heard news from the capital that shook them. The events of that week were part of a chain of events that altered life way beyond the borders of Czechoslovakia. They were part of a geopolitical earthquake that shook the world. Watching everything unfolding in front of him, Jan Reindl decided to become part of something that would forever change his little country.[1]

In the years that followed the 1968 invasion of Czechoslovakia, Soviet leader Leonid Brezhnev's health deteriorated. Over the 1970s, he developed various forms of cancer as well as heart and circulatory diseases. He also suffered several minor strokes. He had his first heart attack in 1975. His insomnia led to an addiction to sleeping pills and tranquilizers. Over time, he suffered from memory loss, became physically unsteady, and increasingly had difficulty speaking. Although he remained in power, he gradually withdrew from public life. Doctors remained constantly by his side and had to save him from death multiple times. Throughout it all, he turned more and more to Soviet hockey, which he watched obsessively while the country's economy stagnated under the weight of poor policy making.

On November 10, 1982, a heart attack struck Brezhnev dead, plunging the Soviet leadership into an unsteady period. The country's next two leaders, Yuri Andropov and Konstantin Chernenko, each died after little more than a year in power, and during that time each appeared unwilling or unable to address the country's growing crisis. The economy scarcely grew at all. The USSR produced inferior goods, and faced frequent shortages of food and other consumer items.

On March 11, 1985, fifty-four-year-old Mikhail Gorbachev became the country's new Communist Party leader. As he took charge, Gorbachev indicated that he intended to continue the Soviet Union's control over its Eastern Bloc satellites, but it also soon became clear that he planned to do things in a new way at home. He introduced political reforms that brought greater freedom into the USSR, hoping to undercut stale, hard-line Soviet programs that seemed to stifle the economy. These moves looked familiar to Czechs and Slovaks who remembered Dubček's efforts in 1968.

However, even as Gorbachev pushed his *glasnost* ("openness") and *perestroika* ("restructuring") reforms in the USSR, little changed in Czechoslovakia. When Gorbachev first spoke about his new policies, Czechoslovakia actually censored the portions of the Soviet Communist newspaper *Pravda* that described them. In the months that followed, Czechoslovakia enacted modest economic reforms, but remained as repressive as ever. Gorbachev visited Czechoslovakia in April 1987, but everything appeared to remain business as usual after he left. Czechs and Slovaks despaired, convinced that nothing would ever change.[2]

In late 1987, after a power struggle, Czechoslovakia's Communists replaced the aging Gustáv Husák at the top of the Party with Miloš Jakeš, who had overseen the purges of countless Party members following the 1968 invasion. Jakeš claimed to be a supporter of Gorbachev's types of changes, but anyone with a sense of the inner workings of Prague knew that Czechoslovakia's new leader had no interest in real reform, even though the country confronted significant problems. The government had prioritized the manufacturing industry and the use of agrochemicals to such a degree that by the 1980s Czechoslovakia faced serious air, water, and soil pollution. Rigid Communist Party policy left the manufacturing and technology sectors of the economy suffering from massive inefficiencies. Unable to purchase basic staples of life, citizens quietly expressed total distrust of the government. The problem eventually became so great that the government had to devote major attention to the country's toilet paper shortage.[3] Even still, Czechoslovakia's hard-liners remained entrenched in power, expressed little interest in serious reform, and showed no patience with moves to challenge their regime. Nevertheless, the new Jakeš regime would soon confront such a challenge, one that was kickstarted by, of all people, a hockey player.

After Marián Šťastný joined his brothers, Peter and Anton, in Canada in 1981, he had a fine five-year career in the NHL and then sought to make his mark off the ice. In July 1987, he was elected vice president of the Slovak World Congress, a body representing Slovak émigrés who sought to promote the cause of their people back home. Czechoslovakia's Communist authorities had always repressed organized religion in their country, and over the years they had threatened, beaten, and even murdered Catholic priests, who were especially prominent and influential in Slovakia. When a popular Catholic priest was murdered there in October 1987, many believed the secret police were responsible.

Heartbroken, Marián sought to raise awareness of the problems of religious freedom and human rights in Slovakia. He laid out a plan in a letter, which his mother-in-law smuggled inside a bar of Swiss chocolate to one of Slovakia's leading dissidents who, in turn, organized citizens on the ground for a major demonstration. The plan, the "Candle Manifestation," began as light rain fell on the evening of March 25, 1988. Over 3,000 Catholics and secular supporters of human rights snuck into Hviezdoslav Square in the center of Bratislava, Slovakia's capital. On adjacent streets, nearly 10,000 demonstrators, unable to get around the line of security forces, set up as well. At six o'clock, standing under brilliantly colored umbrellas, the demonstrators lit candles and sang a hymn. The crowd then began a disciplined half hour of quiet prayer and reflection, many focusing on their rosaries, as the police moved in. The yellow-and-white police cars first disrupted the event with loud sirens and shouting as they pushed into the demonstrators' backs. Then they pounded the kneeling participants with water cannons and clubs. The more than 1,000 security forces arrested 141 demonstrators and injured 14, but the crowd refused to budge until it concluded its full thirty minutes of silent prayer. News of the event made it to the West, which condemned the act of aggression against peaceful protesters. The Candle Manifestation had been the largest direct confrontation in Czechoslovakia between citizens and the country's security forces since the beginning of normalization.

In the months that followed, more people stood up to the Czechoslovak authorities—and the regime continued to quash efforts to challenge it. Earlier in 1988, the country's leading Catholic priests had started a petition demanding greater religious freedoms, which more than 600,000 people signed by May. The regime sent the organizer of the petition to a psychiatric hospital for anti-hallucination treatment.[4] Small-scale altercations between students and dissidents, on one side, and security forces, on the other, popped up throughout the year. The largest clash occurred on August 21, the twentieth anniversary of the Warsaw Pact invasion. In the days leading up to the anniversary, the secret police began arresting potential protesters, but large demonstrations broke out throughout the country anyway, with 10,000 ultimately marching in Prague. As thousands chanted "Freedom! Democracy!" and "Dubček! Dubček!" in Wenceslas Square, the police attempted to control the crowd with truncheons, water cannons, and tear gas. Additional, smaller demonstrations occurred on key anniversaries throughout the remainder of the year.

January 1989 marked a major uptick in street demonstrations during "Palach week," the twentieth anniversary of Jan Palach's self-immolation. For six days, protesters demanded that the government democratize, further provoking the security forces to detain well-known dissidents. Most prominently, the authorities arrested Václav Havel after he tried to lay flowers at the site of Palach's suicide. Since 1985, the police had held Havel multiple times, but they always released him quickly. Now, though, the regime was clearly getting spooked and sentenced Havel to eight months in prison for "disorderly conduct."[5]

As Czechoslovakia's leadership sought to contain the growing dissent, Gorbachev found that his attempts to solve his own country's economic problems were not succeeding, so he decided to push more extensive political reforms. In addition, he withdrew from foreign policy and military commitments that drained Soviet resources. Gorbachev felt personally disturbed by superpowers' reliance on nuclear weapons, but he also believed that the arms race with the United States was too expensive and now harmed the USSR's economy. He worked to create arms control agreements with the West and pulled the USSR out of its costly occupation of Afghanistan.

In 1988, as Soviet analysts increasingly expressed regret over how the country had bullied its satellite states in years past, Gorbachev sought to further cut back USSR financial commitments and announced in December that the country would unilaterally reduce its military presence in Eastern Europe. As he looked at the Eastern European economies and political arrangements, Gorbachev believed that the USSR's satellite states faced the same general problems as the Soviet Union and that only through reform might they save themselves. Indeed, Czechoslovakia's economy and environment were in serious trouble, leaving residents increasingly restless. By early 1989, Gorbachev decided that the Soviet Union would not intercede to halt moves away from communism in the Eastern European countries.

Czechoslovakia's hard-line Communist leaders watched with fear in 1989 as dramatic changes shook the world just beyond them. The Communist parties in Poland, directly to the north and northeast, and Hungary, directly to the south and southeast, had confronted powerful opposition movements for years. Without the Soviet Union acting as a backstop anymore, in spring and summer of 1989 these movements were finally able to flip the trajectory of their countries' politics. Eventually, in genuine democratic elections in Poland, the opposition resoundingly defeated the Communists, leading in August to a new government led by Prime Minister Tadeusz Mazowiecki, an anti–Communist regime activist. In the months that followed, Communists in Hungary overhauled their country's constitution, and in October they adopted legislation to provide free and fair elections.

Still, Czechoslovakia's leaders took solace from the fact that Poland and Hungary were different from Czechoslovakia because of their long experience with opposition movements. Surely nothing so dramatic could happen in Czechoslovakia, where the Communists controlled the population much more tightly.

But fear turned to horror among Czechoslovakia's hard-line authorities as they watched the events that followed in East Germany, directly to the north and northwest. Like Czechoslovakia, the East German government had maintained an iron grip on its people, but control became more difficult in 1989. Earlier in the year, Hungary had opened its border to Austria, creating an escape route to the West for people behind the Iron Curtain. In turn, tens of thousands of East Germans traveled through Czechoslovakia to Hungary, from which they then crossed into Austria. Thousands of other East Germans traveled to Czechoslovakia to camp out at the West German Embassy, where they sought asylum. In September, major pro-democracy demonstrations erupted in East Germany and proceeded to spread and grow larger in early October, when the country's leaders tightened the restrictions on border crossings to Czechoslovakia to stem the wave of emigration.

The East German Communists hoped to use physical force to crush the protesters, but found themselves dissuaded as Gorbachev refused to back such extreme measures. In the hopes of calming the unrest, the East German regime started to create new travel regulations. But on November 9, 1989, a regime spokesman misspoke, stating that all borders would be opened for everyone "immediately, without delay." Immediately and without delay, hundreds of thousands of East Germans crossed the borders. Many celebrated euphorically atop the Berlin Wall, even beginning to tear the monstrosity down with hammers and chisels. It was only a short matter of time until the Communists in East Germany lost their grip on power just as those in Poland and Hungary had lost theirs.

But even as they saw what was happening just across their borders, many in Czechoslovakia found it difficult to truly believe that anything would change for them. Change seemed to be everywhere *except* in Czechoslovakia. There just didn't seem to be much open dissent in Czechoslovakia. Plus, they remembered 1968, when their incredibly high hopes had been so cruelly dashed. It was difficult to imagine that this time would be any different.

The evening of Friday, November 17, 1989, brought a sort of magic to the country, as a stunning red glow appeared in the night sky. For the first time in decades, people in Czechoslovakia witnessed aurora borealis, the northern lights.[6] The lights weren't visible from the capital city, but in Prague a large group of students had a different reason to take to the streets. The students had received state approval to march in commemoration of the fiftieth anniversary of the day that the Nazis stormed a university campus in the city, murdered nine campus leaders, and sent over 1,200 students to concentration camps. The 1989 event began with speeches at a cemetery, but then organizers decided to march to Wenceslas Square. As the group headed to the city center, more residents of all ages joined in. The group began to chant in unison, "We don't want the Communist Party," "Forty years are enough!"

As they began to walk up Wenceslas Square, the demonstrators, several thousand strong, found themselves face-to-face with red-bereted anti-terrorist forces and riot police. The police carried shields and truncheons and wore white helmets on their heads. It was a look that would be replicated many years later in the film *The Hunger Games*, which portrayed the security forces of a totalitarian regime in a cruel, dystopian world. Czechoslovakia's security forces soon had the marchers surrounded and unable to move forward or retreat. Chanting "Freedom!" the demonstrators offered flowers to the police. Placing lit candles on the ground, they chanted "We have bare hands" as they raised their open palms into the air. The police squeezed in, leaving the marchers feeling suffocated. Then the security forces attacked, beating the screaming, helpless protesters.

The brutality left Prague residents sickened. Adults cried at the idea of students, barely older than children, being so viciously attacked by government forces. As (inaccurate) rumors spread that the attack had killed one of the youths, students and theater groups took action, planning general strikes and taking to the streets. Theaters halted their performances and instead invited the public inside to discuss how to proceed. Dissident groups joined in as well. Václav Havel rushed to Prague to help with the plans.

Over the weekend, tens of thousands of youths parked themselves in Wenceslas Square, waving Czechoslovak flags and chanting slogans. By the afternoon of Monday, November 20, 200,000 demonstrators pressed into the Square chanting "Now's the time." Simultaneously, marches took place in Bratislava, Brno, and other cities across the country. The following evening, the crowds grew larger everywhere. Dissidents arrived at a balcony in Wenceslas Square and took turns addressing the crowd, who stood before them holding their fingers aloft in a "V for victory" (and peace) pose. Looking at the extraordinary view below them, speakers on the Prague balcony laid out a list of demands, most notably that the most hard-line members of the Communist government resign immediately.

As they learned about events in Prague, Dukla Jihlava's players—who, as soldiers, had to swear an oath to serve the Communist government—knew they could not speak out openly. But Dominik Hašek thought to himself, *A revolution doesn't happen too many times in your life . . .* On Tuesday, November 21, Hašek, along with teammates František Kučera, Petr Hrbek, Milan Kastner, and Tomáš Sršeň, hopped into the goalie's green Škoda and snuck out of town. They drove to Prague—to Wenceslas Square!—where they were barely able to move amid the sea of humanity, in which people carried signs like "Long Live the Revolution and Down with Communism." They felt a thrill, but also the sense of an unsettled atmosphere. Something big was happening, but having grown up in the shadow of 1968, they didn't know whether that something would be good or not. As members of the army, they risked imprisonment if they were caught. There were also rumors that the army or even militias of armed factory workers might arrive at any moment and carry out a massacre. Yet a stronger feeling also permeated the area. Everywhere the Dukla men went, they saw people determined to put an end to the Communist regime once and for all. Eventually, the players headed to Holešovice to take in a hockey match between Trenčín and host Sparta Prague. The Jihlava men didn't stay long—they were much too likely to be recognized—but what transpired was unlike anything anyone there had ever before experienced.

When the men from Sparta Prague listened to the radio on the bus coming home from Jihlava on November 18, they were heartbroken by the news they heard about the attack on the students the night before. With each detail, Jan Reindl felt a debilitating bitterness and a sense of shame for his country. *To brutally attack a group of young people who simply wanted to express their opinions? This is cowardice* . . . When they got home, the Sparta men could feel Prague buzzing, and with every passing hour the tension mounted. When Reindl and his teammates saw video footage of the attack, they decided to show their solidarity with the students. Reindl received word that a student group wished to speak with him about what he and the hockey players could do for the cause.

On November 21, Reindl and his teammates arrived at their home stadium early as always for their game against Dukla Trenčín. Ordinarily, before matches, the players listened to music in the locker room, but on this Tuesday evening they insisted upon playing the radio news. As they digested each piece of new information, the Sparta men realized that the cause had progressed way beyond the students. This was about the very future of their country. While the players continued to talk, Coach Wohl brought a student representative into the room, whom he introduced to Reindl. The student asked the Sparta men to consider sitting out the match in support of the movement that was playing out in the streets and gave Reindl a statement of support that he might read to the crowd.

Reindl looked at the room and announced, "It seems that we are not playing tonight." He hurried to speak to the men from Trenčín to iron out the details. To his shock, when Reindl arrived in the visitors' locker room, he discovered that the opposing players, who lived far from Prague, in an army town in Slovakia, had no idea about the events in the streets and had no interest in anything at that moment other than playing a hockey match. Besides, as members of an army team, the men from Dukla Trenčín couldn't make an anti-regime statement anyway.

Looking up from the Trenčín players, Reindl saw a group of officials from both the Trenčín and the Sparta teams approach him. They chided Reindl. "What are you doing? They'll lock you up!" The Sparta team captain was apoplectic: "Why would they?! We have to make a statement. What's going on is unacceptable!"

Flummoxed, Reindl returned to the Sparta side to discuss what they should do. The group fell to arguing. Many, like Reindl, thought it essential to make a statement. But some refused, worrying they would lose their bonuses for the game, or worse. There were rumors of tanks and militias preparing to attack. Someone in the locker room said, "The students can handle it without us, right? The world won't change just because of something we do, so are we really going to give up our pay for this?" Reindl understood what was going on. For years now, the regime had clamped down so hard on any act of public disobedience that most people in Czechoslovakia had turned inward, completely avoiding sticking their necks out, no matter how important the cause.

Reindl pondered his options. He had never taken a major political stand in his life. But then again, living where he did, he had never had the opportunity to do so before either. Standing there in his locker room, Reindl thought to himself that he had long felt something was rotten in his country and now he could give a voice to that feeling. *The Communists can go to hell!* He spoke to Horešovský and Wohl. The coaches were deeply worried that armed militias supporting the regime might decide to make an example of protesters. But at this moment, the coaches didn't feel they could express such fears to their team captain. They told him that he had their support.

Reindl stepped out to the ice in his full Sparta uniform—white jersey with red numbers and red pants. Carrying the statement he had received from the students, he skated to the timekeeper's box to ask if he might use the microphone to address the crowd. The timekeeper could not believe that Reindl would ask such a thing. *No way!* With no other option, Reindl decided that he would skate to the middle of the ice, try to quiet the 13,000-person capacity crowd, and attempt to yell out the statement loudly enough for some to hear. But when he skated to center ice and prepared to begin, out of the blue, one of the referees brought him a microphone. Mic in hand, Reindl felt oddly calm, not thinking about any possible repercussions. He focused on the moment and the message that he was to deliver. The Cicero of Czechoslovakia hockey took a deep breath and spoke:

> *We do not want to remain indifferent to the events that are currently moving our republic. That is why we, the Sparta hockey players, hereby join the statement of the Prague students . . .*
>
> *. . . We demand an immediate investigation into the repressive action against the participants in the demonstration on November 17th. We*

*condemn the brutal intervention of the Ministry of the Interior and*
*demand the punishment of those responsible for these acts . . .*
*. . . We also demand that an indefinite popular debate on the current*
*situation be launched and conducted, which will include the search for*
*solutions to the catastrophic social, political, economic, and environmental*
*situation. We call on all fellow citizens to show their solidarity by par-*
*ticipating actively in the forthcoming events.*

Then Reindl did something that stunned the assembled. He sang the national anthem.

His beautiful baritone, emotional, somehow on-key voice floated throughout the arena. At first, the crowd couldn't quite tell what he was saying, but then it hit them. As the crowd, the Sparta coaches, and the Sparta players came to understand what he was doing, they joined in—not in allegiance to the government, but in solidarity against the repressive regime. As they did, tears streamed down many a face, especially as Reindl sang a second stanza, which is part of the anthem but was usually left out in renditions sung at the time:

*Where is my home?*
*Where God self to man had spoken:*
*Gentle be, but never broken,*
*Ever cheerful, hopeful, strong,*
*Bravely thwarting any wrong.*

As Reindl finished singing, there was a second of silence, as everyone wondered, *Will there be more?* And then, in a sudden electrifying moment, the crowd erupted with applause. Not everyone, of course. Some yelled that there would be consequences—years of imprisonment—awaiting Reindl and Sparta for such treasonous behavior. But they were drowned out as thousands began to chant in unison, over and over, *Freedom!*

Amazingly, even after all that had just transpired, the puck dropped and the match began. Sparta's goalie, Petr Bříza, who later addressed a crowd of 750,000 demonstrators in nearby Letna Park, was so shaken that he feared he wouldn't be able to handle a single shot sent his way. Fortunately for him and Sparta, he didn't need to. Trenčín appeared completely flabbergasted and let in three quick goals by Sparta before Bříza faced a serious challenge. The home team went on to win a wild match 7–5.

In the immediate aftermath of the attack on the students, little was known outside the capital about what was happening in Prague. Many who lived farther away, especially in smaller towns, continued to support the regime, but as days passed, the mood against the regime shifted faster and faster. Even in small towns like Havlíčkův Brod. Jan Suchý watched television to see everything that was happening. *I've seen this before, in 1968*, he thought, *but this time it really feels different.*

Under normalization, anti-regime demonstrations had been rare in Jihlava. But now, in November 1989, even in Jihlava everyone felt the political earthquake that shook the country.

Bobby Holík felt it. Throughout his eighteen-plus years, Bobby's life revolved around hockey and his family. Nothing more. But now, as the world directly in front of him—in Jihlava—bounced off its axis, Bobby couldn't help but take notice. In the days after Dukla Jihlava's home match against Sparta, every day at lunchtime Bobby and a teammate walked the five minutes from the hockey rink to the town square. Ordinarily, Bobby felt impervious to weather, but this November was unusually cold. The young men froze as they strode across the cobblestones in the square wearing little but their light-gray team tracksuits with red stripes down the side. Even shivering in the frosty temperatures, Bobby and his teammate were transfixed by the scene before them. In the midst of subzero wind and sideways-swirling snow, an extraordinary, exhilarating chaos of thousands of people bounced and swayed beneath flags and signs that urged the end of the regime. Each day, Bobby and his teammate came back to see the events in the square, and each day the crowd grew larger and more ebullient.

On November 22, the day after Hašek and his teammates joined the demonstrations in Prague, Jihlava played its next match against Pardubice. The Dukla players who went to the capital had received tricolor pins—blue, white, and red, representing Czechoslovakia's flag—from demonstrating soccer players in Prague and wanted to wear them on their uniforms. "Lads, you can't do this," the lead referee told them. "It's too dangerous, you could prick yourselves!" "Geez, all right, we'll take them off," Hašek moaned, but then another player came up with the idea to sew what was effectively a tricolors patch directly onto their jerseys to show their support for the people. The Dukla men had a staff member sew them on just before game time. Coach Augusta looked deeply concerned. They were players on an *army* team, and there was no telling what the Communist leadership might do.

In Jihlava, meanwhile, the demonstrations picked up speed, mostly thanks to the energy of thousands of young people. Jiří and Jaroslav Holík and their wives mostly watched the events unfold on television, but sometimes they headed to a pub in the town square to discuss, in awe, the latest movements. "If only Dad were alive to see this," they said, as they watched hundreds of thousands, if not millions, take to the streets to push back against the regime that had stolen Jaroslav Sr.'s butcher shop nearly forty years before.

Jiří coached a school hockey team and took the squad to a tournament one hundred miles from Jihlava. As the kids hit the ice to play, Jiří turned his head to catch television's latest news of Prague. His daughter was a student there who had been going from factory to factory since November 17, trying to mobilize workers to stand up against the regime. Jiří didn't much like participating in big crowds, but he decided to drive her to a number of these factories and stand at the ready for the secret police to arrest them both. Nothing happened to them, and with each passing day, it seemed to him that the outcome of 1989 really might be different from what had happened in 1968.[7]

People took to saying that "89" was "68" turned upside down and backwards. Indeed, the idea took on greater truth as Marta Kubišová appeared on a balcony in Wenceslas Square. It was Kubišová who in the late 1960s had recorded the Czechoslovak people's peace anthem and then found herself banned from the music industry as a result. Now, in 1989, Kubišová stood before hundreds of thousands of people in Prague singing the very song that had been banned along with her.

Many in the regime became convinced that the key to staying in power was to maintain the support of the country's workers, perhaps by driving a wedge between them and the student and theater groups causing all the mayhem in the streets. Even this strategy soon fell flat. On the afternoon of Thursday, November 23, a Prague Communist leader spoke to a group of large-machine factory workers at a pro-state rally and told the assembled that the government would not let "15-year-old children"—that is, the protesting students—determine who would hold power in Czechoslovakia. Realizing that the Communists were not interested in their opinions either, the thousands of workers hearing the message whistled wildly, and chanted in angry unison *WE ARE NOT CHILDREN! WE ARE NOT CHILDREN!* As the Communist leader tried to continue speaking, the crowd began to chant *ABDICATION! ABDICATION!* The assembled then marched to the Wenceslas Square demonstration to declare its opposition to the government.

The next day, Friday, November 24, the Pilsen team came to play Sparta in Prague. Student representatives and Josef Vinklář, a famous actor at the time, visited the two teams. "In support of the movement in the streets, would you consider not playing tonight's game?" To Reindl and many of the men from Sparta, speeches were no longer sufficient. They, as high-profile athletes, had the power to do more. The administrators of both teams pressed the players to hold the game as scheduled, but the Pilsen and Sparta players weren't having any of it. Pilsen's captain, Pavel Setikovský, and Reindl took to the ice and announced that, given everything going on outside the building, they would not play that day. The two captains shook hands, briefly greeted the small number of fans there, and left the arena to join the people of Czechoslovakia outside.[8]

Many headed to Wenceslas Square, where something occurred that just days earlier had been unthinkable. As the size and energy level of the crowd in the Square continued to grow, the throng looked toward the fourth-floor balcony, where the movement's leaders often addressed them. As they cast their eyes anxiously toward the speakers' platform, the Wenceslas congregation of hundreds of thousands of people began to chant a man's name. The TV crew's spotlights lit the balcony space, and into the freezing night air, seemingly out of nowhere, that man appeared before them.

Alexander Dubček.

Since 1970, Alexander Dubček had lived in Bratislava, constantly watched by the secret police. Slovakia's Communist leadership assigned Dubček to a position as a mechanic in the Forest Administration just outside Bratislava. The leader of the Prague Spring took charge of the maintenance of bulldozers and chain saws and welded broken equipment. He also found himself expelled from every organization in which he had been a member, even the Hunters' Association. The police constantly surveilled him. They kept tabs on him from a car parked outside his home and at times even prevented visitors from entering to see him. The authorities planted bugs in his telephone, television, and even stove. As he rode a streetcar to work, plainclothes officers followed him. When Alexander vacationed with friends and went swimming in a lake, the policeman who tailed them took out a rowboat to maintain contact with the subjects. When locals approached Dubček to offer him sympathy for his plight, they found themselves called in for interrogation and threatened with the loss of their jobs. Others who provided Dubček kindnesses, including a trade union official who gave Alexander's wife, Anna, a permit to get medical care, were fired from their positions.

In 1974, Dubček wrote to Czechoslovakia's Federal Assembly and to the Communist leadership, complaining about the harassment, the utter lack of real discussion within the country's Communist Party, and the country's suppression of basic civil rights. The letter found its way to the Western press. Following its publication, the police stepped up its open surveillance and harassment of Dubček. Communist leader Husák called him a traitor and an enemy of the people. The government published a claim that the CIA had organized the Prague Spring and had sent money directly to Dubček's personal bank account. Dubček became a pariah. He refused to participate in any dissident groups, rarely saw friends, and focused his private life on gardening. The world heard nothing from him for more than a decade.

However, the rise of Gorbachev sparked something in Dubček, especially as the Soviet leader's reforms took hold. In November 1987, Dubček sent a message of congratulations to Gorbachev on the seventieth anniversary of the Soviet Communist Party. He then openly expressed himself on politics for the first time since his banishment, giving an interview that was published in January 1988 in the Italian Communist newspaper *L'Unita*. In the interview, he expressed "unequivocal" support for the Soviet Union's reforms. It was easy to see why. After Gorbachev had visited Czechoslovakia in 1987, a Soviet Foreign Ministry spokesman had been asked to explain the difference between Dubček's and the Soviet leader's reforms. The answer was shocking: "Nineteen years." As the twentieth anniversary of the 1968 Prague Spring arrived, Alexander began to speak out more, decrying the "moral crisis and economic collapse" that had followed the invasion. Czechoslovakia's state-run media responded with a propaganda campaign against him, accusing Dubček of "megalomania."

Yet, no matter what Czechoslovakia's authorities said or did, Dubček became increasingly prominent as the winds of change swept across Czechoslovakia. As larger numbers of people took to the streets to voice their displeasure with the regime, they shouted the name "Dubček!" with greater frequency and volume. When Czechoslovak authorities, under pressure from domestic and international voices, released Václav Havel in May 1989 after he had been imprisoned for "disorderly conduct" earlier in the year, Dubček went to Prague to congratulate the dissident. Just months later, Hungarian television broadcast an interview in which Dubček lashed out at Czechoslovakia's authorities for besmirching his good name. But he did not speak in public to a crowd in Czechoslovakia until the week following the attack on the students. As the revolution raged, he spoke to demonstrators in Bratislava. Following the address, he boarded a bus to Prague and then, on that cold evening of Friday, November 24, he made the biggest splash imaginable when he took to the fourth-floor balcony of the building in Wenceslas Square. [9]

As Alexander Dubček emerged, the hundreds of thousands of demonstrators filling the Square roared, as did many of the millions watching at home on television. Dubček wore his reading glasses, clearly planning to begin speaking immediately from a written text. But when he felt the force of the crowds' adulation, the leader of the Prague Spring beamed beatifically. With his right hand, he snatched the glasses off his face and elatedly thrust them upward. He moved forward and pantomimed an embrace to show how much he loved the crowd before him. As he did, the assembled chanted with great fervor—much as the Swedish crowd had in the Stockholm hockey arena twenty years before, but now with more than twenty times the number of voices—*DUBČEK! DUBČEK!* Over and over. With his silver hair and a frame that had grown frailer, it was clear that the previous twenty years had aged the now sixty-seven-year-old man. Still, he pulled himself up to his full six feet, four inches and spoke. "Why should the country live in the dark, as it does now?" he asked. "Soon, there should be light!" And that light, he said, would end the era that had begun with the invasion of Warsaw Pact troops twenty-one years earlier.

Václav Havel walked out to the balcony to join Dubček, and the crowd cheered for both men. *DUBČEK! HAVEL! DUBČEK! HAVEL!* Other speakers came out to address the crowd and then, seemingly spontaneously, everyone in the sea of 300,000 that filled the Square took out their key rings and jangled them, sending the chimes echoing across the night. In that moment, a third of a million tiny bells tolled, letting Czechoslovakia's Communist leaders know that their time in power was over.

Later that evening, Havel and Dubček sat together on a press conference stage. As Dubček answered a question from the gallery, someone approached Havel urgently from behind. While Dubček continued speaking, Havel, the other man, and a third crouched just inches to the side of Dubček and talked intensely. Somehow the others on the stage composed themselves enough to let Dubček finish his thoughts. The moment he stopped speaking another member of the panel on the stage hurriedly announced, *The entire leadership of the Communist Party has resigned!* The assembled broke into wild applause. Havel and Dubček embraced. Someone brought in champagne.

Havel toasted, "To a free Czechoslovakia!"[10]

# PART V

## THE PEOPLE OF WHOM WE KNOW NOTHING

*I used to always laugh whenever someone said or wrote that athletes were fighting for their entire nation. But since that trip to Stockholm, I cannot laugh at this ever again.*
—Miloslav Jenšík, *The Chronicle of Czech Hockey*[1]

CHAPTER 17

# The Wild, Wild West

W hat happens when, suddenly, anything is possible?
       In October 1989, the end of the Communist regime was unthinkable. Then on November 17, 1989, almost out of nowhere, what later became known as the "Velvet Revolution" began—so named because it was nonviolent, seemingly soft, and smooth. With millions of people taking to the streets and even carrying out a general strike, over the coming weeks Czechoslovakia's Communists realized that they had no other options available and capitulated on nearly all issues. On November 28, the regime formally relented, giving up the Communists' monopoly on power. On December 10, the president appointed a "government of national understanding," in which non-Communists outnumbered Communists for the first time since 1948. On December 28, the federal parliament chose Alexander Dubček to be its new speaker. The following day, the parliament unanimously elected Václav Havel to be Czechoslovakia's new president.

The word "revolution" paints an image of a world turned upside down, with everything dramatically altered in the blink of an eye. But the reality of a "velvet," peaceful revolution is quite different. Most of Czechoslovakia rejoiced over the fall of the Communists, but woke up the next day to find the basics of daily life unchanged. There were no devastated villages to rebuild. No orphaned children to rescue. No dead combatants to mourn. On the morning after the Communists stepped down, Czechs and Slovaks had breakfast with their families, went out to buy groceries, and paid the cashier behind the shop counter with Czechoslovak crowns. All just as they always did.

So it was for Bobby Holík, Robert Reichel, and Jaromír Jágr, who got right back on the ice, just as they always did. As Czechoslovakia's federal parliament went through the process of placing Dubček and Havel into their new seats of power, a group of Czechoslovak youngsters hopped on a plane to Helsinki, Finland, to compete in the high-profile 1990 World Junior Championships (held December 26, 1989 through January 4, 1990), contested by the best under-twenty-year-old hockey players in the world. It was an event that Czechoslovakia had never won.

Led by Reichel, Jágr, and Bobby, Team Czechoslovakia was stacked.[1] For five games it appeared unstoppable, outscoring opponents 45–7. Then it was time to play the USSR, led by Pavel Bure. The Soviets won yet again. Just as they nearly always did.

Yet as the boys headed back to Czechoslovakia, it became clear that real changes were actually occurring all around their home country. The changes were massive. And they were coming fast. The government moved swiftly to permit all the standard freedoms present in democracies, including freedom of speech and association, freedom of the press, freedom to choose one's work, and even the freedom to choose whether to work at all.

The fall of the Communists also meant freedom to challenge authority and, almost immediately, a tragedy encouraged Czechoslovakia's hockey players to tap into this newfound freedom. On January 5, 1990, Zlín defenseman Luděk Čajka collided with an opposing player as he sprinted to grab a loose puck. The collision knocked Čajka headfirst into the boards, where the young man went limp. After rushing him to the hospital, doctors diagnosed a severe spinal cord injury. Čajka never woke up, and a little over a month later he passed away. The immediate aftermath illustrated just how much Czechoslovakia had changed in just two months. Whereas in the past, the players were controlled by the hockey federation, they now forcefully asserted their rights. The precipitating event was less the injury itself than the discovery that the league's insurance did not sufficiently cover the players against serious accidents on the ice. Players began sitting out games and, in the new frontier of post-communist hockey, they pushed for a slew of new rule changes that would do more to protect their interests. After representatives of a nascent players' association made some headway on these issues, especially insurance, the players returned to the ice.[2]

Čajka had previously played two seasons in Jihlava, and many with the team were deeply shaken by his death, but Dukla Jihlava still finished the regular season in mid-February with the league's best record. Bobby had become

Dukla's star forward, but there was no question about the biggest factor driving the team's success: The previous season, with Dominik Hašek in the goal, the Pardubice team had taken the league crown. But now, with Hašek forced to fulfill his military duty, and for the third time in four years winning the award for best player in the league, Dukla Jihlava had jumped to the top of the league.

With Hašek gone, Pardubice tumbled in the standings and, as the end of the season approached, found itself in danger of being dropped from the top league unless it performed better. Making matters worse, it was slated to take on the Hašek-led Dukla squad in one of its final games. Unwilling to harm his hometown team, which he planned to return to after his military service ended, Hašek worked out an agreement with Coach Augusta to skip the game. But someone in the Dukla administration suddenly put the screws to the coach, forcing the goalie to play against Pardubice.

Hašek opened at goal for Dukla, but after his first save twenty seconds into the game, he removed himself, feigning injury. On the bench, Hašek practically had smoke coming out of his ears as the game continued. During the locker room break between the first two periods, he couldn't contain himself anymore. "Fuck all of this!" he screamed, violently hurling his yellow Dukla jersey into a pile of tape and orange peels in a nearby trash bin. Once they regained their ability to speak, Coaches Augusta and Holík yelled at the star goalie to "Pack up and get the hell out!" Augusta sent Hašek to serve with a regular fighting unit for two weeks, where he marched through the cold winter mountains carrying a gun. Augusta also reported Hašek's insurrection to the national hockey federation, which banned the goalie from playing in the team's next eight games.

Dukla never fully recovered and Sparta Prague ultimately won the league championship in the playoffs that March. Jan Reindl couldn't help but think that his team's victory was a sort of karmic reward for its role in the revolution.[3]

Of all the new freedoms introduced in Czechoslovakia, none was more tangible than the freedom to travel beyond the country's borders. Anticipation and excitement tore across the country's hockey league as NHL scouts arrived and Czechoslovakia's top players all began contemplating their next move—to North America! In January, with a month left in the season, national team captain and superstar Vladimír Růžička headed to the NHL with the full permission of Czechoslovakia's authorities. NHL officials appeared giddy at the possibility of other Czechoslovak players. Players like Hašek, Bobby, Jágr, and Reichel.

In late February Ivan Lendl came to Prague for the first time in six years to play a tennis exhibition, but he also had another reason for his return—to free up Bobby Holík. Bobby still had over a year left on his military service, leaving him unavailable to Lendl's Hartford Whalers hockey team until the fall of 1991. Lendl set up a meet-and-greet in Prague with Bobby and his parents, the minister of defense, and President Havel. Although the event was filled with considerable small talk, Lendl made the point of the meeting clear: the Whalers needed Bobby that year. The government released the Holík boy from his military service, and the Whalers sent $100,000 to the Dukla team as compensation. That summer Bobby Holík was free to begin his NHL career.[4]

But before his NHL dream commenced, Bobby headed to Switzerland in April for the 1990 World Ice Hockey Championships, where he and his teammates showed the world the talented group of Czechoslovak players that was about to descend on the NHL. Czechoslovakia had the youngest squad in the tournament, and the games were particularly thrilling for the team's three youngest players, Bobby, Reichel, and Jágr, each playing in his first adult World Championship.[5] The three teens took the championships by storm, combining to knock in a quarter of the team's scores. Reichel, who at just eighteen years of age had already completed one of the greatest league seasons in Czechoslovakia's history that year, finished fourth among all players in the World Championships in total points. Along with Hašek, he was named to the tournament all-star team.

It was a World Championships unlike any held before as even more NHL scouts and team executives came to watch. For the first time, they could scout the young players from both Czechoslovakia and the Soviet Union with the knowledge that at last those young men would be able to come west. In past tournaments, the Czechoslovak players had fixated on doing all they could to challenge the Soviets, but now many appeared distracted by the NHL crowd coming to check them out.

Seeing his world change right in front of him, Hašek thought *It's like the Wild, Wild West.* Everything seemed new and utterly unpredictable. Every conversation at the tournament turned quickly to *Where are you going to sign next year? How much is your contract?* Instead of talking team strategy, the players drifted into conversations about what scout or agent would be at each game. Roommates Bobby and Jágr spent much of their free time in their room, with Holík explaining to the younger boy everything he knew about the NHL. On the team bus, the two gave Hašek fits as they sat behind him talking nonstop about the NHL. Frustrated, Hašek complained about the boys' obsessive conversations. *"Here's how the NHL is structured. Here's how the draft works." All on repeat! "Did you see that great NHL player? Isn't it amazing how great he skates?!" All. The. Time!!*

Despite the distractions, the talent of the young players helped lead Czechoslovakia to a strong performance and, once again, Czechoslovakia faced the Soviet Union in the final game, with the winner taking the tournament gold medal. The two sides locked into a tight match for half the game before Czechoslovakia lost to its hated rival.[6] Just as it nearly always did.

But this time, Czechoslovakia's players gave little thought to regrouping and girding themselves for future encounters with the Red Machine. The Soviets no longer held Czechoslovakia captive. And Czechs and Slovaks could protest injustice any way that they liked, not just by cheering for their boys in a hockey match. Now, they were free. And they could embark on their own individual adventures. Anything was possible now.

Seven months later, Bobby Holík stood atop the Hartford ice readying himself for the referee to drop the puck. Just two and a half months into his NHL career, the Czech rookie decided to send a message to the Buffalo Sabres' eleven-year veteran defenseman in front of him. Pulling himself up to his full six feet, seven inches on skates and 250 pounds in his hockey gear, Bobby announced, "You will not stop me."

NHL observers and participants were fascinated by the sudden arrivals from the Eastern Bloc. In February of 1991, *Sports Illustrated* ran the story of Holík's intimidation tactic as the lede in a feature it published on the early success of Czechoslovakia's rookie hockey players, especially Bobby, Jágr, and Reichel. The boys' arrival was part of a wave that would shake up the world's greatest hockey league.

For decades, the NHL had included very few players from the east end of the Atlantic. North American hockey had long been famous for its rough play, which contrasted with Europe's greater emphasis on finesse. However, events of the early 1970s began to open the minds of some in the West. Canadians were shocked when the Soviet national team essentially played the top players from Canada to a standstill in the famed 1972 Summit Series. Still, the NHL had little interest in European players, all the more so since the Communists refused to let their players head west. But when the WHA formed in the 1970s, the new league's Winnipeg Jets built a juggernaut founded in part on outstanding players from Sweden, and Czechoslovakia's Nedomanský joined the WHA as well. Seeing the success of these Europeans, the NHL rosters increasingly diversified. When WHA players began to shift to the NHL in the 1978–79 season, there were no Soviets in the National Hockey League and just a single Czechoslovak player (Nedomanský), but there were sixteen Swedes. The following year, five players from Finland joined the NHL, as the number of players from Sweden also continued to grow.

Over time, the occasional defector (or past-his-prime player allowed to briefly come to the West) added to the ranks of men from Czechoslovakia in the NHL, so that in the 1989–90 season thirteen participated in the world's top hockey league. In 1990–91, the first full season after the Velvet Revolution, Bobby, Jágr, Reichel, Hašek, and a smattering of other talented Czechs and Slovaks came west. Suddenly a total of twenty-three players (including thirteen rookies) from Czechoslovakia were playing in the NHL, more than any other country except Canada and the US.[7]

The transition was exceptionally difficult for many players from the Eastern Bloc. They were very young men—some teenagers, even—in a totally foreign world. Even seemingly simple parts of life like bank accounts, check-writing, and ATMs were new and required serious adjustment.[8] The move west was especially hard for the eighteen-year-old Jágr, who missed home and felt desperately alone. The language barrier was particularly tough. In one case, the coaches of his Pittsburgh Penguins' squad tried to explain an NHL rule about hockey stick curvature and Jágr became disconsolate, believing that they were chastising him for his play.[9]

But the players from the Eastern Bloc had to face more than just culture shock and homesickness. Some in North America had never taken too kindly to Europeans entering the NHL. Many thought that pushing around the newcomers on the ice was a good tactic, believing that the foreigners couldn't handle physical play. Many wanted retribution for Europeans coming to "steal" their jobs. And many simply were xenophobes, hating anyone from other places.

Europeans in the NHL had to face a constant barrage of physical attacks far beyond what North Americans had to confront.

The abuse foisted upon the Eastern Bloc players beginning in 1990 took on a different and even more intense flavor. There had been no significant Soviet players in the NHL until 1989, when the USSR, facing heavy financial difficulties, started permitting its aging stars to head west. In 1989–90, ten Soviets entered the NHL, with thirty-one-year-old USSR legend Sergei Makarov winning the league's Calder Trophy as rookie of the year. After years of viewing the Soviets as the enemy, it was difficult for many North Americans to get over their Cold War enmity. One Canadian hockey analyst was particularly bitter: "The Russians. No way! I don't want 'em over here! The players don't want 'em here! And you're going to be sorry they're over here." When Vyacheslav "Slava" Fetisov, the captain and face of the USSR's national team, first played in New York's Madison Square Garden as a member of the New Jersey Devils, the crowd booed him as if he were a felon.

This animosity extended to players from Czechoslovakia. To many North Americans, they were all just "dirty Communists." From the stands, on the ice during games—even from teammates in their own locker room—Bobby Holík heard the same refrain. *You fucking commie!* Those who spat the epithets had no idea that former US president Ronald Reagan—the man who had fought the Soviet Union as the "Evil Empire"—had called Jágr on the phone to express his admiration for the youngster after discovering a *Sports Illustrated* article that detailed how the hockey player had carried around a picture of Reagan. The xenophobes had no clue that Bobby's father had taped over the Communist star on his hockey jersey.

Many in the West had little understanding of the fact that Czechoslovakia and the Soviet Union were totally different countries and that the people of Czechoslovakia had been victims of Soviet oppression. Indeed, many North Americans thought that the Czechoslovak players *were* "Russians." Bobby found himself described in articles as "Ivan Drago on skates," referring to the enemy Soviet boxer in the film *Rocky IV.* Over and over, many NHL players tried to give the Soviet and Czechoslovak players a world-class beating for the crime of having been born and raised in countries that had been run by authoritarian Communist regimes.[10]

Despite the beatings, the Eastern Bloc players made an instant impact on the NHL. As usual, Soviets found a way to dominate. In the 1990–91 season, former Soviet star Sergei Fedorov finished second in rookie of the year voting. In 1991, the Soviet Union's Communists agreed to permit a more open, democratic system of government, and the USSR promptly split into multiple independent countries, including the sovereign state of Russia. As it did, Russia's Pavel Bure joined the NHL and won the league's 1991–92 rookie of the year award. In 1992–93, Alexander Mogilny—Bure and Fedorov's linemate in the USSR—led the NHL in goals scored. In 1993–94, Bure scored more goals than any other player in the league, and Fedorov won the Hart Trophy as the NHL's most valuable player.

Czechoslovakia's players in the NHL made their presence felt as well. Peter Šťastný had been one of the league's greatest players in the 1980s, and a number of the other defectors from Czechoslovakia had fine NHL careers. None played in the NHL longer than Petr Svoboda, the Litvínov boy who, as a terrified eighteen-year-old in 1984, had left his Czechoslovak junior team behind in West Germany to ply his trade in the West. After defecting, Svoboda went on to have a solid NHL career, playing until 2001.

Still, none reached anything close to the stardom of Šťastný. That would change with the new group of players from Czechoslovakia.

None received more attention than Jágr, whom the Pittsburgh Penguins had selected with the fifth pick in the 1990 draft. Seeing the language barrier Jágr confronted in moving to the US, the Penguins' team leadership soon acquired Jiří Hrdina, a veteran Czechoslovak player who helped create a bridge between the teen from Kladno and the team. Jágr grew increasingly comfortable with his new life and his play improved. He found himself in the ideal situation as the coaches teamed him with Mario Lemieux, one of the greatest offensive players in NHL history, which dramatically reduced the pressure on Jaromír. Wearing number 68 on the back of his jersey to remember the Soviet invasion of his country, Jágr began to make a habit out of spectacular offensive moves, often leaving longtime hockey observers dumbstruck by his genius. Even in the NHL, Jágr's combination of size and speed stood out, as did his extraordinary puck control and ability to beat the defense with either a shot or a pass. Adding in his rock-n-roll dark brown mullet, Jágr quickly became a fan favorite. It especially helped that, in each of Jágr's first two years in Pittsburgh, the Penguins won the Stanley Cup, the NHL championship.[11] Jágr exploded in the years that followed, becoming one of the NHL's biggest stars. In 1994–95, he led the league in points—the first of five times that he would do so—and finished second in MVP balloting.

For Bobby Holík, the situation in Hartford turned out to be less than ideal. The team wasn't very good and Bobby wasn't the solo instant goal scorer the Whalers had hoped for. The coaching staff and Bobby didn't see eye-to-eye on how best to use his skills. Prior to his third year in the league, Hartford traded Bobby to the New Jersey Devils. After a brief adjustment period, he became a fan favorite because of his intelligence and intensity, his ferocity in fighting for the puck, and the way he wore down opponents with his ceaseless tough play. With his constant hitting, poking, and prodding, opposing players constantly found themselves wanting to fight him. The problem for them, though, was his enormous size, which left opponents both intimidated and unable to do much to faze him. When the New York Rangers were in the locker room preparing to play the Devils, the team listed the opponents' numbers and names on their strategy board. But rather than "HOLIK" next to Bobby's number 16, the Rangers listed "ASSHOLE." Like his dad, Bobby became a target for opposing fans. In one stadium, posters popped up, declaring, "Holik eats babies." In New Jersey, he became deeply valued as a strong veteran presence and an essential member of the Devils when the team won the 1995 Stanley Cup championship. In the following years, he became the top point producer on the team, which remained among the best squads in the league, and he was twice named to the league's all-star team. [12]

North Americans, though, never ended up getting to witness the brilliance of the third of the three great Czechoslovak teens. In his third season, Robert Reichel looked like he was entering the NHL's goal-scoring elite group. But unlike Slovakia's Peter Bondra who, during the 1990s, would twice lead the league in goals scored, Reichel never became the player in the NHL that people back in Czechoslovakia had known. After missing time because of a contract disagreement and a league labor dispute, Reichel never returned to form in North America. [13] Amazingly, though, Robert Lang, Martin Ručinský, and Jiří Šlégr, the three boys who had grown up playing with Reichel as kids in Litvínov, all made it to the NHL as well, where each became a first-rate player.

It appeared for a time that Dominik Hašek's NHL career was going to be exceedingly disappointing. He started off in Chicago, which decided to go with a different goalie. After two seasons, Hašek found himself traded to the Buffalo

Sabres, who were already overloaded at his position. However, in the 1993–94 season, Hašek's fourth year in the league, Buffalo's lead goalie injured his knee, giving Dominik an opportunity to show what he could do. What that turned out to be was the finest netminding of any player in the world. That season, Hašek was named the top goalie in the league and finished second in balloting for the most valuable player. In each year that followed, he continued to get better. In the 1996–97 season, the top goalie and MVP awards both went to the man nicknamed "The Dominator."[14]

As the 1990s progressed, the NHL got used to the influx of foreign players and the game changed. Many North American players saw their teams get better thanks to the new arrivals. The Europeans, including and especially the Soviet and Czechoslovak players, brought an advanced system of skating, passing, and stickhandling that led to vastly increased scoring. The North American players needed to improve their offensive skillsets or they would be skated off the ice by the young men from the Eastern Bloc.[15]

Following the Communists' fall, it felt like anything had become possible for the people of Czechoslovakia. For many, including the young men who took their talents to the NHL, this meant opportunities to succeed in ways that had previously been kept out of their reach. Yet, as countless people back in the Czech and Slovak lands learned in the 1990s, freedom offered no guarantee of success. If anything is possible, then failure is as well.

Thanks to Jaroslav's stardom, the Holíks had a pretty good life under communism, but naturally they were overjoyed at the regime's fall. They had never gotten over the arbitrary rule, the political persecutions, and the corrupt and vengeful regime that threatened them if they stepped out of line. They had felt suffocated, as the Communists constrained them from speaking or traveling freely.[16] After the revolution, it was this freedom of movement that brought them the greatest joy, as Andrea and Franta could return home and Bobby could legally head to the NHL.

And there was more good news. Following the 1989–90 season, an army commander came to see Jaroslav. "You couldn't be the head coach before because you weren't in the Party. But now you can take over!" Jaroslav felt a weight lift from his shoulders as he finally took the reins of Dukla Jihlava. Under Jaroslav, even with Hašek and Bobby gone, in the 1990–91 season, Dukla Jihlava cruised to its first title in six years. [17]

But not all the changes that followed for Jaroslav were welcome ones. Moving to the cold-weather American state of Minnesota, Andrea saw far fewer opportunities to maintain her tennis. It was even more difficult when she and Franta decided to start a family. Just when Jaroslav took over the Dukla team in 1990, Andrea retired from tennis, leaving her father bitter and flummoxed. Yes, of course part of the goal of tennis was to find freedom in the West. But, he wondered, didn't she also still feel that all-consuming competitive drive!?

In early 1992, Jaroslav went with Czechoslovakia's backup national team to a tournament in France, where one morning blood began to drip from his nose. Within moments, the drip turned to a steady stream and he lost consciousness. As people rushed to help, they heard Jaroslav mumbling over and over, "But I will never meet my granddaughter . . ." Andrea had just given birth to her first child, a baby girl. Team officials debated whether they should call an ambulance because of the high cost of hospital bills. The team doctor couldn't believe what he was hearing. "Fuck the money. I'm not going to let him bleed out here." Jaroslav heard nothing of the debate. All the pain had disappeared and he felt peaceful. He found himself walking through a tunnel toward a shining light.

Jaroslav awakened in an emergency room, where his pulse pounded at a blistering 220 beats per minute. He had burst a blood vessel. Eventually the doctors were able to halt the bleeding and return his vital signs to their normal levels. However, the fix proved to be temporary and, after three days in the hospital in which he received several blood transfusions, it was decided that he should be transferred back to Czechoslovakia. The hockey federation planned on the cheapest but also slowest solution of transporting him by bus until an incensed Jiří Holík made a well-placed phone call. The federation agreed to fly Jaroslav home, where he was checked into a military hospital for three weeks.

Between the birth of his granddaughter and his illness, Jaroslav completely changed how he viewed Andrea's decision to end her tennis career: grandchildren were a hundred times more valuable than even a dozen Wimbledon titles.

But his health problems were only just beginning. Within months of his return, red circles appeared all over Jaroslav's body and a dangerously high fever overwhelmed him. Confused about the cause, the doctors checked Holík into the hospital for ten days, where they eventually tried a corticosteroid treatment. The worst of the symptoms disappeared, but the doctors called in a rheumatology specialist, who told Jaroslav that the best explanation for his ailments was that he had contracted the exceedingly rare Kikuchi Disease. From that point on, he had to rely on a daily dose of corticosteroids, which had the side effects of thinning his skin and weakening his body's ability to heal wounds. But it was better than the alternative. Without the medication, the pain became unbearable.[18]

Precisely as Jaroslav faced these dramatic challenges, the entire country of Czechoslovakia confronted its own. In June 1990, Czechoslovakia at last held truly free and fair elections, with more than 95 percent of eligible voters turning out to cast ballots for a wide array of parties, especially the country's leading anti-regime organization.[19] Czechoslovakia dove headfirst into legislation to transform the government-controlled economy that had underpinned the country for more than forty years. It implemented a system of restitution, whereby it returned to individuals the property that the Communist government had confiscated from them years earlier. The new government auctioned off small state-owned businesses to Czechoslovak citizens and sold vouchers for a nominal fee to enable them to purchase shares of large state-owned businesses.[20]

Once Czechoslovakia's Communist government fell, negotiations over the Soviet troop exit began quickly. Soviet forces started to leave Czechoslovakia in February 1990, and by the summer of 1991 the withdrawal was complete, as the last of the 73,500 soldiers, 1,220 tanks, 2,505 armored vehicles, 77 combat aircraft, and 146 helicopters stationed in Czechoslovakia finally departed.[21]

With the departure of the Soviets, who had forced them to remain together, Czechoslovakia confronted the tensions between the Czech and Slovak parts of the country. Hardly surprising, Czech and Slovak leaders disagreed on a variety of issues, including how to protect both sides' interests in future policy making. Slovak leaders pushed harder than ever to place their republic on an equal footing with the Czech lands. Czech leaders actively promoted a uniform free market, while Slovak leaders feared what that would mean for their less-developed economy. Nevertheless, even as late as June 1992, overwhelming majorities of the public in both the Czech and Slovak lands expressed a desire to remain as a unified Czechoslovakia. Despite public opinion on the issue, leaders on both sides began negotiating a split, and within a few months the plan to divide the country was complete. By January 1, 1993, the peaceful

"Velvet Divorce" was consummated as two independent countries were born.[22] In the southeast sat the independent country of Slovakia, with the capital city Bratislava and a population of around five million.

In the northwest, a country of roughly ten million contained many of Czechoslovakia's most famous cities, including Brno and the capital, Prague, as well as lesser-known ones like Jihlava, Kladno, Litvínov, Pardubice, and Havlíčkův Brod. A Czech bureaucratic office standardized its country's name in English as "Czechia," but it didn't catch on. Most of the world would know it as the Czech Republic. Over time, Slovakia began to lean in an authoritarian direction, but the Czech Republic moved fairly easily into stable democratic rule.[23]

The move away from communism sharply altered the foundation of the Czech Republic's top hockey league. By 1991, Jaroslav faced a very different system from what he had been used to. Dukla Jihlava could no longer get top players. The de facto elimination of compulsory military service cut off much of the pipeline that previously delivered quality players to Jihlava, but in addition hockey players could earn a lot more money abroad, even in other European countries. Making things more difficult, Dukla now needed to find new ways to finance the team. The Dukla administrators pressured Jiří Holík to help. Under duress, Jiří left his job as a teacher to take on the daunting role of team CEO.

Jiří despised the new job almost immediately. He had to go hat-in-hand to ask the country's newly private corporations to sponsor the team. He made the rounds of local companies, where the bosses hemmed and hawed and finally offered a pittance. Begging for cash stood completely outside his personality, and his body literally ached with each pitch he made. He began to hide away in his office, and within a few years resigned from the CEO position.

Because of the increase in individual rights in the democratic Czech Republic, as well as the greater power that players had because they could play elsewhere, the new hockey order didn't fit with Jaroslav's dictatorial coaching style. Beginning in the 1992–93 season, Dukla Jihlava fell to near the bottom of the league, where it stayed for the next few years. It was time for Jaroslav to move on. In 1995, he became Pardubice's coach, but team infighting forced him out within his first months on the job. He decided to return to his original home, Havlíčkův Brod, where he reunited with an old friend.

After returning from his hockey career in Western Europe in 1984, Jan Suchý had scrambled to find employment. By the late 1980s, his local connections helped him get a position as a technician supervising the distribution of fertilizers for an agro-company. The job required him to lead a group of workers who unloaded the supply all night and often throughout the weekend. After the revolution, though, environmentalists began to push back against many questionable practices that the Communists had turned a blind eye to, including the heavy use of pesticides and chemicals in fertilizer. Suchý was one of the few people in the company to keep his job, but that only meant more work for him, so he jumped at the chance to leave when a new opportunity arose.

Suchý took charge of trying to rebuild Havlíčkův Brod's hockey program. One of his main jobs was to find team sponsors, but, over time as businesses went bankrupt or moved away, raising funds became difficult. In 1995, Jaroslav joined him, taking over as Brod's coach. The problem, however, was that Jaroslav was accustomed to coaching military players who had no choice but to accept his constantly berating them, and the older players on Brod had no patience for such treatment. After a brief rise in the standings, by January 1998 the team had fallen to the bottom half of the league and Jaroslav was on his way out.[24]

As Czechoslovakia began its transition to a democratic, capitalist system, the expectation was that, after a difficult period, the country would find economic success. In fact, within just a few years after the revolution, the world marveled at the speed with which the Czech Republic had become a stable democracy and how quickly its economy had been transformed. By 1994, the economy was clearly growing and unemployment remained low.[25] Observers the world over described it as the most successful free-market economy among the post-communist countries.[26]

However, as time went by, it became clear that serious problems were emerging. In the new market economy, some people became wildly rich, but in some instances did so by manipulating the new systems of business privatization in ways that smacked of corruption.[27] In addition, some, such as future billionaire and prime minister Andrej Babiš who, unlike Suchý, made a killing in the agro-fertilizer field, appeared to use their connections from the communist era to amass fortunes after 1989.[28] Such moves infuriated people like Jan Reindl, who openly called out former Communists who had transformed quickly after the revolution into democratic supporters and successful capitalist entrepreneurs. Ironically, as a result of his outspokenness regarding such hypocrisy, Sparta's former team captain had difficulty gaining a coaching position in the Czech Republic.[29]

Although the new capitalist Czech Republic helped some people grow wealthy, at the opposite extreme others experienced unemployment and devastating bankruptcies for the first time ever. The regional Communist Party secretary, who years earlier fought with Jaroslav over a tennis court, now inherited a ceramic and porcelain factory through restitution. Unable to afford needed renovations, he approached Jaroslav, of all people, to ask for money. Jaroslav refused him. Unable to handle the debt that befell him, the former Party bigwig shot himself to death.[30]

In 1997, the Czech economy began to decline, and devaluation of the country's currency made it more expensive for Czechs to buy foreign goods. Simultaneously, it turned out that the country's banks, which the state controlled, held huge amounts of debt. When public funds were used to bail out the banks, the public held the government responsible for permitting bank mismanagement and fraud.[31] From there, things only got worse: the government budget deficit ballooned, economic and wage growth slowed, and unemployment rose.

The bad news was hardly restricted to the economy. By July 1997, the results of one survey indicated that 81 percent of the public was dissatisfied with the government. And then things got uglier. The media reported that large anonymous contributions had been made to the country's leading political party, leading many to suspect that the government was accepting bribes. Under attack for what was perceived as dishonest behavior at a minimum and outright corruption at the worst, the prime minister resigned in November 1997.

A deep malaise settled over the country. By 1998, Czechs viewed their country's leaders as corrupt political opportunists and their economy as a mess. Only 5 percent of Czechs said that they were satisfied with the economic transformation of the country, and 45 percent doubted that the economic situation was better than it had been prior to the revolution.[32] The result was a widespread loss of confidence in politics. President Havel himself described a country whose people felt deeply uneasy, "as if the Czech society was in a bad mood." Others later described it all as a "betrayal of dreams."[33]

As President Havel came to office in 1989, he spoke of building a new community that would bring everyone together.[34] The years that followed seemed to produce the opposite outcome. Czechs bemoaned the nationwide rise in individualism and consumerism. In the 1990s, even family ties loosened. Fewer people got married or had children. By the start of 1998, Czechs felt increasingly disconnected from one another.[35]

The changes that afflicted the country appeared to shake even the national hockey team.

Because the Winter Olympics were held during the NHL regular season, countries with NHL players couldn't put forward their best squads at the quadrennial games. As a result, after 1990, when most of its best players had headed to North America, the Czech Republic was no longer able to send top-notch hockey rosters to the Olympics. In addition, the NHL playoffs coincided with the World Championships, thus making it difficult for many of the top players to represent their country in international play. Hardly surprising, therefore, in the initial years after the revolution, the teams—first from Czechoslovakia and then from the Czech Republic—showed less of their old magic in the major world tournaments, and, multiple times, finished without a medal.

In the spring of 1996, though, the available players for the national team caught fire and carried the Czech Republic to its first world ice hockey championship as a new country. But everyone knew that the real challenge would come that summer, when most of the world's top players would actually compete with one another.

August and September 1996 saw the birth of the World Cup of Hockey, contested by many of the best players from the leading hockey-playing countries in the world. In the upcoming 1996–97 season, thirty-eight Czechs would play in the NHL, more than any other country except Canada, the US, and Russia, and the Czech Republic came into the World Cup ready to take down the giants. The Czech press, the people at home, and the Czech players all knew that this was the greatest team the country had ever put together, led by Jágr, Bobby, and Reichel. Hašek didn't participate, but more than a dozen NHL players stacked the Czech roster.[36]

The result was a disaster. With a squad composed of men in their early-to-mid-twenties, much of the team partied throughout the tournament. Even worse, the players appeared poorly trained and out of shape, and they simply didn't work very hard. Rather than performing as a team, they played selfishly and never developed any real chemistry. Finland squashed them 7–3 in the first game. The Czechs played game two at home in Prague against the Swedes. As the match came to a close with Sweden shutting out the Czech Republic 3–0, the hometown fans rained down boos, whistles, and empty beer cans upon their heroes. A leading Czech hockey magazine mocked the team as a "collection of wilted roses." Then, the lowly Germans defeated them 7–1. The Czech Republic finished the tournament dead last out of the eight teams. The Czech sports press slammed its squad, and the players felt overwhelmed with shame. [37]

Back in the Czech Republic, people felt enormous pride as they saw the success of their individual star players in the NHL, but the failure of the national hockey team seemed emblematic of something happening more generally at home. Many Czechs had done very well in the new country, but others felt left out. Sure, they now were free of the Communists, but that freedom had been accompanied by a malaise and an increasing sense that they were not part of something larger than their own individual lives.

When things at home had turned darkest in the past, the hockey team had brought the people of Czechoslovakia together. They had often been overlooked by the global powers, but major international hockey victories had helped the people of Czechoslovakia assert to the world that they could not be ignored.

Nothing seemed to provide that spark now. Czechs felt disconnected at home and invisible on the global stage.

As the Czech men playing in the NHL in the late 1990s saw how their individual successes had not translated into something for their country as a whole, as they witnessed the problems their country faced, and as they generally matured over the course of the decade, they began to reflect on their own legacies. They knew that they owed their place in the NHL to the people and the place that had raised them. Czechoslovakia's population had been only fifteen million people. The Czech Republic held only ten million. But because of what hockey had meant to the people, *millions* of Czech and Slovak children—an entire generation—grew up in the 1970s and 1980s with hockey at the center of their lives. As kids, they played together for years at Czechoslovakia's "school" of hockey, where there was so much high-quality play that it couldn't help but raise the game of everyone. It was this school and the players and teams that came before them that made Czech and Slovak players' moves to the NHL possible in the 1990s.

By the late 1990s, Dominik Hašek had become the elder statesman of the NHL's Czech players. As the years had passed, Hašek increasingly reflected on how it was only thanks to that Czechoslovakia school of hockey, and the support of his teachers, parents, and coaches back home, that he had been able to achieve his dreams in the West. As he saw the difficult times his country now faced, Hašek wondered whether it might be possible to give something back. [38]

# CHAPTER 18

# Nagano

O n February 7, 1998, the world was introduced to the beautiful city of
Nagano, Japan, whose pristine, snow-covered mountains, lush forests,
and rolling rivers offered a stunning backdrop for that year's Winter Olympics.
Sports fans eagerly awaited the chance to watch the fearless Japanese ski
jumpers and a thrilling women's figure-skating battle between Americans Tara
Lipinski and Michelle Kwan. However, for the millions of hockey enthusiasts
around the world, there was but one overriding reason to watch the games: The
1998 Olympic hockey tournament was going to be unlike anything ever before
tried in the sport.

When Gary Bettman got the job of commissioner of the National Hockey
League in 1993, he immediately thought big. It was time for the NHL to become
a global brand. In the early 1980s, Bettman had joined the National Basketball
Association's marketing and legal departments and rapidly climbed the league
office's ladder. By the time he turned forty, the year before he took the NHL
job, he had become the NBA's senior vice-president and general counsel. The
capstone on his career had occurred in 1992, when the NBA created one of
the greatest sports marketing campaigns in history. In the late 1980s, the IOC
began to permit professional athletes to participate in the Olympics. The NBA
jumped at the opportunity to send a collection of its charismatic superstars to
represent America at the 1992 Barcelona summer games. Fans, media, and even
players from other countries treated the US basketball "Dream Team" like rock
stars, generating unprecedented attention for the league. The years that followed
witnessed a dramatic globalization of basketball and the emergence of a huge
worldwide market for the NBA.

When Bettman took the reins of the NHL, he sought to create a similar splash. Nearly three years later, in September 1995, the NHL announced that it would make all its players available to participate in the 1998 Olympics in Nagano, Japan. The greatest logistical difficulty was the fact that—unlike the NBA, whose season didn't overlap with the timing of the summer games—the NHL was in midseason during the Winter Olympics. To handle the issue, the NHL would take a seventeen-day break in February 1998 to allow its players to compete for their home countries. For the first time ever, the Olympics would include the very best players—each in midseason form—from each country, thus producing the first true world championship in the history of hockey. People called it "The Tournament of the Century."[1]

From the moment the NHL season ended in spring of 1997, Dominik Hašek thought constantly about Nagano. He found himself daydreaming about how the games would go. As the Olympics approached, the daydreams became detailed. In his mind's eye, he saw how his teammates would jump into shots and even how his helmet would fly off his head midplay. He imagined beating the Americans in the semifinal and the Canadians in the final.

Despite the daydreams, Hašek and the Czech men faced a cold reality. It seemed unlikely that someone other than Canada or the US would win. Made up entirely by NHL players, the Canadian and American squads were stacked with big, fast players and exceptional depth. The two teams had staged a battle in the World Cup final in 1996 in which the US had come out on top, and the majority of the Czech team saw the US as the most talented. When Hašek reflected on what hockey meant to the entire Canadian nation, however, he felt confident that the United States' northern neighbor would take the title.

On February 7, 1998, the NHL played its final games before the break, giving most of its players only a few days to fly to Asia and get acclimated before the heart of the Nagano hockey schedule began on February 13. In Japan, the arrival of the NHL stars caused a media crush. TV crews, photographers, fans, even screaming girls tried to get a piece of the Canadian hockey team and especially the iconic face of the group, Wayne Gretzky. Known simply as "The Great One," Gretzky was the most outstanding hockey player in world history. Many times over in his storied career, he had won nearly every hockey award imaginable—save one. Now thirty-seven years old and approaching the end of his time as a player, Gretzky was participating in the Olympics for the first and, surely, only time. As the Canadians disembarked from the bullet train that took them to Nagano, the throng surrounding Gretzky and his mates appeared like something out of 1960s Beatlemania. In its haste to get to the superstars, the crowd nearly shoved Canada's third-string goalie onto the track.

Other countries sent spectacular squads as well. Everyone expected the Russians to challenge the Americans and the Canadians. All but one player on the Russian team came from the NHL, and eight had been named to the 1998 NHL all-star game. The squad was captained by the incomparable Pavel Bure. Some analysts made a case for Sweden's team, which was almost completely composed of players from NHL rosters, including four from that year's all-star game. Other experts highlighted the medal threat offered by Finland, which included fourteen NHL players, a spectacular offense, and four 1998 all-stars. [2]

No one seemed to notice when the Czech players arrived in Nagano. Hockey analysts viewed the Czech Republic as a solid team, but not a serious threat. ·Pavel Barta, a Czech team spokesman and media coordinator, found himself chatting with a group of American journalists. "Pavel, you guys have no shot. The players on your team are too small and they're just not tough enough." [3] One Czech player had been told by his NHL teammates as he left for Nagano that his team had the same chance of winning as the Jamaican bobsledders. [4] If all went according to most predictions, the Czechs would finish in fifth or sixth place, eliminated in the quarterfinals.

Back in the Czech Republic, people talked nervously about the upcoming games. Like the players, most just wanted to avoid the humiliation of 1996, but even that seemed to depend on how well Hašek could play. After a slow start in the 1997–98 NHL season, the Czech goalie had become the league's dominant player in the months of December and January. When Czechs thought about their team's chances, they mostly just prayed that Hašek could continue his magic. When Jiří Holík talked about the team, he generally finished his conversations, "With Hašek, there is always hope." But even that hope was pretty slim. The Western sports press saw a shallow Czech roster of players who could skate fast but did not score well, and were too small on defense.

After the Czechs' 1996 World Cup catastrophe, a familiar face had taken charge of their national team. No one in Czech hockey was more respected than Ivan Hlinka. Lauded as a player for both his phenomenal skill and his mental acuity, in the 1970s the man helped bring glory to Litvínov, starred on the national squad that won three world titles, and served as national team captain. In 1981–83, he was among the first players Czechoslovakia's Communists permitted to play legally in the NHL, where he performed at a high level with the Vancouver Canucks. In 1987, he took over as Litvínov's head coach and in 1992–94 also helmed the national team. The players adored Hlinka, swearing they would skate through a brick wall for him. In 1996, he attended the World Cup in an unofficial capacity and watched the disastrous final match against Germany from the stands. Following the game, as Hlinka drove his Litvínov boys Martin Ručinský and Jiří Šlégr back to the Czech Republic from Germany, he lit into them. "What a disaster. We have to change things." When they got to the border, Hlinka handed everyone's passports to the Czech guard, who promptly got a look on his face. "Oooh, look! The embarrassments are coming home!" The players felt humiliated. But there was a bright spot. Hlinka had said, "*We* have to change things." He was coming back as head coach. [5]

When Hlinka began in 1997, his biggest focus was on creating a squad that could compete in Nagano. Naturally, he named Hašek and Jágr to the roster. But in a significant blow to the team's chances, Bobby Holík was not available. From his arrival in the US in 1990, Bobby had felt a deep connection to his new home. In late 1996, the young man from the iconic Czech hockey family became an American citizen, leaving him ineligible for the team of his birth country, even as he made his first NHL all-star team in 1998. Hlinka had to get creative to fill the void. He loaded up on players from Litvínov. In all, he filled *eight* of the twenty-three slots with players from the little town, including all four boys—Reichel, Lang, Ručinský, and Šlégr—who had grown up together in the 1970s and 80s.

When Hašek saw the Czech roster, one name especially bothered him: Petr Svoboda, the Litvínov boy who had defected to the West in 1984, at the age of eighteen, and had spent the past fourteen years in the NHL. Hašek worried that Svoboda wasn't enough of a team player. [6] Another name concerned Hašek as well: another former Litvínov player, Vladimír "Rosie" Růžička, whom Hlinka named as team captain. Růžička had made his Czechoslovak professional debut nearly twenty years earlier in 1979 and had been the top scorer for Czechoslovakia on the 1984 Olympic team. He had been one of the greatest players in Czechoslovakia in the 1980s. But he hadn't been on the national team for nearly a decade—not since 1989, when the country was still communist Czechoslovakia. Růžička had gone to the NHL following the revolution and had become one of the league's goal-scoring leaders, but North American coaches had no patience for his lackluster defense. In early 1994 he found himself back in Europe for good. Now thirty-four years old, Růžička had the respect of all the young Czech players, but when Hašek and Rosie first got together in Nagano the goalie jokingly addressed the big concern. "So you really decided to come back? You know, I didn't know you could still skate!" However, all fears disappeared the first moment the old-timer took to the ice. Růžička could still skate at a high level, and his hands were as quick as they had ever been.[7]

Still, aside from Hašek and Jágr, the Czech team contained no star power. In fact, the team had far fewer NHL players than the rest of the top group. Only eleven of the Czech Republic's twenty-three players were drawn from NHL rosters and the rest came from lesser European leagues.[8] Most Western analysts had never heard of many of the Czechs, and Hašek didn't even recognize some of his teammates. Unable to remember all their names at first, he had to refer to a few by their jersey numbers.

Since his arrival on Czechoslovakia's hockey scene thirty years earlier, Hlinka had been famed for his ability to lead and bring people together. Never before had this asset been so valuable; his welcoming, relaxed approach to the group became contagious. "We came here to play hockey. Don't turn it into rocket science, okay? We will play the best hockey we can. If things go right, they go right." Feeling at home under Hlinka, the group quickly bonded.

Developing team chemistry was essential after the 1996 World Cup. Eleven players on the Czech Nagano team had been part of that debacle. They had learned that acting simply as a collection of individuals wouldn't work. The men became more focused on trying to play together as a group. The leaders—even Hašek and Růžička, the old guys of the team—worked extra hard in practice to set an example for the rest of the squad.

On Friday the 13th, the Tournament of the Century began in earnest. For the top group of eight teams, the opening round of three matches per team would merely set the seeding for the medal round. A team could lose all three and still make the quarterfinals. Even so, it was the Olympics with the greatest collection of talent in hockey history and, as they arrived at the arena to play the opening match against Finland, the Czech players were as anxious as they had ever been at an ice rink. A teammate asked Svoboda how he felt. Set to turn thirty-two years old the following day, Svoboda was among the most experienced of the Czech players. He was also about to play his first-ever game for the national team. "I'm nervous as fuck."

Even Hašek felt more nervous than he could ever remember. The stakes of the tournament had the Dominator anxious, but there was something else. Unbeknownst to anyone, Dominik Hašek, the greatest goalie in the world and his team's only hope if it was to win a medal, was injured. Ten days prior to the Czech Republic's first match in the Olympics, Hašek had gotten into an altercation with a teammate on the Buffalo Sabres. After the men were pulled apart, Hašek realized that he had dislocated his left thumb. The day of the injury, the Sabres' trainer produced a special brace that made play possible. But it was also critical to tape the hand thoroughly, and in Nagano Hašek sweated so much that, after each period, the national team trainer had to quickly—within just three minutes—secretly retape him. With his taped-up finger, he couldn't use his favorite glove and instead had to use an ill-fitting practice mitt that constrained his movements.[9]

As game time approached, Hašek began to pace around the locker room. He stared down at the beautiful bright red jersey laid out in front of him. He thought about how it had been nearly seven years since he last represented his country on the ice and how much he wanted to repay the place that had made him into a hockey player. In 1969, the players had been forced to wear a jersey emblazoned with the hated Communist star. Now, though, the front of the team's jersey bore the Czech Republic's new coat of arms. The crest included two lions and two eagles, each with a crown, and not a star to be seen. As he went through his final preparations, Hašek kissed the crest and pulled the jersey into position. He would repeat the ritual before every match.

As the players prepared to take to the ice, the team's massage therapist, Václav Šašek, halted them. It was said that one of the most important jobs of a team's massage therapist was to select a talisman. Šašek had chosen a glass elephant, which he had specially handmade by a Czech glassblower and smuggled into Japan. Now, Šašek moved to the doorway, where each player gently rubbed the statue on his way out to take on Finland. The men would repeat the ritual prior to every game for the rest of the tournament.[10]

Despite the Czech players' nerves and the high-powered Finnish offense, the first match went smoothly and the Czechs came away with a surprisingly easy 3–0 victory. The second game against Kazakhstan proved even easier. The Czech Republic took the game 8–2, but the team played sloppily. In the locker room afterward, Robert Reichel lit into the other players. "Guys, you can't play like this. Everyone wants to score! Everyone plays for themselves! You can't bloody do that!" The men knew that they would need to play more as a team if they were going to compete with the big boys.

It would not take long to find out how true that was. On February 16, just one day after the match against Kazakhstan, the Czech Republic took on Russia. Thanks to brilliant play by Hašek and a second period goal by Reichel, the Czechs led 1–0 going into the final frame. But then everything flipped. Just over three minutes into the third period, Russia scored twice within ten seconds and then held on to win 2–1 to complete the opening round.

Thus far, the quality of play across most of the teams had been really high, but as they moved to the medal round, everyone would see how the players performed under real pressure. From now on, each team that lost would be eliminated from the tournament. The opening round loss to Russia hadn't knocked the Czech Republic out, but it created a nightmare for the Czechs in the medal round: they would have to open against the terrifying American team. The US had won only one of three games in the first round, but Hašek believed that had just been bad luck. The Americans' shots simply hadn't gone in during the opening round, and the US was the overwhelming favorite against the Czech Republic.

To beat a team as great and as rough as the United States, the Czech coaches knew that they would need more than just their all-world goalie. Jaromír Jágr, the Czech team's superstar forward, had been devastated by his and the team's miserable play in the 1996 World Cup and decided to make amends in Nagano. Jágr's play in Japan had been above reproach, as he worked tirelessly and self-lessly. As always, he skated all out, constantly pushing the pace to make things happen, but he also worked harder on defense than anyone could remember him doing before. To get the most out of their limited roster, the Czech coaches decided to double Jágr's playing time.

The Czechs arrived at Nagano's Big Hat Arena well before their 2:25 P.M. start time on Wednesday, February 18. As Hašek went through his final preparations, he feared that the bad luck that had afflicted the US would run out and the Americans would overwhelm him with a scoring deluge. With a real sense that the Olympics could be over for them at any moment, tension in the Czech locker room mounted. As Hašek stared at the jersey he was about to put on, he thought to himself, *It is very likely that this is the last time you will ever play in this jersey.* Yet again, he gently kissed the coat of arms, feeling that he might be saying goodbye to much more than an article of clothing.

Everything started off wrong for the Czechs. They felt an energy around the arena unlike anything that they had ever experienced before. It *felt* like it was the Tournament of the Century. And that energy seemed to backfire on them. They knew that in the Czech Republic nearly everyone, quite literally, was watching and begging them to succeed. Calling the game for Czech TV, play-by-play announcer Robert Záruba opened the broadcast by offering greetings to the audience in "all the households, factories, receptions, bars and restaurants, corner stores, waiting rooms, kindergartens, and the President's Office." The players felt the weight of their entire country. And if that wasn't enough pressure already, they had to play against the favorites of the entire tournament.

The Czechs took to the ice feeling tight and it showed. From the moment the puck dropped, they felt tentative, quickly losing their composure as everything seemed to move faster than they had ever seen in hockey. The Americans buzzed. Attack. Attack. Attack. Before anyone could catch their breath, the US had smacked six powerful shots. For most of the first period, only Hašek's acrobatics kept the US scoreless, but sixteen minutes in American Mike Modano scored. As the opening period ended, the Czech Republic knew that it was lucky to be down only 1–0.[11] The Czech men headed to their locker room with their heads slightly drooped, looking befuddled as they silently sipped their water and wiped the sweat from their faces. They knew that they were about to be sent home.

After a minute, Rosie Růžička spoke. Until this match, the Czechs had not really required him to rally them, but now they needed something to snap themselves out of their trance. "We cannot worry about their team. . . . We cannot be afraid."[12] The Czech men were ashamed that they had allowed themselves to get psyched out. "I mean, the Americans, they are not gods! They are just normal hockey players!"[13] The room remained silent for a moment until Reichel and some of the younger leaders on the team began shouting for the men to get fired up. Czech coach Hlinka finished it off by simplifying the plan. "Don't shit yourselves! It's just hockey!"

The Czechs took to the ice like a different team in the second period. As Hašek continued to hold off the swarming American offense, eight minutes into the period old man Růžička suddenly snuck in a goal to tie things up. Less than a minute later, Jágr scored on a beautiful move that had everyone in the crowd gasping in disbelief. Coach Hlinka loved placing the Litvínov boys who had grown up together in a single group on the ice. Robert Reichel, Martin Ručinský, and Robert Lang had played alongside one another for so long that each seemed to know instinctively what the others would do at any moment.[14] As the period neared its end, Ručinský took a pass from Lang to score again. The Czech Republic led 3–1.

In the final period, the Americans desperately tried to close the deficit. They attacked and, following a missed shot, one of the Americans threw himself at Hašek's head, leaving the Czech goalie down. Seeing the country's hopes sprawled out on the ice, the entire Czech Republic team froze. But after a few seconds, Hašek shook out the cobwebs and returned to his feet. For the remainder of the game, he continued his masterpiece, flummoxing the Americans as he held them to just one goal in the entire match despite a blitzkrieg-like thirty-nine shots. One late final goal for the Czech Republic left the final score at 4–1.[15]

In shock, the players from the Czech Republic moved on to the semifinals of the Tournament of the Century, where the party was almost certain to end for them. It was time to play the undefeated Canadians, who had outscored their opponents in Nagano 16–4. Canada worked as a disciplined unit, following the coaches' instructions precisely. No prima donnas. Everyone on the Canadian squad appeared to play entirely for the team. The roster was exceptional, not surprising given that more than half of all NHL players, and sixteen out of the forty-six players who made that year's league all-star game, hailed from Canada. By contrast, Czechs made up only five percent of all NHL players, and their squad included just two 1998 all-stars. The Canadian players were some of the greatest in history and included thirteen future hall of famers.[16] Names like Eric Lindros, Steve Yzerman, Brendan Shanahan, and Ray Bourque. And then there was Wayne Gretzky. No longer as skilled as he once had been, Gretzky's presence on the team gave the Canadians an even greater sense of the importance of the tournament. Nearing the end of his career, it would be the only chance for "The Great One" to win an Olympic gold medal.

At least as important, there was also Canada's goalie, Patrick Roy, one of the best in hockey history and still in his prime. Roy had won NHL's top goalie honors three times. His teams had won three Stanley Cups. He had been sensational throughout the Olympics, allowing an average of just one goal per game. Hašek had been the NHL's dominant goalie, but his teams had never won the biggest games. As the media played up the matchup between the two great goalies, Hašek anxiously imagined the headlines: *Roy Once Again Shows His Dominance in the Playoffs. Hašek Can't Handle the Pressure.*

Surprisingly, though, the Czech players as a group felt pretty relaxed entering the semifinal. Nobody expected them to win this game. All the pressure was on Canada, for whom Nagano was gold or bust. The Czech players also knew that the big international ice played on in the Olympics—larger than the space allocated to NHL games—helped reduce one of their greatest disadvantages. The Canadians were physically enormous and tough. The Czech Republic could never hope to compete in a shove-fest against them, but with the larger ice the Czechs could focus on their speed and passing.

At 2:25 P.M., Japan time, on Friday, February 20, the referee dropped the puck, beginning the battle between the Canadians in red and the Czechs wearing white for the first time in the tournament. From the get-go, both teams played disciplined, unselfish, and mistake-free hockey. The world's two best goalies put on a show, not letting a single shot through. For the first forty minutes, the Czechs had a few more shot attempts than the Canadians, but neither side could score.

With just a single period left to play, the score remained knotted at zero. Hašek felt the weight of it all on his shoulders. There were constant battles in front of each of the goals, and the tiniest error could effectively end the tournament for one of the teams.

Opening the period, the Canadians hammered the puck at the Czech goalie, but despite his increasing nervousness, Hašek stopped them without great difficulty. After seven minutes, the tide shifted slightly, and the Czechs now found themselves with multiple chances to score. But none panned out.

With just under eleven minutes left to play, the Czech Republic's Pavel Patera won a face-off on the left side facing the Canadian goal and tapped the puck back to one of the Litvínov boys, Jiří Šlégr. An offensive-minded defenseman, Šlégr calmly set himself. He briefly had a lane to shoot through a few players, and then the window closed as a Canadian stepped into his path. However, when the Canadian player slid over to cover one of Šlégr's teammates, the Litvínov boy launched a missile. Roy stepped up to try to cut off the angle and suddenly looked back over his own right shoulder. Before the goalie even had a chance to react properly, the puck had flown past him into the net! On the Czech TV broadcast, Záruba screamed "GOOOOOOOOALLL!" sounding out the vowels for so long that it seemed that he might never stop. The Czechs on the ice jumped all over Šlégr as the pro-Czech fans in the stands leaped up and down and screamed.

Still, ten whole minutes remained and a great Canada hockey team was ready to swarm. Hašek felt exhausted, but also heartened by how hard his teammates were working. Back in the Czech Republic the entire country seemed to hold its breath for minutes on end as Canada sent all possible attackers at Hašek. During a brief break from play, the Czech goaltender noticed an extraordinary feeling. *We are fighting to make the Olympic final! And we are playing well!* He began to wonder how the people back home were processing the whole experience. He suddenly snapped out of it. *What the hell am I doing? Concentrate!* He focused on the moment in front of him. The scoreboard. The bench. The Czech wives in the stands, all wearing replicas of the team jerseys. He noticed that the Canadians appeared shocked. Then as play resumed, he saw Gretzky throw his all into the game, trying to control the puck and make something happen for his team.

With just under two minutes left, the Canadians launched a torrid offensive, red jerseys pounding at Hašek. The Czechs got the puck and drove with it to the opposite end of the ice, far from the goal that the Canadians needed to penetrate. The Czech Republic just needed to hold on for ninety seconds. But suddenly, with just seventy-seven seconds to go, the Canadians got the puck back at their own end. They drove toward Hašek with controlled urgency. They launched a powerful shot. Ordinarily, Hašek would have caught it easily, but his movements were hampered by the poor-fitting backup glove he had been forced to use because of his injured finger. He dropped the puck. Lindros chased it down and sent a perfect pass to Trevor Linden, standing ten feet directly in front of the net. Linden swung. Hašek knew that he had the play under control, but the puck willed itself into the stick of one of the Czech defensemen, rico-cheting away from the Czech goalie and into the goal with sixty-three seconds left. Tie score! The pro-Canada crowd went berserk.

All the air went out of the Czech men. Before Canada's goal, they had all but secured a trip to the gold medal game. Then, poof. It was gone. Somehow the Czechs managed to make it through the final minute without further damage, but their spirits had turned to ash. Even the Czech faithful in the crowd looked ill, with many clutching their faces in agony. The two teams would now play a ten-minute sudden death overtime period. Canada looked rejuvenated and a single Canadian score would end the Czech Republic's dreams.

Hašek, his gloves drenched through with sweat, returned to the bench. "We can do this!" But his teammates could scarcely bring themselves to even look at him. As play resumed, the Czechs focused on playing as a team, without anyone getting too aggressive. They looked shaken and had difficulty controlling the puck. The Canadians repeatedly grabbed it and took it to Hašek.

The Czechs should have known that it just wasn't going to go their way. Early in the overtime Svoboda headed to the locker room after injuring his right elbow. Then, partway through the ten-minute overtime, Hašek felt awful. The pressure was overwhelming, far beyond anything he had ever felt in a hockey match. His helmet bothered him. He felt exhausted. His head started to spin and he saw imaginary floaters in front of him. He called time out and headed to the bench.

Hašek looked spent, as he removed his helmet and wiped his face and hair with a towel. Knowing that he had to be at his absolute best or everything would be lost, he focused on pulling himself together. He returned to his net and bent down, ready for the next red wave, which came momentarily. The Canadians took control and Lindros made a goal try just feet in front of Hašek, who, along with a gaggle of Czech skaters, threw himself in front of the puck. Crisis averted. From there, play continued, with no team scoring. Then, out of nowhere, with just under two minutes remaining in the overtime period, Canada's Theo Fleury bumped into Hašek, sending the skinny Czech man to the ice. Slowly, very slowly, Hašek returned to his feet, leaning heavily on the net for support.

After the short break that followed, play grew desperate. Players from both teams took turns grabbing opposing skaters and pulling them down to the ice. Rosie Růžička's helmet flew off, forcing the other skaters to navigate around it. And, still, the Canadians continued to fire away. Hašek had little choice but to throw his body all over the crease to stop the shots. But nothing found its way into the net. The Czechs somehow survived the overtime with the score still tied. Hašek moved slowly to the bench.

The game would be decided by a shootout, in which the teams took turns sending a player one-on-one with the puck against the opposing team's goaltender until five men from each team had a try. This tie-break approach was not used at the time in NHL games, but the NHL included shootouts as part of a skills competition during the yearly all-star game. Hašek felt a bit dazed and completely gassed, but he also recalled that he had outperformed Roy in blocking shooters in such competitions.

Franta Musil had spent the 1990s as a first-rate NHL player and dreamed of joining the Czech Olympic team in 1998. He had been heartbroken when he hadn't been invited to Nagano. Unable to do anything but watch from North America, Musil cheered on his childhood pal Hašek. Now, as the shootout approached, Musil remembered how unbeatable Hašek had always been on one-on-one breakaways. *That's it! The Canadians cannot win now.* But knowledge of Hašek's past successes did nothing to ease the suffering of a viewer back in the goalie's hometown of Pardubice. Dominik's mother, who had been watching the game on the television in her second-floor apartment, simply couldn't bear the stress of the shootout. She walked out her front door and began pacing up and down the three stories of the building. Despite the wild screams everywhere around her, she wouldn't stop to find out what happened until her daughter went to get her when it was all over.[17]

When each team's coaches put together their list of five shooters, one of the Canadians' choices flummoxed the entire world of hockey fans. Wayne Gretzky, the greatest hockey player in history, was not on the list. Gretzky had never been great at breakaways, but he was by far the most prolific scorer of all time. Hašek later found the omission baffling, but in the moment he didn't notice. He was too busy trying to grapple with the mind-crushing pressure. *One mistake and we lose!*[18]

Hašek also didn't notice the extraordinary energy on his bench. Without anyone saying a word first, the Czech players came together in one long line along the length of the bench, arms across each other's shoulders, embracing their sense of shared teamwork, and supporting their teammates, who one at a time took to the ice. Czech assistant coach Slavomír Lener felt his heart swell as he took in the brotherhood shared by his team's men.[19]

Canada had the first chance. Theo Fleury drove toward Hašek, who came out a yard or two to meet him and easily snuffed out the shot attempt.

Now it was the Czech Republic's turn. Skating first was Reichel. Robert Reichel, who during the late 1980s had been the greatest of all the talented young players in Czechoslovakia. Reichel, who in the NHL had never quite lived up to the lofty expectations held for him. North American fans had no idea how totally Reichel had dominated Czechoslovak and international competition when he first started out. As his teammates cheered him on, Reichel drove toward Roy, and then toward the right side of the goal. As the Canadian goalie waited for him, Reichel suddenly gave a quick jerk of the wrist, flipping the puck toward the opposite side of the net, where it hit the post and caromed in for a score. He skated back over to his teammates, who calmly congratulated him before they returned to watching the next Canadian skater. Reichel climbed in to be part of the arm-across-arm group on the bench.

The Czechs now led by a goal, but at least four more Canadians still had a chance. The two goalies took turns snuffing out attempts by each side until Canada's fourth skater, Eric Lindros, stepped onto the ice. The Canadian team captain drove his six-foot, four-inch, 240-pound body forward toward Hašek, moving faster and faster. As Lindros came within twenty-five feet of the net, Hašek slid out six feet to meet the much bigger man. Lindros subtly slid slightly to the left, while tapping the puck a foot to the right, and then abruptly pulled himself and the puck sharply to the left. He had Hašek beat!

As Lindros made his final motion, Hašek threw himself down to the ice. His legs splayed out to the right side of Lindros, and he thrust his stick hand—his right—straight forward, just in front of the Canadian. Continuing the motion, the Czech goalie threw himself onto his back, throwing his glove-covered left hand over his shoulder to his own right as Lindros smacked the puck at the net. In the years that followed, countless people would watch the replay, but none could agree on just what happened after the puck left Lindros's stick. Some insist that Hašek's glove hand barely tipped the puck. Others say that Hašek missed it entirely. They all agree on one thing: The puck hit the left post of the net and bounced to the side. *NO GOAL!!*

Next, Jágr tried the exact move that Reichel had scored on earlier, but the puck hit the post and bounded out. No goal. Canada had one last chance to tie.

Brendan Shanahan skated toward Hašek, tried a quick fake, slid to the right, and shot. The puck bounced harmlessly off Hašek's pads.

Hašek raced to the center of the rink, throwing his arms over and over into the air. The Czechs became entangled in a joyful embrace on the bench. When they finally pulled themselves apart, they flew to Hašek. The Canadians went out to the ice and patiently waited to congratulate the Czechs. Except for one man. Gretzky sat forlornly, chinstrap dangling, lower lip covering the upper, as he stared out at the spectacle. It was his last international competition and he later told people, "It's devastating, the worst feeling I've ever had in hockey." After a minute, he got up to join his teammates.

For several more minutes, the Czechs remained in their swirling dogpile. Hašek told his teammates, "Don't get up just yet. I want to savor this moment. Please stay with me here just a bit longer." When they finally rose, Hašek bent down and kissed the ice.

Back home in the Czech Republic, the entire country came to a halt. It was a Friday morning but there was celebrating in the streets. Businesses and schools shut down for the day.

By noon, everyone knew whom they would play in the gold medal game.

Throughout Czechoslovakia's history, in four separate Olympics—in 1968, 1972, 1976, and 1984—the country's hockey team had gone into its final match simply needing a win to take the gold medal. All four times the team came up short. And in the final three of those opportunities, the devastating loss in the finale came at the hands of Czechoslovakia's most hated rival and occupier, the Soviet Union. Now, in 1998, in the Tournament of the Century, the Czechs had gone on a fairy tale run all the way to the Olympic gold medal game. Fairy tale as it was, there could be no doubt about whom they would need to defeat in that game. Behind the *five goal* performance of Pavel Bure, the Russians had blown Finland away in the other semifinal. The gold medal match-up now seemed preordained. Czechs versus Russia.

The match-up didn't have the overwhelming political overtones that Czechoslovakia-USSR did during the Cold War, but the shared history was far from forgotten. It was the icing on the cake that the gold medal would only come if they could take down Russia.[20]

The press played up the two countries' history with one another. It didn't need to exaggerate. Countless articles and television segments talked about how Jágr wore number 68 as a reminder of the Soviet invasion. Even the timing of the tournament was noteworthy. The year 1998 marked the thirtieth anniversary of the USSR-led invasion, and the gold medal match would be played during the week-long fiftieth anniversary of the Soviet-backed coup that thrust the Communists into power in Czechoslovakia. Given that context and the way hockey had always been a part of Czechoslovakia's resistance to the Soviets after 1968, it was little wonder that Czechs saw this match as something different. All over the Czech Republic, people proclaimed: *This isn't just sport! We'll bury the Russians in ice for what they did in 1968!*[21]

The press also played up the meaning of the Nagano tournament for Czechs' ability to build a national identity and national pride during their country's difficult transition away from communism.[22] Just as countless telegrams were sent to the Czechoslovak players in Stockholm in 1969 as they awaited their matches against the Soviet Union, thousands of faxes arrived in 1998 for the Czech players in Nagano. They expressed the people's longing for a gold medal and a Czech Republic that might be relevant in the world.[23] The team had the day off on Saturday, February 21, so the Czech players each grabbed stacks of faxes and brought them back to their apartments in the Olympic Village, where they spent much of the day reading and sharing them with one another. One of the men came across a fax from an elderly Czech woman, leading Reichel to pipe up, "If this old lady wants us to win, we're gonna win it for her!"[24]

That evening, the Czech team held its final meeting to prep for the Russians. Hašek had given up only six goals in five games, but the Russian offense had been unstoppable, averaging five goals per game. The Russians were undefeated in their five games, and within a ten-second span in their previous match-up, they had scored twice on Hašek. The Czechs' planning focused on Bure, whose nine goals led all players in the tournament by four. When the meeting adjourned, Hašek returned to his apartment, packed, and went to bed. He couldn't sleep, though, as the floors below pounded with the music of the athletes who had already finished their competitions. After hours of tossing and turning, he gave up trying to sleep and just read faxes from home until 2:30 A.M. When he finally drifted off, he had been able to read only about a tenth of all the messages in the tall stack.

As Hašek traveled to Big Hat Arena the next morning, he thought about all the people back in the Czech Republic who were gathering to watch the match.

Then he started thinking about how many times the Czechs had come in second. Were they destined to always be the bridesmaid? Would they have anything left after all that they had done in the last two games? When he entered the locker room, his fears about the team's energy level dissipated as he watched Robert Reichel pump the group up: "We can't let this go after we made it so far! We won't let the gold slip away!"

The match was set to commence at 1:45 P.M. in Nagano, which was 5:45 *in the morning* in the Czech Republic. Nearly four and a half million out of the country's ten million people pulled themselves out of bed to watch. Ninety-seven percent of all televisions in the country were turned on for the game. In corner stores, neighborhood residents huddled to squint at tiny screens. School was open that Sunday for kids to watch as a group. In the country's beautiful public squares in cities big and small, organizers erected giant monitors for tens of thousands of people to view the event together.[25] A group of four teenagers left their suburban home shortly after midnight to walk the four hours to Prague's Old Town Square, where organizers had set up three giant viewing screens amid the old Baroque buildings. In the square, the teens were joined by an additional 70,000 Czechs who wanted to experience the freezing predawn viewing party with as many of their country-mates as possible.[26] In Havlíčkův Brod, Jan Suchý had shared every single game of that year's Olympics with buddies in his favorite pub, where for years hockey players had gone after practice. On that particular morning, the owner of the pub started work at 1 A.M. to have the soup ready for the packed crowd that arrived at 4 o'clock.[27]

On the Czech television coverage, announcer Záruba cut to the chase: "Looking at the trophy case of Czech hockey reminds us that one big success, one big win, one big trophy is missing: the Olympic gold medal." He talked about how the Soviets had been the winningest hockey team in Olympic history. And he spoke of the many close calls Czechoslovakia had over the years in its quest to win Olympic gold, especially against the Soviet Union, and how those chances had not once gone Czechoslovakia's way.

The Czech team received some good news. It had been feared that Petr Svoboda's injured right elbow would keep him out of the gold medal game. Losing Svoboda would hurt. He was one of the team's elder statesmen, a great leader who had kept the team's spirits up, and he had been a big part of the team's strong defensive play. Fortune smiled—Svoboda showed up ready to go.

In the locker room, the Czech men followed their rituals. Hašek kissed the Czech coat of arms on his jersey. The men lined up. As they walked through the door to exit the locker room, they gently touched the glass elephant.

The Russian men had started the march to the ice a few seconds before the Czechs. To those with a sense of hockey history, the view of the two teams was eerie. The match was held eighteen years to the day after the famous "Miracle on Ice" match from the 1980 Olympics, in which a group of American college kids had achieved a seemingly impossible upset over the mighty Soviet hockey team. Just as the Soviets had in 1980, the Russians marched out in their bright red helmets, jerseys, and pants. The Czechs came out in uniforms that had far more than just a passing resemblance to the Americans' uniforms from 1980: blue helmets, white jerseys with blue lettering and patches of red and blue, and red pants. Noticeably, unlike the 1980 American jerseys, which prominently featured a star on each shoulder, the Czechs had no sign of one on their uniforms.

Coming out through the tunnel, team captain Pavel Bure led the way for the Russians, walking a few paces ahead of Hašek. Otherwise, the teams largely moved together side-by-side to hit the ice. All the Czechs could see the brilliant Russian scorer in front of them, and they silently pledged to keep their eyes on him until the final horn sounded. Those watching from behind the players got a reminder of what the game meant to the Czech Republic. The last player to hit the ice for either team was Jaromír Jágr, with his number *68* screaming out in bright blue on the back of his pristine white jersey.

Rosie Růžička won the faceoff to open the game and quickly tapped it back to his mates to begin the most important match of their lives. Both teams started somewhat slowly, with the Czechs in particular moving almost timidly at times. The Russians pounded numerous shots at Hašek, including more than one where the skater had nothing but open space between himself and the Czech goalie, but the Dominator stopped them all. Bure *flew* around the ice in never-ending pursuit of the puck, but the Czechs kept track of him, even when they were on offense, fearing what he might do if they lost the puck. Midway through the period, the speedy Russian smacked multiple tries at Hašek, but the Czech goalie handled each in turn.

The Russians' defensive firepower was devastating. The referees largely let the players hit without penalty, so the Russians were able to play rough. They hit Jágr, in particular, hard and often. Between his brilliant offensive moves, his size and skill, his charismatic flair, and of course his hair, Jágr was unmistakable all over the ice. He constantly pushed toward the Russian goal, whether he had the puck or drove to grab a loose ricochet. Jágr would pay for his efforts. With under a minute to go in the first period, Jágr nabbed the puck in the Russian zone and looked to attack. As he did, a Russian defender flew toward him at full speed, obliterating Jágr with a brutal left elbow to the head. The Czech Republic's best offensive player went down hard. Jágr pulled himself off the ice to the bench, where he bent over in pain clutching his face. The Czech faithful looked on in horror as Jágr, still holding a bright orange towel to his face, walked to the locker room ahead of all the other players during the break between the first two periods.

Jágr was able to return with his team to the ice for the second period and the pace of play picked up. The Russians opened on the offensive with great opportunities, but they were unable to get a good angle on a shot. Moments later, the Czechs had a two-on-one breakaway. Czech forward Pavel Patera flipped the puck to Jágr on the right near the goal, and only a great tip by a Russian defenseman kept it out of the net. Just a couple of minutes later, the Czechs again went on the attack but weren't able to score as the Russian netminder flew onto his back to block the attempt.

Eight minutes into the period, the Russians got their big break with a beautiful pass to forward Andrei Kovalenko, who was standing with plenty of time to score just a few feet in front of Hašek. Across the Czech Republic, hundreds of thousands, if not millions, of team fanatics gasped. Kovalenko, who had already scored four goals in the tournament, readied himself for goal number five and the lead. Hašek bent way down toward Kovalenko and did the splits, looking like a bizarre multijointed beetle as his arms supported him in front. Kovalenko prepared to shoot, and Hašek—now nearly flat on his stomach—threw his legs to the left as he flopped his upper body to the right and blocked with the stick in his right hand. The entire action took less than a second and kept the game scoreless.

Throughout the first half of the game, the puck had mostly stayed on Hašek's side of the ice. Partway through the second period, the Czech players tried to move play to the other end of the rink and hold it there. The increasingly pro-Czech crowd began to chant *My chceme gól!* ("We want a goal!"). Jágr got the puck and began one of his patented drives. Four red jerseys moved to surround Jágr as he slid right and pulled up just thirty feet from the crease. The shot flew past the Russian goalie before he even had a chance to react . . . and banged off the post and back into play. In the following minutes, the Czechs continued on the offensive and were met time and again with vicious hits by the Russians. Eleven and a half minutes into the period, just seconds after a particularly violent hit on Reichel by the Russians, the Czechs centered the puck to Martin Ručinský, who looked to have a breakaway just in front of the net. As Ručinský reached for it, Bure hooked the Litvínov boy from behind, bringing him down onto the ice and ending the scoring threat. The crowd whistled with displeasure.

By the end of the second period, it was clear that the Czechs were playing better than earlier. They had had five solid chances in the period to score. But after a couple of Czech shots hit the post, thus just missing, Hašek thought that it just might not be his team's day. *Damn, so many chances. I hope it doesn't turn against us.* Still, he continued to violate the laws of human flexibility as he flopped down onto the ice, practically standing upside-down, blocking shots with every part of his body. The Russians could only shake their heads.

The Czechs came out for the third period anxiously aware that all they needed was a single goal. Hlinka always encouraged his players not to take hockey too seriously, but as he sat on the bench with his arms crossed across his chest and his face pinched tight, the Czech coach looked miserable, just as he had throughout the game. The Czechs opened the third period playing their best hockey of the game, constantly on the attack. Six minutes in, Litvínov boys Martin Ručinský and Robert Lang passed the puck back and forth to each other in a beautiful series of weaves that turned into high-quality shots. But no luck.

The Russians regained the puck and launched a rocket at Hašek. The shot bounced out. As Jágr flew in to grab the ricochet, Czech Republic fans everywhere realized that they were watching a man who intended to win the gold medal for them. Jágr sprinted straight up the ice, hair flying behind him. He moved so fast that he left most of his charging teammates far behind. As he drove directly toward the net, he suddenly passed the puck to the left to Josef Beranek, who hit a blistering slap shot, which bounced back toward him. As the crowd chanted *Do toho!* ("Let's go!"), Beranek took the bounce and tried to backhand it in, but the Russian goalie and Bure smothered the puck.

A face-off was set to the left, facing the Russian goal. While the Czechs got set up, defensemen Svoboda and Roman Hamrlík quickly strategized. If the Czech Republic won the face-off, the puck was to go to Svoboda. He was a great skater, but didn't shoot with much power. Svoboda agreed that if he got the puck he would pass it to teammate Hamrlík, who had stronger offensive skills. When play began, the Czech Republic's Pavel Patera won the face-off and sent the puck to Martin Procházka, who tapped it back to Svoboda. Svoboda stood on the left side, some fifty feet from the Russian goal, and decided not to pass the puck. Seeing an open lane in front of him, he bounced his stick on the ice, reared back as far as his arms would move, and let it fly. Then he watched.

Almost magically, nearly every major event in Czechoslovak history has had some sort of time stamp with the number eight on it: from the birth of Czechoslovakia in 1918, to the German annexation of the country in 1938, to the Communist coup in 1948, to the Prague Spring and Soviet invasion in 1968, to the Revolution in 1989 ("89" as the upside-down and backwards "68").

As he looked at what was going on in front of him, Petr Svoboda was not thinking about any of this. Svoboda was also not thinking about the fact that as an eighteen-year-old he had escaped into the night in West Germany with nothing but the clothes on his back so that he might be free to go chase his dreams in the NHL. He wasn't thinking about the fact that he was playing for the Czech adult national team for the only time in his life, nor that he had never before scored a goal for his country. He wasn't thinking about how his birthplace had never won an Olympic gold medal in this, the beloved sport of the country. He was not thinking about how the winner of this match could truly declare itself the greatest team in the greatest hockey tournament of all time. He wasn't thinking about the fact that the world had overlooked his country for far longer than he had even been alive, and had sacrificed it to world powers who had abused it. He wasn't even thinking now about the fact that this match was against Russia, which had held his own land captive for decades.

And he certainly was not thinking about the fact that *his* name—"Svoboda"—means *freedom*.

In the 1998 Olympics, 8 minutes and 8 seconds into the final period of the final match of the Tournament of the Century, Petr Svoboda was thinking that his shot had just sailed past the Russian goalie and into the back of the net.

Czech announcer Záruba bellowed, "Goal! It's in! It's in! Justice exists after all!"[28]

Back in the Czech Republic, millions in homes, and schools, and corner markets, and rail stations, and pubs, and squares screamed, jumping up and down, rejoicing. Hundreds of thousands hugged the people closest to them, even strangers. Tens of thousands waved their country's flag. Thousands cried.

However, Czech viewers had seen this movie before. In the 1976 Olympics, a great Czechoslovak team had the lead and needed to hold the Soviets scoreless for a mere five final minutes to at long last take the Olympic crown—but then, less than a minute later, the Soviet Red Machine had scored, snatching gold from Czechoslovakia at the last moment. With this history in the back of their minds, with the way the Canadians had scored with just a minute left in regulation in the previous game, and the way that Russia had come back to win after being down 1–0 late in their previous match-up in this year's tournament, no one on the Czech side could rest easy with the knowledge that nearly twelve minutes remained in the game.

When play resumed after Svoboda's goal, the Czech Republic continued to attack, but it also stayed disciplined. On the bench, the Czech players appeared poised and unflustered. The Russians meanwhile looked uncomfortable, leaning forward on their bench, as if they were trying to use their tension to will a score. On the ice, Bure turned to solo attack mode, trying over and over to score by himself. But the Czechs refused to let one man beat them. And the clock continued to move.

Hašek found himself daydreaming about what could be. His heart swelled at the incredible effort of his teammates. He wondered how everyone at home was celebrating. He caught himself. *Stop messing around, Goddamnit! Focus on the game!*

The Russians appeared increasingly desperate, swarming, maintaining their physical play, sending a pair of Czechs to the bench in agony from the hits they received. But walls of Czech defenders kept swallowing up would-be scorers, and Hašek easily stopped anything that came his way.

The crowd continued the Czech chant of *Do toho!* ("Let's go!") as the seconds ticked away, and the Czech Republic clung to its 1–0 lead. Hlinka sent

Reichel, Lang, Ručinský, and Šlégr—the four Litvínov boys who had grown up together—back out to the ice one last time. On the bench, the Czech players took to their feet in anticipation. Hašek began to jump up and down in celebration as Hlinka barked instructions to the skaters. The Russians wildly aimed the puck toward the Czech goalie at the other end of the ice. Just as the puck passed the net without doing any damage, time expired.

Czech Republic–1, Russia–0!

Hašek threw his stick and glove into the air as he slid out from the crease. As he did, the first of his teammates arrived, wrapping the goalie up in the most heartfelt of embraces. A half-second later, a second skater flew in and within five seconds Hašek was at the bottom of a pile of two dozen men in white jerseys. On the bench the coaches hugged. So did the Czech faithful in the crowd. Back in the Czech Republic, millions appeared to enter an out-of-body state of exhilaration as Záruba boomed, "We are opening the golden gate of the Olympic tournament! We are the Olympic champions! Rewrite the history!"

It was the stuff of legend. During the years when the country was under the thumb of the Soviet Union, it came close over and over again to winning Olympic gold in the sport that it held so dear. Yet each time it fell short. Now, having thrown off the Soviet yoke but crushed by national growing pains, the people were again lifted up by their hockey team. But this time the team had achieved something that no one in the country had ever done before. Indeed, something that no country in the world had ever done before. And a man named "Svoboda"—a man named *Freedom!*—had scored the goal that pushed the team and the country over the top.

Freedom to win.

# Too Good to be Denied

*Victories in sport do more to cement the nation than one hundred
political slogans.*

—Vladimir Putin

B obby Holík's absence in Nagano felt odd. Given the central role the Holíks
played in battling the Soviet Union on the ice, in the Hollywood version it
would have been Bobby who scored the winning goal against the Russians and
then raced into the stands to embrace his father, Jaroslav. But in the real-world
version of the story, Bobby wasn't in Japan. In the real-world version of the story,
Bobby Holík didn't go to Nagano because, for Czechs and Slovaks—even for
the players themselves—the story of hockey in Czechoslovakia had never been
just about hockey.

Someone paying close attention on July 15, 1990, seven and a half years
before the Tournament of the Century, might have realized that Bobby's path
would ultimately diverge from the one most young Czechoslovak hockey stars
were on. Nineteen-year-old Bobby always ate more than just about anyone in
his orbit, so when he rose in his parents' home in Jihlava that Sunday morning,
he made sure to eat a big breakfast. It was going to be a long day. When he
finished eating, he got dressed. Jeans and a t-shirt as always, along with a pair
of impressively unfashionable eyeglasses. He double-checked to make sure he
had everything he needed in his two bags. One suitcase with the bare necessities and a bad polyester suit. One hockey bag with his gear. Bobby, Marie, and
Jaroslav climbed into their car to begin the hour-and-a-half drive from Jihlava

to the Prague airport. Marie was emotional. That was expected. But Jaroslav appeared to be overcome as well. That was out of the ordinary. From the moment he had kids, Jaroslav had maniacally structured his life, and theirs, to make this moment possible. And now it was really happening.

The aim had been to make Bobby too good to be denied. No matter how everything else unfolded, the goal had always been to get Bobby out of the country and into the NHL. Not even a revolution could change that. As the family exchanged goodbyes, Bobby told his mother, "You can come visit me, but I'll never come back here."

Bobby settled into the Lufthansa jet seat, which hardly fit his six-foot, four-inch, 220 pound—and still growing—frame. As he looked out the window, he thought about the hockey players of his dad's generation. Their battles against the Soviets had been more than just games, and had inspired Bobby's generation. As he flew over Western Europe and then the Atlantic Ocean, Bobby reflected on how, for decades, athletes like Big Ned, Martina Navrátilová, Peter Šťastný, and Ivan Lendl had to defect in order to reach the goal that he was now free to pursue. They had paved the way for him. Most of all, though, as Bobby neared the East Coast of the United States, he thought about what his family—especially his father—had done to make the flight he was now on possible.

Bobby meant it when he told his mother that he would never return. Part of it was that the person closest to him was no longer there. Throughout Bobby's life, Marie's father—his beloved grandfather—had come to his games. Marie always sat behind the Dukla bench, and Grandpa sat across from her on the other side of the rink. In a 1988 match in Jihlava, Bobby had a breakaway with the puck, and only the other team tripping him prevented a goal. But the referee didn't call a penalty. Furious, Grandpa stood up in his third-row seat and shook his cane. Suddenly, he collapsed. Trying to tend to the old man, the surrounding group began removing his jacket. Seeing only the disrobing, Marie chuckled. *Ah, Dad is overdressed again.* Soon, she realized that there was a problem and rushed to the first aid station, where she learned that her father had passed away. Devastated, she sent word to her husband. As the game ended, Jaroslav pulled Bobby aside and, in his typical Jaroslav way, bluntly told him: "Grandpa died." A million things went through Bobby's head, but one stood out. *He died defending me!*

But the absence of his grandfather wasn't the only reason that Bobby didn't plan to return home; there was also the long shadow of the single person who had dominated his life. Bobby had never resented his father's tough training. He believed that no one else could have unlocked the talent within him as effectively. Nevertheless, Bobby had a constant feeling that in Czechoslovakia people believed that he received special treatment because of his dad. In North America, Bobby's path was his own.

More than anything, though, Bobby didn't plan to return because, aside from his family, the single thing he most associated with his birthplace was a regime that had run roughshod over his family for four decades. What the regime had done to his grandparents, and to his father, and then ultimately to his sister, and even himself—it was deeply personal.

To Bobby Holík, growing up under Czechoslovakia's communist system had been a gift. To demonstrate the "superiority" of the system, the regime had supported the efforts of athletes like Bobby to succeed at the highest level. Just as important, Bobby had used his hatred of the Communists as fuel. That "gift" affected his life way beyond the ice. His NHL dreams had never been only about hockey. Making it to the NHL meant escaping Czechoslovakia's oppressive regime.

But the dream had never included the possibility that one day the Communists might fall. By the time that they did, it was too late to alter Bobby's perspective. He had lived under the regime his entire life, and he couldn't flip a switch and alter his view of the place just because of changes during his final half year there.

Growing up, Bobby had been different from most other hockey players, and that was even more true in North America. He didn't party. He never consumed alcohol until the celebratory champagne after the New Jersey Devils won the 1995 Stanley Cup championship, and even then he hated the taste. He was an intellectual, loved reading history, and spent his road trips going to museums. He was political, outspoken on every topic, and expressed his views without filter. Finding him forthright, funny, and a great interview, reporters loved him. Major American periodicals like *ESPN the Magazine*, *Sports Illustrated*, and the *New Yorker* all ran features on him.

To a greater degree than most Czech hockey players, Bobby embraced life in America. He remained grateful to the Czechs and Slovaks who had paved the way for him. He loved the Czech lands, the Czech people, and most of all his family, but he never overcame his memories of the regime that governed his childhood. The regime he hated didn't even exist anymore, but it was in America that he achieved everything he had ever dreamed of. He made it in the NHL. He met and married a woman who gave his life deeper meaning. And he had freedoms that had never existed for him during the first nineteen years of his life. As soon as he was permitted, Bobby submitted paperwork. On November 4, 1996, he became an American citizen. He was no longer eligible, therefore, to play for the Czech national hockey team.[1]

Even following the Nagano victory, Bobby didn't regret the decision. To the Holíks, hockey had always been about more than the game or winning matches. Hockey afforded them the freedom and opportunity for a better life. Under communism, sports offered one of the few ways that people could stand out as individuals and make something of themselves outside the Party. It was for that reason that Jaroslav's own father had driven Jaroslav and Jiří to become athletes. It was also through hockey that Bobby's dad found a way to channel his ferocious rage and fight back directly against the Soviet Union that he despised. Most of all, hockey provided a place where Jaroslav could become too good to be denied. If he was great, ultimately he could inoculate himself against the Communists. And if his kids were great, they could create a safe place for themselves in the world. Yet, as Jaroslav told Bobby, "When you play hockey, you give it everything you've got. But when you are away from the game, you remember that there is more to life."

Despite the central role it played in their lives, the Holíks and Jan Suchý had always put hockey in perspective. In 1979, the year Suchý decided to retire from Czechoslovakia's hockey league, he ran into Vladimír Kostka, who lamented, "If you didn't smoke and drink, you could play for at least another ten years at the top level." Suchý responded in his inimitable way. "Professor, if I didn't drink and party, that would be no life. What kinds of memories would I have then, only that I was good at hockey? That wouldn't be enough for me."[2]

Jiří Holík had long felt it in his own ways. As a player, he had retired from the national team because the training camps kept him away from his family so much. In the 1990s, he had become a hockey team executive and then a coach for lower tier teams, but found the jobs to be a constant source of stress. He retired from all positions in hockey in 2002 and discovered a new sort of peace. He became obsessed with reading about impressionist artists, especially how many had lived life in poverty and only gained fame after their death. He found daily joy in working on odd jobs around his home. Whenever he visited friends and family in Jihlava, he loved to travel by foot and, upon arriving at his destination, tell his hosts with a smile about the wonderful walk that had brought him there. Unannounced, Jaroslav decided to visit his brother late one afternoon. He found Jiří in front of the house, totally contented, relaxing and looking at the sky. Seeing Jaroslav, he asked, "Oh, is it evening already?"[3]

The Holíks would even have to put Nagano in perspective.

The entire family adored Jaroslav's mother-in-law, who, like her daughter, was named Marie. Born in 1922, the elder Marie had always been an exceptionally empathetic figure, noted for initially dating her future husband, Josef, because she felt sorry for him. As she got older, she moved in with Jaroslav and her daughter, where they could all look after one another. She took particular care of Jaroslav, who was so inept in the kitchen that he couldn't even make a cup of tea for himself.

On the day of the victory over Russia in Nagano, the younger Marie was visiting Andrea in the US, but Jaroslav was home in Jihlava. His morning began gloriously with the Czech victory, and that night he celebrated with friends at the annual Dukla Ball. But as the Dukla faithful raised a toast that evening to the hockey team, Jaroslav's mother-in-law, who had stayed at home, took ill. Her condition worsened and her children who were with her called the paramedics. The ambulance arrived at 8 P.M. and rushed her to the hospital. To no avail. At 9 o'clock she passed away. The younger Marie's siblings knew how important the Olympic victory was, so they agreed not to interrupt Jaroslav in his celebration. But, unable to reach his mother-in-law at home, he grew anxious and headed back to the house early. There he learned the tragic news.

To the Holíks, Nagano was monumental, but of course it meant nothing by comparison. It gave the younger Marie a whole new take on the magical eights in Czech history. To her, they were filled with tragedy. Andrea was born in early 1968, but seven months later the joy of that moment was overtaken by the Soviet invasion. As Marie thought about her mother's death, she couldn't miss the bizarre numerical coincidences in her own life. *It's just so strange: Jaroslav's father died in '78. My father died in '88. And my mother died in '98. All those stupid eights.*[4]

Still, hockey would always dominate Jaroslav Holík's life. For years, he had lobbied officials to hand him the reins to the country's national junior team. Despite its history of great young players, Czechoslovakia's team had never won gold in the World Junior Championships, and the Czech Republic had never even medaled. Jaroslav complained that "they always give the junior team job to such nobodies, but if you give it to me, I could get them to win World Championships." Soon after Nagano, the Czech Hockey Federation relented and let Jaroslav take over. Sure enough, in the 2000 tournament, the Czech Republic, under Coach Jaroslav Holík, won the world junior title in a thrilling overtime shootout over, of all teams, Russia. With Jaroslav still at the helm the following year, the Czech Republic won the championship again.

However, Jaroslav's time with the team ultimately led him into new troubles. In 2010, when he was sixty-eight years old, reports in the Czech media alleged that Jaroslav had possibly solicited bribes in his role as national junior team coach. Specifically, when agents lobbied to put a particular player on the team, Jaroslav sometimes asked them for payment to make it happen. When asked about it, Jaroslav explained that the request was simply a test to see if the agent truly believed that the player was worthy, and insisted that he had never actually taken any cash. After all, given Bobby's success as an NHL player, Jaroslav certainly didn't need the money. A police investigation cleared him of any misconduct, but within the Czech hockey community views of the hockey legend became divided.

Soon, Jaroslav had to turn to even more serious matters. Following years of health issues—possibly due to Kikuchi Disease, possibly the treatment for his illness in France in 1992, or possibly both—Jaroslav developed massive headaches. One day he passed out from the pain. As he recovered, the little toe of his left foot developed a crack. When it began to fester, doctors removed a piece of the toe. Spots appeared on his leg and the doctors removed more and more of Jaroslav's limb. Finally, it became clear that he had gangrene and doctors had to amputate his left leg below the knee. In the months that followed, the disease continued to ravage his body, but Jaroslav retained his irrational confidence that he could power through anything. He told people: "I never knew how to lose. I never thought my strength would leave me, but maybe one day the juice will run out. I can't yet imagine that."[5]

Ultimately, even Jaroslav couldn't hold off the illness. He passed away on April 17, 2015.

When a legend dies, hundreds of people usually attend the funeral, but no more than a few dozen attended Jaroslav's service in a Jihlava funeral home. He had told his family that he didn't want people talking insincerely about what a great guy he was. He insisted that the funeral be limited to those who truly knew him and understood what he was really all about.

The funeral shook Bobby in an unexpected way. Jaroslav had built a relationship with his son founded on relentless training. Despite his son's successes, Jaroslav rarely offered praise, leaving Bobby with little sense of what his father actually thought of him. It was for this reason that, as he chatted with the people attending the funeral, Bobby found himself entering a state of shock: One after another, the assembled told him something that he had never known. All his life, his father had constantly and effusively talked about how proud he was of his boy.

At Jaroslav's insistence, only the family's dear friend Dr. Jiří Havránek was invited to address the congregation, but in reality Dr. Havránek's was not the funeral's only eulogy. The second speech was delivered in English, but everyone there knew precisely what it meant. As the assembled paid their final respects to the great hockey legend, the family played over the sound system a song that Frank Sinatra had made famous in 1969, the same year that Jaroslav carried out his most iconic act of rebellion. More than any speech could, "My Way" perfectly described the wild, uncompromising hockey man, with his over-the-top intensity and certainty that he knew precisely how everything ought to be done.

> *But through it all, when there was doubt*
> *I ate it up and spit it out*
> *I faced it all and I stood tall and did it my way*

There is also a more oft-forgotten part of the song, one that talks of living according to a carefully set plan, that represented Jaroslav just as well. Jaroslav Holík had maniacally but methodically plotted a course to ensure that Czechoslovakia's Communist regime would never defeat his family and him. His family would become too good to be denied and, thus, could find a way to live free. When he looked back, Jaroslav knew that his plan had succeeded and that the life his family had been able to live was a testament to that plan. To Jaroslav, there was no need for any other speeches at the funeral because his family, and its life, was the eulogy.

Hockey had been central to that plan, but, to the Holíks, the meaning of hockey changed when communism collapsed in Czechoslovakia in 1989. In the Hollywood version of the story, where Bobby Holík scores the gold-medal-winning goal against the Russians and races into the stands to hug his father, Czechoslovakia would still have been communist. And that winning goal would have inspired the people of the country to rise up and—because it is the Hollywood version—overthrow their oppressors. But, in reality, by 1998, the stakes had changed.

Under communism, especially beginning in 1968, sports had meant something different in Czechoslovakia. When the Soviets invaded, hockey helped the occupied people of Czechoslovakia overcome their feelings of demoralized impotence. Overwhelmed by the military might of a bullying superpower, it was the opportunity to battle their occupiers in hockey matches that gave the people a way to feel that they could fight back. And it was victories on the ice that gave people a sense that not *all* their freedoms were lost.

In the 1990s, after the fall of communism, it became easier to see hockey matches as, first and foremost, "just" sporting events. A position on the national team no longer held the same political importance. The greatest victory had come with the fall of the Iron Curtain in 1989, after which the battles against the Russians on the ice didn't have the same meaning. As Bobby thought about the Czech Republic's gold medal, he remembered the era he had grown up in. About how Jaroslav had devoted his life to helping his children escape their country's authoritarian regime and go someplace where they had the ability to make their own choices. To Bobby, an Olympic gold medal would be nice, but . . . as he recalled everything his sister, his brother-in-law, his father, and his grandfather had gone through at the hands of Czechoslovakia's government, what was most important was that, whatever the consequences, he was now free to make his own decisions.[6]

Even still, there were other people—literally millions of others—for whom hockey matches continued to be much more than just games, even after the Iron Curtain fell. Citizens of little countries like Czechoslovakia can't help but question their very place in a world that has repeatedly ignored them and at times even used them as disposable pawns. To people living in such countries, standing out on the global stage means no longer feeling invisible, as they force the rest of the world to recognize not just that they exist, but that they matter.

For years, this dynamic had even existed between people *within* Czechoslovakia. Throughout the country's history, many Slovaks had felt that their country favored the Czechs and the Czech lands at their expense and that much of the rest of the world overlooked that they were even part of Czechoslovakia. Then, when Slovakia became its own independent country in 1993, it seemed to many Slovaks that few people outside of Eastern Europe even noticed.

But it would be through hockey that the world would come to see that the independent country of Slovakia was very much there.

Following the 1993 Velvet Divorce, Slovakia found itself practically erased from the hockey world. Because a majority of Czechoslovakia's national team had been made up of Czechs, the Czech Republic was instantly placed in the top pool in international hockey, eligible to compete in the 1993 World Championships. Despite a rich hockey tradition that produced a number of NHL stars, Slovakia was treated as a brand-new competitor and therefore ineligible for major international play.

When Slovakia became independent in 1993, no one felt greater joy than Peter Šťastný. Throughout his time as an NHL superstar in the 1980s, almost no one he met in North America had even heard of Slovakia. After the Velvet Divorce, he was speechless at the thought that his beloved Slovakia was now independent, that it had its own government, its own capital, its own flag, its own anthem, and its very own hockey team. Šťastný returned to the land that he had always felt was home to help build the new independent country. He sought to draw attention to Slovakia abroad and, in turn, to build pride at home. In future years, Peter would play a central role in trying to get the new country into the European Union and NATO, and he would represent the independent Slovakia in the European Parliament. But first, he focused on returning Slovakia to its rightful place among the world hockey powers.

Along with leaders of the country's hockey federation and even members of the national government, Peter fought to get Slovakia's hockey team into the 1994 Olympics. Based on their previous success in World Championships, eleven teams already had spots in the games locked up. The Slovak contingent passionately lobbied everyone it could think of for an opportunity to compete for the one remaining open slot. After a split vote, the selection committee gave the go-ahead to Slovakia's hockey team, which made quick work of four other teams to qualify for the Olympics for the first time as an independent country. [7]

As the February 1994 winter games in Lillehammer, Norway, opened, Peter Šťastný became the first person ever to carry Slovakia's flag in the Olympics. The Slovak hockey squad quickly showed that it belonged. People following the Olympics had no choice but to take notice as the little country played both Sweden and the US, two of the world's hockey powerhouses, to a tie. Following the match against the Americans, Peter, the team captain, openly wept. When he had played for Czechoslovakia, he had always felt that he represented the Slovak people, and for nearly a decade he had been banned from his homeland. Now he exulted, "This is the greatest thing that's ever happened, to play for your own country."

The public relations dream continued as Slovakia won its next three games. Every day the world's media told the story of the tiny new country, born just one year earlier, that had fought its way into the Olympics. The run ended in a loss in the next match to Russia, but the plan had worked to perfection. Not only did the games draw worldwide attention to Slovakia, but they also helped build national unity and a sense of identity and pride at home. Slovakia went mad with Olympic hockey mania. It had become the little country with the hockey team that could stand toe-to-toe with the greatest in the world.

Thanks in large part to Peter's playing and recruiting efforts, in 1996 Slovakia became a regular in the top pool of international hockey participants, eligible for both the World Championships and the Olympics, but the slights continued. For the 1998 winter games, the NHL had halted its schedule on February 7 to give plenty of time for the top six international hockey teams (including the Czech Republic) to get their players to Japan for the start of major tournament play on February 13. However, lower-ranked countries such as Slovakia were forced to begin an earlier round of Olympic play on February 7, before the NHLers were available. As a result, the tiny country was missing a number of its best players and eliminated early in Nagano.

Nevertheless, Slovakia continued to build its hockey program, and in 2000 something extraordinary occurred. Slovakia had an excellent tournament in the World Hockey Championships and made it all the way to the finals. In a bizarre twist, its opponent was the defending world champion . . . the Czech Republic. It felt like the Czech Republic, with its ten and a half million citizens, was a giant compared to Slovakia, with its five and a half million people and only eight indoor rinks. The Czechs won 5–3.

In 2001, Šťastný took over as general manager of Slovakia's national hockey team and went into overdrive recruiting the country's best players. Peter appealed to their sense of nationalism, pushing them to think about what it would mean to represent their country. He was able to add elite NHL players, including Peter Bondra, Miroslav Šatan, Žigmund Pálffy, Michal Handzuš, and Ľubomír Višňovský. With its best team in years ready for the 2002 World Championships, Slovakia looked forward to another chance to take on the Czech Republic, but the Czechs were eliminated in the quarterfinals. Slovakia got the next best thing: Russia in the final. The score was tied at three with a mere one hundred seconds left in regulation when Bondra found himself driving toward the net with the puck. He slapped it hard off the inside post and watched it bound in for the game-winning score.

The goal instantly became part of Slovak lore, not just among hockey fans, but among all Slovaks. People across all of Slovakia took to the streets, waving national flags, singing victory songs, and calling the hockey players gods. A thousand Slovaks who attended the game celebrated as if they had just gained their independence. And in a sense they had. The tiny country had been born just nine years earlier, and still countless people around the world didn't even know it existed. The hockey victory put it on the map. [8]

For Slovakia, the world title was central to the creation of something new, but for the Czech Republic, the victory in Nagano appeared to be more of a final chapter in a multigenerational epic. The Czech Republic was very much the heir to Czechoslovakia, a little country in the middle of Europe that repeatedly carved out an independent and prosperous place for itself only to see the so-called good guys of the world willingly sacrifice it to their most powerful enemies in order to keep the peace.

In the midst of these dynamics, hockey had never been just hockey. In Czechoslovakia, hockey had been intertwined with the country's history. That became clear in 1950 when, soon after coming to power, the country's Communist authorities imprisoned the national hockey team, sending a message that no one was beyond the reach of the government. And following the 1968 Soviet invasion, it had been the national hockey team that helped buoy the people's spirits in March 1969 in Stockholm. It therefore hurt that much more when, every time the people's hockey heroes appeared set to take the Olympic gold medal, they found their hopes dashed at the last moment. Between its geopolitics and its beloved hockey, Czechoslovakia was the country equivalent of Charlie Brown about to kick the football. Every time it thought that it had finally found a path to success, Lucy pulled it away.

But not in Nagano.

Little wonder, then, that in February 1998 President Havel sent his airplane to pick up the victorious hockey players from Japan to bring them home to celebrate with their people. As the team landed in Prague, a massive crowd waited on the runway. Untold numbers of Czechs rushed to the players as they moved toward the terminal. And then thousands more surrounded the bus that was to take them to the heart of the city. The traffic of onlookers kept the bus moving at a bare crawl, so it took an hour to travel the few miles needed to reach the president's villa. After a brief meeting with President Havel, they headed to Prague's beautiful Old Town Square. When they neared the Square, the bus had to slow down because of all the people. At least 140,000 of them, including many who had been waiting since the game ended twenty hours earlier. Not since the 1989 revolution had anyone seen anything like it. [9]

The impact of Nagano carried on well beyond that week. For years, everyone in the country could remember exactly where they were when the team won the gold medal. In 2004, an opera commemorating the victory premiered. It ran for five years. All over the country, pubs opened bearing the name "Nagano," as did a business park in Prague. [10]

It might be tempting to chalk up the people's reactions to the country's hockey victories as just another case of what a Roman poet nearly two millennia ago referred to as "bread and circuses," where those in power keep people in line by providing them with food and entertainment. To be sure, there is something to that idea, as Nagano provided a distraction from all the difficulties facing the Czech Republic at the time. But in reality it was deeper than simply a "circus."

At the end of the gold medal game, when Czech announcer Robert Záruba exclaimed, "Rewrite history!" he didn't mean that the world, and especially Czechs, should ignore the difficult history Czechoslovakia had experienced. He meant that, with the Olympic victory, it could no longer be said that the Czech Republic had never won a gold medal in the sport that defined the country. But Záruba's exclamation really went way beyond hockey. "Rewrite history!" was a reminder that Czechs no longer needed to define themselves by their past. That was the story of a different country. In 1989, that country had become free and, with freedom, its people could find ways to move forward and write a new story for themselves. Like Bobby Holík, the country could now make its own choices.

Most of all, "Rewrite history!" meant rethinking Czechs' place in the world. It seemed that *everyone* in the country had thrown their heart into the events at Nagano, just as they had when Czechoslovakia's hockey team defeated the Soviets in Stockholm nearly thirty years earlier. Líba, the woman who had no interest in hockey but watched the 1969 games and took to the streets afterward, even as pregnancy weighed her down, watched every moment of the 1998 match against the Russians and then turned on the television again to watch the celebrations as the team returned to the Czech Republic. Far beyond "just" sports, these were moments that made people across the country feel noticed, and even empowered. Speaking twenty years after Nagano, Záruba reflected, "Since 1989, I've never seen such an upsurge of national pride like after our hockey victory in Nagano. Some people laugh about this, that we Czechs only wave the flag when we win in hockey or soccer. But I don't think this was insignificant. I think it's nice to feel equal to the rest of the world."[11]

People all over the Czech Republic knew instinctively what Záruba meant. Celebrating in Prague, a middle-aged man talked of the link between hockey and the country's difficult experience. "Sports have always been sort of a healing patch in our history. People were venting feelings of humiliation, which we had suffered through in the past."[12] Nearby, a pensioner became overwhelmed and exclaimed, "This triumph shows that a tiny country like ours can have some significance in the world."[13]

For people in the Czech Republic, the 1998 victory carried so much weight because of what it said about them and their place in the world. In 2017, a Prague taxi driver spoke of her love for Czechoslovakia's hockey teams of the Cold War years. Then she paused. "Oh . . . and Nagano . . ." she said, as she wiped the tears from her eyes. "It's that the country is so small and draws from such a small pool of players that any medal just means so much."

In 1998, Russia's population was nearly 150 million, the US's nearly 300 million. Even Canada had thirty million people. The Czech Republic had a mere ten million. The people of Czechoslovakia felt that, ever since their country's birth, they had been cast aside and even trampled time and time again. In 1938 when they were handed over to Nazi Germany, at the end of World War II when the allies permitted the Soviets to "liberate" the country, in

1948 when the Communists took power in a coup, and in 1968 when half a million Warsaw Pact soldiers occupied their country.

In 1938, British prime minister Neville Chamberlain made it clear that he had ceded much of the Czech lands to Nazi Germany because he was unwilling to risk war for "people of whom we know nothing." Little wonder, then, that when the Czech Republic's 1998 national hockey team came to visit following the Nagano victory, President Havel expressed gratitude to the players for much more than a sporting victory. "Thanks to you, billions of people know now what the Czech Republic is."[14] For the people of such a small country to win the first true world hockey championship over the behemoths of the hockey universe meant that the world couldn't just overlook them. In this moment at least, they had become too good to be denied.

# Acknowledgments

T his book came about because I was terrified of disappointing my students.
     I am a professor at UC Davis, and, in 2016, I thought it would be fun to teach a new course, "Politics & Sports." I began with lectures on civil rights and sports in the US. And then I panicked. How would I fill the many weeks of lectures I'd promised on other countries?! One evening, I grew so anxious that I couldn't sleep, got out of bed, and spent half the night going down unproductive internet rabbit holes. Suddenly, I found a book that looked promising: Tal Pinchevsky's *Breakaway*.

Pinchevsky's terrific book chronicles Eastern Bloc hockey players who, during the Cold War, sought to escape to pursue their dreams in the NHL. The book opens with eight and a half mesmerizing pages on how the entire country of Czechoslovakia had turned to the 1969 World Ice Hockey Championships as the chance for revenge after the Soviet Union invaded in 1968, and how seemingly every Czech and Slovak in the country had taken to the streets following the hockey matches. It was emotionally moving, thrilling, and the most perfect example of overlap between politics and sports that I had ever come across. But *Breakaway* was primarily a book about hockey defectors and there was little in the rest of the wonderful narrative about the story that had captivated me at the start.

Eventually, I found enough other material to cover the rest of my class, but over the following months, I couldn't stop thinking about the story of Czechoslovakia and hockey. I started doing bits of research here and there until eventually I learned: (1) The story was even more incredible than I had originally thought. (2) There was almost nothing in English on it. (3) I *had* to know more. One morning, I told my wife about it and, seeing the crazed look in my eyes, she told me, "This is obviously your next book." Well, it wasn't obvious to me—I don't speak Czech or Slovak and didn't even know that much about hockey, but . . . I couldn't *not* do this project and the years that followed became an adventure.

The adventure truly began in 2017. I had learned that two of the central characters in the story shared a relative, Bobby Holík, a former NHL player, who lived in the US. I wrote Bobby a letter, asking if we could talk, and then assumed that I would never hear from him. A couple weeks later I received a phone call: "Ethan, I *love* your project. I'd be so happy to talk with you." Five days later, I was on a plane to see him.

Bobby has been the single person who has most helped make this book happen. In our many conversations since that first trip, he has been knowledgeable, deeply informative, and honest. He has been beyond generous with his time, always willing to do anything to help. He also vouched for me with his wonderful family—his mother, Marie, and his uncle, Jiří, whom I flew off to see in the Czech Republic. In turn, Marie then introduced me to Jan Suchý.

Bobby, thank you for everything you have done for a guy that you didn't even know when this process began. Without you, I would never have been able to tell the world this story in the detail it deserves.

Marie (Holíková), thank you so much for your extraordinary hospitality and your willingness to so generously share your time and your memories. I wish I could have met your husband, but thanks to all of you, I feel like I know him. Thank you as well for introducing me to Jiří (Holík) and Jan (Suchý). I am beyond grateful.

Jiří and Jan, thank you so much for all your time and for sharing with me these amazing stories about your lives. I was deeply saddened when I learned that Jan passed away in 2021.

Another group of people also deserves special thanks:

David Lukšů of Czech TV (and the brilliant author of multiple books on hockey in Czechoslovakia) spent literally *dozens* of hours generously answering my questions, offering sharp insights, helping me access and acquire photos and resources, and introducing me to key figures. Admittedly, I bought him more than a few beers, but I don't see how I can ever truly repay him.

The amazing Dr. Pavel Bačovský helped me more than I can describe. Pavel is not only Czech and a hockey fan, but also earned his Ph.D. in political science in the US. Pavel translated the bulk of the Czech sources I used, reached out on my behalf to people in the Czech Republic and Slovakia, read an entire draft of the manuscript, and did countless hours of research. His work was of the highest quality and the detail with which I told this story is a testament to Pavel's tireless commitment. I couldn't have written the book the way I did without Pavel.

Kristina Slezacek was the single person most responsible for making all my initial interviews in the Czech Republic and Slovakia a success. Kristina helped me connect with the people I needed to talk with and acted as the interpreter. Later, when we set up follow-up interviews with Marie, Jiří, and Jan, after I returned to the US, the Wi-Fi in the meeting site didn't work, so Kristina kindly carried out the interviews, asking my questions for me.

Martina Navratilova graciously spoke to me about her recollections of the 1969 hockey matches. She provided the very words that became the title of the book: "The hockey games went beyond sports. They gave people hope. They let us know that we had the *freedom to win*."

I interviewed many people associated with Cold War-era hockey, people who lived under Czechoslovakia's communist system and scholars of Cold War Czechoslovakia. I am so grateful for their time and detailed reflections. I would especially like to thank Pavel Bárta, Luděk Bukač, John Connelly, Marian Gmitter, Jozef Golonka, Dominik Hašek, Jan Havel, Jiří Holeček, Miloslav Jenšík, František Kučera, Liba, Morris Mott, Vashi Nedomanský, Terry O'Malley, Tal Pinchevsky, Jan Reindl, Martin Ručinský, Jana Slezacek, Peter Šťastný, Michal Stehlík, Oldřich Tůma, and Zdenka. Special thanks to Renée Holik for her generous hospitality in Wyoming and to Frank Musil and Andrea Musilová for their kindness in Jihlava. I would like to offer extra thanks to Josef Horešovský, who met with me twice for many hours and helped set up other interviews. Special thanks as well to Štefan Nižňanský, who put in extraordinary work to provide me with detailed information on the return of Slovakia to international hockey.

I also feel here a need to apologize: there are many great players from the era I discuss who don't get the attention they deserve. Sadly, keeping the manuscript within a manageable number of pages meant that some important figures didn't get their due here.

There is another group of people who dramatically improved the substance and presentation of the book.

Professor Kieran Williams, one of the world's leading scholars of Czech and Slovak politics, generously read the *entire* manuscript and gave me outstanding, detailed feedback.

Marcel Lang graciously sent me his (and Katharina Focht's) translations of Russian work on Soviet hockey and the rivalry between the USSR and Czechoslovakia on the ice and shared his own research on the topic. He also gave me terrific feedback on my early draft on Soviet sports and hockey.

Betsey Scheiner's edits of the entire first draft of the manuscript hugely improved the language and storytelling in every chapter. Melanie Hurley's suggestions for revising and reorganizing the first three chapters created a crisper and more accessible opening to the book.

My editor, Jessica Case of Pegasus Books, has been a pleasure to work with. She has been wonderfully helpful and responsive throughout the process. She was stupendously patient with me when I sent her an obscenely long first draft. And best of all, she has repeatedly offered great suggestions on how best to improve the manuscript.


Huge thanks also to:

My wonderful agent, Jill Marr, was an early believer in the project and is always willing to do whatever is necessary to help it succeed. Thanks also to Andrea Cavallaro for her work with Jill and the Sandra Dijkstra Literary Agency on behalf of the book's rights.

David Priess has been enthusiastic about the project from its infancy. He helped me make connections that led to my work on sports and political resistance in Czechoslovakia appearing in popular outlets. He gave me early feedback on the proposal. And he has worked hard to attract greater attention to this story, including by having me on his terrific Lawfare Blog *Chatter* podcast.

Briana Megid provided wonderful research assistance.

Charles Brock's jacket design was brilliant! It took my breath away the first time I saw it.

Thank you to Victoria Rose for substantially improving the manuscript with her copy edits, to Stephanie Marshall Ward for her terrific proofreading work, and to Maria Fernandez for coordinating production and her beautiful interior book design. Thank you to Suzie Tibor, who did spectacular work helping me acquire the book's photos, to Emily Torres for creating the excellent map of Czechoslovakia, and to Nicole Maher for her great work publicizing the book.


In addition, so much thanks to the following people who helped out in a variety of ways: Bruce Berglund, Sean Conboy, Silvester Filkorn, Pete Fitzmaurice, Amy Greene, Patrick Houda, Cornelia Levine, Lisa Little, Andrew Maraniss, Laura Mazur, Asher Minkoff, Jon Minkoff, Julian Minkoff, Miroslav Nemčok, Joe Pelletier, Yuri Slezkine, Matthew Stenberg and the UC Berkeley Eastern Europe working group, Jason Turbow, Abby Weil, and Jeremy Weinstein. Thanks also to Corrine Dugan, who lent me Daniel James Brown's *The Boys in the Boat*, which taught me a whole new way to write.

At UC Davis, I would like to acknowledge funding I received from the Department of Political Science, the Publication Assistance Fund, and the Small Grant in Aid program. I would especially like to thank my colleagues and friends Jim Adams, Jo Andrews, Amber Boydstun, Ben Highton, John Scott, Matthew Shugart, and Randy Siverson for their support. And thanks to my students whom I so feared disappointing that I ended up finding this project. Thanks also to Andy Baker for his friendship and for first introducing me to John Carlin's masterful *Playing the Enemy*, which inspired my initial interest in the overlap between politics and sports.

Most important, I thank my wonderful family. Coco, Cody, Dash, Derek, Finn, Jessica, Joe, Polly, Posie, Sarah, Scott, and Talia, I love you all. Dick and Nila Hurley, thank you for always treating me like I was your son from birth and for your never-ending support. Margaret (Buela) Chowning, thank you for all the wonderful Sunday dinners that let me escape from the madness of this project every week and for your love and friendship. BB (Mom), thank you for your love and for letting me prattle on endlessly about the project. I'm so grateful for you. My dad (Dida) died a year and a half before I completed the manuscript. In our last phone conversation, he told me how he couldn't wait to read the book. That he'll never see it is my only regret about the project, but I will forever cherish his encouragement, warmth, and love.

Melanie, Casey, and Serena (Googie/Percy), you are my world. The worst part about this book was the time I had to spend away from you. But I will be forever grateful for how you supported me throughout the journey.

Finally, I would be remiss to close without noting, *plus ça change, plus c'est la même chose* ("the more things change, the more they stay the same"). Every day, as I put the final touches on my book on the tragedy of the 1968 Soviet invasion of Czechoslovakia, I pick up the newspaper and read the latest account of the tragedy of the Russian invasion of Ukraine. All I can do is hope that it takes far less than twenty-one years for the people of Ukraine to be free of their own nightmare.

# Endnotes

**PART I: FROM WINTER TO SPRING**
1     Simon Mawer, *Prague Spring* (New York: Other Press, 2018), 214.

**CHAPTER 1: THE BUTCHER SHOP ON THIN ICE**
1     Jiří Sochr and Marie Sochrová, *Havlíčkův Brod a okolí* [Havlíčkův Brod and its surroundings] (Havlíčkův Brod: Gradat, 1992).
2     František Jirků, "Okupace 1939. Brod ovládla tichá lhostejnost." *Mladá fronta Dnes.* April 27, 2019. MAFRA.
3     Sochr and Sochrová, *Havlíčkův Brod a okolí.*
4     Jirků, "Okupace 1939."
5     Interview with Jiří Holík, September 21, 2019.
6     David Lukšů, *Žít jako Holík: Životní a hokejové zápasy Jaroslava Holíka* [Live Like Holík: The Hockey Matches of Jaroslav Holík] (Prague: Nakladatelství Epocha, 2015), 10.
7     Interview with Jiří Holík, September 21, 2019; Sochr and Sochrová, *Havlíčkův Brod a okolí*, 42.
8     Sochr and Sochrová, *Havlíčkův Brod a okolí.*
9     Lukšů, *Žít jako Holík*, 9.
10     Interview with Jiří Holík, September 21, 2019.
11     Lukšů, *Žít jako Holík*, 30.
12     Interview with Jiří Holík, September 21, 2019.
13     Lukšů, *Žít jako Holík*, 9.
14     Sochr and Sochrová, *Havlíčkův Brod a okolí*, 43.
15     Post Bellum Institute, March 21, 2016, "Jiří Holík," *Memory of Nations.* Retrieved July 11, 2019, from https://www.memoryofnations.eu/cs/Holík-Jiří-20160321-0.
16     Interview with Jiří Holík, September 21, 2019.
17     Sochr and Sochrová, *Havlíčkův Brod a okolí.*
18     Interview with Jiří Holík, September 19, 2017.
19     Interview with Jiří Holík, September 21, 2019.
20     Interview with Jiří Holík, September 21, 2019; Lukšů, *Žít jako Holík*, 9.
21     Lukšů, *Žít jako Holík*, 31.
22     Interview with Marie Holíková, September 18, 2017.
23     Lukšů, *Žít jako Holík*, 27.

24    Jaroslav Kirchner, *Dynastie Holíků* [The Holík Dynasty] (Prague: ZEMS, 2006), Jiří
      Holík, ch1; interview with Jiří Holík, September 19, 2017.

25    Interview with Jiří Holík, September 19, 2017.

26    Lukšů, *Žít jako Holík*, 18–22.

27    Lukšů, *Žít jako Holík*, 18–19; Kirchner, *Dynastie Holíků*, Jiří Holík, ch1.

28    Lukšů, *Žít jako Holík*, 31–35; Kirchner, *Dynastie Holíků*, Jiří Holík, ch1.

29    Kirchner, *Dynastie Holíků*, Jiří Holík, ch1; interview with Jiří Holík, September 19, 2017.

30    Lukšů, *Žít jako Holík*, 43.

31    David Lukšů and Aleš Palán, *Souška: Životní příběh Jana Suchého* [Souška: The Life Story
      of Jan Suchý] (Prague: Nakladatelství Epocha, 2015), ch2; Kirchner, *Dynastie Holíků*,
      Jiří Holík, ch1; Lukšů, *Žít jako Holík*, 36; interview with Jiří Holík, September 19, 2017;
      Dušan Vrbecký, *Dukla Jihlava 1956-2006: Půl století legendy* [Dukla Jihlava 1956-2006: A
      Half Century of Legends] (Jihlava: Parola, 2006), 152; Lukšů and Palán, *Souška*, ch2.

32    Kirchner, *Dynastie Holíků*, Jiří Holík, ch1; *Lukšů, Žít jako Holík*, 43; interview with Jiří
      Holík, September 19, 2017.

33    Interview with Jiří Holík, September 19, 2017.

34    Lukšů and Palán, *Souška*, chs1–2.

35    Lukšů, *Žít jako Holík*, 31; Lukšů and Palán, *Souška*, ch2; interview with Marie Holíková,
      September 18, 2017.

36    Lukšů and Palán, *Souška*, chs1–2.

37    Interview with Jiří Holík, September 21, 2017; interview with Jan Suchý, September 28,
      2019; Lukšů and Palán, *Souška*, ch2.

38    Lukšů, *Žít jako Holík*, 28; Vrbecký, *Dukla Jihlava 1956–2006*, 152; Lukšů and Palán,
      *Souška*, ch2; interview with Jan Suchý, September 18, 2017.

39    Kirchner, *Dynastie Holíků*, Jiří Holík, ch1; Vrbecký, *Dukla Jihlava*, 152; Lukšů, *Žít jako
      Holík*, 39.

40    Sochr and Sochrová, *Havlíčkův Brod a okolí*.

41    Igor Lukes, "The 1948 Coup d'État in Prague Through the Eyes of the American
      Embassy," *Diplomacy & Statecraft*, 22:3 (2011), 431–449; Tad Szulc, *Czechoslovakia Since
      World War II* (New York: The Viking Press, 1971), 29–40.

42    Szulc, *Czechoslovakia Since World War II*, 29–40.

43    Robert Evanson, "Political Repression in Czechoslovakia, 1948-1984," *Canadian Slavonic
      Papers*, Vol. 28, No. 1 (March 1986), 2–3; Igor Lukes, "Rudolf Slánský: His Trials and
      Trial," The Cold War International History Project, Working Paper #50, Woodrow
      Wilson International Center for Scholars, 14.

44    Robert Evanson, "Political Repression in Czechoslovakia, 1948-1984," *Canadian Slavonic
      Papers*, Vol. 28, No. 1 (March 1986), 5.

45    Szulc, *Czechoslovakia Since World War II*, 79–80.

46    Kirchner, *Dynastie Holíků*, Jiří Holík, ch1; interview with Jiří Holík, September 19,
      2017.

47    Interview with Jiří Holík, September 19, 2017.

48    Szulc, *Czechoslovakia Since World War II*, 79–81.

49    Hana Pichova, "The Lineup for Meat: The Stalin Statue in Prague," *Modern Language
      Association*, Vol. 123, No. 3 (May 2008), 614–631.

50    Igor Lukes, "Rudolf Slánský: His Trials and Trial," The Cold War International History
      Project, Working Paper #50, Woodrow Wilson International Center for Scholars, 16;
      Alexander Dubček, *Hope Dies Last: The Autobiography of Alexander Dubcek*, edited and
      translated by Jiří Hochman (New York: Kodansha International, 1993), 84–5.

51    Tom McEnchroe, "'Operation K'—How the Communists wiped out Czechoslovakia's monasteries in one brutal stroke," *Radio Prague International,* April 13, 2020. Viewed on June 4, 2020 at https://www.radio.cz/en/section/czech-history/operation-k-how-the -communists-wiped-out-czechoslovakias-monasteries-in-one-brutal-stroke.

52    Richard Askwith, *Today We Die a Little: The Inimitable Emil Zátopek, the Greatest Olympic Runner of All Time* (New York: Nation Books, 2016), 13–15.

53    Lukšů, *Žít jako Holík*, 10, 13–14.

54    Sochr and Sochrová, *Havlíčkův Brod a okolí*, 45-6.

55    Interview with Jiří Holík, September 21, 2019; Kirchner, *Dynastie Holíků,* Jiří Holík, ch1; Lukšů, *Žít jako Holík*, 11–12.

56    Interview with Jiří Holík, September 21, 2019.

57    Szulc, *Czechoslovakia Since World War II*, 93.

58    Szulc, *Czechoslovakia Since World War II*, 99–100.

59    Igor Lukes, "Rudolf Slánský: His Trials and Trial," The Cold War International History Project, Working Paper #50, Woodrow Wilson International Center for Scholars, 54–58.

60    Lukšů, *Žít jako Holík*, 12–14.

## CHAPTER 2: ENORMOUS FISH ON A TINY POND

1    Lukšů, *Žít jako Holík*, 26; Kirchner, *Dynastie Holíků,* Jiří Holík, ch1; interview with Jiří Holík, September 19, 2017.

2    Askwith, *Today We Die A Little*, 115–21; http://archiv.ucl.cas.cz/index.php?path =RudePravo/1950/6/10/3.png; https://echo24.cz/a/S3F7k/zatopek-spolupracoval -s-stb-podle-historiku-by-nemel-byt-modlou.

3    Askwith, *Today We Die A Little*, 97–98, 125–6, 150.

4    Askwith, *Today We Die A Little*, 98–9.

5    Askwith, *Today We Die A Little*, 106, 158–160, 195–6.

6    Lukšů, *Žít jako Holík*, 26.

7    Stephen Hardy and Andrew C. Holman, *Hockey: A Global History* (Urbana: University of Illinois Press, 2018).

8    Denis Gibbons, "The Origins of European Hockey," in *The Official Encyclopedia of the National Hockey League*, eds. Dan Diamond et al. (New York: Total Sports, 1998), 18–19.

9    Interview with Miloslav Jenšík, March 14, 2018.

10    Birger Nordmark, "Les Avants and the Bohemians: The Birth of International Hockey," in *World of Hockey: Celebrating a Century of the IIHF*, eds. Szymon Szemberg and Andrew Podnieks (Bolton: Fenn Publishing Company Ltd., 2007), 4.

11    Andrew Podnieks et al., *Kings of the Ice: A History of World Hockey* (Richmond Hill, Ontario: NDE Publishing, 2002), 287.

12    Podnieks et al., *Kings of the Ice*, 287–8; interview with Miloslav Jenšík, March 14, 2018.

13    Jaroslav Drobny, *Champion in Exile: The Autobiography of Jaroslav Drobný, Wimbledon Champion 1954*, (London: The Sportsman's Book Club, 1957), 152–5.

14    Bruce Berglund, *The Fastest Game in the World: Hockey and the Globalization of Sports* (Oakland: University of California Press, 2021), 104–108; Igor Kuperman, "The Lost Generation: The Czechoslovakian National Team of 1950," in *The Official Encyclopedia of the National Hockey League*, eds. Dan Diamond et al. (New York: Total Sports, 1998), 462–3.

15    Jonathan Bolton, *Worlds of Dissent* (Cambridge: Harvard University Press, 2012), 74–6.

16    Česká televize [Czech Broadcasting Corporation], December 11, 2008, *Milujeme hokej* [We love hockey]. Retrieved July 11, 2019, from https://www.ceskatelevize.cz/ivysilani /10170070745-milujeme-hokej and https://www.youtube.com/watch?v=cxXlBfqaZVw.

17 Interview with David Lukšů, September 27, 2017.

18 Lukšů and Palán, *Souška*, ch1; interview with Jiří Holík, September 21, 2019; Post Bellum Institute, Jiří Holík interview.

19 Lukšů, *Žít jako Holík*, 43–46; Kirchner, *Dynastie Holíků*, Jiří Holík, ch1; Vrbecký, *Dukla Jihlava*, 152.

20 Kirchner, *Dynastie Holíků*, Jiří Holík, ch1; interview with Jiří Holík, September 19, 2017.

21 Lukšů, *Žít jako Holík*, 30; Kirchner, *Dynastie Holíků*, Jiří Holík, ch2.

22 Lukšů, *Žít jako Holík*, 36.

23 Lukšů, *Žít jako Holík*, 32–33.

24 Interview with Jiří Holík, September 19, 2017.

25 Kirchner, *Dynastie Holíků*, Jaroslav Holík, 13; interview with Jan Suchý, September 18, 2017.

26 Lukšů, *Žít jako Holík*, 34; Kirchner, *Dynastie Holíků*, Jiří Holík, ch1.

27 Lukšů, *Žít jako Holík*, 31; Kirchner, *Dynastie Holíků*, Jaroslav Holík, 11–13; interview with Jiří Holík, September 19, 2017; Vrbecký, *Dukla Jihlava*, 152.

28 Lukšů, *Žít jako Holík*, 31.

29 Lukšů, *Žít jako Holík*, 29.

30 Interview with Jan Suchý, September 28, 2019; interview with Jiří Holík, September 19, 2017; Lukšů and Palán, *Souška,* ch3; Vrbecký, *Dukla Jihlava*, 146–50.

31 Lukšů and Palán, *Souška*, ch3.

32 Lukšů, *Žít jako Holík*, 18–23.

33 Lukšů, *Žít jako Holík*, 28–29; Lukšů and Palán, *Souška*, ch2; interview with Jan Suchý, September 18, 2017; Kirchner, *Dynastie Holíků*, Jiří Holík, ch1.

34 Lukšů, *Žít jako Holík*, 52–3.

35 Lukšů, *Žít jako Holík*, 51.

36 Lukšů, *Žít jako Holík*, 113.

37 Lukšů and Palán, *Souška,* chs2-3.

38 Lukšů and Palán, *Souška,* ch5.

39 Interview with Jiří Holík, September 19, 2017, September 21, 2019.

40 Lukšů and Palán, *Souška*, ch3.

41 Interview with Jan Suchý, September 18, 2017; interview with Jiří Holík, September 19, 2017; Lukšů and Palán, *Souška*, ch2; Kirchner, *Dynastie Holíků*, Jiří Holík, ch1; Lukšů, *Žít jako Holík*, 38.

42 Kirchner, *Dynastie Holíků*, Jiří Holík, ch1; Lukšů, *Žít jako Holík*, 22.

43 Lukšů, *Žít jako Holík*, 47–9.

44 Lukšů, *Žít jako Holík*, 41–2.

45 Interview with Bobby Holík, June 2017.

46 Lukšů, *Žít jako Holík*, 47.

47 Lukšů, *Žít jako Holík*, 50.

## CHAPTER 3: THE BOYS FROM BROD IN ARMY TOWN

1 Zdeněk Meitner, Petr Fiala, and Milan Řepa, *Kometa: Příběh hokejového klubu* [Kometa: Story of the Hockey Club], (Brno: Jota, 2011).

2 Interview with David Lukšů, September 24, 2017.

3 Renata Pisková, et al., *Jihlava: Historie, kultura, lidé* [Jihlava: History, Culture, People] (Prague: Nakladatelství Lidové Noviny, 2009), 657–9.

4 Citations for background on Jihlava: Interview with Michal Stehlík, March 14, 2018. Michal Stehlík, "Jihlavský kraj v procesu kolektivizace 1948–1960" ["Jihlava region during the collectivization process, 1948–1960"], in *Závěrečná fáze kolektivizace zemědělství v Československu, 1957–1960* [Final phase of agriculture collectivization in Czechoslovakia,

1957–1960], eds. Vladimír Březina and Jiří Pernas (Brno: Stilus, 2009); Pisková, et al., *Jihlava*, https://jihlava.cz/en/vismo/dokumenty2.asp?id_org=100405&id=1001; https ://mahlerfoundation.org/mahler/locations/czech-republic/jihlava/upper-square/.

5     Jaroslav Pitner, *Pohledy ze střídačky* [The Views from the Bench] (Prague, Czechoslovakia: Magnet, 1972).

6     Vrbecký, *Dukla Jihlava*, 14–15.

7     Pitner, *Pohledy ze střídačky*; Jaroslav Pitner and Pavel Novotny, *Hokejový generál vzpomíná* [The Hockey General Remembers] (Jihlava: Madagaskar, 1997); Vrbecký, *Dukla Jihlava*, 16–21, 141–5.

8     Lukšů, *Žít jako Holík*, 55–61; Lukšů and Palán, *Souška*, ch4.

9     Lukšů, *Žít jako Holík*, 62–64; Lukšů and Palán, *Souška*, ch3; interviews with Jiří Holík, September 19, 2017, September 21, 2019.

10    Miloslav Jenšík, Preface, in Lukšů, *Žít jako Holík*, 5–7; interview with Miloslav Jenšík, March 14, 2018.

11    Kirchner, *Dynastie Holíků*, Jiří Holík, ch2; interviews with Jiří Holík, September 19, 2017, September 21, 2019; Lukšů and Palán, *Souška*, ch4.

12    Kirchner, *Dynastie Holíků*, Jiří Holík, ch2; Lukšů, *Žít jako Holík*, 66–71, 74.

13    Lukšů and Palán, *Souška*, ch5.

14    Lukšů, *Žít jako Holík*, 55, 72–6, 125; interview with Jiří Holík, September 19, 2017; Pitner and Novotný, *Hokejový generál vzpomíná*, ch35.

15    Lukšů and Palán, *Souška*, 124–128.

16    Interview with Josef Horešovský, September 21, 2017; Lukšů, *Žít jako Holík*, 127–135; Lukšů and Palán, *Souška*, 110.

17    Lukšů, *Žít jako Holík*, 94–104; Lukšů and Palán, *Souška*, ch4; Kirchner, *Dynastie Holíků*, Jiří Holík, ch2; Vrbecký, *Dukla Jihlava 1956-2006*, 161–5.

18    Interview with Michal Stehlík, March 14, 2018.

19    Jaromir Jagr and Jan Smid, *Jagr: An Autobiography*, (Pittsburgh: 68 Productions, Ltd., 1997), 68; Lukšů, *Žít jako Holík*, 82–4; Lukšů and Palán, *Souška*, ch4.

20    Lukšů, *Žít jako Holík*, 86–8; Lukšů and Palán, *Souška*, ch6; Vrbecký, *Dukla Jihlava 1956-2006*, 31–3.

21    Kirchner, *Dynastie Holíků*, Jiří Holík ch2; Vrbecký, *Dukla Jihlava 1956-2006*, 34–7.

22    Kirchner, *Dynastie Holíků*, Jiří Holík, ch3

23    Lukšů, *Žít jako Holík*, 117.

24    Lukšů, *Žít jako Holík*, 85.

25    Lukšů, *Žít jako Holík*, 169; interview with Marie Holíková, September 18, 2017.

## CHAPTER 4: POKING THE BEAR

1     Pitner and Novotný, *Hokejový generál vzpomíná*, ch4.

2     Jim Riordan, "Rewriting Soviet Sports History," *Journal of Sports History*, vol. 21, number 3 (Winter 1993), 247–250; John Sanful, "The Reign of the Red: 1963–1971 Soviet National Team," in *The Official Encyclopedia of the National Hockey League*, eds. Dan Diamond et al. (New York: Total Sports, 1998), 465–8.

3     Berglund, *The Fastest Game in the World*, 98–9; Hardy and Holman, *Hockey*, 328–40; Riordan, "Rewriting Soviet Sports History," 247–250; Sanful, "The Reign of the Red."

4     I'm grateful to Marcel Lang for highlighting this point for me.

5     Lawrence Martin, *The Red Machine: The Soviet Quest to Dominate Canada's Game* (Toronto: Doubleday Canada Limited, 1990), 35; Riordan "Rewriting Soviet Sports History," 247–250.

6     Paul Harder, "Developing World Championship Ice Hockey in the U.S.S.R.: The Inside Story, 1946–1972," Master's Thesis, The Institute of European and Russian Studies,

Carleton University, Ottawa, Ontario, March 19, 2004, especially p. 8; Hardy and Holman, *Hockey*, 329; Igor Kuperman, "The Fall of the Maple Leaf and the Rise of the Star: The Soviets Blaze onto the International Scene," in *World of Hockey: Celebrating a Century of the IIHF*, eds. Szymon Szemberg and Andrew Podnieks (Bolton, Ontario: Fenn Publishing Company Ltd., 2007); Sanful, "The Reign of the Red"; https://sihr hockey.org/2020/columns/article.cfm?aid=669; Martin, *The Red Machine*, 19, 24–7; written correspondence with Marcel Lang; Podnieks et al., *Kings of the Ice*, 309–11.

7   Written correspondence with Marcel Lang; "Czechs Not Allowed to Bodycheck Russians," *Montreal Gazette*, May 1, 1948, 9; articles by Vladimir Nikanorov and Sergei Savin in *Sovietsky Sport*, March 4, 1948—translation produced by Katharina Focht and Marcel Lang; Drobny, *Champion in Exile*, 109–117; Kuperman, "The Fall of the Maple Leaf and the Rise of the Star," 36–7. Thanks to Marcel Lang for providing me with terrific descriptions of the games. Viktor Dubinin, "Great Success of the Soviet Hockey Players," *Komsomolskaya Pravda*, March 5, 1948, translation produced by Katharina Focht and Marcel Lang.

8   Harder, "Developing World Championship Ice Hockey in the U.S.S.R.," ch5; Kuperman, "The Fall of the Maple Leaf and the Rise of the Star."

9   Martin, *The Red Machine*, 19, 32, 50.

10  Hardy and Holman, *Hockey*, 330; Martin, *The Red Machine*, 33–4.

11  "Anatoly Tarasov," in Podnieks et al., *Kings of the Ice*, 355–7.

12  Berglund, *The Fastest Game in the World*, 103; Martin, *The Red Machine*, 50; Pitner, *Pohledy ze střídačky*.

13  Hardy and Holman, *Hockey*, 343; Martin, *The Red Machine*, 52; "Anatoly Tarasov," in Podnieks et al., *Kings of the Ice*, 355–7; Sanful, "The Reign of the Red."

14  Hardy and Holman, *Hockey*, 343; Martin, *The Red Machine*, 18, 82; "Anatoly Tarasov," in Podnieks et al., *Kings of the Ice*, 355–7; Sanful, "The Reign of the Red."

15  Berglund, *The Fastest Game in the World*, 101-4; Robert Edelman, *Serious Fun: A History of Spectator Sports in the USSR* (New York: Oxford University Press, 1993), 117; Harder, "Developing World Championship Ice Hockey in the U.S.S.R.," 117; Martin, *The Red Machine*, 33–4.

16  On both Chernyshev and the comparisons to Tarasov: Martin, *The Red Machine*, 26–7; Podnieks et al., *Kings of the Ice*, 309–11; Harder, "Developing World Championship Ice Hockey in the U.S.S.R.," ch5; Pitner and Novotný, *Hokejový generál vzpomíná*, ch4; correspondence with Marcel Lang; Marcel Lang, "Stalinist Purge and Canadian Hockey: The Life and Times of Arkadi Ivanovich Chernyshov," https://hfboards.mandatory.com /articles/stalinist-purge-and-canadian-hockey-the-life-and-times-of-arkadi-ivanovich -chernyshov.2620/.

17  Berglund, *The Fastest Game in the World*, 96–7; Edelman, *Serious Fun*, 139; Harder, "Developing World Championship Ice Hockey in the U.S.S.R."; Hardy and Holman, *Hockey*, 331; Kuperman, "The Fall of the Maple Leaf and the Rise of the Star"; Podnieks et al., *Kings of the Ice*, 289–292.

18  Kuperman, "The Fall of the Maple Leaf and the Rise of the Star;" Podnieks et al., *Kings of the Ice*, 289–292.

19  Berglund, *The Fastest Game in the World*, 103; Edelman, *Serious Fun*, 139–40; Harder, ch5; Sanful, "The Reign of the Red."

20  John Soares, "Cold War, Hot Ice: International Ice Hockey 1947–1980," *Journal of Sport History*, Vol. 34, No. 2 (Summer 2007), 207–230.

21  Harder, ch5; Berglund, *The Fastest Game in the World*, 121.

22  Harder, ch5; Hardy and Holman, *Hockey*, 340; Igor Kuperman, "Tarasov's Unstoppable Dynasty: The 'Big Red Machine' Wins Nine Consecutive Gold Medals," in *World of*

*Hockey: Celebrating a Century of the IIHF*, eds. Szymon Szemberg and Andrew Podnieks (Bolton, Ontario: Fenn Publishing Company Ltd., 2007); Martin, *The Red Machine*, 80; Sanful, "The Reign of the Red"; "Arkady Cheryshev" and "Anatoly Tarasov" in Podnieks et al., *Kings of the Ice*, 309-311, 355-358; Pitner, *Pohledy ze střídačky*.

23    Berglund, *The Fastest Game in the World*, 100, 121–2; Edelman, *Serious Fun*, 139–40; Martin, *The Red Machine*, 21, 52–3; Sanful, "The Reign of the Red."

24    Martin, *The Red Machine*, 71, 85; *Kings of the Ice*, 351–4.

25    Interview with Jan Havel, September 21, 2017; *Kings of the Ice*, 457–8; Robert Záruba from the Czech TV commentary accompanying the 50th anniversary replay of the March 30, 1969, World Championships match between Czechoslovakia and Sweden.

26    Berglund, *The Fastest Game in the World*, 108.

27    Mikhail Prozumenschikov, "Soviet-Czechoslovak Ice Hockey Politics," Woodrow Wilson International Center for Scholars Cold War International History Project Working Paper #69 (2014); *The (Inter-Communist) Cold War on Ice: Soviet-Czechoslovak Ice Hockey Politics, 1967–1969*, 94; Katharina Focht and Marcel Lang translation of Stanislav Gridasov blog at https://www.sports.ru/tribuna/blogs/prosport/2944995.html that draws from "Notes of the Commitee for Physical Culture and Sports under the Council of Ministers of the USSR in the Central Committee of the CPSU on the results of the participation of the Soviet sports delegation in the 7th Winter Olympic Games." February 27, 1956. Secret. RGANI F. 5. O 47. D. 167. L. 31-41. (RGANI = Rossiyskiy gosudarstvenny arkhiv noveyshey istorii / Russian State Archive of Contemporary History).

28    Katharina Focht and Marcel Lang translation of Alexander Gorbunov, *Anatoly Tarasov* (Moscow: Molodaya gvardiya, 2015); Hardy and Holman, *Hockey: A Global History*, 341–2; Kuperman, "The Fall of the Maple Leaf and the Rise of the Star"; Szymon Szemberg, "The Unheralded Miracle of 1960," in *World of Hockey: Celebrating a Century of the IIHF*, eds. Szymon Szemberg and Andrew Podnieks (Bolton, Ontario: Fenn Publishing Company Ltd., 2007), 39.

29    Prozumenschikov, "Soviet-Czechoslovak Ice Hockey Politics," 93; interview with Oldřich Tůma, March 13, 2018; Oldřich Tůma (translated by Jiří Mareš), "'They had no tanks this time and they got four goals': The hockey events in Czechoslovakia in 1969 and the fall of Alexander Dubček," Woodrow Wilson International Center for Scholars Cold War International History Project Working Paper #69 (2014), *The (Inter-Communist) Cold War on Ice: Soviet-Czechoslovak Ice Hockey Politics, 1967-1969*, 15-6.

30    Jim Coleman, "World of Sport" column, *Calgary Herald*, March 24, 1969, 9.

31    Kirchner, *Dynastie Holíků* Jiří Holík, ch2.

32    Pitner and Novotný, *Hokejový generál vzpomíná*, ch4.

33    Tal Pinchevsky, *Breakaway: From Behind the Iron Curtain to the NHL—The Untold Story of Hockey's Great Escapes* (New York: HarperCollins Publishers, 2013), 10.

34    Dubček, *Hope Dies Last*, 105–6, 114–5; Mark Kurlansky, *1968: The Year That Rocked the World* (New York: Ballantine Books, 2003), (Kindle location 575–576); Kenneth N. Skoug, Jr., *Czechoslovakia's Lost Fight for Freedom, 1967–1969: An American Embassy Perspective* (Westport: Praeger, 1999), 29; Szulc, *Czechoslovakia Since World War II*, 242–7.

35    Interview with Jan Suchý, September 18, 2017; interview with Jiří Holík, September 19, 2017; interview with Peter Stastny, March 7, 2018; Lukšů, *Žít jako Holík*, 82.

36    Lukšů, *Žít jako Holík*, 82–84.

37    Interview with Miloslav Jenšík, March 14, 2018.

38    Pitner and Novotný, *Hokejový generál vzpomíná*, ch4.

39    Interview with Jiří Holík, September 19, 2017.

40   https://theathletic.com/1315421/2019/11/11/Václav-Nedomanskýs-hall-of-fame
     -journey-started-with-a-secret-dash-to-freedom-in-1974/; https://www.si.com/hockey
     /news/meet-big-ned-the-international-hockey-legend-you-never-knew.

41   Pitner, *Pohledy ze střídačky*; Pitner and Novotný, *Hokejový generál vzpomíná*, ch4; https
     ://icehockey.fandom.com/wiki/1967_Centennial_Tournament.

42   Pitner, *Pohledy ze střídačky*; Pitner and Novotný, *Hokejový generál vzpomíná*, ch4.

43   Podnieks et al., *Kings of the Ice*, 401–2; Sanful, "The Reign of the Red."

44   Kuperman, "Tarasov's Unstoppable Dynasty," 52.

45   The Czech TV rebroadcast of the game with commentary from recent years can be found
     at https://www.youtube.com/watch?v=BisXp5fzjFU.

46   Lukšů and Palán, *Souška*, ch9.

47   Kirchner, *Dynastie Holíků*, 11.

48   Lukšů, *Žít jako Holík*, 182.

49   Lukšů, *Žít jako Holík*, 153–7; Pitner and Novotný, *Hokejový generál vzpomíná*, ch5; Tůma,
     "They had no tanks this time and they got four goals," 16.

50   Mark Kramer (translation and introduction), "Cable from the Soviet Embassy in Prague
     about Soviet-Czechoslovak Tensions, April 1, 1967," Woodrow Wilson International
     Center for Scholars Cold War International History Project Working Paper #69 (2014);
     *The (Inter-Communist) Cold War on Ice: Soviet-Czechoslovak Ice Hockey Politics, 1967–
     1969*, 114.

51   Robert Záruba commentary at the Czech TV rebroadcast of the game at https://www
     .youtube.com/watch?v=BisXp5fzjFU.

## CHAPTER 5: THE PRAGUE SPRING

1    Pavel Barta and Robert Záruba commentary (at the 1:56:00 mark) on the re-airing of the
     match at Czech TV: https://www.youtube.com/watch?v=BisXp5fzjFU; Pitner, *Pohledy ze
     střídačky*; Kirchner, *Dynastie Holíků*, Jiří Holík, ch2.

2    Cable from the Soviet Embassy in Prague about Soviet-Czechoslovak Tensions, April 1967,
     Translated and Introduced by Mark Kramer in Woodrow Wilson International Center
     for Scholars Cold War International History Project Working Paper #69 (2014), *The
     (Inter-Communist) Cold War on Ice: Soviet-Czechoslovak Ice Hockey Politics, 1967-1969*,
     110-6.

3    Tůma, "They had no tanks this time and they got four goals," 15–8.

4    Lukšů, *Žít jako Holík*, 158-60; interview with Miloslav Jenšík, March 14, 2018.

5    Pitner and Novotný, *Hokejový generál vzpomíná*.

6    Lukšů, *Žít jako Holík*, 158–60.

7    Dubček, *Hope Dies Last*, 49, 61.

8    Dubček, *Hope Dies Last*, 70.

9    Dubček, *Hope Dies Last*, 71–3.

10   Dubček, *Hope Dies Last*, 74-85; Igor Lukes, "Rudolf Slánský: His Trials and Trial,"
     The Cold War International History Project, Working Paper #50, Woodrow Wilson
     International Center for Scholars, 59.

11   Dubček, *Hope Dies Last*, 74–83.

12   Dubček, *Hope Dies Last*, 85.

13   Karel Hrolik, "Reds Reduce Czechoslovakia to Status of Mission Land," *The Catholic
     Transcript*, July 4, 1963, 8; Kurlansky, *1968*, location 643–650.

14   Tůma, "They had no tanks this time," 16.

15   Szulc, *Czechoslovakia Since World War II*, 225–235.

16    Michael Polák, "Street Politics: Student Demonstrations in Prague in the 1960s and the
      Disintegration of the ČSM University Structures," *Czech Journal of Contemporary History*,
      Vol. 8 (2020), 63–4; Szulc, *Czechoslovakia Since World War II*, 247–50.

17    Kieran Williams, *The Prague Spring and its Aftermath: Czechoslovak Politics 1968-1970*
      (New York: Cambridge University Press, 1997), 63–4.

18    Phil Carradice, *Prague Spring 1968: Warsaw Pact Invasion* (South Yorkshire: Pen & Sword
      Books, 2019); Kurlansky, *1968*.

19    Vladimír Kostka, "Czechoslovakia," in James Riordan (ed.) *Sport Under Communism: The
      U.S.S.R., Czechoslovakia, The G.D.R., China, Cuba* (Montreal: McGill-Queen's University
      Press, 1978), 65; Berglund, *The Fastest Game in the World*, 140.

20    Karel Gut and Jaroslav Prchal, *100 let českého hokeje* [100 years of Czech hockey] (Prague:
      AS Press, 2008), 177.

21    Lukšů and Palán, *Souška*, ch9.

22    Interview with Jiří Holík, September 19, 2017; interview with Jan Suchý, September 28,
      2019; Lukšů and Palán, *Souška*, ch9.

23    Pitner, *Pohledy ze střídačky*; Pitner and Novotný, *Hokejový generál vzpomíná*, ch4.

24    Interview with Jiří Holík, September 19, 2017; Lukšů, *Žít jako Holík*, 153–7; Pitner and
      Novotný, *Hokejový generál vzpomíná*, ch4; Jaroslav Pitner in Dušan Vrbecký, *Dukla Jihlava
      1956-2006: Půl Století legendy* [Dukla Jihlava 1956-2006: A Half Century of Legends].
      (Jihlava: Parola 2006), 141–5.

25    Lukšů, *Žít jako Holík*, 150; interview with Bobby Holík, June 22, 2017; interview with
      Jiří Holík, September 19, 2017; interview with Marie Holíková, September 18, 2017;
      interview with Peter Stastny, March 7, 2018.

26    https://www.youtube.com/watch?v=UYRX2qNrECI.

27    Lukšů, *Žít jako Holík*, 158–60.

28    Pitner, *Pohledy ze střídačky*.

29    https://www.youtube.com/watch?v=UYRX2qNrECI.

30    https://www.youtube.com/watch?v=UYRX2qNrECI.

31    Pitner, *Pohledy ze střídačky*; "Canada Can Win Gold Medal With Victory Over Russia,"
      *Ottowa Journal*, February 16, 1968, 17; "Czechs 'Spoil' Russians: Hockey Streak Broken,"
      *The Argus*, Friday, February 16, 1968, 11; "Russians Upended By Czechs," *Calgary Herald*,
      February 16, 1968, 25.

32    Pitner and Novotný, *Hokejový generál vzpomíná*.

33    Pitner, *Pohledy ze střídačky*.

34    https://www.youtube.com/watch?v=UYRX2qNrECI.

35    Pitner, *Pohledy ze střídačky*; *Kings of the Ice*, 353.

36    Pitner, *Pohledy ze střídačky*; interview with Jan Havel, September 21, 2017; interview with
      Josef Horesovsky, September 21, 2017.

37    Williams, *The Prague Spring and its Aftermath*, 14, 67.

38    https://www.theguardian.com/world/2018/jul/22/observer-archive-the-prague-spring
      -27-july-1968.

39    Kurlansky, *1968*, (Kindle location 699-706); Skoug, Jr., *Czechoslovakia's Lost Fight for
      Freedom*, 61–3.

40    Kurlansky, *1968*, ch17 (Kindle location 4421–4423).

41    Pisková, et al., 2009; *Jihlava*, 651–6.

42    Dubček, *Hope Dies Last*, 101, 169.

43    Carradice, *Prague Spring 1968*, 52; Dubček, *Hope Dies Last*, 137–73; Kurlansky, *1968*,
      (Kindle location 4304–5), 746–747.

44    Jiri Valenta, "The Bureaucratic Politics Paradigm and the Soviet Invasion of
      Czechoslovakia," *Political Science Quarterly*, Vol. 94, No. 1 (Spring, 1979), 66.
45    Dubček, *Hope Dies Last*, 173–5; Kurlansky, *1968*, ch17.

**PART II: THEY'RE HERE**
1     Bolton, *Worlds of Dissent*, 7–8.

**CHAPTER 6: INVASION**
1     Interviews with Marie Holíková, September 18, 2017, September 28, 2019.
2     Alan Levy, *So Many Heroes* (New York: The Permanent Press, 2015), ch12 (Kindle
      location 3877).
3     Robert Littell (ed.), *The Czech Black Book: An Eyewitness Documented Account of the Invasion
      of Czechoslovakia*, (New York: Praeger, 1969), 6; Levy, ch12 (Kindle location 3683–3704).
4     Kurlansky, *1968*, ch17 (Kindle location 5139).
5     Pinchevsky, *Breakaway*, 1.
6     Rudiger Wenzke, "The Role and Activities of the SED, the East German State and Its
      Military During the 'Prague Spring' of 1968," in M. Mark Stolarik, ed., *The Prague Spring
      and the Warsaw Pact Invasion of Czechoslovakia, 1968: Forty Years Later* (Mundelein, IL:
      Bolchazy-Carducci Publishers, Inc., 2010), 151–8.
7     Ruud Van Dijk (ed.), *Encyclopedia of the Cold War* (New York: Routledge, 2008), 718; Jan Kaplan
      and Krystyna Nosarzewska, *Prague: The Turbulent Century* (Cologne: Konemann, 1997), 325.
8     William Shawcross, *Dubček* (New York: Simon and Schuster/Touchstone, 1990), 152;
      Szulc, *Czechoslovakia Since World War II*, 380.
9     Szulc, *Czechoslovakia Since World War II*, 381-2; Kurlansky, ch17 (Kindle location 5145).
10    Dubček, *Hope Dies Last*, 181.
11    Szulc, *Czechoslovakia Since World War II*, 381; Levy, ch12 (Kindle location 3933).
12    Kurlansky, *1968*, ch17 (Kindle location 5101–5109).
13    Szulc, *Czechoslovakia Since World War II*, 385.
14    It was widely reported that the young man was killed, but according to state police reports
      no one was killed in front of the headquarters. It seems likely that the young man was
      hit in the head, brought to the hospital, and then lived several more years. See Milan
      Barta, Lukas Cvrcek, Patrik Kosicky, and Vitezslav Sommer, *Victims of the Occupation:
      The Warsaw Pact Invasion of Czechoslovakia: 21 August-31 December 1968* (Prague: The
      Institute for the Study of Totalitarian Regimes, 2008), 35, 70, fn. 8.
15    Zdeněk Mlynář, *Nightfrost in Prague: The End of Humane Socialism*, trans. Paul Wilson
      (New York: Karz, 1980), 176–177; Bolton, *Worlds of Dissent*, 9.
16    Szulc, *Czechoslovakia Since World War II*, 384–5.
17    Littell, *Czech Black Book*, 19.
18    Dubček, *Hope Dies Last*, 182–3; Williams, *The Prague Spring and its Aftermath*, 51.
19    Shawcross, *Dubček*, 154.
20    Dubček, *Hope Dies Last*, 183–6.
21    Shawcross, *Dubček*, 154.
22    Williams, *The Prague Spring and its Aftermath*, 121–7; Kurlansky, ch17 (Kindle location
      5093–5099, 5120–5127).
23    Williams, *The Prague Spring and its Aftermath*, 132.
24    Szulc, *Czechoslovakia Since World War II*, 383–4.
25    Levy, *So Many Heroes*, ch11 (Kindle location 3775–3824). The general idea is also
      reproduced in Mawer, *Prague Spring*, 330.

26   Szulc, *Czechoslovakia Since World War II*, 390-1

27   Clyde Farnsworth, "People of Prague Scream Defiance at the Tanks," *New York Times*, August 22, 1968, 1.

28   Kurlansky, *1968*, ch17 (Kindle location 5155); Szulc, *Czechoslovakia Since World War II*, 390–1; Bolton, *Worlds of Dissent*, 10.

29   Szulc, *Czechoslovakia Since World War II*, 385–6.

30   Farnsworth, "People of Prague Scream Defiance at the Tanks," 16.

31   Levy, *So Many Heroes*, ch12 (Kindle location 4058–4065).

32   Szulc, *Czechoslovakia Since World War II*, 392–3; *Czech Black Book*, 31.

33   Barta et al., *Victims of the Occupation*, 35; Levy, ch12 (Kindle location 4109); Kurlansky, ch17 (Kindle location 5154–5168).

34   Farnsworth, "People of Prague Scream Defiance at the Tanks," 1, 16.

35   Farnsworth, "People of Prague Scream Defiance at the Tanks," 1.

36   Farnsworth, "People of Prague Scream Defiance at the Tanks," 16.

37   Littell, *Czech Black Book*, 50.

38   Littell, *Czech Black Book*, 50.

39   Littell, *Czech Black Book*, 39.

40   Skoug, Jr., *Czechoslovakia's Lost Fight for Freedom*, 143.

41   Williams, *The Prague Spring and its Aftermath*, 128.

42   Szulc, *Czechoslovakia Since World War II*, 394; Littell, *Czech Black Book*, 35.

43   Amos Chapple, "Invasion: the Crushing of the Prague Spring," *Radio Free Europe Radio Liberty*, August 10, 2018. https://www.rferl.org/a/crushing-of-prague-spring-1968/29420107.html; Farnsworth, "People of Prague Scream Defiance at the Tanks," 1, 16.

44   Bolton, *Worlds of Dissent*, 10.

45   Barta et al., *Victims of the Occupation*, 165; Kurlansky, ch17 (Kindle location 5168–5176).

46   Interviews with Josef Horešovský, September 21, 2017, March 8, 2018; interview with Jan Havel, September 21, 2017.

47   Alan Taylor, "Photos: 50 Years Since a Soviet Invasion Ended the Prague Spring," *The Atlantic*, August 20, 2018. https://www.theatlantic.com/photo/2018/08/photos-50-years-since-a-soviet-invasion-ended-the-prague-spring/567916/.

48   Szulc, *Czechoslovakia Since World War II*, 395.

49   Farnsworth, "People of Prague Scream Defiance at the Tanks," 16.

50   Levy, *So Many Heroes*, (Kindle location 4503).

51   Littell, *Czech Black Book*, 70–1.

52   Pinchevsky, *Breakaway*, 3

53   Littell, *Czech Black Book*, 60; Levy, ch14 (Kindle location 4576–4589).

54   Harold Gordon Skilling, *Czechoslovakia's Interrupted Revolution* (Princeton: Princeton University Press, 1976), 776.

55   Kaplan and Nosarzewska, *Prague*, 327.

56   M. Mark Stolarik, "Introduction," in M. Mark Stolarik, ed., *The Prague Spring and the Warsaw Pact Invasion of Czechoslovakia, 1968: Forty Years Later* (Mundelein, IL: Bolchazy-Carducci Publishers, Inc., 2010), xiii.

57   Levy, *So Many Heroes*, (Kindle location 4170–4192); Kurlansky, *1968*, ch17 (Kindle location 5184); Barta et al., *Victims of the Occupation*, 15.

58   Kurlansky, *1968*, ch17 (Kindle location 5237); Szulc, 395.

59   Kaplan and Nosarzewska, *Prague*, 324.

60   Levy, *So Many Heroes*, ch14 (Kindle location 4668).

61   Levy, *So Many Heroes*, chs13–14 (Kindle location 4213, 46970).

62    Interview with Miloslav Jenšík, March 14, 2018.

63    Skilling, *Czechoslovakia's Interrupted Revolution*, 773.

64    Barta et al., *Victims of the Occupation*, 134, 151; Pisková, et al., *Jihlava*, 651–656.

65    Interviews with Marie Holíková, September 18, 2017, September 28, 2019.

66    Kirchner, *Dynastie Holíků*, Jaroslav Holík, ch3, 30; interviews with Marie Holíková, September 18, 2017, September 28, 2019.

67    Interview with Jiří Holík, September 21, 2019; Kirchner, *Dynastie Holíků*, Jaroslav Holík, ch3, 30.

68    Interview with Jan Suchý, September 28, 2019; Kirchner, *Dynastie Holíků*, Jiří Holík, ch3.

69    Interview with Jan Suchý, September 28, 2019; Interview with Jiří Holík, September 21, 2019; Kirchner, *Dynastie Holíků*, Jiří Holík, ch3.

70    Kirchner, *Dynastie Holíků*, Jaroslav Holík, ch3, 30.

71    Interview with Jiří Holík, September 21, 2019; interview with Jan Suchý, September 28, 2019; Lukšů, *Žít jako Holík*, 109–110; Kirchner, *Dynastie Holíků*, Jiří Holík, ch3.

## CHAPTER 7: ON FIRE

1    Kaplan and Nosarzewska, *Prague*, 775; Williams, *The Prague Spring and its Aftermath*, 132–3.

2    Kurlansky, *1968*, ch17 (Kindle location 5189–5202).

3    Kurlansky, *1968*, (Kindle location 5247–5279).

4    Mitchell Lerner, "'Trying to Find the Guy Who Invited Them': Lyndon Johnson, Bridge Building, and the End of the Prague Spring," *Diplomatic History*, Vol. 32, No. 1 (January 2008), 77–103.

5    Szulc, *Czechoslovakia Since World War II*, 399–400.

6    https://www.upi.com/Archives/1968/08/21/LBJ-urges-Soviets-to-leave-Czech -soil/3214613850584/.

7    Szulc, *Czechoslovakia Since World War II*, 400–1.

8    Williams, *The Prague Spring and its Aftermath*, 132–3.

9    Dubček, *Hope Dies Last*, 187–214.

10   Dubček, *Hope Dies Last*, 187–214; Kurlansky, *1968*, ch17 (Kindle location 5312–5413); Shawcross, *Dubček*, 155–61; Skilling, *Czechoslovakia's Interrupted Revolution*, 803–8; Szulc, *Czechoslovakia Since World War II*, 413–33; Williams, *The Prague Spring and Its Aftermath*, 135–143.

11   Szulc, *Czechoslovakia Since World War II*, 433.

12   Szulc, *Czechoslovakia Since World War II*, 436–7; Williams, *The Prague Spring and Its Aftermath*, 146.

13   Williams, *The Prague Spring and Its Aftermath*, 147, 158.

14   Szulc, *Czechoslovakia Since World War II*, 455–8.

15   Harry Blutstein, *Games of Discontent: Protests, Boycotts, and Politics at the 1968 Mexico Olympics* (Montreal & Kingston: McGill-Queen's University Press, 2021), ch10; https ://www.idnes.cz/wiki/sport/vera-caslavska.K459064; https://www.latimes.com /archives/la-xpm-1990-04-05-sp-900-story.html; https://www.politico.com/magazine /story/2018/09/05/nfl-players-anthem-protest-cold-war-219632/; https://www.nytimes .com/2016/09/01/sports/olympics/vera-caslavska-gymnast-soviets-czechoslovakia-dead .html; https://www.wilsoncenter.org/blog-post/forgotten-protest; https://www.bbc.com /sport/olympics/45900544.

16   Szulc, *Czechoslovakia Since World War II*, 463–4.

17   Carradice, *The Prague Spring*, 91-102; Dubček, *Hope Dies Last*, 215-36; Shawcross, *Dubček*, 161-176; Skilling, *Czechoslovakia's Interrupted Revolution*, 801-819; Szulc,

*Czechoslovakia Since World War II*, 435–473; https://sg.news.yahoo.com/fifty-years-ago
-soviet-tanks-crush-prague-spring-042500956.html; Williams, *The Prague Spring and Its
Aftermath*, 144–198.

18  Shawcross, *Dubček*, 175–6.

19  Lukšů and Palán, *Souška*, ch7; interview with Jiří Holík, September 21, 2019; interview
with Jan Suchý, September 28, 2019.

20  Pisková, *Jihlava*, 651–656.

21  Interview with Jan Suchý, September 28, 2019.

22  Kirchner, *Dynastie Holíků*, Jiří Holík, ch3; interview with Jiří Holík, September 21, 2019;
Lukšů and Palán, *Souška*, ch5.

23  Vrbecký, *Dukla Jihlava*, 146–50.

24  Dubček, *Hope Dies Last*, 236.

25  Interview with Josef Horešovský, September 21, 2017.

26  Interview with Jiří Holík, September 19, 2017, September 21, 2019; interview with Josef
Horešovský, September 21, 2017.

27  Pitner and Novotný, *Hokejový generál vzpomíná*, ch9; Vrbecký, *Dukla Jihlava 1956–2006*,
141–5.

28  Josef Černý and Jozef Golonka from the commentary accompanying the 50th anniversary
replay (March 21, 1969) of the first game against the Soviets on Czech TV.

29  Dan Diamond, et al., *The Official Encyclopedia of the National Hockey League* (New York:
Total Sports, 1998), 505.

30  Interview with Terry O'Malley, September 13, 2017.

31  Pitner and Novotný, *Hokejový generál vzpomíná*, ch9; Lukšů, *Žít jako Holík*, 162.

32  Martin, *The Red Machine: The Soviet Quest to Dominate Canada's Game* (Toronto:
Doubleday Canada Limited, 1990), 92.

33  Martin, *The Red Machine*, 97.

34  Martin, *The Red Machine*, 157.

35  Martin, *The Red Machine*, 93.

36  Kirchner, *Dynastie Holíků*, Jiří Holík, ch3.

37  Interview with Morris Mott, July 6, 2017.

38  Documentary video *Razítko na normalizaci* [*Stamp on Normalization*] at https://www
.ceskatelevize.cz/porady/12387474945-archiv-d/219471294071011/.

39  Interview with Jiří Holík, September 21, 2019.

40  Josef Černý and Jozef Golonka from the commentary accompanying the 50th anniversary
replay (March 21, 1969) of the first game against the Soviets on Czech TV; interviews
with Jiří Holík, September 19, 2017, September 21, 2019; interview with Morris Mott,
July 6, 2017; interviews with Jan Suchý, September 18, 2017, September 28, 2019.

41  Documentary video *Razítko na normalizaci* [*Stamp on Normalization*] at https://www
.ceskatelevize.cz/porady/12387474945-archiv-d/219471294071011/.

42  Lukšů, *Žít jako Holík*, 185.

43  Kirchner, *Dynastie Holíků*, 32.

44  Lukšů, *Žít jako Holík*, 162.

## CHAPTER 8: YOU SEND TANKS, WE BRING GOALS

1  Interview with Terry O'Malley, September 13, 2017.

2  Martin, *The Red Machine*, 94.

3  http://webarchive.iihf.com/iihf-home/the-iihf/100-year-anniversary/100-top-stories
/story-18/.

4    For two of many examples, see "Czechs Upset Russians in Hockey 'Hate Match.'" *Chicago Tribune*, March 22, 1969, 1. "Czechs win hate match, refuse to shake with Russian losers: 'Tonight, Even Tanks Won't Help,'" *Toronto Globe and Mail*, March 22, 1969, 1.

5    John Soares, "Complexity in Soviet-Czechoslovak Hockey Relations," *The (Inter-Communist) Cold War on Ice: Soviet-Czechoslovak Ice Hockey Politics, 1967–1969*, 10; "Fires Burn Late in Wenceslas Square: Czechs Upset Russians 2-0," *Ottowa Journal*, March 22, 1969, 14.

6    Shawcross, *Dubček*, 177.

7    Peter Dahlen and Tobias Stark, "Political Resistance on Ice: The 1969 Ice Hockey World Championship in the Swedish and Norwegian Press," in *The Nordic Media and the Cold War*, eds. Henrik G. Bastiansen and Rolf Werenskjold (Goteborg: Nordicom, 2015), 173.

8    Tůma, "They had no tanks this time."

9    Robert Záruba from the commentary accompanying the 50th anniversary replay (March 21, 1969) of the first game against the Soviets on Czech TV.

10   Dahlen and Stark, "Political Resistance on Ice," 173.

11   Interview with Jan Suchý, September 18, 2017.

12   Soares, "Complexity in Soviet-Czechoslovak Hockey Relations," 10.

13   Václav Pacina, "Hokejová pomsta za okupaci" ["Hockey Revenge for the Occupation"], *iDNES Sport*, March 25, 2004, available at https://www.idnes.cz/hokej/ms-2004 /hokejova-pomsta-za-okupaci.A040325_111628_reprezentace_rav. Also, Robert Záruba from the commentary accompanying the 50th anniversary replay of the game on Czech TV.

14   "Fired-up Czechs upset Russia 2-0," *The Montreal Gazette*, March 22, 1969, 26; "Fires Burn Late in Wenceslas Square: Czechs Upset Russians 2-0," *Ottowa Journal*, March 22, 1969, 14.

15   Martin, *The Red Machine*, 94.

16   Jim Coleman, "World of Sport" column, *Calgary Herald*, March 21, 1969, 14.

17   Jozef Golonka from the commentary accompanying the 50th anniversary replay (March 21, 1969) of the first game against the Soviets on Czech TV; documentary video *Razítko na normalizaci* [Stamp on Normalization] at https://www.ceskatelevize.cz/porady /12387474945-archiv-d/219471294071011/.

18   Lukšů, *Žít jako Holík*, 121.

19   *Of Miracles and Men*, directed by Jonathan Hock (part of ESPN's *30 for 30* series).

20   https://www.iihf.com/IIHFMvc/media/Downloads/Regulations/2019/2019-IIHF -Championship-Regulations-FINAL-VERSION.pdf: "5.5.4 Pre-Game Ceremony Approximately 2 minutes before the scheduled starting time of a game and during the playing of the Championship music, both teams will enter the ice surface one after the other, and stand on their respective blue lines with the referee(s) and linesmen standing in front of the timekeeper's bench. Team captains will come forward to the game officials, exchange pennants, and shake hands while the announcer introduces the starting line ups. Then the teams skate to their goalies and then back to the bench, with only the starting players remaining on the ice. The opening faceoff shall take place at the exact game start time. For precise timing see the IIHF Pre- and PostGame Countdown."

21   Jan Havel from the commentary accompanying the replaying of the game on Czech TV.

22   Pitner and Novotný, *Hokejový generál vzpomíná*, ch9; interview with Jiří Holík, September 19, 2017; interview with Josef Horešovský, September 21, 2017.

23   Interview with Oldřich Tůma, March 13, 2018.

24   Pacina, "Hokejová pomsta za okupaci." Also, Robert Záruba from the commentary accompanying the 50th anniversary replay of the game on Czech TV.

25 Interview with Jiří Holík, September 21, 2019; Kirchner, *Dynastie Holíků*; Lukšů, *Žít jako Holík*, 162.

26 Lukšů, *Žít jako Holík*, 162.

27 Lukšů and Palán, *Souška*, ch9; Lukšů, *Žít jako Holík*, 162.

28 Jiří Holík from the commentary accompanying the 50th anniversary replay (March 28, 2019) of the second game against the Soviets on Czech TV.

29 Interview with Josef Horešovský, March 8, 2018.

30 Josef Černý and Jozef Golonka from the commentary accompanying the 50th anniversary replay of the game on Czech TV.

31 Josef Horešovský from the commentary accompanying the 50th anniversary replay (March 28, 2019) of the second game against the Soviets on Czech TV.

32 Interview with Canadian player Morris Mott, July 6, 2017, and Canadian player Terry O'Malley, September 13, 2017.

33 Interview with David Lukšů, March 14, 2018.

34 Lukšů, *Žít jako Holík*, 182.

35 Lukšů, *Žít jako Holík*, 113.

36 Interview with Jozef Golonka, March 12, 2018; interview with David Lukšů, September 24, 2017.

37 Oldřich Tůma, "'They had no tanks this time"; documentary video *Razítko na normalizaci* [*Stamp on Normalization*] at https://www.ceskatelevize.cz/porady/12387474945 -archiv-d/219471294071011/.

38 Interview with Canadian player Morris Mott, July 6, 2017.

39 Robert Záruba from the commentary accompanying the 50th anniversary replay (March 21, 1969) of the first game against the Soviets on Czech TV

40 Jan Havel in "Cold War On Ice: How Czechoslovakia's Hockey Team Avenged Soviet Invasion 50 Years Ago," created by Stuart Greer for Radio Free Europe Radio Liberty, released on March 21, 2019 at https://www.rferl.org/a/cold-war-on-ice-how -czechoslovakia-hockey-team-beat-soviets/29832512.html.

41 Robert Záruba from the commentary accompanying the 50th anniversary replay (March 21, 1969) of the first game against the Soviets on Czech TV.

42 Interview with Miloslav Jenšík, March 14, 2018.

43 Martin, *The Red Machine*, 94-5.

44 Martin, *The Red Machine*, 94.

45 Martin, *The Red Machine*, 95.

46 Martin, *The Red Machine*, 95.

47 Robert Záruba from the commentary accompanying the 50th anniversary replay (March 21, 2019) of the first game against the Soviets on Czech TV.

## CHAPTER 9: BLACKED OUT STARS

1 Pitner and Novotný, *Hokejový generál vzpomíná*, ch9.

2 Interview with Jan Suchý, September 18, 2017.

3 Interview with Canadian hockey player Terry O'Malley, September 13, 2017.

4 Interview with Jan Havel, September 21, 2017; "Cold War On Ice," Radio Free Europe Radio Liberty.

5 Interview with Jiří Holík, September 21, 2019; interviews with Jan Suchý, September 18, 2017, September 28, 2019; Kirchner, *Dynastie Holíků*, Jiří Holík, ch3; Jan Suchý autobiography, ch9.

6 Gorbunov, *Anatoli Tarasov*; Pitner and Novotný, *Hokejový generál vzpomíná*, ch9.

7   Martin, *The Red Machine*, 95.

8   Česká televize [Czech Broadcasting Corporation]. (December 11, 2008). *Milujeme hokej* [We love hockey]. Retrieved July 11, 2019, from https://www.ceskatelevize.cz/ivysilani/10170070745 -milujeme-hokej and https://www.youtube.com/watch?v=cxXlBfqaZVw.

9   Pitner and Novotný, *Hokejový generál vzpomíná*, ch9.

10  Pitner, *Pohledy ze střídačky*.

11  Martin, *The Red Machine*, 95–6.

12  Interview with Josef Horešovský, September 21, 2017.

13  Robert Záruba from the commentary accompanying the 50th anniversary replay (March 21, 2019) of the first game against the Soviets on Czech TV.

14  "Fired-up Czechs upset Russia 2–0," *The Montreal Gazette*, March 22, 1969, 26.

15  "Czechs Upset Russians in Hockey 'Hate Match,'" *Chicago Tribune*, March 22, 1969, 1.

16  "Czechs win hate match, refuse to shake with Russian losers: 'Tonight, Even Tanks Won't Help,'" *Toronto Globe and Mail*, March 22, 1969, 1.

17  Quoted in unpublished 2015 Abigail Weil Harvard University manuscript, "'Jásot se proměnil, v co musel': The 1969 World Ice Hockey Championships and the Struggle for Control Over the Czechoslovak Press."

18  Josef Černý from the commentary accompanying the 50th anniversary replay of the game on Czech TV.

19  As told by Jan Havel in "Cold War On Ice," Radio Free Europe Radio Liberty.

20  Skoug, Jr., *Czechoslovakia's Lost Fight for Freedom*, 228.

21  Pitner and Novotný, *Hokejový generál vzpomíná*, ch9.

22  Josef Horešovský from the commentary accompanying the 50th anniversary replay (March 28, 2019) of the second game against the Soviets on Czech TV.

23  Pitner and Novotný, *Hokejový generál vzpomíná*, ch9.

24  From the commentary accompanying the 50th anniversary replay (March 28, 2019) of the second game against the Soviets on Czech TV.

25  From the commentary accompanying the 50th anniversary replay (March 28, 2019) of the second game against the Soviets on Czech TV.

26  Miloslav Jenšík, *Kronika českého hokeje*, 1894–2000 [Chronicles of Czech Hockey], (Prague: Olympia, 2001), 241–2.

27  Interview with Miloslav Jenšík, March 14, 2018.

28  Lukšů and Palán, *Souška*, ch9.

29  Pacina, "Hokejová pomsta za okupaci."

30  Lukšů, *Žít jako Holík*, 163–4.

31  Lukšů and Palán, *Souška*, 124–128.

32  Robert Záruba and Jan Havel from the commentary accompanying the 50th anniversary replay (March 28, 2019) of the second game against the Soviets on Czech TV.

33  Interview with Miloslav Jenšík, March 14, 2018.

34  Interview with Miloslav Jenšík, March 14, 2018.

35  Interview with Jan Suchý, September 18, 2017; Lukšů and Palán, *Souška*, ch9.

36  Dino Numerato, "Between small everyday practices and glorious symbolic acts: sport -based resistance against the communist regime in Czechoslovakia," *Sport in Society*, 13:1 (2010), 112, DOI: 10.1080/17430430903377920.

37  Interview with Martina Navratilova, September 24, 2018.

38  Interview with Jiří Holík, September 19, 2017.

39  Interview with Josef Horešovský, September 21, 2017. Pacina, "Hokejová pomsta za okupaci."

40  "Cold War On Ice," Radio Free Europe Radio Liberty.

41  I spoke to a number of the players involved in the taping of the stars and there was not total consistency across their stories. Journalists Miloslav Jenšík and David Lukšů spoke to even more people and heard many more tales, with Jenšík even hearing them as the players first put the tape on. The stories are all sufficiently different that it is impossible to know who came up with the idea to tape the stars and how it was decided. Jiřík, Havel, Jaroslav Holík, and even Golonka would each later suggest that the idea was his own. Both Jenšík and Lukšů agreed that, although it is impossible to know for sure at this point, many of the stories involve Jaroslav leading the act and that the act was consistent with Jaroslav's personality. It also remains unclear as to when the players first wore the tape. Jaroslav Holík almost certainly wore it during a game against the Canadians on March 23, 1969. Some people also insist that Suchý wore the tape in games prior to his injury and some say that Golonka also wore it.

42  Lukšů and Palán, Souška, 190; Jiří Holík from the commentary accompanying the 50th anniversary replay (March 28, 2019) of the second game against the Soviets on Czech TV.

43  Interview with Marie Holíková, September 18, 2017.

44  Interview with Jiří Holík, September 19, 2017.

45  Interview with Josef Horešovský, September 21, 2017.

46  Tomáš Řanda, "Vy nám tanky, my vám branky aneb Padesát let od hokejové pomsty za okupaci, část druhá" ["You bring the tanks, we bring the goals or Fifty Years since the hockey revenge for the occupation, part two"], Czech Television Sport (March 27, 2019), https://sport.ceskatelevize.cz/clanek/hokej/vy-nam-tanky-my-vam-branky-aneb -padesat-let-od-hokejove-pomsty-za-okupaci-cast-druha/5c9c07c88b0b334bdbbb06a4.

47  Interview with Miloslav Jenšík, March 14, 2018.

48  Interview with Miloslav Jenšík, March 14, 2018.

49  Pacina, "Hokejová pomsta za okupaci."

50  Marika Studeničová, Jozef Golonka—Rebel s číslom 9 [Jozef Golonka—Rebel with the number 9] (Bratislava: Verbis, 2008), 133-141.

51  "Czechs edge Big Bear again—move closer to title," Brandon Sun, March 29, 1969, 7.

52  "Cold War On Ice," Radio Free Europe Radio Liberty.

53  Lukšů and Palán, Souška, ch9.

54  Lukšů, Žít jako Holík, 31.

55  "Czechs edge Big Bear again—move closer to title," Brandon Sun, March 29, 1969, 7.

56  Jim Coleman column, Calgary Herald, March 29, 1969, 15.

57  Jim Coleman column, Calgary Herald, March 29, 1969, 15.

58  Jan Havel from the commentary accompanying the 50th anniversary replay (March 28, 2019) of the second game against the Soviets on Czech TV.

59  Josef Horešovský from the commentary accompanying the 50th anniversary replay (March 28, 2019) of the second game against the Soviets on Czech TV.

60  Interview with Canadian hockey player Terry O'Malley, September 13, 2017.

61  Lukšů and Palán, Souška, ch9.

62  Interview with Josef Horešovský, March 9, 2018.

63  Jan Havel from the commentary accompanying the 50th anniversary replay (March 28, 2019) of the second game against the Soviets on Czech TV.

64  Lukšů, Žít jako Holík, 31.

65  Jan Havel from the commentary accompanying the 50th anniversary replay (March 28, 2019) of the second game against the Soviets on Czech TV.

66  Jan Havel from the commentary accompanying the 50th anniversary replay (March 28, 2019) of the second game against the Soviets on Czech TV.

67  Studeničová, *Jozef Golonka*, 133–141.

68  Pacina, "Hokejová pomsta za okupaci."

69  Pacina, "Hokejová pomsta za okupaci."

70  Jim Coleman column, March 29, 1969, 15.

71  Documentary video *Razítko na normalizaci* [*Stamp on Normalization*] at https://www.ceskatelevize.cz/porady/12387474945-archiv-d/219471294071011/; Pinchevsky, *Breakaway*, 7.

72  "A Great Moment for Czech Pride," *Vancouver Province*, March 29, 1969, 15.

73  "Czechs stage own overthrow, tip Russians," *Windsor Star*, March 29, 1969, 27.

74  "Czechs defeat Russians 4–3," *Montreal Gazette*, March 29, 1969, 45.

75  Jiří Holík from the commentary accompanying the 50th anniversary replay (March 28, 2019) of the second game against the Soviets on Czech TV.

76  Skoug, Jr., *Czechoslovakia's Lost Fight for Freedom*, 228-9.

## PART III: THE RETURN TO WINTER

1   Václav Havel, "Dear Dr. Husák," in *Open Letters: Selected Writings, 1965–1990*, selected and edited by Paul Wilson (New York: Vintage Books, 1992) 50–83.

## CHAPTER 10: QUASHED

1   Shawcross, *Dubček*, 177.

2   Berglund, *The Fastest Game in the World*, 142; Jan Kalous, "ČSSR—okupanti 4:3—Analýza jedné březnové noci" [Czechoslovakia 4, Occupiers 3: Analysis of One March Night], *Paměť a dějiny. Revue pro studium totalitních režimů*, (2009), 22–43; Alvin Shuster, "Aeroflot Office Burned in Prague: Crowd Celebrates Hockey Victory Over Soviet," *New York Times*, March 29, 1969, 5; Woodrow Wilson International Center for Scholars Cold War International History Project Working Paper #69 (2014), *The (Inter-Communist) Cold War on Ice: Soviet-Czechoslovak Ice Hockey Politics, 1967–1969*: Tůma, "'They had no tanks this time," 20–9; Report on Visit of Soviet ambassador Stepan Chervenenko to Czechoslovak Foreign Ministry, 29 March 1969 (translation by Jiří Mareš), 40–2, Czechoslovak Interior Minister Jan Pelnář, Report on Security Situation in Czechoslovakia on night of 28–29 March 1969 (Pelnář Report), March 31, 1969 (translated by Jiří Mareš), 43–54; Record of Conversation, Czechoslovak Defense Minister Martin Dzúr and Soviet Defense Minister Andrei Grechko, Prague, April 1, 1969 (translated by Mark Kramer), 55–65; "Czechoslovakia: The High Price of Victory," *Time*, April 11, 1969; Pinchevsky, *Breakaway*, 6–8; Williams, *The Prague Spring and its Aftermath*, 198–9.

3   Josef Horešovský from the commentary accompanying the 50th anniversary replay (March 28, 2019) of the second game against the Soviets on Czech TV; Jan Havel and Robert Záruba commentary accompanying the 50th anniversary replay on Czech TV of the second game against Sweden; interview with Miloslav Jenšík, March 14, 2018; Lukšů, *Žít jako Holík*, 166.

4   Pitner and Novotný, *Hokejový generál vzpomíná*, ch9.

5   Kirchner, *Dynastie Holíků*, Jiří Holík, ch3.

6   Pitner and Novotný, *Hokejový generál vzpomíná*, chs9–10; Pitner, *Pohledy ze střídačky*.

7   Interview with Jan Suchý, September 18, 2017.

8   Pacina, "Hokejová pomsta za okupaci."

9    Pacina, "Hokejová pomsta za okupaci;" Kirchner, *Dynastie Holíků*, Jiří Holík, ch3.

10   Vladimír Bednar commentary accompanying the 50th anniversary replay on Czech TV of the second game against Sweden; Pitner and Novotný, *Hokejový generál vzpomíná*, ch10.

11   Szulc, *Czechoslovakia Since World War II*, 474; Williams, *The Prague Spring and its Aftermath*, 199.

12   Szulc, *Czechoslovakia Since World War II*, 474; Williams, *The Prague Spring and its Aftermath*, 202, 206.

13   Petr Zídek, "Záhada pochodně č. 3" [The mystery of torch no. 3], *Lidové Noviny*, 11, April 2009, https://www.lidovky.cz/domov/zahada-pochodne-c-3.A090411_000087_ln_noviny_sko.

14   Pisková, *Jihlava*, 651-656.

15   Pitner and Novotný, *Hokejový generál vzpomíná*, ch10; Vrbecký, *Dukla Jihlava*.

16   Interview with Miroslav "Harry" Martínek in the Czech TV documentary *Razítko na normalizaci* [Stamp on Normalization], https://www.ceskatelevize.cz /porady/12387474945-archiv-d/219471294071011/.

17   This information is drawn from reports acquired from the Czech *Archive of Security Forces [Archiv bezpečnostních složek]: Collection "Central administration of military counterintelligence SNB—personal files,"* archival file no. KR-18188 VKR. See also Lukšů, *Žít jako Holík*, 168.

18   Lukšů and Palán, *Souška*, ch9.

19   Czech TV documentary *Razítko na normalizaci* [Stamp on Normalization], https://www .ceskatelevize.cz/porady/12387474945-archiv-d/219471294071011/; Jan Dvořák, "1969: Dvě výhry nad Rusy, dvě hodiny svobody a pak ještě větší temno [1969: Two victories over the Russians, two hours of freedom, and then even deeper darkness], *Česká Televize Sport* (October 14, 2018), https://sport.ceskatelevize.cz/clanek/hokej/1969-dve-vyhry-nad -rusy-dve-hodiny-svobody-a-pak-jeste-vetsi-temno/5bca04c059841d79e18a8ab0; Pinchevsky, *Breakaway*, 7.

20   Kevin McDermott, *Communist Czechoslovakia, 1945–89: A Political and Social History* (London: Palgrave, 2015), 158.

21   Szulc, *Czechoslovakia Since World War II*, 14; Williams, 48.

22   Bolton, *Worlds of Dissent*, 78–9; Shawcross, *Dubček*, 56; Szulc, *Czechoslovakia Since World War II*, 14; Williams, *The Prague Spring and its Aftermath*, 48.

23   Kevin McDermott and Klára Pinerová, "The rehabilitation process in Czechoslovakia: Party and popular responses," http://shura.shu.ac.uk/10473/.

24   Szulc, *Czechoslovakia Since World War II*, 263–4.

25   Bolton, *Worlds of Dissent*, 57, 78–9; Williams, *The Prague Spring and its Aftermath*, 49.

26   Dubček, *Hope Dies Last*, 239–241; Williams, *The Prague Spring and its Aftermath*, 202–9.

27   Bolton, *Worlds of Dissent*, 57; Dubček, *Hope Dies Last*, 242–4; Williams, *The Prague Spring and its Aftermath*, 237–9, 245.

28   Martina Navratilova with George Vecsey, *Martina* (New York: Ballantine Books, 1985), 81.

29   Bolton, *Worlds of Dissent*, 59–62; Maria Dowling, *Czechoslovakia*, (London: Arnold Publishers, 2002), 123; Rick Fawn, *The Czech Republic: A Nation of Velvet* (Taylor & Francis Group, 2000), 21–2; Williams, *The Prague Spring and its Aftermath*, 228–236.

30   Bolton, *Worlds of Dissent*, 58, 88–9; Dowling, *Czechoslovakia*, 122-3; Williams, 252–3; McDermott, *Communist Czechoslovakia*, 158.

31   Askwith, *Today We Die A Little*, 276–304.

32   Williams, *The Prague Spring and its Aftermath*, 239–241.

33   Dubček, *Hope Dies Last*, 248–252; Williams, *The Prague Spring and its Aftermath*, 241–2.

34    Interview with Jan Havel, September 21, 2017; Jan Havel commentary accompanying the
      50th anniversary replay on Czech TV of the 1969 World Championships second game
      against Sweden.
35    John Soares, "Our Way of Life against Theirs: Ice Hockey and the Cold War," in
      Heather L. Dichter & Andrew L. Johns (eds.). *Diplomatic Games: Sport, Statecraft, and
      International Relations Since 1945* (Lexington: The University Press of Kentucky, 2014),
      (Kindle location 5356–5366).
36    Williams, *The Prague Spring and its Aftermath*, 249–251.
37    Lukšů, *Žít jako Holík*, 168; Martin, *The Red Machine*, 92–6. I acquired a copy of
      the file from the Czech *Archive of Security Forces [Archiv bezpečnostních složek]:
      Collection "Central administration of military counterintelligence SNB—personal files,"*
      archival file no. KR-18188 VKR.

## CHAPTER 11: CROSSING THE LINE

1     Pitner and Novotný, *Hokejový generál vzpomíná*, ch3; Lukšů, *Žít jako Holík*, 196.
2     Lukšů and Palán, *Souška*, Ch9.
3     Soares, "Our Way of Life against Theirs," (Kindle location 5694–5706).
4     Interview with Jiří Holeček, September 22, 2017.
5     Interview with Jan Suchý, September 18, 2017; Vrbecký, *Dukla Jihlava*, 146–50; Lukšů
      and Palán, *Souška*, ch10.
6     Gorbunov, *Anatoli Tarasov*.
7     Kirchner, *Dynastie Holíků*, Jiří Holík, ch2.
8     Interview with Jiří Holík, September 19, 2017; interview with Josef Horešovský,
      September 21, 2017; Lukšů, *Žít jako Holík*, 178-80.
9     Gorbunov, *Anatoli Tarasov*; Paul Harder, "Developing World Championship Ice Hockey in
      the U.S.S.R.", 139–44; Martin, *The Red Machine*, 111–113; Soares, "Our Way of Life against
      Theirs," (Kindle location 5139, 5337–5342); written correspondence with Vashi Nedomanský,
      March 14, 2022; https://www.sports.ru/tribuna/blogs/prosport/2944995.html.
10    Interview with Jan Suchý, September 18, 2017; written correspondence with David
      Lukšů, March 23, 2022; Lukšů and Palán, *Souška*, ch10; Lukšů, *Žít jako Holík*, 118–120;
      Vrbecký, *Dukla Jihlava*, 146-50.
11    Lukšů, *Žít jako Holík*, 185; Kirchner, *Dynastie Holíků*, 37; commentary by Jiří Holeček,
      Josef Horešovský, Vladimír Martinec, František Pospíšil, and Robert Záruba with Czech
      TV rebroadcast of April 20, 1972 World Championship match Czechoslovakia-U.S.S.R.
12    Interview with Miloslav Jenšík, March 14, 2018.
13    Tůma, "They had no tanks this time," 34.
14    Interview with Josef Horešovský, September 21, 2017.
15    Interview with Miloslav Jenšík, March 14, 2018.
16    Kirchner, *Dynastie Holíků*, Jaroslav Holík, 37.
17    Lukšů, *Žít jako Holík*, 188–191.
18    Lukšů, *Žít jako Holík*, 191.
19    Interview with Jiří Holík, September 19, 2017; interview with Marie Holíková, September
      18, 2017; Kirchner, *Dynastie Holíků*, Jiří Holík, ch4; Lukšů, *Žít jako Holík*, 191.
20    Tůma, "They had no tanks this time," 34.
21    Vrbecký, *Dukla Jihlava*, 158–60.
22    Lukšů, *Žít jako Holík*, 191; commentary by Jiří Holeček with Czech TV rebroadcast of
      April 20, 1972 World Championship match Czechoslovakia-U.S.S.R.
23    Lukšů, *Žít jako Holík*, 29.

24    Kirchner, *Dynastie Holíků*, Jiří Holík, ch4; interview with Marie Holíková, September 18,
      2017; Lukšů, *Žít jako Holík*, 191.

## CHAPTER 12: UP, UP, AND . . . AWAY

1     Lukšů, *Žít jako Holík*, 191.
2     Bolton, *Worlds of Dissent*, 59; "CZECHOSLOVAKIA: Wave of Arrests," *Time*, Monday,
      March 6, 1972, http://content.time.com/time/subscriber/article/0,33009,910213,00.html;
      "Prague Sentences Three in Leaflets Trial," *New York Times*, August 2, 1972; Williams, 205.
3     McDermott, *Communist Czechoslovakia*, 159.
4     Blutstein, *Games of Discontent*, 150–2; Paul Hoffman, "Czech Party Ousts Champion
      Runner," *New York Times*, October 25, 1969, 15.
5     Thanks to Kieran Williams for highlighting this point.
6     Bolton, *Worlds of Dissent*, 12–13, 19-20, 74; Fawn, *The Czech Republic*, 21–4; Williams,
      39-46; interview with Oldřich Tůma, March 13, 2018; Navratilova, *Martina*, 74;
      McDermott, *Communist Czechoslovakia*, 155.
7     McDermott, *Communist Czechoslovakia*, 159–160; 258 in Tomas Sobotka, Krystof Zeman,
      and Vladimira Kantorova, "Demographic Shifts in the Czech Republic after 1989:
      A Second Demographic Transition View," *European Journal of Population* 19 (2003), 258.
8     Bolton, *Worlds of Dissent*, 73–4; Dowling, *Czechoslovakia*, 129; Paulina Bren,
      "Weekend Getaways: The *Chata*, the *Tramp*, and Politics of Private Life in Post-1968
      Czechoslovakia," David Crowley and Susan E. Reid (eds.), *Socialist Spaces: Sites of
      Everyday Life in the Eastern Bloc* (Oxford: Berg, 2002), 123-140; McDermott, *Communist
      Czechoslovakia*, 168.
9     Interview with Jan Suchy, September 28, 2019.
10    Interview with Jan Suchy, September 28, 2019; Lukšů and Palán, *Souška*, ch10.
11    Written correspondence with David Lukšů, March 23, 2022.
12    Jenšík, *Kronika českého hokeje, 1894–2000*, 258–262.
13    Soares, "Our Way of Life against Theirs," (Kindle location 5717–5722).
14    Lukšů, *Žít jako Holík*, 191–2; Kirchner, *Dynastie Holíků*, Jaroslav Holík, 41.
15    Lukšů, *Žít jako Holík*, 118–120; Lukšů and Palán, *Souška*, ch10; Jenšík, *Kronika českého
      hokeje, 1894–2000*, 262–265.
16    Interview with Jan Suchý, September 18, 2017.
17    Interview with Jan Havel, September 21, 2017; interview with Josef Horešovský,
      September 21, 2017.
18    Dowling, *Czechoslovakia*, 127.
19    Interview with Vashi Nedomansky, May 24, 2022; Berglund, *The Fastest Game in the
      World*, 164; Scott Burnside, "Vaclav Nedomansky's Hall of Fame journey started with a
      secret dash to freedom in 1974," *The Athletic*, November 11, 2019, https://theathletic
      .com/1315421/2019/11/11/vaclav-nedomanskys-hall-of-fame-journey-started-with
      -a-secret-dash-to-freedom-in-1974/; George Gross, "Czech Hockey Star Defects to
      Canada," *Toronto Sun*, July 18, 1974, 1, 32; "Czechoslovak hockey star defects to Canada,"
      *Cold War Conversations* podcast, episode 132, July 24, 2020; interview with Jan Havel,
      September 21, 2017; interview with Josef Horešovský, September 21, 2017; Kirchner,
      *Dynastie Holíků*, Jiří Holík, ch4; Lance Hornby, "Vaclav Nedomansky followed his
      dream to play in North America," *Toronto Sun*, November 15, 2019, https://torontosun
      .com/sports/hockey/vaclav-nedomansky-followed-his-dream-to-play-in-north-america;
      Lukšů and Palán, *Souška*, ch10; Mark Mulvoy, "Check And Double-Czech: A Couple of
      Canadian Tycoons With A Yen For Signing Stars For Super Salaries Have Landed Two

More And Stirred Up A World Controversy," *Sports Illustrated*, July 29, 1974, https ://vault.si.com/vault/1974/07/29/check-and-doubleczech; Mark Mulvoy, "Payoff On A Big Czech: One Reason Toronto's Toros Are Still Unbeaten Is A Burly Center Who Arrived Via The Underground," *Sports Illustrated*, November 4, 1974, https://vault.si.com /vault/1974/11/04/payoff-on-a-big-czech; Pinchevsky, *Breakaway*, 9-28; Tal Pinchevsky, "Vaclav Nedomansky paved the way for hockey defectors who followed," ESPN.com, March 14, 2016, https://www.espn.com/nhl/story/_/id/14972472/nhl-vaclav -nedomansky-was-hockey-first-true-defector; Soares, "Our Way of Life against Theirs," (Kindle location 5366–5373); Dave Stubbs, "Nedomansky paved way for European players on way to Hockey Hall of Fame: Defection from Czechoslovakia in 1974 helped change game in North America," *NHL.com*, November 13, 2019, https://www.nhl.com /news/hall-of-fame-nedomansky-paved-way-for-european-players/c-311086082; interview with Jan Suchý, September 18, 2017.

20   Dowling, *Czechoslovakia*, 127.

21   Interview with Martina Navratilova, September 24, 2018; Navratilova, *Martina*, 10–29, 73–103, 132–151.

22   Lukšů and Palán, *Souška*, ch10; Kirchner, *Dynastie Holíků*, Jaroslav Holík, ch4; Jenšík, *Kronika českého hokeje, 1894–2000*, 266–269.

23   Interview with Jiří Holík, September 19, 2017; interview with Jiří Holeček, September 22, 2017; Gut and Prchal, *100 let českého hokeje*, 180-191; Jenšík, *Kronika českého hokeje, 1894–2000*, 269–75; Koubek, "RETRO: Ne olympiádě! Kvůli strachu o přírodu i finance zaskakoval Innsbruck" ["RETRO: No to the Olympics! Due to the worries about nature and finances, Innsbruck had to step in"], *Idnes.cz/Sport* (December 29, 2021), https ://www.idnes.cz/oh/peking-2022/retro-serial-idnes-premium-zimni-olympijske-hry -innsbruck-1976.A211220_110108_olympiada-peking-2022_mkou?zdroj=olympiada -peking-2022_hp; https://www.cbc.ca/sports/2.722/1976-innsbruck-austria-1.779950; Jim Coleman column, *Calgary Herald*, February 16, 1976, 20.

24   Kirchner, *Dynastie Holíků*, Jiří Holík, ch3.

25   Joe Pelletier and Patrick Houda, *The World Cup of Hockey: A History of Hockey's Greatest Tournament* (Toronto: Warwick Publishing, 2003), 13, 35–6, 41–6.

26   Gut and Prchal, *100 let českého hokeje*, 191; Thomas Whalen, *Kooks and Degenerates on Ice: Bobby Orr, the Big Bad Bruins, and the Stanley Cup Championship That Transformed Hockey* (London: Rowman & Littlefield Publishers, 2021); Soares, "Our Way of Life against Theirs," (Kindle location 5140–5146).

27   Gut and Prchal, *100 let českého hokeje*, 192–201; Jenšík, *Kronika českého hokeje*.

28   Interview with Jiří Holeček, September 22, 2017; interview with Josef Horešovský, September 21, 2017; Post Bellum Institute, Jiří Holík interview.

29   Interview with Peter Šťastný, March 7, 2018.

30   Fawn, *The Czech Republic*, 22–4.

31   Pinchevsky, *Breakaway*, 40.

32   Lukšů, *Žít jako Holík*, 199–202; Lukšů and Palán, *Souška*, chs10–11.

33   Jenšík, *Kronika českého hokeje*; *TIP magazine*, 1980 issue noted at https://hfboards .mandatory.com/threads/hockey-in-czechoslovakia-and-europe-from-1968-to -1990-some-awards-and-stats.2395399/page-2#post-139429813; https://history .vintagemnhockey.com/page/show/1166356-1980-pre-olympic-tour-schedule-results.

34   Interview with Luděk Bukač, March 13, 2018.

35   Interview with Peter Šťastný, March 7, 2018; Jenšík, *Kronika českého hokeje, 1894–2000*.

36   Kieran Williams, *Václav Havel* (London: Reaktion Books, 2016), 116.

37  "Enemy of the People," *Guardian*, March 24, 1999, https://www.theguardian.com/the
     guardian/1999/mar/25/features11.g2.
38  Bolton, *Worlds of Dissent*, 27–8, 115–6, 239–42; Dowling, *Czechoslovakia*, 128–134; Fawn,
     *The Czech Republic*, 21–4.
39  Robin Herman, "Europe's Icemen Cometh," *New York Times*, January 3, 1982, https://www
     .nytimes.com/1982/01/03/magazine/europe-s-icemen-cometh.html.
40  Interview with Peter Šťastný, March 7, 2018; Scott Burnside, "Vaclav Nedomansky's Hall
     of Fame journey started with a secret dash to freedom in 1974," *The Athletic*, November 11,
     2019, https://theathletic.com/1315421/2019/11/11/vaclav-nedomanskys-hall-of-fame
     -journey-started-with-a-secret-dash-to-freedom-in-1974/; Mike Delnagro, "Speaking A
     New Language The Word On The Multilingual Nordiques Is That They're Now Big
     Winners," *Sports Illustrated*, December 14, 1981, https://vault.si.com/vault/1981/12/14
     /speaking-a-new-language-the-word-on-the-multilingual-nordiques-is-that-theyre-now
     -big-winners; Robin Herman, "Europe's Icemen Cometh," *New York Times*, January 3,
     1982, https://www.nytimes.com/1982/01/03/magazine/europe-s-icemen-cometh.html;
     Jeff Jacobs, "This is the Year of the Czechs," *Hartford Courant*, October 7, 1990; Dave
     Naylor, "The triumphs and challenges of the Šťastnýs," https://www.tsn.ca/naylor-the
     -triumphs-and-challenges-of-the-stastnys-1.133234?tsn-amp; Filip Pavčík and Robert
     Hric, Post Bellum Project, November 12, 2020, "Peter Šťastný: K veľkému hokeju som sa
     dostal úplne omylom] [Peter Šťastný: I only accidentally ended up great playing hockey],"
     *Týždeň.sk* [The Week/Weekly], https://www.tyzden.sk/spolocnost/68754
     /peter-stastny-k-velkemu-hokeju-som-sa-dostal-uplne-omylom/; Tal Pinchevsky,
     *Breakaway: From Behind the Iron Curtain to the NHL—The Untold Story of Hockey's Great
     Escapes* (New York: HarperCollins Publishers, 2013), ch2; E.M. Swift, "Don't Call Us,
     We'll Call You: Two Czech Stars Got On The Phone To Quebec, And Came In From
     The Cold," *Sports Illustrated*, November 17, 1980, https://vault.si.com/vault/1980/11/17
     /dont-call-us-well-call-you-two-czech-stars-got-on-the-phone-to-quebec-and-came-in
     -from-the-cold; "Marián Stastny Defects, Joins Brothers In Canada," *Associated Press*,
     June 7, 1981, https://www.nytimes.com/1981/06/07/sports/Marián-stastny-defects-joins
     -brothers-in-canada.html; The Cam & Strick Podcast, Peter Šťastný interview, July 6,
     2020; "Hockey Escape of the Century—Stastnys Land in Quebec," https://webarchive
     .iihf.com/iihf-home/the-iihf/100-year-anniversary/100-top-stories/story-46/index.html;
     Stastny documentary, *The Sports Network*, https://vimeo.com/118611552; "3d Stastny
     Brother Joins the Nordiques," *UPI*, June 8, 1981, https://www.nytimes.com/1981/06/08
     /sports/3d-stastny-brother-joins-the-nordiques.html.
41  The Cam & Strick Podcast, Peter Šťastný interview, July 6, 2020.

**PART IV: CHILDREN OF THE OCCUPATION**

1   Pinchevsky, *Breakaway*, 72.

**CHAPTER 13: TRAINING TO GO**

1   Interviews with Marie Holíková, September 18, 2017, September 28, 2019; Robert
     Sára, "STALO SE 17. DUBNA: Zemřel Jaroslav Holík, bouřlivák I zničený
     maratonec" [What happened on April 17: Jaroslav Holík, a wild spirit and destroyed
     marathon runner, passed away], *iDnes.cz* (2020), https://www.idnes.cz/hokej
     /reprezentace/stalo-se-pred-lety-vzpominani-jaroslav-holik-umrti-pet-let-vyroci-2015
     .A200416_150239_reprezentace_ten.
2   Lukšů, *Žít jako Holík*, 103.

3     Lukšů, *Žít jako Holík*, 170-1; Lukšů and Palán, *Souška*, 117.

4     Interview with Marie Holíková, September 18, 2017; interview with Bobby Holík, August 16, 2021.

5     Drobny, *Champion in Exile*, 126–7; Kirchner, *Dynastie Holíků*, Jiří Holík, ch1.

6     Drobny, *Champion in Exile*, 156.

7     Lukšů, *Žít jako Holík*, 173–7.

8     Kirchner, *Dynastie Holíků*, Andrea Musilová, ch1.

9     Kirchner, *Dynastie Holíků* Andrea Musilová, ch1.

10    Kirchner, *Dynastie Holíků*, Andrea Musilová, ch1; Lukšů, *Žít jako Holík*, 113.

11    Lukšů, *Žít jako Holík*, 226.

12    Kirchner, *Dynastie Holíků*, Jaroslav Holík, ch1, 49, Bobby Holík, ch1; Lukšů, *Žít jako Holík*, 173; interview with Bobby Holík, June 22, 2017.

13    Jaroslav Kirchner, *Dynastie Holíků*, Andrea Musilová, ch1; Lukšů, *Žít jako Holík*, 222.

14    Lukšů, *Žít jako Holík*, 177.

15    Lukšů, *Žít jako Holík*, 172–7.

16    Lukšů, *Žít jako Holík*, 226–233.

17    Interview with Marie Holíková, September 28, 2019.

18    Interview with Bobby Holík, June 22, 2017; interview with Marie Holíková, September 18, 2017; Lukšů, *Žít jako Holík*, 242.

19    Interview with Bobby Holík, August 17, 2021; https://www.espn.com/magazine/vol5no01Holík.html.

20    Lukšů, *Žít jako Holík*, 16–17; interview with Bobby Holík, June 22, 2017.

21    Kirchner, *Dynastie Holíků*, Jaroslav Holík, 49, Andrea Musilová, ch1; Lukšů, *Žít jako Holík*, 173.

22    Interview with Jiří Holík, September 21, 2019; Gut and Prchal, *100 let českého hokeje*, 189; https://sport.ceskatelevize.cz/clanek/hokej/Jiří-Holík-slavi-sedmdesatiny-klid-hleda-na-golfu/5bded0000d663b6fe8e381d8; Kirchner, *Dynastie Holíků*, Jiří Holík, ch4; Post Bellum Institute, Jiří Holík interview.

23    Gut and Prchal, *100 let českého hokeje*, 177; Lukšů and Palán, *Souška*, ch11, 294–303.

24    Lukšů, *Žít jako Holík*, 199-206; interview with Bobby Holík, June 22, 2017; https://web.archive.org/web/20060221210630/http://historie.hokej.cz/index.php?view=clanek&lng=CZ&id=242&menu_id=242&open_id=0.

25    Archiv bezpečnostních složek [Archive of the Security Forces]. 2020. *Scans of the Ministry of Interior File on Jaroslav Holík*, multiple reports from 1979 and 1985 1985.

26    Drawn from the report from July 24, 1985 acquired from the Czech *Archive of Security Forces [Archiv bezpečnostních složek]: Collection "Central administration of military counterintelligence SNB—personal files*," archival file no. KR-18188 VKR."

27    Lukšů, *Žít jako Holík*, 222.

28    Lukšů, *Žít jako Holík*, 207.

29    Lukšů, *Žít jako Holík*, 232; interview with Bobby Holík, June 22, 2017.

30    Interview with Bobby Holík, August 16, 2021; https://english.radio.cz/love-or-labour-significance-may-day-czech-republic-8620251.

31    Lukšů, *Žít jako Holík*, 177.

32    Lukšů, *Žít jako Holík*, 175.

33    Kirchner, *Dynastie Holíků*, Andrea Musilová, ch1.

34    Lukšů, *Žít jako Holík*, 173-5; interview with Marie Holíková, September 18, 2017.

35    http://www.tennisabstract.com/cgi-bin/wplayer-classic.cgi?p=AndreaHolikova&f\=ACareerqq.

36    Kirchner, *Dynastie Holíků*, Andrea Musilová, ch1.

37    http://www.tennisabstract.com/cgi-bin/wplayer-classic.cgi?p=AndreaHolikova&f
      =ACareerqq; https://wikivisually.com/wiki/Andrea_Hol%C3%ADkov%C3%A1.

## CHAPTER 14: HOMEBOUND

1     https://oilersnation.com/2017/11/30/top-10-unsung-heroes-frank-musil-7/; Kirchner,
      *Dynastie Holíků*, František Musil, ch1; Lukšů, *Žít jako Holík*, 208.
2     Vrbecký, *Dukla Jihlava 1956–2006*, 161–5.
3     Kirchner, *Dynastie Holíků*, František Musil, ch1; Lukšů, *Žít jako Holík*, 129–30, 211–4.
4     Robin Herman, "Europe's Icemen Cometh," *New York Times*, January 3, 1982, https
      ://www.nytimes.com/1982/01/03/magazine/europe-s-icemen-cometh.html; Pinchevsky,
      *Breakaway*, 69–70; https://www.eliteprospects.com/draft/nhl-entry-draft/nation/svk;
      https://www.eliteprospects.com/draft/nhl-entry-draft/nation/cze.
5     Kirchner, *Dynastie Holíků*, František Musil, ch2; Pinchevsky, *Breakaway*, ch3; Lisa
      Dillman, "To Them, America Means Togetherness: Young Lovers Leave Czechoslovakia
      to Pursue Fame, Fortune," *Los Angeles Times*, January 23, 1987; interview with Dominik
      Hašek, September 20, 2017.
6     Kirchner, *Dynastie Holíků*, František Musil, ch2; Kirchner, *Dynastie Holíků*, Andrea
      Musilova, ch1; Kirchner, *Dynastie Holíků*, Jaroslav Holík, 52; Lukšů, *Žít jako Holík*,
      214–5; Dillman, "To Them, America Means Togetherness."
7     https://english.radio.cz/asanace-communists-infamous-clearance-operation-left-indelible
      -stain-dissidents-8090221.
8     https://www.nytimes.com/1979/10/25/archives/a-thoroughly-politicized-czech-playwright
      -vaclav-havel-man-in-the.html.
9     Dowling, *Czechoslovakia*, 134–6.
10    Kirchner, *Dynastie Holíků*, František Musil, ch2, Andrea Holíková, ch1; Pinchevsky,
      *Breakaway*, 97–99; Brian Murphy, "František Musil has returned to the Twin Cities for
      another big moment," *Twin Cities Pioneer Press*, June 23, 2011, https://www.twincities
      .com/2011/06/23/František-musil-has-returned-to-the-twin-cities-for-another-big
      -moment/; Bob Showers, *Minnesota North Stars: History and Memories with Lou Nanne*
      (Beaver's Pond Press, 2007); https://www.ahaonline.cz/clanek/sport/12060/František
      -musil-jak-jsem-emigroval.html; https://www.irozhlas.cz/sport/hokej/hokej-František
      -musil-slozka-stb-snb-emigrace-minnesota_1805170822_vman.
11    Frank Deford, "Yes, You Can Go Home Again: Martina Navrátilová Went Home To
      Czechoslovakia And Found Fans Plentiful At The Federation Cup," *Sports Illustrated*,
      August 4, 1986; Mike Downey, "Navrátilová Czechs In on Her Past," *Los Angeles Times*
      (July 23, 1986), 1; John Feinstein, "Federation Cup," *Washington Post*, July 27, 1986; Jane
      Brown Grimes interview "The Girl Who Got Away" (Episode 19, May 16, 2016) in the
      Wilson Center History and Public Policy Program's Sport in the Cold War podcast.
      https://digitalarchive.wilsoncenter.org/resource/sport-in-the-cold-war/episode-19
      -the-girl-who-got-away; Roy Johnson, "U.S. Open; Mandlíková: From the Heart,"
      *New York Times*, August 25, 1986; George Pendle, "The Daily Match points—When
      tennis collided with the cold war," *1843 magazine | The Economist*, July 27, 2016; Roger
      Williams, "Navrátilová Gets Discreet Welcome," *New York Times*, July 21, 1986; "Martina
      Navrátilová, returning to Czechoslovakia," *Los Angeles Times*, July 20, 1986; "Czech
      Fans Roar for Navrátilová," *New York Times*, July 23, 1986; http://www.asapsports.com
      /show_interview.php?id=100923.
12    František Musil, Secret Police File; https://www.ahaonline.cz/clanek/sport/12060
      /František-musil-jak-jsem-emigroval.html; https://www.irozhlas.cz/sport/hoke
      j/hokej-František-musil-slozka-stb-snb-emigrace-minnesota_1805170822_vman.

13    Interview with Bobby Holík, June 22, 2017; Kirchner, *Dynastie Holíků*, František Musil,
      ch2; Kirchner, *Dynastie Holíků*, Andrea Musilova, ch1; Kirchner, *Dynastie Holíků*,
      Jaroslav Holík, 52; Lukšů, *Žít jako Holík*, 215-17, 233; Kurt Chandler, "Czech athlete to
      seek asylum within weeks," *Minneapolis Star Tribune*, November 21, 1986, 10B; Kurt
      Chandler, "Tennis player's tourney plans await asylum ruling," *Minneapolis Star Tribune*,
      December 5, 1986, 6B; Kurt Chandler, "Defector finds life here makes for perfect
      match," *Minneapolis Star Tribune*, June 26, 1988, 1B; Lisa Dillman, "Czech Tennis Player
      Holíková, 18, Seeks Political Asylum in U.S.," *Los Angeles Times*, November 22, 1986,
      B15; Dillman, "To Them, America Means Togetherness"; Andrea Holíková Secret Police
      file; https://www.irozhlas.cz/sport/hokej/hokej-František-musil-slozka-stb-snb-emigrace
      -minnesota_1805170822_vman.

## CHAPTER 15: INSPIRATION FOR A GENERATION

1     Interview with Marie Holíková, September 18, 2017.
2     Interviews with Bobby Holík, June 22, 2017; August 17, 2021; Lukšů, *Žít jako Holík*, 228.
3     Pinchevsky, *Breakaway*; https://theathletic.co.uk/344005/2018/05/06/filip-zadina-part
      -of-new-wave-of-czech-talent-giving-hope-to-a-once-great-hockey-nation/?redirected=1.
4     Pinchevsky, *Breakaway*, ch3.
5     Petr Pavlinek and John Pickles, *Environmental Transitions: Transformation and Ecological
      Defence in Central and Eastern Europe* (London: Routledge, 2000), ch5; interview with
      Martin Ručinský, September 29, 2017; interview with Ludek Bukac, March 13, 2018;
      Litvínov club website: https://www.hcverva.cz/zobraz.asp?t=kronika-klubu; interview
      with Bobby Holík, September 17, 2021; commentary by Lang, Reichel, and Ručinský in
      Czech TV 20th anniversary rebroadcast of 1998 gold medal Olympic hockey game; Karel
      Knap, "Sen litvínovských legend. Vyhraj titul za nás, vzkazují Ručinskému" [Dream of
      the Litvínov legends: "Win the title in our stead" they tell Ručinský], *Lidovky.cz*
      (April 11, 2015). https://www.lidovky.cz/sport/hokej/Šlégr-Ručinský-Litvínov
      -finale-extraliga-titul.A150411_132201_ln-sport-hokej_vlh; Karel Knap, "Šlégr, Reichel,
      Ručinský. Kamarádi navždy. Legendy vyprávějí oblíbené historky" ["Šlégr, Reichel,
      Ručinský. Best friends forever. Legends tell their favorite stories"], *iDnes.cz/Sport* (2021),
      https://www.idnes.cz/hokej/ms-2021/Jiří-Šlégr-robert-reichel-martin-Ručinský
      -pribeh-hokejovi-musketyri.A210520_608921_ms-hokej-2021_tof; https://theathletic
      .com/1905292/2020/07/02/stories-from-Litvínov-inside-the-czech-hockey-factory-I
      -never-heard-of/?redirected=1&redirected=1.
6     Jágr and Smid, *Jágr*, 41.
7     Lukšů, *Žít jako Holík*, 228.
8     Interview with Bobby Holík, March 8, 2022.
9     Jágr and Smid, *Jágr*, 58–62.
10    Berglund, *The Fastest Game in the World*, 199.
11    Interview with Dominik Hašek, September 20, 2017; William Nack, "A Prague Summer
      After Dominating The Olympics and the NHL Season, Sabres Goalie Dominik Hasek
      Returned To His Hometown, Near The Czech Capital, For A Hero's Welcome," *Sports
      Illustrated*, August 10, 1998; https://slapshot.blogs.nytimes.com/2008/06/09/the
      -morning-skate-the-two-sides-of-dominik-Hasek/; Randi Druzin, *Between the Pipes:
      A Revealing Look at Hockey's Legendary Goalies* (Vancouver: Greystone Books, 2013);
      interview with Bobby Holík, August 17, 2021; Berglund, *The Fastest Game in the World*, 198.
12    Mike Beamish, "Swede likely top NHL pick," *Vancouver Sun*, June 15, 1989, D1; "Czech
      Hockey Star, 18, May Have Defected," *Los Angeles Times*, June 15, 1989; interview with
      Bobby Holík, August 17, 2021.

## CHAPTER 16: 89 IS 68 TURNED UPSIDE DOWN AND BACKWARDS

1   https://www.bezfrazi.cz/pribehy/jan-reindl/co-se-bude-dit; interviews with Josef
    Horešovský, September 21, 2017, March 8, 2018; Jenšík, *Kronika českého hokeje*, 337-8;
    interview with Jan Reindl, March 15, 2018.

2   https://www.nytimes.com/1988/09/04/magazine/prague-waits-for-a-thaw.html; Fawn,
    *The Czech Republic*, ch1.

3   F.W. Carter, "Pollution Problems in Post-War Czechoslovakia," *Transactions of the Institute
    of British Geographers*, 1985, Vol. 10, No. 1, 17–44; Lubomír Kopeèek and Stanislav Balík,
    "Market reforms, society, and the main features of Czech capitalism," in Stanislav Balík, Vít
    Hloušek, Lubomír Kopeèek, Jan Holzer, Pavel Pšeja and Andrew Lawrence Roberts (eds.),
    *Czech Politics: From West to East and Back Again* (Verlag Barbara Budrich, 2017), 185.

4   John F.N. Bradley, *Czechoslovakia's Velvet Revolution: A Political Analysis* (New York:
    Columbia University Press, 1992); Oskar Gruenwald, "Toward an Open Society:
    Reflections on the 1989 Revolution in Eastern Europe," in Stanslav J. Kirschbaum (ed.),
    *Central European History and The European Union* (New York: Palgrave Macmillan, 2007),
    42; Padraic Kenney, *A Carnival of Revolution: Central Europe 1989* (Princeton: Princeton
    University Press, 2002), 215–7; https://enrs.eu/article/candle-manifestation-of-1988;
    https://spectator.sme.sk/c/22083731/candle-manifestation-anniversary-31-years
    .html; https://spectator.sme.sk/c/20788579/candle-manifestation-anniversary-slovakia
    -miklosko-carnogursky-bratislava-30years.html?ref=av-center.

5   Kieran Williams, *Critical Lives: Václav Havel* (London: Reaktion Books, 2016), 157.

6   https://www.novinky.cz/historie/17-listopad/clanek/sametovou-revoluci-doprovazela-polarni
    -zare-40303788; https://www.astro.cz/clanky/ukazy/sametovou-revoluci-pred-30-lety-prova
    zela-jasna-polarni-zare.html; https://ct24.ceskatelevize.cz/veda/2979455-listopad-1989-kdyz
    -zacaly-prvni-demonstrace-nad-ceskem-zazarila-vyjimecna-ruda-polarni

7   Interview with Jiří Holík, September 21, 2019.

8   https://www.bezfrazi.cz/pribehy/jan-reindl/co-se-bude-dit; Dominik Hašek and Robert
    Záruba *Chytám svůj život* [Catching My Life] (Prague: Terra, 1999), ch13; https://vault
    .si.com/vault/1998/08/10/a-prague-summer-after-dominating-the-olympics-and-the-nhl
    -season-sabres-goalie-dominik-hasek-returned-to-his-hometown-near-the-czech-capital
    -for-a-heros-welcome; interviews with Jiří Holík, September 19, 2017, September 21,
    2019; interview with Marie Holíková, September 28, 2019; interviews with Bobby Holík,
    June 22-23, 2017, August 15-18, 2021; interviews with Josef Horešovský, September 21,
    2017, March 8, 2018; email correspondence with Franticek Kucera, October 8, 2017;
    interviews with Jan Suchy, September 18, 2017, September 28, 2019; Jenšík, *Kronika
    českého hokeje*, 337–8; Lukšů, *Žít jako Holík*, 246; interview with Jan Reindl, March 15,
    2018; https://sport.lidovky.cz/listopad-1989-ocima-sportovcu-d16-/hokej.aspx?c
    =A141116_174855_ln-sport-hokej_lso; http://www.hcsparta.cz/clanek.asp?id=Prvni
    -novodoby-titul-Sparty-pred-25-lety-9563.

9   https://www.nytimes.com/1988/09/04/magazine/prague-waits-for-a-thaw.html; https
    ://www.nytimes.com/1987/04/12/world/gorbachev-alludes-to-czech-invasion.html;
    https://www.rferl.org/a/1092649.html.

10  Timothy Garton Ash, *The Magic Lantern* (New York: Vintage Books, 1990), ch5;
    Dowling, *Czechoslovakia*, 137-159; Fawn, *The Czech Republic*, ch1; https://www
    .theguardian.com/world/from-the-archive-blog/2019/nov/13/czechoslovakia-velvet
    -revolution-november-1989; https://www.nytimes.com/1989/11/23/world/Dubček-talks
    -to-rally-outside-bratislava-trial-clamor-in-the-east.html; https://www.youtube.com
    /watch?v=cBoIF-1YOu8; Mark Kramer, "The Demise of the Soviet Bloc," *Journal of Modern
    History*, Vol. 83, No. 4 (December 2011), 788–854; Dubček, *Hope Dies Last*, 254–71.

**PART V: THE PEOPLE OF WHOM WE KNOW NOTHING**

1    Jenšík, *Kronika českého hokeje*, 242. In Czech, Jenšík uses the word *sever* ("north"). I translate it as "Stockholm" here to specify what he really means: the 1969 World Championships.

**CHAPTER 17: THE WILD, WILD WEST**

1    Jágr and Smid, *Jágr*, 79.

2    Gut and Prchal, *100 let českého hokeje*, 236; Vrbecký, *Dukla Jihlava*, 86–7; Hašek and Záruba, *Chytám svůj život*, ch13; Jágr and Smid, *Jágr*, 67–8; https://www.idnes.cz/hokej/extraliga/nhl-cekala -ale-prisla-smrt-od-zraneni-hokejisty-cajky-uplynulo-dvacet-let.A100104_230031_hokej_par.

3    Interview with Jan Reindl, March 15, 2018.

4    Interviews with Bobby Holík, June 2017 and August 17, 2021; Jágr and Smid, *Jágr*, 71; Andrea Peirce, "Lendl tops Mecir in return to Prague courts" (February 27, 1990), https://www.upi.com/Archives/1990/02/27/Lendl-tops-Mecir-in-return-to-Prague -courts/5660636094800/; "For Lendl, a homecoming," *Tampa Bay Times* (February 28, 1990), https://www.tampabay.com/archive/1990/02/28/for-lendl-a-homecoming/.

5    https://www.quanthockey.com/whc/en/teams/team-czechoslovakia-players-1990-whc -stats.html.

6    Lukšů, *Žít jako Holík*, 230; Jágr and Smid, *Jágr*, 74-8; interview with Dominik Hašek, September 20, 2017; Hašek and Záruba, *Chytám svůj život*, ch13; Jeff Jacobs, "This Is the Year of the Czechs," *Hartford Courant*, October 7, 1990.

7    https://www.quanthockey.com/nhl/nationality-totals/nhl-players-1978-79-stats.html; https:// www.quanthockey.com/nhl/nationality-totals/nhl-players-1990-91-stats.html; Podnieks et al., *Kings of the Ice*, 543; Dan Diamond et al., *Total Hockey: The Official Encyclopedia of the National Hockey League* (New York: Total Sports, 2000), 134.

8    Pinchevsky, *Breakaway*, 190.

9    E.M. Swift, "The KID From Kladno: By achieving NHL stardom, the Penguins' Jaromír Jágr has realized the dream he had as a youth in Czechoslovakia," *Sports Illustrated*, October 12, 1992.

10   Pinchevsky, *Breakaway*, 189; *Nagano Tapes*, Olympic Channel documentary; Jay Greenberg, "Czeching In: The future looks very bright for four NHL rookies from Czechoslovakia," *Sports Illustrated*, February 25, 1991; Lukšů, *Žít jako Holík*, 236; interview with Bobby Holík, August 17, 2021; Jerry Kirshenbaum, "Scorecard," *Sports Illustrated*, November 16, 1992.

11   Greenberg, "Czeching In;" Swift, "The KID From Kladno."

12   Interviews with Bobby Holík, June 2017 and August 17, 2021; Kirchner, *Dynastie Holíků*, Bobby Holík, ch3; Jeff Jacobs, "This Is the Year of the Czechs," *Hartford Courant*, October 7, 1990; Ben McGrath, "Think Positive," *The New Yorker*, March 24, 2003; Shaun Assael, "That Holík," *ESPN the Magazine*, October 1, 2001; Michael Farber, "Czech Point To Get Past The Devils, The Penguins First Must Get Past New Jersey's Chippy And Worldly Star, Bobby Holík," *Sports Illustrated*, May 21, 2001.

13   https://thehockeywriters.com/whatever-happened-to-robert-reichel-edition/; https://www.matchsticksandgasoline.com/2020/12/4/21574831/calgary-flames-robert -reichel-nhl-hockey-26.

14   Druzin, *Between the Pipes*, ch11.

15   Larry Wigge, "New World Order: As the Olympics have shown, the influx of players from across the Atlantic has brought a sea change to the NHL game," *The Sporting News*, February 25, 2002, 24–6; interview with Bobby Holík, August 17, 2021; *Nagano Tapes*, Olympic Channel documentary.

16   Lukšů, *Žít jako Holík*, 272.

17  Kirchner, *Dynastie Holíků*, Jaroslav Holík, ch4; Lukšů, *Žít jako Holík*, 244.

18  Interviews with Jiří Holík and Marie Holíková, September 19, 2017; Lukšů, *Žít jako Holík*, 265–268; Kirchner, *Dynastie Holíků*, chapters on Jaroslav Holík, Frantisek Musil, and Andrea Musilova.

19  Miloš Brunclík and Michal Kubát, "The Crisis Of The Czech Politics 25 Years After The Velvet Revolution," *Politeja*, No. 28 (2014), 163–180; Fawn, *The Czech Republic*, 27.

20  Fawn, *The Czech Republic*, ch3.

21  https://english.radio.cz/ten-years-ago-last-russian-soldiers-left-czechoslovakia-8045146; https://apnews.com/article/774bedc743abe759737785aa0edfeba9; https://www.jstor.org /stable/23615731?seq=1#metadata_info_tab_contents.

22  Fawn, *The Czech Republic*, 28–33.

23  Brunclík and Kubát, "The Crisis Of The Czech Politics," *Politeja*, No. 28 (2014), 163–6.

24  Lukšů, *Žít jako Holík*, 244–250; Kirchner, *Dynastie Holíků*, Jaroslav Holík, chs4–5; Jiří Holík, chs4–5, Lukšů and Palán, *Souška*, ch12; Vrbecký, *Dukla Jihlava*, 90–113, 156–8, https://www.idnes.cz/zlin/zpravy/krimiserial-sef-hokejoveho-vsetina-roman-zubik-byl -odsouzeny-za-podvody.A151231_140126_zlin-zpravy_ras.

25  Fawn, *The Czech Republic*, ch3.

26  Kristian Palda, "Czech Privatization and Corporate Governance," *Communist and Post-Communist Studies* Vol. 30, No. 1 (1997), 83.

27  Lubomír Kopeèek and Stanislav Balík, "Market reforms, society, and the main features of Czech capitalism," in Stanislav Balík, Vit Hloušek, Lubomir Kopeček, Jan Holzer, Pavel Pšeja, and Andrew Lawrence Roberts (eds.), *Czech Politics: From West to East and Back Again* (Opladen: Verlag Barbara Budrich, 2017), 195.

28  Ola Cichowlas and Andrew Foxall, "Now the Czechs Have an Oligarch Problem, Too: How the rise of a powerful businessman threatens to undermine democratic institutions in the heart of Europe," *Foreign Policy*, April 10, 2015. https://foreignpolicy .com/2015/04/10/now-the-czechs-have-an-oligarch-problem-too-andrej-babis/.

29  Interview with Josef Horešovský, March 8, 2018.

30  Lukšů, *Žít jako Holík*, 221.

31  Fawn, *The Czech Republic*, ch3.

32  Andrew Roberts, "Five ways of looking at Czech politics," in Stanislav Balík, Vit Hloušek, Lubomir Kopeček, Jan Holzer, Pavel Pšeja, and Andrew Lawrence Roberts (eds.), *Czech Politics: From West to East and Back Again* (Opalden: Verlag Barbara Budrich, 2017); Fawn, *The Czech Republic*, chs2–3; Lubomír Kopeèek and Stanislav Balík, "Market reforms, society, and the main features of Czech capitalism," in Stanislav Balík, Vit Hloušek, Lubomir Kopeček, Jan Holzer, Pavel Pšeja, and Andrew Lawrence Roberts (eds.), *Czech Politics: From West to East and Back Again* (Verlag Barbara Budrich), 2017.

33  Brunclík and Kubát, "The Crisis Of The Czech Politics," *Politeja*, No. 28 (2014), 9.

34  Fawn, *The Czech Republic*, 40–1.

35  Tomas Sobotka, Krystof Zeman, and Vladimíra Kantorova, "Demographic Shifts in the Czech Republic after 1989: A Second Demographic Transition View," *European Journal of Population* 19 (2003), 249–277.

36  Diamond, *Total Hockey*, 481–3.

37  *Nagano Tapes*, Olympic Channel Documentary; interview with Martin Ručinský, September 29, 2017; Lukšů, *Žít jako Holík*, 278; Kirchner, *Dynastie Holíků*, Bobby Holík section; "Jágr's Homecoming Turns Sour," *Associated Press*, August 30, 1996; http://bigmouthsports.com/wp-content/uploads/2016/09/1996-world-cup.pdf; Gut and Prchal, *100 let českého hokeje*, 269–270; Jenšík, *Kronika českého hokeje*, 374–375.

38  Interview with Dominik Hašek, September 20, 2017.

**CHAPTER 18: NAGANO**

1   https://en.wikipedia.org/wiki/Gary_Bettman; https://www.nytimes.com/1992/11/29
    /sports/hockey-nhl-considers-an-nba-officer.html; https://www.nytimes.com/1995/09/30
    /sports/hockey-in-the-nhl-s-future-olympics-labor-peace.html; https://www.nytimes
    .com/1997/09/16/sports/hockey-nhl-s-olympic-gamble-stars-participation-nagano-could
    -raise-sport-s.html.

2   https://vault.si.com/vault/1998/02/09/instant-replay-how-could-underdog-sweden-win
    -the-olympic-title-again-let-us-count-the-ways.

3   Interview with Pavel Barta, September 25, 2017.

4   Diamond, *Total Hockey*, 483.

5   Knap, "Šlégr, Reichel, Ručinský. Kamarádi navždy. Legendy vyprávějí oblíbené historky."

6   Hašek and Záruba, *Chytám svůj život*, ch21.

7   Hašek and Záruba, *Chytám svůj život*, ch21; https://web.archive.org/web
    /20150225005019/http://www.praguepost.cz/archivescontent/31399-passing-the-puck
    .html; http://bruinslegends.blogspot.com/2010/12/Vladimír-Růžička.html.

8   Diamond, *Total Hockey*, 482; Podnieks, et al., *Kings of the Ice*, 860.

9   Vrbecký, *Dukla Jihlava*, 188–191; Hašek and Záruba, *Chytám svůj život*, ch21.

10  https://ustecky.denik.cz/hokej_region/zemrel-vaclav-sasek-maserska-legenda-z
    -nagana-a-kamarad-ivana-hlinky-20200110.html; https://www.lidovky.cz/sport/hokej
    /kdyby-ses-lip-ucil-mohl-jsi-delat-masera-a-taky-dostavat-prsteny-zadarmo-rikal
    -zesnuly-sasek-jagrovi.A200109_203226_ln-sport-hokej_lar.

11  Interview with Martin Ručinský, September 29, 2017.

12  https://www.si.com/hockey/all-access/how-Hasek-led-the-czech-republic-to-glory
    -a-look-back-at-the-nagano-olympics.

13  Hašek and Záruba, *Chytám svůj život*, ch21.

14  Diamond, *Total Hockey*, 483.

15  https://archive.nytimes.com/www.nytimes.com/specials/olympics/nagano/hkm
    /021898oly-hkm-czech.html.

16  https://www.si.com/hockey/all-access/how-Hasek-led-the-czech-republic
    -to-glory-a-look-back-at-the-nagano-olympics.

17  William Nack, "A Prague Summer After Dominating The Olympics and the NHL
    Season, Sabres Goalie Dominik Hasek Returned To His Hometown, Near The Czech
    Capital, For A Hero's Welcome," *Sports Illustrated*, August 10, 1998.

18  https://archive.nytimes.com/www.nytimes.com/specials/olympics/nagano/hkm
    /022198oly-hkm-mens.html; https://www.washingtonpost.com/wp-srv/sports/longterm
    /olympics1998/sport/hockey/articles/czkcan20.htm.

19  https://www.washingtonpost.com/wp-srv/sports/longterm/olympics1998/sport/hockey
    /articles/czkcan20.htm

20  *Nagano Tapes*, Olympic Channel Documentary on the 1998 Olympic hockey; interview
    with Martin Ručinský, September 29, 2017.

21  *Nagano Tapes*, Olympic Channel Documentary on the 1998 Olympic hockey; https
    ://www.nytimes.com/1998/02/23/sports/the-xviii-winter-games-ice-hockey-in-prague
    -70000-fans-gather-to-savor-moment.html.

22  https://www.washingtonpost.com/wp-srv/sports/longterm/olympics1998/sport/hockey
    /articles/czkcan20.htm.

23  *Nagano Tapes*, Olympic Channel Documentary on the 1998 Olympic hockey.

24  *Nagano Tapes*, Olympic Channel Documentary on the 1998 Olympic hockey.

25   *Nagano Tapes*, Olympic Channel Documentary on the 1998 Olympic hockey; Czech TV replaying
     of the 1998 gold medal game on the 20th anniversary of the match, with commentary.
26   https://www.nytimes.com/1998/02/23/sports/the-xviii-winter-games-ice-hockey-in
     -prague-70000-fans-gather-to-savor-moment.html.
27   Interview with Jan Suchý, September 28, 2019.
28   *Nagano Tapes*, Olympic Channel Documentary on the 1998 Olympic hockey; Czech
     TV replaying of the 1998 gold medal game on the 20th anniversary of the match, with
     commentary; https://theathletic.co.uk/344005/2018/05/06/filip-zadina-part-of-new
     -wave-of-czech-talent-giving-hope-to-a-once-great-hockey-nation/?redirected=1.

**EPILOGUE: TOO GOOD TO BE DENIED**

1    Interview with Bobby Holík, August 17, 2021; Lukšů, *Žít jako Holík*, 233; Kirchner,
     *Dynastie Holíků*, Bobby Holík, ch2.
2    Lukšů and Palán, *Souška*, ch9.
3    Interview with Jiří Holík, September 21, 2019; Kirchner, *Dynastie Holíků*, Jiří Holík, ch5;
     Lukšů, *Žít jako Holík*, 35.
4    Interview with Marie Holíková, September 28, 2019.
5    Lukšů, *Žít jako Holík*, 268-271; Sára, "STALO SE 17. DUBNA: Zemřel Jaroslav Holík,
     bouřlivák I zničený maratonec."
6    Interviews with Bobby Holík, June 22, 2017, August 17, 2021; interview with Marie
     Holíková, September 28, 2017.
7    Written correspondence with Štefan Nižňanský.
8    Interview with Peter Šťastný, March 7, 2018; https://www.nj.com/olympics/2014/02
     /sochi_olympics_2014_former_devil_peter_Šťastný_watches_his_son_star_against
     _his_native_slovakia.html; Jerry Sullivan, "No question of loyalty for Peter Šťastný,"
     *Buffalo News*, February 13, 2014; https://buffalonews.com/sports/no-question-of
     -loyalty-for-peter-Šťastný/article_4d4be709-a3b3-58c6-8100-9ca1e210306e.html; Jerry
     Sullivan, "Šťastný Finally Competing in the Name of Slovakia," *Buffalo News*, February
     16, 1994; https://buffalonews.com/news/Šťastný-finally-competing-in-the-name-of
     -slovakia/article_e2bfb3c1-7180-5067-9c02-92881a11a64c.html; Szymon Szemberg
     and Andrew Podnieks, "Story #22—Bondra's bomb—the biggest thing for Slovakia
     since independence," in *IIHF Top 100 Hockey Stories of All-Time* (Bolton: H.B. Fenn &
     Company, Ltd., 2008). Also available at http://webarchive.iihf.com/iihf-home
     /the-iihf/100-year-anniversary/100-top-stories/story-22/.
9    Hašek and Záruba, *Chytám svůj život*; interview with Dominik Hašek, September 20,
     2017; interview with Martin Ručinský, September 29, 2017; email correspondence with
     František Kučera, October 8, 2017.
10   Tomáš Řanda, "1998: The Nagano Myth. Hockey success caused euphoria that
     transcended the boundaries of sport," *Czech Television*, October 29, 2018, https://sport
     .ceskatelevize.cz/clanek/hokej/1998-mytus-nagano-hokejovy-uspech
     -spustil-euforii-prekracujici-hranice-sportu/5bd71b1b0d663b6fe857846c.
11   *Nagano Tapes*, Olympic Channel Documentary, 1998.
12   *Nagano Tapes*, Olympic Channel Documentary, 1998.
13   https://www.nytimes.com/1998/02/23/sports/the-xviii-winter-games-ice-hockey-in
     -prague-70000-fans-gather-to-savor-moment.html.
14   Tomáš Řanda, "1998: The Nagano Myth," https://sport.ceskatelevize.cz/clanek/hokej
     /1998-mytus-nagano-hokejovy-uspech-spustil-euforii-prekracujici-hranice-sportu
     /5bd71b1b0d663b6fe857846c.

# Index